From the Land of Hibiscus

From the Land of Hibiscus

Koreans in Hawai'i, 1903–1950

Edited by Yŏng-ho Ch'oe

University of Hawai'i Press   Honolulu

11 10 09 08 07   5 4 3 2 1

Library of Congress Cataloging-in-Publication Data
    From the land of hibiscus : Koreans in Hawaii, 1903–1950 /
edited by Yong-ho Ch'oe.
    p. cm.
    Includes bibliographical references and index.
    ISBN-13: 978-0-8248-2981-0 (cloth : alk. paper)
    ISBN-10: 0-8248-2981-6 (cloth : alk. paper)
    1. Koreans—Hawaii—History—20th century.
2. Koreans—Hawaii—Social conditions—20th century.
3. Hawaii—History—1900–1959. 4. Hawaii—Ethnic
relations—History—20th century. I. Ch'oe, Yong-ho, 1931–
    DU624.7.K67F76 2007
    305.895'7096909041—dc22

                                    2006006222

University of Hawai'i Press books are
printed on acid-free paper and meet the
guidelines for permanence and durability
of the Council on Library Resources.

Designed by Leslie Fitch
Printed by Edwards Brothers Inc.

To the first-generation Korean Americans,
whose pioneering spirit and sacrifice opened
new opportunities for their descendants

Contents

Yŏng-ho Ch'oe

Introduction

T HE HIBISCUS IS the national flower of Korea. From ancient times, Korea has been known as the Land of Hibiscus *(kŭnhwa hyang* or *kŭn'yŏk)*, as hibiscus flowers adorned all corners of the country with varying colors and beauty. In modern Korea, the hibiscus has symbolized, in addition to its beauty, longevity and endurance as Korea struggled to cope with the dark days of Japanese colonial rule and the tragedies of the division of the country and of the fratricidal Korean War. Koreans nowadays affectionately call their land *mugunghwa tongsan* (land of hibiscus). It so happens that the hibiscus is the state flower of Hawai'i as well, symbolizing the ever-present beauty of the Island State.

It was from the Land of Hibiscus that the first group of 102 Koreans, dressed mostly in their traditional costumes, landed at Honolulu harbor on January 13, 1903. Thereafter, approximately 7,200 Koreans came to Hawai'i to work as laborers on sugar plantations. About a thousand of them moved on to the mainland United States in search of better opportunities while about the same number returned to Korea. Although there have been some important and significant studies made recently on certain aspects of Koreans in Hawai'i, their history has not yet been fully studied, and many aspects of Korean experiences in Hawai'i still remain largely unexplored.

It was to remedy this regrettable situation that the Center for Korean Studies of the University of Hawai'i held two academic conferences—one in January 2000 and another in May 2001—inviting scholars from the United States and Korea. Selected papers from those conferences examining the achievements and experiences of Koreans in Hawai'i are included in this book. As the Koreans in Hawai'i have left rich and diverse legacies in the past hundred years, the works in this book scratch only the surface of Korean experiences in the Islands. It is hoped that the publication of this book will provide an impetus for more serious research toward a better and fuller understanding of the Koreans in Hawai'i.

Like many immigrants who came to the United States, the Koreans in Hawai'i encountered many adversities, such as racism, cultural shock, and economic exploitation and hardship, that were common to most immigrants. Unlike others, the Koreans in Hawai'i had to bear additional handicaps that were unique to them during the first half of the twentieth century. To begin with, numerically, the Koreans remained a small minority within the Hawai'i community, as their number never exceeded 2 or 3 percent of the total population. This numerical disadvantage deprived them of the ability to exercise meaningful political or social power in protecting and promoting their rights and interests. Moreover, their tiny minority status made it extremely difficult for them to succeed in the economic sector, as they had been obliged to find their clients beyond their own ethnic group and compete against non-Korean businesses that had already established their roots in Hawai'i ahead of them.

Second, the Koreans were latecomers to Hawai'i. Arriving in the years between 1903 and 1905, they were the last group to reach Hawai'i from Asia, except the Filipinos. As late starters, they discovered that many opportunities—economic and otherwise—had already been taken by Chinese and Japanese immigrants. Often they were obliged to content themselves with finding small niches not yet filled by their Asian counterparts.

The most serious handicap, however, was the loss of their country. With Japan's forcible annexation of Korea in 1910, Korea was reduced to a colony, and the Koreans in Hawai'i lost their home government. Without their own government to protect their interests, the Koreans in Hawai'i became "international orphans," so to speak, and there was no governmental authority that could look after their well-being or help redress their grievances. In addition, with the loss of the Korean nation, the recovery of Korean sovereignty became the foremost priority for most Koreans in Hawai'i. Much of their energies and resources were directed toward nationalist activities to regain Korean independence. Had these energies and resources been utilized toward promoting their own well-being, the fortunes of the Koreans in Hawai'i would have been drastically different from what they were. The original dream of the Korean immigrants was to make a quick fortune in Hawai'i and return home. With Korea under Japanese occupation, however, they had no country to which to return and were obliged to set aside their search for personal wealth and happiness in favor of supporting the Korean independence movement.

In the course of dealing with their adversities and handicaps, Koreans in Hawai'i encountered many difficulties. Unable to cope, many became victims of dysfunctional families and even lawless elements, adding considerably to the public burden. In the end, however, with their typical resourcefulness and indefatigable determination, Koreans were able to overcome their adversities, and in less than two generations they became the most successful minority group in Hawai'i. By 1970, their median family income was highest among all ethnic groups in the Islands, according to a Hawai'i state study.

In Chapter 1, "The Early Korean Immigration: An Overview," Yŏng-ho Ch'oe gives the historical background of the early Korean immigration to Hawai'i, such as the conditions surrounding their arrival, problems they encountered, and how they overcame their adversities. Accurate statistics are fundamental to a correct understanding of the conditions of the immigrants' life in Hawai'i. The tables and figures in the chapter cover such issues as the number of Korean arrivals in Hawai'i, their occupational backgrounds in Korea, gender and age distributions, hours and wages of plantation workers, number of Koreans working on sugar plantations, rate of juvenile delinquency, illiteracy, interracial marriages, and the like. One notable point of this chapter is that it challenges previous contentions about the social and occupational backgrounds of the Korean immigrants. Both Bernice Kim and Wayne Patterson, perhaps the two foremost authorities on Korean immigration, concluded in their important studies that most Korean immigrants to Hawai'i were drawn from a nonagrarian urban background in Korea. Ch'oe, however, disputes this conclusion. Analyzing the contemporary socioeconomic conditions of Korea at the turn of the twentieth century and relying on job descriptions immigrants themselves gave to the immigration authorities in Honolulu, the author believes that a majority of the Korean immigrants came from a rural agrarian background.

American missionaries played a key role in persuading the Korean government to permit Koreans to migrate to Hawai'i and in the initial recruiting of Korean laborers. Horace N. Allen, the first Western missionary in Korea, who later became the U.S. minister in Korea, was largely responsible for guiding the Korean emperor to give permission for Korean immigration to Hawai'i. And when the initial Korean response to the call for labor recruitment was tepid, Rev. George Heber Jones, an American missionary working in the Inch'ŏn area, exhorted the congregations of the Naeri Church and others to go to Hawai'i. Persuaded by Rev. Jones's sermon, perhaps as many as half of the first group of 102 Koreans who went to Hawai'i were members of the churches under Jones's missionary charge, and they included some leading members of the Inch'ŏn-area churches. In Chapter 2, "Korean Immigration to Hawai'i and the Korean Protestant Church," Mahn-Yol Yi (Yi Man-yŏl) gives us a fascinating account of the role Korean churches played in Korean immigration and its impact upon the Protestant churches in Korea. As a large number of church members joined the Hawai'i emigration, according to Yi, strong criticisms were raised by the Western missionaries in Korea as well as by the Korean church leadership, who feared that the Hawai'i migration might drain off those whom they had painstakingly converted to Christianity only recently. Another noteworthy aspect of this chapter is that it shows how Christians among the Korean immigrants played leadership roles in political and social activities in Hawai'i.

Arguably the most prominent and controversial person in Hawai'i was Syngman Rhee, who used the Pacific islands as his home base for his political and nationalist activities. "Syngman Rhee in Hawai'i: His Activities in the Early Years, 1913–1915" (Chapter 3) is a study of Rhee's early work in Hawai'i. When Rhee arrived in Honolulu in 1913, the American Methodist Mission in Hawai'i was in deep trouble with island Koreans, as American Methodist leaders had publicly uttered remarks favoring Japanese control over Korea, causing a furor within the Korean community. Hoping to mitigate the Koreans' anger, the Methodist Mission entrusted Rhee to take charge of the education of Korean youths in Hawai'i. Rhee's initial work was enormously successful, and he introduced some innovative programs. Rhee's collaborative work with the Methodist Mission, however, did not last long. By the end of 1915, Rhee broke away from the mission and embarked on educational work with Korean youths on his own. Yŏng-ho Ch'oe examines the reasons behind Rhee's break from the Methodist Mission. The year 1915 was an important turning point not only for Rhee but also for the entire Korean community as well. It was in this year that Rhee first ventured into the politics of the Korean community in Hawai'i. At the time, Rhee's followers challenged the leadership of the most important community organization, the Korean National Association (KNA). At issue in the dispute was who would control the KNA, an organization that claimed virtual jurisdiction over all the Koreans in Hawai'i, acting as a semi-government agency, and who would lead the Korean nationalist movement against the Japanese occupation of Korea. Ch'oe analyzes the issues and causes of the 1915 feud, which splintered the Korean community in Hawai'i irrevocably and whose long-lasting impact is still being felt today.

In the early days of their immigrant life, Koreans had a serious problem with their public image. This negative image was partly of their own making, as lawless elements among them muddied the water, which in turn was compounded by the white-owned newspapers that often portrayed the Koreans with racist overtones as uncivilized and heathen. In Chapter 4, "Images and Crimes of Koreans in Hawai'i: Media Portrayals, 1903–1925," Brandon Palmer examines crimes committed by Koreans in Hawai'i, how the major English-language newspapers handled them, and the ways in which Koreans tried to overcome their negative image. Unfamiliar with the Western legal system, some Koreans attempted to take the law into their own hands in dealing with those who violated their codes of conduct. There were also outright outlaws, who threatened the law and order of both the Hawaiian and the Korean communities, thereby besmirching Korea's good name. With racial overtones, the two Honolulu newspapers—the *Pacific Commercial Advertiser* (now the *Honolulu Advertiser*) and the *Hawaiian Star* (now the *Honolulu Star-Bulletin*)—often characterized crimes committed by Koreans in a prejudicial way. It was indeed a formidable task for the Koreans in Hawai'i to overcome the stereotypical image of the white newspapers while at the same time uplifting the spirit and morale of their compatriots.

On March 1, 1919, Korea exploded with the declaration of Korean independence followed by nationwide demonstrations in what is now known as the March First Movement. Inspired by Woodrow Wilson's peace proposal in Europe, which called for "self-determination" in dealing with those people who were under alien rule, Korea proclaimed itself as an independent nation and the entire population rose up in peaceful, nonviolent demonstrations demanding the end of the Japanese colonial rule. Although the March First Movement failed to achieve its objective of regaining independence for Korea, as Japan mobilized its brutal force to crush the uprising, the movement had a far-reaching impact upon the Korean nationalist movement with the formation of the Korean Provisional Government in exile in China. The news of the outbreak of the March First Movement was received with great excitement by the Koreans in Hawai'i, who immediately moved to help restore independence to their homeland. In Chapter 5, "The March First Movement of 1919 and Koreans in Hawai'i," Do-Hyung Kim (Kim To-hyŏng) and Yŏng-ho Ch'oe examine how Koreans in Hawai'i reacted to the March First Movement and worked toward regaining Korean independence. Hungry for any news from Korea, which was heavily censored by the Japanese authorities, the Koreans in Hawai'i relied mostly on reports appearing in the two major English-language newspapers in Honolulu, which carried relatively detailed accounts of events unfolding in Korea, in general sympathetic to Koreans while critical of the brutal way Japan handled the situation. The enthusiasm aroused by the March First Movement brought unity—though short-lived—to a Korean community that had been bedeviled by feuds.

No doubt the most serious problem the Korean community in Hawai'i encountered was division within, which led to factional strife. After Syngman Rhee challenged the leadership and gained control of the KNA in 1915, the Koreans in Hawai'i were deeply divided. Those who were forced out of the KNA leadership—mostly followers of Pak Yong-man—refused to cooperate with Rhee. Feuds and squabbles were periodic occurrences, plaguing the Korean community, undermining the spirit and morale of the Koreans in Hawai'i, and seriously tarnishing their image. In addition to the personality differences between the two leaders, the division involved divergence in opinions about the best strategy to win Korean independence—Rhee favoring diplomatic efforts to gain support of world opinion and Pak advocating military confrontation against Japan.

In 1931, the Korean community witnessed another bitter feud, once again over the control of the KNA. When the annual delegate convention was con-

vened in January, disputes arose over the proper qualification of the delegates
who attended, which in turn led to physical violence. Again, Syngman Rhee was
a key man behind the disputes as his followers tried to take over the meeting by
force. In Chapter 6, "Local Struggles and Diasporic Politics: The 1931 Court
Cases of the Korean National Association of Hawai'i," Richard S. Kim gives us
a perceptive analysis of the background of the dispute and the outstanding
issues involved. Going beyond local politics, Kim sees the 1931 dispute as part
of a transnational struggle over the control of the Korean nationalist movement
that became increasingly important after the formation of the Korean Provisional Government in exile in Shanghai in 1919. The 1931 feud was in the end
adjudicated by the U.S courts, in which Rhee suffered a humiliating defeat,
resulting in considerable damage to his reputation.

The world witnessed in the 1930s a significant change in the international
climate as Japan provoked war in China with the Manchurian Incident in 1931
and the Sino-Japanese war in 1937. The war in Asia gave rise to an anti-Japanese sentiment in the United States, which was welcomed by the Korean nationalists, who believed such a development might be conducive to the liberation of
Korea from Japan. For such an eventuality, they reasoned that there was a strong
need for all Koreans to unite their energies and resources for the common cause.
Three main groups had vied for leadership in the Korean community. Founded
in 1909 as a representative organization for all Koreans, the KNA came under
the influence of Syngman Rhee in 1915 and was renamed Taehan'in Kyomindan (Korean Residents Association) in 1922, following an ordinance issued by
the Korean Provisional Government. After the bitter court battle over the control of the association in 1931, Rhee lost influence, and in 1933, the Residents
Association reverted to its old name, the KNA, now dominated by those who
either had seceded from Rhee's camp or had opposed Rhee all along. The second group was the Tongjihoe (Dong Ji Hoi), which Rhee organized in 1921 as
his own support organization. Although after the 1931 court battle, some key
members broke away from Rhee, the Tongjihoe remained staunchly loyal to
Rhee throughout the politically tumultuous years he spent in Hawai'i. (The
Tongjihoe even named Rhee as its president for life.) The third group consisted
of followers of Pak Yong-man, who had lost the control of the KNA to Rhee in
1915. They organized the Tae Chosŏn Tongniptan (Korean National Independence League) to provide support for Pak. But with the loss of their leader in
1928 when Pak was assassinated in China, it lost centripetal force. Although
there were many other smaller organizations, these three groups formed the
backbone of the Korean community. In Chapter 7, "The Unification Movement
of the Hawai'i Korean Community in the 1930s," Sun-Pyo Hong (Hong Sŏng-
p'yo) offers us a detailed account of the very complicated and complex efforts to
bring unity within the Korean community during the 1930s.

With the Japanese attack on Pearl Harbor in December 1941, the United States entered the war against Japan. Japan, against whom Koreans had been waging a lonely struggle for more than three decades, now became the common enemy of both Korea and the United States. This was a welcome turn of events that Koreans had long awaited. Identifying their nationalistic aspirations with the military goals of the United States, the Koreans in Hawaiʻi offered their unstinting support for the war. But, to their horror and astonishment, the U.S. martial law authorities in Hawaiʻi declared Koreans "enemy aliens," effectively classifying them as Japanese subjects—a humiliation no Korean could bear. Even though the federal government in Washington exempted Koreans living in the mainland United States from registering as enemy aliens, the military governor in Hawaiʻi refused to do so. Imposition of enemy alien status placed many restrictions on Koreans, such as in bank transactions, travel, and curfews. What were reasons for such a ruling? Was it racially motivated? What were the reactions of the Koreans? In Chapter 8, "How Koreans Repealed Their 'Enemy Alien' Status: Korean Americans' Identity, Culture, and National Pride in Wartime Hawaiʻi," Lili M. Kim offers a perceptive analysis of how Koreans came to receive enemy alien status, the rationale behind the U.S. officials' justification of their decision, and the strategy Koreans in Hawaiʻi pursued to repeal enemy status.

As war clouds loomed over the Pacific with Japan's expansionism, the fractured Koreans in Hawaiʻi and the United States began to realize the importance of presenting a united front to fight for Korean independence. In the spring of 1941, a convention of overseas Koreans was held in Honolulu, where delegates from various organizations in the United States and Hawaiʻi discussed strategy for their nationalist struggle against Japan and agreed to form an umbrella organization that would embrace all Korean nationalist groups so as to present themselves as united for the common cause of regaining Korean independence. This important organization was the United Korean Committee in America (Chae-Mi Hanjok Yŏnhap Wiwŏnhoe). The timing of the Korean unity could not have been more opportune, as shortly thereafter Japan attacked Pearl Harbor, inducing the United States to declare war on Japan. The American entry into the war raised the hope of Korean nationalists significantly as the United States now assumed the main burden of defeating the militaristic Japan. In Chapter 9, Ann Soon Choi gives the first serious study on the activities of the United Korean Committee in America and the various problems it had to deal with. Though launched with great optimism and enthusiasm, the Committee soon encountered serious issues such as the personal political ambitions of certain individual leaders and honest differences over the strategy for winning Korean independence. Organized as a showcase of unity, the United Korean Committee was caught in a bind. On the one hand, it had to demonstrate to the outside world that Koreans were capable of uniting for a common cause; on the other hand, being a volunteer umbrella organization, it lacked any force to coerce those unwilling to abide by its rules and principles. Choi examines and analyzes the work of the Committee in promoting Korean nationalist activities in the United States and at the same time its attempt to coordinate its work with the Korean Provisional Government then in exile in Chungking, China. We learn from Choi's study that in spite of many difficult obstacles, the United Korean Committee, under the leadership of a new generation of Korean Americans who, unlike the earlier generation, had received thorough American educations, worked strenuously and selflessly for the Korean nationalist cause toward achieving Korean independence as well as improving the lot of the Koreans in the United States.

Unfortunately, the cultural aspects of the life of Korean immigrants in Hawai'i have not yet been fully studied. With regard to literature, for example, virtually nothing is known, with the exception perhaps of a manuscript of epic poems left by Yi Hong-gi. Arriving in Hawai'i in 1904 to work as a plantation laborer, Yi Hong-gi wrote poems reflecting the harsh life he experienced as a plantation worker in a strange land and expressing his longing for the homeland. Written in the difficult Sino-Korean classical writing *(hanmun)*, Yi's poems have yet to be studied and introduced to the public. For the Korean immigrants in Hawai'i, music and dance were an integral part of their life. Through music and dance, they could vent their frustration and regain cheerfulness after a hard day's work. In music and dancing, they found solace and comfort from homesickness. Unfortunately, we do not have many records on music and dance. In spite of the paucity of data, we are fortunate in the field of dance that Judy Van Zile is able to present us with her study in Chapter 10, "Korean Dance in Hawai'i: A Century in the Public Eye." Through this valuable study, we learn of important contributions made by three key individuals in preserving and promoting Korean dance in Hawai'i as well as many roles public performance of Korean dance played for the Korean and the Hawai'i communities.

It is a pleasure to express my deep gratitude to the Center for Korean Studies of the University of Hawai'i at Mānoa and its former director, Edward J. Shultz. Dr. Shultz organized and administered the two conferences for our purposes efficiently and smoothly and has given me all the help I needed in preparing this book. I am most thankful to him. Mike Macmillan helped me in many ways to improve this book, ranging from editorial guidance to consultation, for which I am grateful. I was also very fortunate to have had able graduate assistants, Min-woo Shin and Brandon Palmer, who worked with me patiently and effectively. I thank them as well. Finally, I owe my wife, Minja Kim Choe, more than words can express. She has put up with me all this time with patience and love, while carrying out her own busy professional duties at the East-West Center. I am most grateful to her.

Note: Romanization of personal names posed some problems, as many Koreans in Hawai'i used their own ways of spelling their names. In principle, the McCune-Reischauer system is used as much as possible. For those whose spelling is different, the McCune-Reischauer romanization is given in parentheses at the first occurrence. For example, Hyŏn Sun spelled his name as Soon Hyun. Hence, his name is given as "Soon Hyun (Hyŏn Sun)" when it first appears.

I

The Early Korean Immigration
An Overview

Known as a Hermit Kingdom, Korea was the last country in Asia to open its door to the Western world. After repeated rejections of Western overtures to negotiate, in 1882 Korea finally signed a treaty of amity and trade with the United States, the first Western country with which Korea established diplomatic ties. Uncertain of the shifting balance of power surrounding the Korean Peninsula, Korea moved to join the family of nations haltingly and with great reluctance in the last decades of the nineteenth century.

In the meantime, during the latter half of the nineteenth century, unbeknown to Korea, the Kingdom of Hawai'i came increasingly under the influence of the white people as the sugar industry gained dominance in the Hawaiian economy, leading eventually to the overthrow of the Hawaiian Kingdom by the whites in 1893 and the annexation of Hawai'i by the United States in 1898. Constantly in need of cheap labor, the Hawai'i sugar industry sought multiple sources of plantation workers and—after several years of unsuccessful efforts—won Korean governmental approval to allow its citizens to go abroad and work in Hawai'i. Between 1903 and 1905, more than 7,200 Koreans immigrated to Hawai'i to work on sugar plantations. This chapter presents an overview of these early Korean immigrants.

ARRIVAL

As early as 1896, the Hawai'i sugar industry attempted to obtain Korean laborers. The task of securing Korean workers, however, was not easy, as there were strong oppositions and difficulties within Korea. It was not until the intervention of Horace N. Allen, the U.S. minister to Korea, on behalf of the Hawai'i sugar industry that the Korean government finally gave its approval to Korean emigrations. A medical missionary-turned-diplomat stationed in Korea since 1884, Allen had won the confidence and trust of the ever-suspicious Emperor Kojong of Korea and successfully prevailed upon the Korean ruler to permit Koreans to work in Hawai'i.[1] In 1902, Emperor Kojong authorized the setting up of an office called Suminwŏn² to issue passports to those who wished to travel abroad.

As an agent of the Hawaii Sugar Planters Association (HSPA), David W. Deshler established the East-West Development Company (Tongsŏ Kaebal Hoesa) in Inch'ŏn to recruit Korean laborers. The first shipload of Koreans left Inch'ŏn harbor for Japan aboard a Japanese ship, *Genkai-maru*, on December 22, 1902. There are, however, conflicting reports on the exact number of the first group of Koreans who departed Inch'ŏn on that date. Kim Wŏn-yong, who wrote perhaps the most helpful history of Koreans in the United States, claims that 121 workers left Korea as the first group of Korean emigrants for Kobe, Japan, where they underwent a physical examination and that those who passed the physical (101 persons along with interpreters) boarded an American merchant ship, *Gaelic*, on a voyage to Hawai'i.³ Unfortunately, Kim Wŏn-yong gives no source for this information. Thereafter, many scholars accepted Kim Wŏn-yong's number—that is, 121—as the first group of Korean emigrants.⁴ To add to the confusion, *Hwangsŏng shinmun*, a contemporary Korean newspaper published in Seoul, carried the following news article under the heading of "Hawaii Emigration" (Hawaii Imin) on December 27, 1902: "As previously reported, Deshler, an American stationed at Inch'ŏn harbor, was engaged in recruiting Korean emigrants to Hawaii. Fifty-four Koreans who responded to [Deshler's call for] recruitment left on 22nd of this month for Hawaii via Japan." Because this news appeared only five days after the departure of the first Korean emigrant group, this number—fifty-four—would seem to be the most reliable. This, however, is not the case. It may have referred only to the number of adult male workers, not including women and children who accompanied them (as we will see below).

The most credible information comes from a report made by a Japanese consul general stationed at Inch'ŏn. On January 24, 1903, about one month after the departure of the first Korean emigrant group, Katō Motoshirō, the Japanese consul general at Inch'ŏn, made a detailed report (seven pages long, handwritten) to the Japanese foreign minister in Tokyo under the subject of "Koreans Going to Hawaii for Work" (Kankokujin no Hawaii dekasegi). In it, Katō wrote: "On December 22 last year [1902], ninety-seven Koreans (fifty-four males, twenty-one females, and twenty-two children) left this port [Inch'ŏn] aboard *Genkai-maru* to work in Hawaii. This is the beginning of the Korean emigration to work in Hawaii."⁵ Here, Katō gives the specific number of males, females, and children who departed Inch'ŏn on December 22, 1902, and the total number, we are told, was ninety-seven (including fifty-four adult males, as *Hwangsŏng shinmun* reported). As Japan at the time was moving toward gaining dominance over Korea, Japanese officials in Korea were paying meticulous attention to the developments within Korea, scrutinizing every detail of Korea's contacts with foreigners. Hence, it is reasonable to conclude that the report made by the Japanese consul general at the time when the first group of Korean emigrants had departed the port of Inch'ŏn is most reliable. I believe that the first group of Korean emigrants who left Inch'ŏn on December 22, 1902, numbered ninety-seven, contrary to other numbers given elsewhere.

If this is the case, there arises another discrepancy between the numbers of those who departed Inch'ŏn on December 22, 1902—that is, ninety-seven—and those who arrived in Honolulu on January 13, 1903—that is, 102. In view of no other available evidence, a reasonable assumption one can draw is that the first group of ninety-seven emigrants were joined in Japan by other Koreans who had come from other Korean ports at around the same time to undergo physical examinations. One hundred two Koreans who received physical clarification then were allowed to board an American steamship, *Gaelic,* for a trans-Pacific voyage to Hawai'i.

Be that as it may, amid a fanfare of aloha, the first group of 102 Korean laborers arrived at Honolulu harbor on January 13, 1903, and was soon assigned to the Waialua plantation on the island of O'ahu. The second group of 63 Koreans reached Hawai'i on February 8 of the same year and was sent to sugar plantations at Kahuku.[6] Thereafter, Korean laborers continued to arrive and by the end of June 1905, when Korean immigration practically halted, as many as 7,291 Koreans had come to Hawai'i.

From the perspective of Korean history, the Korean immigration to Hawai'i that took place from 1903 to 1905 has special historical significance. First, it was the first officially sanctioned immigration of Korean people to any foreign country in Korean history. Although it is true that a large number of Koreans had migrated to the Maritime Province of Russia and to the present-day Yanbian region of China during the nineteenth century, they did so without formal authorization from the Korean government.

Second, it provided opportunities for Koreans at the grassroots level for the first time in their history to come in contact with the Western world. After Korea signed the treaty of amity and commerce with the United States in 1882, only a handful of high government officials and social elites had opportunities to visit America. The ordinary people at the bottom of the social strata could not even imagine going to the United States until 1903. The immigration of Koreans to Hawai'i marks an important turning point in the relationship between Korea and the United States, whose interactions were greatly stimulated by the contacts the Korean emigrants established with the United States and Hawai'i.

Third, the Korean immigration to Hawai'i signified the first overseas venture to the West. As we look back over the last hundred years, there are perhaps as many as two million Koreans living in the Western world. For these Koreans, those who moved to Hawai'i in 1903–5 were the pioneers in Korea's oversea advancement, acting as agents to enrich the cultures, economies, and other aspects of their respective regions.

Fourth, by sheer historical coincidence, Hawai'i became an important base for Korean nationalism during the first half of the twentieth century. Within a few years after their arrival in Hawai'i, the Koreans learned the tragic news of the demise of their homeland, as Japan forcibly annexed Korea and reduced it to a colony of the Japanese empire in 1910. The Japanese annexation of Korea had a heart-rending impact upon Koreans in Hawai'i, which in turn profoundly influenced the nature of their immigrant life abroad. A Korean American, Ethan Sungkoo Kiehm, who was only five years old at the time, recalls the reactions of Koreans on the island of Kaua'i when they learned of the Japanese seizure of Korea in 1910:

> All I remember of when Korea was taken by Japan was that everybody at our Kauai plantation was crying. I can't forget it. Nobody worked that day. They took us to the gathering. All I knew was that it must have been terrible to lose a country. Just about every person was crying. We cried too when the adults cried. We didn't know what it was all about, but we cried. There were 100 people there. They decided to boycott anything and everything that came from Japan. They all brought out Japanese things from every house and burned them in a big bonfire. And they cried all night. That left quite an impression on me. I was 5 years old.[7]

Obsessed with the goal of restoring the sovereignty of their motherland, the Koreans in Hawai'i developed an intense nationalistic sentiment directed against Japanese imperialism and militarism, and Hawai'i became a crucial base for Korean nationalist activities. Through their direct participation and their generous financial and moral support, the Koreans in Hawai'i made significant contributions to awakening Korea's nationalistic consciousness and sustaining nationalistic spirit and activities throughout the darkest hours in Korean history.

A long-range objective of the sugar industry in bringing Korean laborers to Hawai'i was to secure a continuous supply of cheap labor. A more immediate goal, however, was to counter the preponderance of Japanese labor in Hawai'i. After the enactment of the Chinese Exclusion Act in 1882 and with the annexation of Hawai'i to the United States, the Hawai'i sugar industry was obliged to depend largely on imported Japanese workers as a source of cheap labor. But it soon became clear that relying on just one source of labor entailed serious problems. In 1905, the U.S. Commission of Labor on Hawai'i gave the following assessment of the labor situation in Hawai'i:

Another aspect of the labor situation as it affects the planters arises out of a preponderance among their laborers of a single nationality. As a result of the exclusion of Chinese since annexation, the supply of imported labor for the plantations was confined entirely to the Japanese until the beginning of Korean immigration was brought about in 1903. The Japanese have secured a preponderance among the plantation workers which creates serious difficulties of administration, renders the plantations liable to great loss by strikes, and to a certain extent takes out of the hands of overseers and managers the control of administration.[8]

It was to offset this situation that the HSPA attempted to bring Korean laborers to Hawai'i in 1896 without success, finally succeeding in 1903. In short, the main objective of importing Korean laborers to Hawai'i was to break up the Japanese monopoly of Hawai'i's labor market in the sugar industry.

This factor unfortunately placed the Korean immigrants in an adversarial relationship with the Japanese in Hawai'i from the very beginning of their Hawaiian life, as Japanese laborers came to regard Koreans as unfriendly competitors who would take away their jobs and other opportunities. The strained relationship between the two Asian ethnic groups was further compounded by the Japanese colonization of Korea in 1910, which aroused a strong anti-Japanese sentiment among Koreans in Hawai'i.

From the standpoint of the sugar industry, it was only natural that the HSPA wanted to have a continuous supply of Korean laborers. But to their disappointment, the Korean government formally issued an order prohibiting all further immigration of laborers to foreign countries on April 1, 1905.[9] There have been debates over the true motive of the Korean government in halting Korean emigration. It has often been claimed that reports received by the government about the harsh treatment of Korean laborers who had gone to Mexico at about the same time led to the decision. But evidence indicates that the reported plight of the Koreans in Mexico was tangential in the government decision to halt emigration. The direct reason was the pressure imposed by the Japanese government, and the correct answer must be sought in the existing relationship between Korea and Japan at the time.

Briefly, the fierce rivalry between Japan and Russia over Korea culminated in the outbreak of the Russo-Japanese war in February 1904, and a series of military victories achieved by Japan enabled it to become the dominant power in Korea. As a result, Japan imposed a series of "treaty agreements" upon Korea, one of which, signed in August 1904, stipulated that the Korean government was to employ as diplomatic advisor a foreigner recommended by the Japanese government and that all matters pertaining to Korea's foreign affairs were to be handled only after consulting with him.[10] Thus, by April 1905, Japan had virtual control over Korea, and the treaty reducing Korea to a mere protectorate of Japan would follow in a few months.

One individual who stood to lose most from the prohibition of Korean emigration was an American, D. W. Deshler, who, having obtained sole authorization from the Korean government to recruit Korean laborers, was operating a lucrative labor recruitment company in Inch'ŏn as an agent of the HSPA. As soon as he learned of the prohibition order, Deshler rushed to the Korean foreign minister Yi Ha-yŏng to protest the government's action, whereupon the Korean minister, according to Deshler, stated that "personally he [the minister] was greatly in favor of the emigration" and that "no one [in his government] had any objection to Hawai'i emigration." But when the Korean minister consulted the Japanese minister in Seoul about prohibiting Korean immigration to Mexico, as there had been reports of mistreatment of Korean laborers there, "the Japanese Minister pointed out that it would be unfair to discriminate in favor of any emigration company or country and that if one stopped, all must stop."[11] Thus, on April 1, 1905, the Korean government, under pressure from Japan, formally issued an order prohibiting all further immigration of Koreans to any country.[12]

The true intent of the Japanese government in halting Korean emigration, however, is revealed elsewhere in its instructions given to the Japanese consul general at the port city of Inch'ŏn. Dated April 7, 1905, only a few days after the issuance of the prohibition order, the Japanese instructions read in part:

> Not only is there a fear that the Korean laborers in foreign countries may compete against and come in conflict with our [i.e., Japanese] emigrants, but also these Koreans in their passages abroad go through quarantine at Yokohama or Kobe, in which no small number of patients with communicable diseases have been detected, causing annoyance at our hospitals. Now that the Korean government has prohibited the emigration of laborers, it is a rather opportune occasion for us. Therefore, one should keep in mind to make this order effective as long as possible.[13]

Simply stated, the Japanese government did not want Koreans to compete against its own laborers in Hawai'i.[14]

The Korea Review, a journal published by Westerners in Seoul, made the following observation on the subsequent "Korean Emigration Protection Law" imposed by Japan in 1906:

> There is something pathetic in the way Japan is providing "protection" for Koreans where no protection is required. No one has heard that Koreans have suffered because they went abroad to work. They make very satisfactory workmen and in Hawaii are considered superior to Japanese

laborers. No one would deny that the government should exercise a certain oversight over emigration but these laws seem to be simply putting obstacles in the way of emigration rather than helping the Korean to gain an honest livelihood in the labor market abroad. The Korean has as much right to go abroad and work as has the Japanese but these laws practically prohibit this. It may be that free emigration would result in individual cases of hardship but why not begin at points where the Korean really needs protection? To hold a man down by the throat while you rifle his pockets and at the same time give him a dose of quinine for fear he will catch cold during the process would be a curious case of mixed motive.[15]

In spite of the prohibition order, apparently a small number of Koreans continued to leave for Hawai'i. When Japanese officials in Korea learned about it, they made a strong protest demanding stricter enforcement of the order by the Korean government.[16] Thus, except for the picture brides who were permitted into Hawai'i from 1910 to 1924, Korean immigration to Hawai'i came to an end for all practical purposes by mid-1905, only two and a half years after it had begun.

Also, as Wayne Patterson persuasively argues,[17] Japanese objection to the Korean immigration to Hawai'i was tied to Japan's strained relationship with the United States at the time caused by the race issue. As many Japanese immigrants (and also Koreans) moved on to the West Coast from Hawai'i, there arose a strong anti-Japanese sentiment in California (which culminated in San Francisco's school segregation in 1906), causing serious diplomatic tension between the United States and Japan. There was even a fear of the enactment of a Japanese exclusion act by U.S. Congress that would deal a serious blow to Japan's ambition to become a world power. It was to mitigate such a situation that Japan decided to put an end to Korean immigration to Hawai'i and the United States. Patterson writes: "Ironically, it meant that the Japanese had decided to mount an exclusion campaign against the Koreans in order to prevent their own exclusion from the United States. The right of Korea to send its people abroad would have to be sacrificed to prevent Japan from losing face internationally."[18] In other words, Japan used Korean immigration as a sacrificial lamb on the altar of promoting Japanese interests in dealing with the United States.

Appendix 1 gives an annual breakdown of the number of Koreans who entered the United States, Hawai'i, and California from 1899 to 1932 as reported by the commissioner general of immigration. During this period, 9,483 Koreans entered the United States, and of these 8,320, or 87.2 percent, went to Hawai'i. The number of Koreans who migrated to Hawai'i between 1903 and 1905, however, was 7,291, and they were then followed by several hundred picture brides (as will be explained below). Between 1903 and 1905, a total of

7,400 Koreans entered the United States, and of these, 7,291, or 98.5 percent, were accepted into Hawai'i. This report gives the male/female breakdown for the entire United States, but unfortunately not for Hawai'i.

Another report by the commissioner of labor statistics on Hawai'i, however, offers a gender breakdown of those Koreans who were admitted into Honolulu harbor (see Table 1). According to this report, from July 1, 1900, to June 31, 1915, 8,047 Koreans arrived in Hawai'i, and they were listed as 6,773 males (84.2 percent), 780 females (9.7 percent), and 494 children (6.1 percent). Many of them, however, did not stay in Hawai'i but moved elsewhere. The commissioner of labor statistics on Hawai'i reports that of these 8,047 Koreans, 2,482 (30.8 percent) left Hawai'i either for their homeland in Asia or for the mainland United States between 1900 and 1915 (see Table 2). According to this report, from 1906 to 1915, 660 Koreans moved to the mainland United States, while 1,101 went to Asia, most likely returning to their homeland. For the period from 1900 to 1905, 721 Koreans left Hawai'i, but there is no information on their destinations. It is believed, however, that most of them went to the mainland United States rather than to Korea. If this is so, as many as 1,381 persons may have moved on to the United States. Of those 7,291 Koreans who arrived in Hawai'i between 1903 and 1905, in the end 5,565 remained in the Islands.

OCCUPATIONAL BACKGROUNDS OF KOREAN IMMIGRANTS

Who were these Koreans? The issue of occupational backgrounds of the Korean immigrants prior to their departure from Korea is still debated. Bernice B. H. Kim, who undertook the first serious study of the Koreans in Hawai'i in 1937, believed that most Korean immigrants came from cities and had no agrarian background. In her important University of Hawai'i M.A. thesis, she wrote: "nearly all [Korean immigrants] had been city dwellers" and that "farmers . . . made up less than one-seventh of the total number who came to the Territory [of Hawai'i]." As for the occupations the Korean immigrants held prior to immigrating to Hawai'i, Kim concluded: "In order of descending numerical strength, the largest proportion was common laborers or coolies, who worked

Table 1 *Statistics of the Korean Immigration to Hawai'i, 1900–1915: Arrivals*

	ADULT MALE	ADULT FEMALE	CHILDREN	TOTAL
1900–5	6,717	677	465	7,859
1906–10	24	12	9	45
1911–15	32	91	20	143
Subtotal	6,773	780	494	8,047

Source: *Report of Commissioner of Labor Statistics on Hawaii* (1915), 64.

periodically about port cities and towns; next, ex-soldiers of the Korean Army
. . . then minor governmental clerks, manual laborers, political refugees, students, policemen, miners, wood-cutters, household servants, and a few Buddhist
monks."[19] Unfortunately, Kim gave no specific numbers of these Koreans, nor
did she tell how she had obtained her information. One can only presume that
her claim was based largely on her observations of the Korean community in
Hawai'i at the time of her study, not necessarily on rigorous scientific research.

Wayne Patterson follows Bernice Kim in believing that most of the Korean
immigrants had come from nonagrarian urban backgrounds. In his recent com-
prehensive and important studies on the early Korean immigrants, Patterson
concluded that "the great majority of Korean immigrants had lived in the cities
rather than the countryside before coming to Hawai'i" and that "Korean immigrants toiled in mostly nonagricultural occupations prior to their emigration."[20]

These observations, however, are contradicted by the official report of the
immigration officer. Table 3 gives the breakdowns of the occupations of 7,400
Koreans who entered the United States, including 7,291 who went to Hawai'i,
between 1903 and 1905 as reported by the commissioner general of immigration. Of these Koreans, 6,320, or 84.9 percent, registered their occupations in
Korea as farmers or farm laborers. This figure directly contradicts the observations made by the two foremost authorities on Korean immigrants in Hawai'i.
To be sure, it is entirely possible that many Koreans with no farming background
may have told the immigration officials in Hawai'i when they entered Honolulu
harbor that they had been farmers in Korea and these people may have included
scholars, government officials, former soldiers, students, and the like. (It may
also be possible that they had been coached by Deshler or his agents to hide their
nonfarming backgrounds.) Even if that were the case, it is my belief that the
proportion of such men was relatively small and that a large majority of Korean
immigrants to Hawai'i were men of agrarian backgrounds.

The reason for such a belief is that Korea at the time of the Hawai'i immigration was still overwhelmingly an agrarian society with virtually no industry

Table 2 *Statistics of the Korean Immigration, 1900–1915: Departures*

	TO UNITED STATES			TO ORIENT			TOTAL		
	ADULT MALE	ADULT FEMALE	CHILDREN	ADULT MALE	ADULT FEMALE	CHILDREN	ADULT MALE	ADULT FEMALE	CHILDREN
1900–5	NA	NA	NA	NA	NA	NA	653	40	28
1906–10	568	29	19	758	90	117	1,326	119	136
1911–15	40	4	—	112	15	9	152	19	9
SUBTOTAL	608	33	19	870	105	126	2,131	178	173
TOTAL		660			1,101			2,482	

Source: Report of Commissioner of Labor Statistics on Hawaii (1915), 64.

to speak of. As for the urban origins of the Korean immigrants as claimed by Bernice Kim and Wayne Patterson, urbanization in Korea at the time was extremely limited. There were only a handful of traditional cities, and even these cities had few modern amenities. For example, the only railroad available in the whole of Korea as of 1905 was one trunk line connecting Seoul and Pusan, which had only been completed in 1904, in addition to a short line between Seoul and Inch'ŏn. In this situation, urban/rural differences were meaningless. Considering the objective conditions in Korea at the beginning of the twentieth century, it is difficult to accept that a large majority of the emigrants from Korea came from urban backgrounds.

Also, the ports where Korean emigrants embarked on their journey to Hawai'i may tell us their origins. *Hwangsŏng shinmun,* dated April 3, 1905, reported: "The day before yesterday, the Ministry of Foreign Affairs issued a telegraphic order to the magistrates of these ports—Samhwa, Inch'ŏn, Pusan, Okku, Muan, and P'yŏngyang—to prohibit strictly any Korean from traveling to Hawai'i or Mexico."

From this report, we learn that those Koreans who migrated to Hawai'i used

Table 3   *Occupations of Korean Immigrants to the United States, 1903–1905*

	1903	1904	1905	TOTAL
Professionals	8	4	2	14
Clergy	4	0	1	5
Teacher	2	1	0	3
Actor	0	2	0	2
Physician	0	1	0	1
Official	0	0	1	1
Not specified	2	0	0	2
Skilled	26	1	4	31
Clerk and Accountant	6	1	4	11
Not specified	20	0	0	20
Miscellaneous	434	1,644	4,295	6,373
Farmer	54	0	59	113
Farm laborer	369	1,614	4,190	6,172
Laborer	3	9	23	35
Merchant dealer	7	13	9	29
Servant	1	9	12	22
Housekeeper	0	0	1	1
Agent	0	0	1	1
No occupation (including women and children)	96	258	628	982
TOTAL	564	1,907	4,929	7,400

Sources: *Annual Report of the Commissioner-General of Immigration for the Fiscal Year Ending 30, 1903, 1904,* and *1905.*

these ports for their embarkation. Of the six ports mentioned here, only three
—Inch'ŏn, P'yŏngyang, and Pusan—may be considered urban, and even Pusan
at the time was only slowly shedding the image of a fishing hamlet due to an
increase in contact with Japan. The other three—Samhwa (in P'yŏngan Province), Okku, and Muan (both in Chŏlla Province)—were all located in Korea's
countryside and remain rural to this date. Those who used these ports, although
we have no numbers, must have come from farming backgrounds.

Although the proportion of those who registered as farmers with the immigration office may not have been as high as the official immigration registration
indicates (84.9 percent), I maintain that, until one comes up with contrary evidence, a large majority of the early Korean immigrants to Hawai'i were farmers
as Table 3 indicates (though not necessarily that high a percentage) and that
most of them came from rural backgrounds in Korea.

It is also noteworthy that those who recorded their occupations as "farm
laborers" as distinguished from "farmers" numbered 6,172, or 83.4 percent. In
traditional Korea, the term *farmers* usually referred to those who were independent farmers and owned their own land for cultivation, while farm laborers
were those who, not possessing their own land, worked on someone else's land
as hired workers. They usually belonged to the deprived class of people at the
very bottom of Korean society. It is not clear whether the immigration office
registered them as "farm laborers" to make such a distinction. It is, however,
believed that the classifications of the Korean immigrants' prior occupations
were made while they were still in Korea by either the Korean government,
which had issued passports, or Deshler's company, which had recruited the
Korean laborers. If this was indeed the case, then the "farm laborers" classification would suggest the social origins of the immigrants—that is, a large majority of them came from poor farming backgrounds in the countryside.

There were, on the other hand, a sizable number of Koreans working on the
docks and doing other manual labor in port cities such as Inch'ŏn, Pusan, and
Wŏnsan, and many of them may have joined the ranks of emigrants, as Kim
and Patterson claim. Unfortunately, we have no figures showing how many of
them went to Hawai'i. These people were, as Ch'oe Ch'ang-hŭi points out, those
who had been squeezed out of farming because of severe economic conditions
in Korea and had become vagrants, finding occasional manual work at dock-
yards.[21] As such, their lot had been worse than that of the indigent farmers. But
even these people had their roots in agriculture in Korea.

PROVINCIAL ORIGINS

The "List or Manifest of Alien Immigrants for the Commissioner of Immigration" held by the National Archives and Records Administration gives a com-

plete list of Korean passengers who arrived at Honolulu between 1903 and 1905.[22] Among the information provided in this list is "Last Residence," indicating where the passengers had originated before boarding ships. Although doubt has been raised about the accuracy of this information,[23] my reading of the original is that it is fairly reliable data, whose analysis will give us a good indication as to what provinces the Korean immigrants had come from.

Recorded in this passenger list are 6,740 Koreans who reached Hawai'i. Of these, we can clearly determine the names of counties—that is, their "last residence" in Korea—of 2,842 (42.2 percent). The remaining 3,898 (57.8 percent), however, are not clear: 2,407 (35.7 percent) are not recorded at all, while 1,491 (22.1 percent) give last residences whose whereabouts are unknown. Admittedly, such data are incomplete and cannot yield a completely reliable picture. Nevertheless, in view of the absence of other evidence, an analysis of the data, inadequate though it may be, gives us useful ideas on the geographical origins of the Korean immigrants to Hawai'i.

A breakdown by province of the 2,842 whose last residences are known is given in Table 4. It tells us that every province in Korea contributed to the immigration to Hawai'i and that a large majority, 2,365, or 83.2 percent, came from the city of Seoul (512) and six other provinces—namely, Kyŏnggi (521), South Kyŏngsang (406), South P'yŏngan (282), North Kyŏngsang (249), South Hamgyŏng (228), and Hwanghae (167). As for the city origins, next to Seoul, Inch'ŏn supplied the largest number with 258, followed by P'yŏngyang with 144, Pusan with 113, Taegu with 48, and Wŏnsan with 47. These cities together provided 1,122 immigrants to Hawai'i, which is 39.5 percent of those whose county origins are clearly known. This percentage, however, is reduced to 25.9 percent if

Table 4 *Provincial Origins*

PROVINCE	SEOUL	KYŎNGGI	HWANGHAE	NORTH CH'UNGCH'ŎNG	SOUTH CH'UNGCH'ŎNG
Number	512	521	167	49	83
Percentage	18.0	18.3	5.9	1.7	2.9

PROVINCE	KANGWŎN	NORTH P'YŎNGAN	SOUTH P'YŎNGAN	NORTH HAMGYŎNG	SOUTH HAMGYŎNG
Number	49	74	282	25	228
Percentage	1.7	2.6	9.9	0.9	8.0

PROVINCE	NORTH CHŎLLA	SOUTH CHŎLLA	CHEJU	NORTH KYŎNGSANG	SOUTH KYŎNGSANG
Number	29	81	78	249	406
PERCENTAGE	1.0	2.9	2.7	8.8	14.3

Source: Duk-Hee Lee Murabayashi, comp., "Korean Passengers Arriving At Honolulu, 1903–1905," www.koreancentennial.org/passlist.pdf

we include those whose "last residences" are recorded but whose locations are unknown (totaling 4,333 persons). The latter calculation, I believe, is a fairer estimate of urban origins because the recorded but unknown "last residences" are mostly believed to be in rural areas.[24] Whichever estimate we take, it is clear that a majority of the Korean immigrants who migrated to Hawai'i in 1903–5 were drawn from rural backgrounds. We should at the same time take note of the fact that those who came from cities—though modern amenities were still scarce in Korea then—were a significant minority.

We can also make the additional observation from this analysis that four ports—Inch'ŏn, Chinnamp'o, Wŏnsan, and Pusan—may have been the main magnetic points that attracted a large majority of the Korean emigrants, as these ports were all accessible to Seoul and the six provinces that produced 83.2 percent of the emigrants.

LIFE IN HAWAI'I

The Korean immigrants who went to Hawai'i were apparently led to believe that they could easily make a quick fortune. Yun Ch'i-ho, who inspected the conditions of the Koreans living in Hawai'i in 1905 in his official capacity as the vice foreign minister of Korea, wrote his impressions of his fellow countrymen in Hawai'i: "Most of the Koreans I have asked tell me that they were deceived by the recruiting agent. They (the emigrants) seem to have thought that gold dollars were blossoming on every bush in Hawaii, so that all they had to do to be rich was to pick the dollars into their pockets."[25] Contrary to such optimistic expectations, a harsh life awaited them in Hawai'i.

Most Koreans who went to Hawai'i began their work on sugar plantations on various islands. They lived in plantation camps provided by the planters, usually "in big barracks consisting of one square sleeping room in which there was no privacy."[26] One Korean woman who had married a plantation worker and lived in such a camp told me that she and her husband were assigned to a corner room of a bachelors' barrack and that their room was so poorly partitioned from the bachelors' section by thin strips of wooden board with many openings in between that the couple had virtually no privacy.

Their daily work in the field, except on Sundays, usually began at 6:00 a.m. and ended at 4:30 p.m. with a 30-minute break for lunch. But often they were obliged to work extra hours when such work was demanded. As Table 5 shows, they worked an average of 60 hours a week (or 10 hours a day Monday through Saturday). Most of the Korean males worked as field hands and received 65 cents a day in 1905, which was increased to 73 cents in 1910. Female workers were paid considerably lower wages than their male counterparts, earning 49 cents and 53 cents, respectively, for a day's work. Unable to bear the hardships of sugarcane field work, many Koreans left plantations to look for jobs elsewhere whenever possible. In time, this created some problems for the sugar companies as Koreans came to be regarded as one of the most mobile groups. In order to secure more stable labor, the Hawaiian Agricultural Company on the Big Island wrote the following letter to C. Brewer and Company on October 12, 1915:

> As you are aware we are at present paying $10.00 towards the Korean pastors pay, and I take it that Mr. Fry [the superintendent of the Methodist Mission in Hawai'i] wishes us to add $5.00 to this. We have quite a gang of Koreans here at present (about 40 in all), but they are rather an uncertain bunch, and sometimes we may not have more than 15. Now I am going to ask you to give me authority to try out the idea of regulating the pastors pay, according to the gang holds out. Say $5.00 per month when they dwindle to 15 men and up to $20.00 per month, should the gang hold up to 50 or 60.[27]

There is no information available on what action C. Brewer and Company might have taken on this recommendation.

Because of the severity of the cane field work, Koreans did not stay at the plantations too long. Figure 1 shows the number of Koreans working in the sugarcane fields from 1905 to 1935 (see also Appendix 2). The largest number (4,893) worked in the cane fields in 1905, but in the next 5 years this number was sharply reduced to 1,549. Thereafter, the number fluctuated at around 1,500 until 1921, after which it further declined steadily until 1930, when fewer than 500 worked for the plantations. These figures indicate that most Koreans had left the sugar plantations by 1930 and moved on to engage in other businesses.

Table 5   *Working Hours and Wages of Korean Laborers, 1905, 1910, and 1915*

JOB POSITION, SEX	NUMBER OF WORKERS			AVERAGE HOURS PER WEEK			AVERAGE WAGE PER DAY (IN DOLLARS)		
	1905	1910	1915	1905	1910	1915	1905	1910	1915
Cane Cutter, M	828	432	235	58.7	58.1	60.0	0.665	0.94	1.01
Cane Loader, M	248	17	—	58.2	60.1	—	0.815	0.99	—
Cane Loader & Cutter, M	—	59	56	—	61.0	—	—	0.87	1.02
Contract Cultivator, M	460	912	528	60.9	60.6	—	0.745	0.87	1.33
Field Hand, M	3,039	585	—	59.7	59.9	—	0.65	0.73	—
Field Hand, F	44	12	—	59.4	59.9	—	0.49	0.53	—

Sources: Report of Commissioner of Labor Statistics on Hawaii, 1905, 1910, and 1915.

Wayne Patterson posits the thesis that Koreans, having departed the sugar plantations but being deprived of their motherland to which they had hoped to return, developed a settler mentality (in contrast to the sojourner attitude of the Chinese and Japanese) and were more readily adaptable to the Hawai'i environment, allowing them to seek new opportunities. He observes: "Koreans left plantation work faster than any of [the] other thirty-three ethnic groups in the history of Hawai'i."[28] This view, however, is challenged by Seok-Dae Hong. In his recent master's thesis, Hong made a comparative study of the employment of several ethnic groups on sugar plantations and concluded that Korean workers left the plantations relatively more slowly than the Chinese and Japanese cane field workers. According to Hong, the time of ethnic arrival to Hawai'i and job opportunities available outside plantations were important factors in determining how soon workers departed plantations, and the Korean workers did not abandon cane fields any faster than their Asian counterparts.[29]

Be that as it may, as they left plantations, the Koreans moved to cities. Table 6 shows the Korean population in the Territory of Hawai'i and the City of Honolulu from 1910 to 1950. It indicates a drastic shift of the Korean population to the city of Honolulu. In 1910, only 10.1 percent of the Koreans lived in Honolulu, but this percentage increased to 26.6 in 1920 and 40.3 in 1930. By 1940, it is believed that a majority had moved to Honolulu.

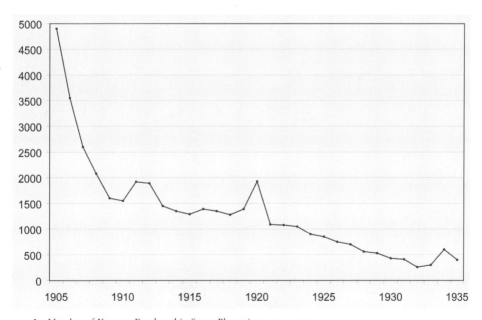

1   Number of Koreans Employed in Sugar Plantations, 1905–1935.

PICTURE BRIDES

Perhaps the biggest problem the early Korean immigrants faced was the extreme imbalance in the gender ratio of the Korean population in Hawai'i. Figures 2, 3, and 4 give the age and sex pyramids of Koreans in Hawai'i based on the national censuses taken in 1910, 1920, and 1930. In 1910, there were 3,931 males but only 602 females; in 1920, there were 3,498 males and 1,452 females; and in 1930, there were 3,999 males and 2,462 females.[30] This gender imbalance is most striking in the age group between 20 and 49, the ages when sex parity is most needed. Table 7 gives the sex distribution of this particular group. In 1910, for those between the ages of 20 and 49, there were 13 men for each woman. The absence of gender parity created many serious problems within the Korean community in its early stage.

Because of the shortage in the number of women, only a very small proportion of the Koreans in Hawai'i were able to maintain ordinary family lives. The bulk of the other Koreans, deprived of home environments, suffered from emotional, psychological, physiological, and other frustrations. This became a source of instability in the Korean community, causing serious anxiety among those who were affected. Not having a warm family to welcome them home from a hard day's work, many Korean workers sought solace and comfort in drinking, gambling, visiting prostitutes, and other activities. Scarcity of women also caused many incidents of a "scandalous nature," such as adultery, elope-

Table 6   *Koreans in Hawai'i and Honolulu*

YEAR	HAWAI'I	HONOLULU	PERCENTAGE IN HONOLULU
1910	4,533	460	10.1
1920	4,950	1,319	26.6
1930	6,461	2,604	40.3
1940	6,851	N/A	—
1950	7,030	4,802	68.3

Sources: Hawaiian Almanac (1915), 19; (1925), 10; (1935), 18; Andrew W. Lind, *Hawaii's People* (1980), 57.

Table 7   *Sex Distribution of Population Between Ages of 20 and 49*

	1910	1920	1930
Male	3,378	2,177	1,104
Female	261	596	740
Number of Men per Woman	12.9	3.7	3.7

Sources: Calculated from Eleanor C. Nordyke, *The Peopling of Hawaii,* 196.

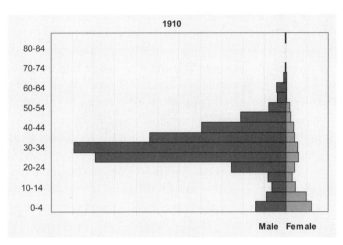

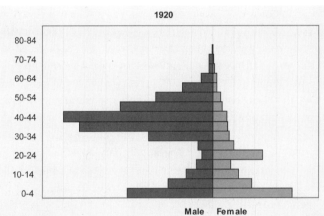

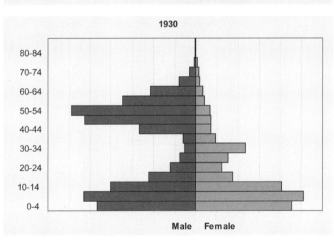

2   Age-Sex Pyramid of Koreans in Hawai'i, 1910–1930.

ment, and fights over women. A more innocuous practice, however, was that Koreans, though not known as frequent bathers, often visited Japanese bath-houses, for Japanese in Hawai'i still practiced mixed bathing at the time.[31]

It was to assuage this situation that the so-called picture bride system was adopted with the encouragement of the Hawai'i government and the sugar plantations. The first Korean picture bride, according to Kim Wŏn-yong, arrived in Hawai'i in November 1910. Thereafter, picture brides were allowed into Hawai'i until 1924, when the Oriental Exclusion Act stopped all emigration from Asia.[32]

Exactly how many picture brides came from Korea is not yet fully established. Kim Wŏn-yong, who is usually reliable, wrote in his invaluable book that as many as 951 Korean women arrived in Hawai'i as picture brides; however, he did not indicate where he obtained this information.[33] Kingsley K. Lyu, on the other hand, estimated the number to be around 600, again with no source.[34] Official U.S. Immigration statistics, however, show that altogether 859 Koreans entered Hawai'i as immigrants from 1910 to 1924, but unfortunately it gives no information on their gender. The same statistics, on the other hand, give the number of Korean women who were allowed into the United States as a whole, including Hawai'i, and that number is 842.[35] If we assume all of them were picture brides, we can then estimate the total number of picture brides who reached Hawai'i to be 842 at most because this number includes those who went to California, where there was a sizable Korean community, and elsewhere in the United States. In the meantime, a demographic analysis of the age group between 15 and 39 (assuming all picture brides belonged to this age group) in the Hawai'i censuses taken in 1910, 1920, and 1930 yields 468 women as having come from outside. This figure has been adjusted for mortality based on an abridged life table for Hawai'i at that period.[36] In view of these conflicting figures, it is difficult at this time to estimate definitively the exact number of Korean picture brides arriving in Hawai'i.

On a personal level, there are cases of both happiness and unhappiness among the picture bride marriages. Many tragicomic situations arose from mutual misunderstandings and from differences in ages between man and wife, in personal and social backgrounds, in regional origins, and in expectations and aspirations. The biggest problem undoubtedly was caused by the difference in ages. Whereas most picture brides were in the age group between 15 and 20 (although there were some who were divorced or widowed in their 30s), their grooms in Hawai'i were mostly in their 30s and 40s. In arranging marriages, it was customary for prospective grooms to send photos that were not current but that had been taken in younger days. Former picture brides with whom I spoke during the 1970s and 1980s almost unanimously complained that they felt they had been cheated when they discovered the ages of their husbands upon arrival in Hawai'i. Some said their husbands were as old as their fathers back home.[37] One 19-year-old picture bride recalled her experience:

> I came to Hawaii and was so surprised and very disappointed because my husband sent his 25 year old handsome looking picture. You know he was tall, six feet high. He came to the pier, but I see he's really old, 25 years more old than I am. My heart stuck. I was so disappointed, I don't look at him again. So I don't eat and only cry for eight days. I don't eat nothing, but at midnight when everybody sleeps I sneak out to drink water, so I don't die. . . . If I don't marry, immigration law send me back to Korea free. Oh, I was thinking, thinking. I came once [to Hawai'i], better I marry and stay here. . . . My parents would be very shame, so I can't go back. So after eight days, I [married him]. . . . Then, I didn't talk to him for three months, living together in the same house.[38]

Such stories were quite common among Korean picture brides. Many tried to escape without success, and still others refused conjugal relationships with their husbands for months. (One woman confided to me that she was too young even to know that conjugal relationships involved sexual intimacy.) With a sense of having been deceived, several former picture brides spoke rather disdainfully of their husbands and former husbands, some with bitter feelings.

Such situations often led to unhappy marriages. One American social worker has given the following depiction of the life of a picture bride in Hawai'i:

> In 1920, a Korean man weary of his lonely life on rural Hawaii negotiated for marriage with a picture bride who was 17 years of age and 15 years his junior. The young girl felt no love for her husband and became homesick and despondent. When her husband died five years later, alone and without resources, she allowed a second marriage to be arranged through a marriage broker. This marriage, too, had nothing of love in it and the case worker, knowing the family, today sees four children who are the targets for a disillusioned mother and a disinterested father. Other marriages of this nature have been accepted by both man and wife as an inevitable part of their culture and there is no thought of rebellion.[39]

Of course, not all the picture bride marriages were as disappointing as this one. There were many cases in which such a marriage brought a happy family life.

From a historical perspective, we can say that the picture brides nevertheless played important roles for the following reasons. First, the picture brides brought stability to the Korean community in Hawai'i by providing "homes" for their husbands. Many restless and insecure bachelors now had for the first time their own homes to return to after a hard day's work, having been freed from the cramped bachelors' quarters of the plantations. Those picture brides I talked to were almost unanimous in claiming that their husbands had stopped, for the time being after their marriages at least, frequenting places of drinking and gambling.

Second, the picture brides contributed greatly to the enhancement of economic conditions of the Koreans in Hawai'i. Resourceful and hardworking, most picture brides started to work gainfully soon after their arrival in Hawai'i as cooks, laundresses, seamstresses, field hands on the plantations, and so forth, thus providing added income to their families. When they moved to cities, they became more enterprising, for example, opening small shops such as laundries and tailor shops, running rooming houses, and managing rental units. Their favorite way of raising needed capital was *kye* (known among Japanese as *tanomoshi*), a traditional practice whereby friends pooled their resources to secure a sum of money for each member in rotation. By the mid-1940s, after the Pearl Harbor attack, many of these Koreans had become rather successful businesswomen in their own right, thus laying a firm foundation for the economic prosperity of the Korean community (as we will see below).

Third, the arrival of the picture brides galvanized Korean nationalist activities in Hawai'i. Having experienced life in Korea under Japanese colonial rule, the picture brides brought firsthand information about the harsh realities of Korea under alien domination. Their reports on the plight of their countrymen under the brutal Japanese rule led the Korean community in Hawai'i to redouble its determination to fight for Korea's freedom. Most of these women became actively involved in nationalistic causes by organizing and participating in a number of organizations, such as the Korean Ladies' Relief Society and the Yŏngnam Women's Business League. These Korean women became important nationalists, willingly sacrificing themselves for the recovery of Korean independence by participating in activities such as raising funds and engaging in charitable works.

Lastly, the most important contribution the Korean picture brides made was their role in continuing the life of Korean ethnic stock in Hawai'i by giving birth to second-generation Koreans. Without these picture brides, Koreans as an ethnic group would have faced certain extinction after the first generation passed away. That Hawai'i today teems with third- and fourth-generation Koreans is due almost wholly to the picture brides. The Korean picture brides thus added a significant new dimension to the rich multicultural life of Hawai'i.[40]

ADVERSITIES

The Korean community, although stabilized after the arrival of the picture brides, faced many other adversities. First, except for the Filipinos, the Koreans were among the last of the Asian ethnic groups to arrive in Hawai'i. The Chinese had been in Hawai'i since 1852 and the Japanese since 1868. By the time the Koreans began to arrive in 1903, both the Chinese and the Japanese already had a significant head start. The Koreans faced a long road in catching up with their fellow Asians.

Second, Koreans were the smallest minority among many ethnic groups throughout their presence in Hawai'i. This smallness in number was of no help for survival in the Hawaiian environment. For example, when a member of a small minority group ventures into business, he is obliged to seek success beyond his own ethnic group, as Romanzo Adams pointed out: "When a young university graduate set up as a printer the fact of his being a Korean was no help. He had to find his business in the general business community. If he got it at all, it was because he was a good printer not because he was a good Korean."[41]

Another problem the early immigrants faced in Hawai'i was racial prejudice. Their arrival at the turn of the twentieth century coincided with the rise of racism in the Western world and the United States, leading to the growing fear of the so-called yellow peril, which culminated in the enactment of the Oriental Exclusion Act of 1924. In Hawai'i, where the *haoles* had maintained dominant control in virtually all fields, the Asian immigrants on the plantations, to borrow sociologist Andrew Lind's words, "were regarded much like draft animals."[42] The Koreans, being of Asian stock, were of course subjected to such racial prejudice.

In addition, Koreans in Hawai'i suffered further racial antagonism arising from the political conflict between Korea and Japan, which led to the unfortunate annexation of Korea by Japan in 1910. The situation in Hawai'i did not help race relations between these two ethnic groups. For one thing, bringing Koreans to Hawai'i with the explicit intention of counteracting the predominance of Japanese labor gave rise to Japanese suspicions about Koreans. Furthermore, frequent use of Korean workers as strike breakers during labor disputes involving Japanese laborers only aggravated strains between these two Asian groups. To be sure, such racial animosity between Koreans and Japanese in Hawai'i was mutual. But it was most unfortunate for the Koreans because not only were the Japanese numerically the largest ethnic group in Hawai'i but also because the particular situation in Hawai'i demanded that Koreans come in contact with Japanese more than any other ethnic group on account of their cultural, economic, and occupational similarity. Koreans thus became the victims of double racial discrimination coming from both whites and the Japanese.

THE SECOND GENERATION

Against this background, the early Korean immigrants in Hawai'i had to go through many difficulties in adjusting to the new environment. Statistical and other records show that the Koreans contributed more than their share in creating social problems and adding to the public burden. A 1930 study of ghettos and slums in Honolulu indicated that the Koreans along with the Puerto Ricans and the Spanish had "the highest rate of public dependency."[43]

Unhappy family lives, lack of social cohesiveness, and economic deprivation also contributed to the high rate of crimes committed by Koreans in the early stages of their life in Hawai'i. The number of criminal convictions per 1,000 men in two 6-year periods, 1919–24 and 1925–30, was 1.562 and 2.914, respectively, for Koreans. For the Japanese, the figures were 0.402 and 0.403 during the same periods, while those for the Chinese were 0.878 and 0.950, respectively.[44] Similarly, the average annual incidents of juvenile delinquency over two periods, 1916–24 and 1929–30, were very high for Koreans—1,926 and 1,391 per 100,000 youths between 10 and 17 years of age, as compared to 376 and 341 for Japanese and 1,546 and 812 for Chinese.[45] Clearly, Koreans had more dysfunctional families than their two Asian neighbors in Hawai'i. We can perhaps attribute this to the late start for Koreans in Hawai'i: whereas both the Chinese and the Japanese were already well settled, having arrived in Hawai'i a few decades earlier, Koreans were going through the pains of cultural shock and adjusting to the new environment.

While going through these difficulties, the Koreans in Hawai'i on the other hand put much of their effort and energy into the education of their children with very impressive results. As shown in Table 8, the percentage of illiteracy among Korean boys and girls between the ages of ten and twenty was progressively reduced, and illiteracy was virtually eliminated by 1930.

The elimination of illiteracy among Korean youths was obviously due to the great emphasis placed on education by their parents and community (as is shown in the efforts of Syngman Rhee in Chapter 3 of this book). The percentage of Korean children between the ages of 6 and 13 attending school increased progressively from 77.3 percent in 1910, to 86.0 percent in 1920, and to 91.6 percent in 1930, as against 80.1 percent, 90.1 percent, and 88.8 percent for the

Table 8 *Percentage of Illiteracy (Boys and Girls 10–20 Years of Age)*

	1910	1920	1930
Koreans	11.8	2.7	0.1
Chinese	6.7	1.3	0.9
Japanese	10.6	2.3	0.5
All Races	9.6	4.0	3.1

Source: Romanzo Adams, *The Peoples of Hawaii,* 43.

Chinese and 83.8 percent, 87.3 percent, and 89.8 percent for the Japanese. By 1930, the rate of Korean children attending school was the second highest among all ethnic groups in Hawai'i, exceeded only by the *haoles*.[46] On the ability to learn English, Romanzo Adams observed: "They [the Koreans] have made more rapid progress in the acquisition of English than the more numerous Japanese. Because of their fewness it was necessary for them to make a greater use of English, but there is a developing myth that they are superior in native linguistic ability."[47]

The education of children has always been a part of the deeply rooted tradition in Korea, and obviously this tradition was carried on strongly in Hawai'i. One scholar studying public education in Hawai'i remarked in 1932: "In general, the Korean group seems to be very able and many of them are making their way into commercial and professional occupations."[48]

On another level, the Koreans in Hawai'i, especially the second and third generations, have shown a remarkable degree of assimilability in Hawaiian society. One sociologist remarked in 1944 that "of the three Oriental groups here, the Koreans, especially the second generation, seem to me to be more completely Westernized in thought and action than the other Orientals."[49] If, as Andrew W. Lind suggested, interracial marriage is "one of the most accurate indices" of assimilability,[50] the Koreans in Hawai'i indeed rank very high, as Table 9 shows. The increasing rate of interracial marriages over the years among Koreans is astonishing. After 1950, more than two-thirds of Koreans in Hawai'i sought their marriage partners outside their own ethnic group. Only Hawaiians had a higher ratio of interracial marriage. If ethnic out-marriage is indeed a good index of assimilation, the Koreans have been certainly most successful in merging into Hawai'i's sociocultural environment.

How can we explain the high ratio of interracial marriages among Koreans in Hawai'i? The first reason obviously is the small number of Koreans in Hawai'i, which obliged them to look for spouses beyond their own ethnic group.[51] The second reason may be weakening nationalistic sentiment among second-generation Koreans. Whereas strong nationalism had been one of the strongest characteristics of the first-generation Koreans, the second generation

Table 9 *Interracial Marriages as Percentage of All Marriages*

	1912–16	1920–30	1930–40	1940–49	1950–59	1960–64
Grooms	26.4	17.6	23.5	49.0	70.3	77.1
Brides	0.0	4.9	39.0	66.7	74.5	80.1

Source: Andrew Lind, *Hawaii's People*, 108.

did not share as strong a sentiment of nationalism as their parents did. Lind observed: "As a group, the second generation Koreans show a distinct lack of interest in the nationalistic aspirations and quarrels of the first generation."[52] Third, related to the weakening of nationalism, a negative image of Korea may have been a factor in alienating second-generation Koreans from identifying themselves with their ancestral land. Experiencing harsh Japanese colonial rule, Korea was a land of abject poverty during the time when the second generation grew up in Hawai'i. As for the Korean community in Hawai'i, it went through periodic turmoil of political infighting largely between those who supported Syngman Rhee and those who opposed him, and media coverage of Korean feuds cast a negative shadow over Korea and the Koreans in Hawai'i. (See Chapter 3 of this book.) In spite of heavy emphasis on inculcating patriotism among the second generation by the first-generation Koreans, Korea's negative image may have made it difficult for many second-generation Koreans to willingly identify themselves with Korea.

CONCLUSION

In the year 2003, Hawai'i celebrated the centennial of Korean immigration. As we look back, the Koreans in Hawai'i have come a long way. When they first arrived, most of them were penniless and uneducated with virtually no skills. They came, as a Korean expression goes, with bare fists *(maenjumŏk)* and started from the deep bottom *(mitbadak)* of Hawai'i society. Uprooted from their ancestors' land and transplanted to a totally unfamiliar environment, the Korean immigrants in Hawai'i had to face seemingly insurmountable odds. In the course of time, they had their share of problems and even contributed in some instances more than their share of burden to the Hawaiian community. But they have shown remarkable resiliency and resourcefulness and in the end overcame the challenges magnificently.

Table 10   *Median Family Income before Tax by Ethnicity, 1970*

ETHNICITY	MEDIAN ANNUAL FAMILY INCOME (DOLLARS)
Korean	16,621
Chinese	14,725
Japanese	13,646
Caucasian	11,539
All Groups	11,650

Source: Dorothy Lee, "Ethnic Structures in Hawaii," *Population Report* 6 (1976): 18.

If the success of a people can be measured in terms of monetary earnings (as is the practice nowadays), Koreans have been far more successful than any other ethnic group in Hawai'i. According to a study conducted by the Department of Health of the State of Hawai'i,[53] the median family income in 1970 was highest for Koreans, as Table 10 shows. The median income of a Korean family was $16,621 as compared to the next highest group, the Chinese family, who earned $14,725, followed by the Japanese family, whose income was $13,646. What the 1970 census data tell us is the coming of age of the second-generation Koreans. Within two generations, Koreans in Hawai'i achieved the greatest economic success. Such an impressive achievement was possible largely due to the selfless sacrifices made by the first-generation Koreans for the sake of their children. Even though they suffered from poverty, lack of education, discrimination, and a host of other adversities, first-generation Koreans put their minds and energy to enhancing the education and well-being of their children. That we now see in Hawai'i a number of Korean Americans occupying key positions in both the public and private sectors—a disproportionately large number, in fact—is testimony to the success the Koreans have attained in their newly adopted land.

In addition to facing the difficult tasks of settling in their newly adopted land, Koreans, unlike other ethnic groups, had to wage an arduous struggle toward recovering the sovereignty of their beloved homeland as well. Foremost in their minds was regaining Korea's independence, for which they willingly and selflessly sacrificed the bulk of their energy and material gains. That a large number of Koreans from Hawai'i have officially been decorated by the Republic of Korea government with national medals for meritorious contributions to the cause of Korean independence is testimony to their sacrifice for the country they left behind.

Looking back over the past hundred years, the Koreans in Hawai'i can justly take great pride in their achievements.

Appendix 1 *Number of Koreans Admitted to the United States, Hawai'i, and California, 1899–1932*

| YEAR | UNITED STATES | | | HAWAI'I | CALIFORNIA |
	MALE	FEMALE	TOTAL		
1899	N/A	N/A	22		
1900	N/A	N/A	71		
1901	N/A	N/A	47	4	N/A
1902	N/A	N/A	28	12	N/A
1903	496	68	564	515	38
1904	1,723	184	1,907	1,884	8
1905	4,506	423	4,929	4,892	22
1906	106	24	127	98	13
1907	36	3	39	9	13
1908	20	6	26	8	6
1909	9	2	11	2	2
1910	14	5	19	7	1
1911	0	8	8	8	0
1912	14	19	33	17	7
1913	15	49	64	45	15
1914	58	94	152	92	36
1915	91	55	146	78	54
1916	70	84	154	80	62
1917	75	119	194	116	61
1918	59	90	149	78	53
1919	6	71	77	66	0
1920	25	47	72	45	8
1921	22	39	61	41	4
1922	31	57	88	58	6
1923	53	51	104	53	17
1924	68	54	122	75	8
1925	22	4	26	7	0
1926	39	13	52	9	3
1927	40	7	47	10	5
1928	19	3	21	0	8
1929	41	8	49	7	4
1930	26	7	33	4	12
1931	19	2	21	0	6
1932	N/A	N/A	19	N/A	N/A
TOTAL	7,700	1,596	9,483	8,320	472

Sources: Reports of Commissioner-General of Immigration.

Appendix 2 *Number of Plantation Workers, 1905–1935*

YEAR	KOREANS	ALL NATIONALITIES
1905	4,893	44,949
1906	3,675	41,303
1907	2,694	44,575
1908	2,058	44,789
1909	1,705	41,748
1910	1,549	42,846
1911	1,925	44,268
1912	1,588	46,930
1913	1,402	45,875
1914	1,365	46,213
1915	1,286	44,299
1916	1,430	46,117
1917	1,370	46,695
1918	1,299	44,708
1919	1,407	45,311
1920	1,982	44,285
1921	1,150	38,707
1922	1,159	46,273
1923	1,063	42,001
1924	990	39,599
1925	877	44,450
1926	715	44,159
1927	641	43,630
1928	571	48,279
1929	520	49,579
1930	484	49,532
1931	468	49,134
1932	442	49,947
1933	458	48,072
1934	522	46,255
1935	491	43,502

Sources: Hawaiian Almanac and Annual, 1906–1936.

NOTES

1. For a good study on this subject, see Wayne Patterson, *The Korean Frontier in America: Immigration to Hawaii, 1896–1910* (Honolulu: University of Hawai'i Press, 1988).

2. There is disagreement with regard to reading the name of this office. Based on Yun Ch'i-ho's diary, Wayne Patterson opted to read it as Yuminwŏn (see his

The Korean Frontier in America, 220–21). Dictionaries and many Korean scholars, however, read it as Suminwŏn. I decided to follow dictionary reading.

3. Kim Wŏn-yong, *Chaemi Han'in 50-nyon sa* (A 50-year History of Koreans in the United States) (Reedley, Calif., 1959), 6.

4. For example, see Bong-youn Choy, *Koreans in America* (Chicago: Nelson-Hall, 1979), 75.

5. "Hawai-koku e Kankokujin dekasegi ikken," Diplomatic Records Office, Japanese Foreign Ministry (Classification No. 3-9-2-6).

6. Hyŏn Sun, *P'owa yuram ki* (Record of Journey to Hawai'i) (Seoul, 1909), 5.

7. K. W. Lee and Dr. Luke and Grace Kim, "Whispers from the Past: The Lonesome Journey of Ethan Sungkoo Kiehm, an American Born Child of Some of the First Korean Immigrant Contingents to Hawaii," *KoreAm Journal* 14, no. 1 (January 2003): 55.

8. "Report of the Commissioner of Labor on Hawaii, 1905," 23–24.

9. *Hwangsŏng shinmun* (Imperial News), April 3, 1905. This report states that the Ministry of Foreign Affairs issued "a strict prohibition" order against further emigration "the day before yesterday," and hence the order must have been given on April 1, 1905.

10. C. I. Eugene Kim and Han-Kyo Kim, *Korea and the Politics of Imperialism, 1876–1910* (Berkeley: University of California Press, 1967), 121–35; Yi Sŏn-gŭn, *Han'guk-sa: Hyŏndae p'yŏn* (History of Korea: Modern Period) (Seoul: Chindan hakhoe, 1963), 905–10.

11. Letter written by D. W. Deshler to Huntington Wilson of the American Legation in Tokyo, which the State Department forwarded to Governor George R. Carter in Hawai'i; now in the Hawai'i State Archives.

12. *Hwangsŏng shinmun*, April 3, 1905.

13. *Jinsen-fu shi* (History of Inch'ŏn City) (Inch'ŏn, 1933), 543.

14. For a more detailed study of the Japanese opposition, see Patterson, *The Korean Frontier in America*, 124–48.

15. "The Korean Emigration Protection Law," *The Korea Review* 6, no. 7 (July 1906): 256–57.

16. *Ku Han'guk oegyo munsŏ* (Diplomatic Documents of the Former Han Empire) (Seoul, 1970), 7:549, 552, 556, and 580; Kuksa P'yŏnch'an Wiwŏnhoe, *Kojong sidaesa* (History of the Kojong Period) (Seoul, 1972), 7:233. For a fuller study on the termination of Korean emigrations, see Patterson, *The Korean Frontier in America*.

17. Patterson, *The Korean Frontier in America*, 124–48.

18. Ibid., 135.

19. Bernice B. H. Kim, "The Koreans in Hawaii" (unpublished M.A. thesis, University of Hawai'i, 1937), 85–86.

20. Wayne Patterson, *The Ilse: First Generation Korean Immigrants in Hawaii,*

1903–1970 (Honolulu: University of Hawai'i Press, 2000), 6. See also his *The Korean Frontier in America,* 103–6.

21. Ch'oe Ch'ang-hǔi, "Han'guk in ǔi Hawaii imin" (Korean Immigration to Hawai'i), *Kuksagwan nonch'ong* 9 (1989): 163–65.

22. See Duk-Hee Lee Murabayashi, comp., "Korean Passengers Arriving at Honolulu, 1903–1905," at www.koreancentennial.org/passlist.pdf.

23. Murabayashi, who painstakingly made the entire passenger list from the near illegible original manifests in microfilm, writes that "information on last residence is ambiguous" because "there is no way to determine whether these entries referred to an individual's residence immediately before passage or to the location of a permanent family domicile." Ibid.

24. Most of the unknown "last residences" are village names, such as "dong" and "ri," suggesting they are from rural regions, and hence it is safe to assume that they are not from cities.

25. Yun Ch'i-ho, *Yun Ch'i-ho ilgi* (Yun Chi-ho's Diary) (Seoul: Kuksa p'yŏnch'an wiwŏnhoe, 1976), 6:167–68 (English original).

26. Morris Pang, "A Korean Immigrant," *Social Process in Hawaii* 13 (1949).

27. In the files of C. Brewer and Co., Ltd., in the possession of Professor (Emeritus) Edward D. Beechert of the Department of History, University of Hawai'i. I am grateful to him for sharing this information with me.

28. Patterson, *The Ilse,* 33.

29. Seok-Dae Hong, "Early Korean Immigrants in Hawaii: A Study of Social Mobility" (unpublished M.A. thesis, University of Hawai'i, 2001), 19–24.

30. Eleanor C. Nordyke, *The Peopling of Hawaii,* 2nd ed. (Honolulu: University of Hawai'i Press, 1989), 196.

31. Yi Hong-gi, handwritten memoir (unpublished), 18. In this memoir, Yi Hong-gi gives an account of his travel to Hawai'i and experiences as a sugarcane worker and other aspects of life in Hawai'i, interspersed with his own classical Sino-Korean poems.

32. Kim Wŏn-yong, *Chae-Mi Han'in 50-nyŏn sa,* 27–29. See also Kingsley K. Lyu, "Korean Nationalist Activities in Hawaii and the Continental United States, 1900–1945; Part I: 1900–1919," *Amerasia Journal* 4, no. 1 (1977): 26–29.

33. Kim Wŏn-yong, *Chae-Mi Han'in 50-nyŏn sa,* 29.

34. Lyu, "Korean Nationalist Activities in Hawaii and the Continental United States, 1900–1945," 27.

35. Based on *Reports of the Commissioner-General of the United States Immigration and Naturalization Service.* See Appendix 1.

36. This analysis was made by Minja Kim Choe, senior fellow, Population Program, East-West Center, Honolulu, Hawai'i.

37. When Yong-Hyun Park (Pak Yong-hyŏn) married his wife Kim Mal-sun in 1924, he was forty-two years old and his bride was sixteen. He immigrated at

first to Hawai'i and then moved on to Montana, where he married his picture bride wife and engaged in farming. My conversation with their daughter, May Park Lafleur, of Gresham, Oregon, on January 13, 2003, and her letter dated January 22, 2003. See also "T'aep'yŏngyang" (The Christian Pacific), newsletter of the Korean Pacific Mission Society, Portland, Oregon, 3 (March–April 1980), 15 and 18.

38. Alice Chai, "A Picture Bride from Korea: The Life History of a Korean American Woman in Hawaii," *Bridge: An Asian American Perspective* (Winter 1978): 38.

39. Eileen Blackey, "Cultural Aspects of Case Work in Hawaii," *Social Process in Hawaii* 5 (1939): 36.

40. For Korean women in Hawai'i, see Esther Kwon Arinaga, "Contributions of Korean Immigrant Women," in *Montage: An Ethnic History of Women in Hawaii*, ed. Nancy Foon Young and Judy R. Parrish (Honolulu, 1977), 73–81.

41. Romanzo Adams, *The Interracial Marriage in Hawaii* (New York: Macmillan, 1937), 182.

42. Andrew W. Lind, *Hawaii's People* (Honolulu: University of Hawai'i Press, 1974), 8.

43. Ibid., 2.

44. Romanzo Adams, *The Peoples of Hawaii* (Honolulu: American Council, Institute of Pacific Relations, 1933), 52.

45. Ibid., 53.

46. Ibid., 45.

47. Adams, *Interracial Marriage in Hawaii*, 187–88.

48. Thayne M. Livesay, *A Study of Public Education with Special Reference to the Pupil Population*, University of Hawai'i Research Publication, No. 7 (1932). Professor Wm. Theodore de Bary of Columbia University told me that when he was serving as a Navy intelligence officer in Hawai'i in the 1940s, the Naval Intelligence Office conducted a survey on various ethnic groups in Hawai'i, in which Koreans ranked at the top in intelligence quotient.

49. Bernice Kim McInervey, "Koreans—A Rapidly Assimilated Group," *The New Pacific* (March 1944): 11.

50. Andrew W. Lind, "Attitudes Toward Interracial Marriage in Kona, Hawaii," *Social Process in Hawaii* 4 (May 1938): 79.

51. Adams, *Interracial Marriage in Hawaii*, 198.

52. Andrew W. Lind, "Some Types of Social Movements in Hawaii," *Social Process in Hawaii* 7 (November 1941): 13.

53. Dorothy D. Lee, "Ethnic Structures in Hawaii," *Population Report* 6 (September 1976): 18.

2

Korean Immigration to Hawaiʻi and the Korean Protestant Church

WITH THE DRAMATIC growth of the sugar industry in Hawaiʻi in the latter half of the nineteenth century, the Hawaii Sugar Planters Association (HSPA) was in constant need of laborers to work on the sugar plantations. Throughout most of its boom years, the HSPA relied heavily on cheap labor from East Asia. At first, the sugar planters imported Chinese laborers, and then Japanese. By the turn of the twentieth century, the Japanese workers began to dominate the labor market, allowing them to wage collective actions such as strikes to demand higher wages and better working conditions.

To counter this domination by Japanese workers the HSPA looked to Korea for a new source of labor. The conduit between the HSPA and Korea was Horace N. Allen. A medical missionary of the Presbyterian Board of Foreign Missions, Allen first went to China, and from there, he was reassigned to Korea. Having arrived in Seoul in September 1884 as a doctor for the U.S. embassy, he was given an opportunity to give medical treatment to Min Yŏng-ik, who had received a serious injury in an assassination attempt in the abortive coup that took place in December 1884. Allen's medical skills saved Min's life and thus won the deep gratitude of the Korean royal family, as Min Yŏng-ik was not an ordinary person: he was a favorite nephew of Queen Min. With the support of the royal family, Allen, in April 1885, opened the first Western medical hospital in Korea. In 1887, when Korea dispatched its first permanent diplomatic envoy to the United States, he accompanied the Korean mission as an escort. In 1897, he was appointed the American minister to Korea stationed in Seoul. By this time, Allen had won the confidence of Emperor Kojong and had become one of the most trusted advisors of the Korean ruler. In 1901, when he returned to the United States on leave, he was approached by William G. Irwin, an HSPA agent, who pleaded for Allen's assistance in securing Korean laborers for Hawaiʻi sugar plantations. Allen consented to this request.

With a poor harvest, Korea was going through economic hardship in 1901. Allen suggested to the emperor that one possible way out of this difficulty was to allow Koreans to immigrate to Hawai'i. Besides, these Koreans might acquire new knowledge of Western civilization that would be of great use to Korea, Allen explained. Persuaded by Allen, Emperor Kojong appointed Min Yŏng-hwan as the president of a new office called Suminwŏn[1] to handle all emigration matters. At the same time, David W. Deshler, a fellow Ohioan who became Allen's protégé in Korea, became responsible for recruiting Korean laborers. For this purpose, Deshler set up the East-West Development Company in Korea and also established a bank, which came to be known as the Deshler Bank.

In the joint name of the Suminwŏn and the East-West Development Company, a public recruiting announcement was circulated. It pointed to Hawai'i's good weather and said that recruits would work ten hours a day with a holiday on Sundays and that the monthly wages would be $15. The announcement was posted in many parts of the country, including Seoul, Pusan, Inch'ŏn, Wŏnsan, and many other harbor towns. As a result, a group of men and women with children left Inch'ŏn on December 22, 1902. At Kobe, Japan, they underwent further physical examinations, and 102 persons of this group finally reached Honolulu on January 13, 1903. Thereafter, 7,226 Koreans immigrated to Hawai'i by the end of 1905,[2] when Japanese interference stopped further emigration.

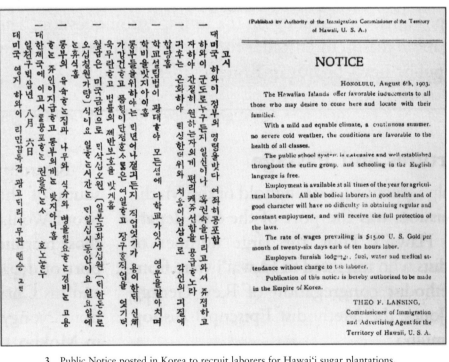

3   Public Notice posted in Korea to recruit laborers for Hawai'i sugar plantations.

CHRISTIANS AMONG EMIGRANTS

The announcement recruiting laborers for Hawai'i was at first met with skeptical responses from the general public in Korea, and not many Koreans applied initially. There was no precedent for official migration of Koreans abroad, and few had accurate information about foreign countries and the proper procedures for applying. The only information available was the announcement of the East-West Development Company, which many learned about through indirect dissemination of information. It was also uncertain whether one could trust either the Suminwŏn or the East-West Development Company. Nor was there information available on the detailed conditions of laborers, other than that contained in the public notice.

Even before the Hawai'i immigration, Koreans had been moving to foreign countries, though with reluctance. As early as the 1860s, many Koreans crossed the Tumen River to settle in the Maritime Province of Russia, where they later

4   Inch'ŏn Harbor, 1903 ("koreanphoto.co.kr" with permission).

provided important bases for Korean independence fighters. Toward the last years of the Chosŏn dynasty, many Koreans crossed the Yalu River to escape economic hardship and harsh exploitive taxation and established new roots in the Yanbian region of China. There, by the early 1880s, some thirty thousand Koreans formed twenty-eight communities. In addition, Korean students and political refugees went to such countries as Japan and the United States. These immigrations, however, were never officially sanctioned by the government, and also there were virtually no students or political refugees among the immigrants.

As Koreans hesitated in responding to the call for immigration to Hawai'i, active promotion of immigration came from the Protestant churches, especially the Methodist Episcopal Church, which was active in the region west of Seoul. That this was the case is confirmed by the following facts.

First, Rev. George Heber Jones, who was active in missionary work in the Inch'ŏn area, energetically encouraged the Korean emigration, explaining the

5   Pusan Harbor, 1903 ("koreanphoto.co.kr" with permission).

advantageous conditions in Hawai'i. When skeptical Koreans responded to the labor recruitment announcement rather tepidly, Deshler requested assistance from Jones.[3] Hyŏn Sun (also known as Soon Hyun), who accompanied Korean migrants to Hawai'i as a Methodist leader in 1903, gave credit to Jones for prompting Koreans to come forward to go to Hawai'i:

> Although the public announcement [for labor recruitment in Hawai'i] was distributed to major counties and harbors, people in general were skeptical and hesitated to apply. Whereupon, Rev. George Heber Jones of Yongdong Church in Inch'ŏn explained the conditions in Hawaii to his congregation. Soon thereafter, 50 men and women of this church as well as 20 laborers volunteered to go there.[4]

This testimony accords with the issue raised by Rev. Shin Hŭng-shik, who was critical of Jones's encouragement of emigration as it allegedly caused problems within the Korean Methodist Church.[5]

Second, D. W. Deshler, who set up the East-West Development Company as an agency to recruit Korean emigrants, had been active along with the Korean church in relief work in the Inch'ŏn area.[6] Moreover, many Korean church leaders were employed by Deshler's company as interpreters and office staff. They included such men as Chang Kyŏng-hwa, An Chŏng-su (An Chung Su), Yuk Chŏng-su, Song Ŏn-yong, and Hyŏn Sun, who were close associates of Jones.[7] As for Hyŏn Sun, he began to work for Deshler's company as an interpreter soon after his return from study in Japan in April 1902. On his first day at work for the East-West Development Company, Hyŏn learned many things about the company from An Chŏng-su. He then attended Yongdong Methodist Church (now Naeri Methodist Church), where he was eventually introduced to Jones, who spoke Korean fluently. Hyŏn wrote in his autobiography that "he [Deshler] told me also that I should go to Hawaii with the Korean emigrants as interpreter."[8] Jones also encouraged his church members to go to Hawai'i.[9]

Newly uncovered evidence indicates that those Koreans who worked for the East-West Development Company, such as Chang Kyŏng-hwa, An Chŏng-su, Yuk Chŏng-su, and Hyŏn Sun, were closely associated with the Methodist churches. (Song Ŏn-yong was an exception.) That these men were active in Chemulp'o[10] suggests that they had maintained certain ties with Jones. Born in Kaesŏng, Chang Kyŏng-hwa (1857–1904) studied at a Christian school, worked as a preacher, and made significant financial contributions to the church.[11] An Chŏng-su was also a preacher of the Methodist Church in the Chemulp'o area[12] and became the head of the communication department of the Chemulp'o youth organization.[13] He, along with Chang Kyŏng-hwa, led the youth group in Chemulp'o in "celebrating the birthday of the great emperor" in August 1901[14] and acted as the general secretary of the first western regional conference of the

Methodist churches.[15] Yuk Chŏng-su, on the other hand, was a member of the youth group of Chŏngdong Church in Seoul and was also a member of a committee that initiated a campaign to erect a monument for Henry G. Appenzeller, the first Methodist missionary in Korea and the founder of the Paejae School, who died in 1902 in a ship accident.[16] It is probable that these people too may have encouraged Korean church members to go to Hawai'i, and their work may have been involved with the immigration of Koreans to Hawai'i as well.

Third, as members of the Korean churches immigrated to Hawai'i, many church leaders also migrated as interpreters, and perhaps they wanted to make sure that their fellow congregation members continued in the newly acquired faith by accompanying them. Both An Chŏng-su and Chŏng In-su joined the first group that went to Hawai'i as interpreters, and Hyŏn Sun followed them in the second group.[17] Thereafter, groups of Koreans who immigrated to Hawai'i included leaders who had been active in the Methodist churches in the western region of Korea. As we will see below, these people played a leading role in organizing Korean churches in Hawai'i.

THE ORDEAL OF THE METHODIST CHURCHES IN KOREA'S WESTERN REGION

As a result of their involvement in the Korean immigration to Hawai'i, the Methodists in the Chemulp'o area began to encounter serious problems within their own churches. Above all, the number of Methodist church members in the Chemulp'o region declined drastically as many who joined the migration to Hawai'i were drawn from church congregations. The churches in the western region of Korea went through an especially serious ordeal. On this issue, Rev. Shin Hŭng-shik, the minister of Naeri Methodist Church, offered the following account:

> In 1902, because of the encouragement of our pastor, the Rev. Cho Wŏn-shi [George Heber Jones], an emigration company was organized and through this, no small number of our church members joined the emigration. As a result, the size of congregations decreased significantly not only in our own church but also in other churches as well. There were some among the Western missionaries who strongly criticized the Rev. Cho Wŏn-shi for the decline in the congregations.[18]

Because of the Hawai'i emigration, the Methodist churches in Korea encountered hitherto unprecedented problems. Lured by the promise of salaries that were excessively high compared to those in Korea at the time, leading members of the churches such as local preachers and exhorters took up head positions in the emigration project. As a result, they not only lost interest in their church work, but also, exercising their influence, worked hard for the success of immigration to Hawai'i, harming the Korean churches as a whole in the end. Missionary work in Korea suffered serious damage, and the number of congregations was reduced significantly. In one extreme case, a church in the Kyodong district on the island of Kanghwa was wiped out completely because of emigration. In a report submitted in May 1904, Rev. E. M. Cable, who replaced Jones as the new superintendent of mission work in the region, severely criticized his predecessor for urging members of his congregation to migrate to Hawai'i, which Cable regarded as a cause of decline in church membership.[19]

The damaging effects of the Hawai'i emigration are attested by a report submitted by the Women's Foreign Missionary Society:

> The Exodus to Hawaii in consequence of efforts from planters there to secure laborers has caused much more anxiety and loss to our work. Not only common laborers, which class includes many of our most reliable Christians, but teachers and interpreters were called for, and such inducements held out to them that the people in their poverty believed Hawaii to be a land in which milk and honey flows and for a time it seemed as if we were to lose all of our best trained workers. The only comfort is in the thought that the Spirit of the Lord will be with them and use them to the saving of souls in these plantations.[20]

In the following year, the same missionary board wrote: "The loss of so many of the brightest and best trained helpers who had emigrated to Hawai'i is of course still felt, and the total inadequacy of the missionary force impresses itself more and more upon our workers, so that at times they seem to be almost in despair."[21] These reports tell us how seriously the Hawai'i emigration damaged the churches in the Inch'ŏn area.

Among Korean church leaders, Yi Kyŏng-jik and Hong Sŭng-ha are noteworthy, in addition to An Chŏng-su and Hyŏn Sun, mentioned above. Yi Kyŏng-jik's name is often mentioned in various sources. Hong Sŭng-ha, on the other hand, boosted the church's position by cleansing an evil spirit from a woman in 1903, according to a church journal,[22] and worked very effectively as a preacher before moving to Hawai'i late in the same year. His departure was a great loss for the Korean churches.[23]

At about this time, the Rev. Jones, who had been heavily involved with the Korean immigration to Hawai'i, had to take a leave of absence because of health reasons, and Chang Kyŏng-hwa, who had assisted Jones and worked as a general executive of the East-West Development Company, died. These two events caused a severe strain on the churches, raising the suspicions of many who were skeptical of the Korean emigration, believing that it contributed to the trouble Korean churches were experiencing.

ORGANIZING KOREAN CHURCHES IN HAWAI'I

The first Christian activity among Koreans in Hawai'i was started by Hong Ch'i-bŏm (Chi Pum Hong), Im Chŏng-su, Hyŏn Sun, and others at the Waialua and Kahuku plantations on the island of O'ahu soon after their arrival in 1903, when they began to proselytize and set up churches according to the American Methodist Church rules. Soon thereafter, Hong Sŭng-ha, who had been active in mission work at Namyang, and Yun Pyŏng-gu, who had worked at Kaesŏng with the Methodist Episcopal Conference South, moved to Honolulu and began proselytization work in cooperation with Rev. George L. Pearson of the Methodist Mission in Hawai'i.[24]

Pearson resigned in December 1904 and was succeeded by Rev. John Wadman. Working directly with the Korean laborers at various sugar plantations, Wadman worked strenuously on proselytization. Inspired by Wadman's hard work, the number of Koreans who came to "accept the Lord" increased daily. By 1906, there were as many as thirteen churches and thirty-five mission stations (chŏndoso) along with several dozen Korean pastors and preachers, according to Hyŏn Sun, who was on the island of O'ahu at the time. Starting with Min Ch'an-ho in Honolulu, Kim Yu-sun, Im Chŏng-su, Kim Yŏng-sik, Hong Ch'i-bŏm, Yi Kyŏng-jik, Kim Ŭi-je, Ch'oe Chin-t'ae, Shin P'an-sŏk, and others were leaders of the Korean churches on various islands in Hawai'i.[25]

Hong Sŭng-ha migrated to Hawai'i in late 1903 and continuously carried out church work. He also founded the Shinminhoe (New People's Association), which subsequently became the first political organization for Koreans in Hawai'i, and was elected its first president. Unable to adjust to the Hawaiian climate and environment, he suffered from health problems and was in the end obliged to return to Korea after a little over one year. Hyŏn Sun, on the other hand, met George Heber Jones again in Hawai'i in the winter of 1906, when the American missionary was on his way back to Korea after a leave. After receiving Jones's promise that he would be given a very important position if he returned to Korea, Hyŏn went back to Seoul in May 1907.

From these accounts, we can say that gospel work for the Koreans in Hawai'i was started by the leaders of the Korean Methodist churches who accompanied the first emigrants and that the first Korean churches in Hawai'i were founded and expanded under the leadership of these individuals. The churches in Korea continued to show interest in the Koreans in Hawai'i and dispatched church leaders to the Islands. Sending Grace Moon, along with her husband, to Hawai'i to guide Korean women is a case in point. A missionary report said of Moon:

> Grace Moon, a most reliable native helper, was obliged to leave to go
> with her husband to Hawaii. It was long before her place was satisfacto-

rily filled. At last just the one for the place seems to have been found an earnest, true Christian, one of the best educated women that Korea affords, able to command the respect and obedience of the girls. Her history is so remarkable that it seems as if the Lord had been preparing her for years for this work.[26]

CONCLUSION

Naeri Methodist Church in Inch'ŏn claims it was solely responsible for starting the missionary work for the Koreans in the United States. Its church history states that Naeri Church was "the fountainhead of the Korean emigration to and the mission work in the United States."[27] Although we can take issue with such a claim of sole responsibility, no one can deny that in a larger perspective the Methodist churches in Korea were the mothers of Korean churches in Hawai'i. The Methodist churches in Korea were closely involved in the immigration to Hawai'i from the very beginning, ranging from recruitment of laborers to their spiritual guidance. Because of their involvement, many of these churches suffered pains as a consequence for many of their leaders' and congregation members' joining the emigration, resulting in a significant decline in the vitality of the churches in Korea, especially in the western region. It is, therefore, no exaggeration to say that the Korean churches in Hawai'i were founded largely on the self-sacrifice of the Methodist churches in Korea.

Because of the close ties between the churches in Korea and the Korean churches in Hawai'i, the Koreans in Hawai'i did not hesitate to make monetary contributions to worthy causes in Korea. When a new school was established by the Epworth League at Sangdong Church in Seoul in 1904, with Syngman Rhee as its principal, the Koreans in Hawai'i donated "a no small amount of hard-earned money" even though they were still in the stage of struggling to settle down in the new alien environment.[28] In another case, upon learning that his hometown church was building a new school, Ch'oe Chin-yong, who immigrated to Hawai'i from Pongsan in Hwanghae Province, contributed money to this church from his "pennies and dimes savings" that he accumulated from the meager wages of plantation work.[29] There must have been hundreds, if not thousands, more similar cases that have not been recorded for posterity.

The churches in Korea played a crucial role in the immigration of Koreans to Hawai'i. They helped recruit laborers bound for Hawai'i and provided many key leaders for the Koreans in Hawai'i. As soon as they arrived in Hawai'i, these Korean followers of Christianity established their own churches on various islands with the help of American missionaries to proselytize and minister to the increasing number of new converts among the Koreans. These Korean churches played a vital role not only as places of worship and spiritual guidance but also as important centers for social and nationalist activities in Hawai'i. That Hawai'i was an important center for the Korean nationalist activities before Korea's liberation in 1945 is well known, and the Korean churches and their congregations in Hawai'i were the backbone of the Korean nationalist movement.

NOTES

This chapter was written in Korean and was translated into English by Yŏng-ho Ch'oe.

1. The Suminwŏn was established in 1902 to handle those who traveled to foreign countries, but this office was abolished in the same year and hence had very little to do in reality with Korean immigration to Hawai'i.

2. According to "Hawaii Governor's Reports, 1905–1909," 7,388 Koreans arrived in Hawai'i between January 1903 and April 1905.

3. Hong Ki-p'yo, *Naeri 95-nyŏnsa* (95-year History of Naeri [Church]) (Inch'ŏn, 1980), 106.

4. Hyŏn Sun, *P'owa yuram ki* (Record of Journey to Hawai'i) (Seoul, 1909), 5.

5. Shin Hŭng-shik, *Inch'ŏn Naeri Kyohoe Yŏksa* (History of Naeri Church in Inch'ŏn) (Inch'ŏn, 1923), 16.

6. Hong Sŏk-ch'an, *Chemulp'o chibang kyohoesa charyo chip, 1895–1930* (Historical Sources of Church History in the Chemulp'o [Inch'ŏn] Area) (Eimen, 1995), 142.

7. That these men were active leaders of the early Korean Methodist churches appears in various historical sources. For example, Yuk Chŏng-su was active in Chŏngdong Church in Seoul and appears to have begun to work for the East-West Development Company around this time, while Chang Kyŏng-hwa and An Chŏng-su may have been active in Inch'ŏn. The names of both Chang and An appear in the October 1901 issue of *Shinhak wŏlbo* (Theological Monthly) as leaders of the Chemulp'o youth group that sponsored "the celebration of the Korean emperor's birthday."

8. Soon Hyun [Hyŏn Sun], "My Autobiography," 59 (typewritten).

9. Ibid., 61.

10. Chemulp'o is an old name of Inch'ŏn.

11. Kim Ki-bŏm, "Chemulp'o kyou Chang Kyŏng-hwa ssi pyŏlseham" (Chemulp'o Church Member Mr. Chang Kyŏng-hwa Passed Away), *Sinhak wŏlbo* (November 1904): 432–35. Hong Ki-p'yo writes in his *Naeri 50-nyŏn sa* (107) that Chang Kyŏng-hwa, as a general secretary, led the first group of Koreans to Hawai'i. This, however, is wrong. This mistake is probably due to an incorrect

reading of Rev. Shin Hŭng-shik's account given in *Inch'ŏn Naeri Kyohoe yŏksa* (16), which reads: "Preacher Chang Kyŏng-hwa worked as a general secretary of an emigration office and was engaged in work dealing with emigration."

12. *Shinhak wŏlbo* (June 1901): 267–68.

13. An Chŏng-su, "Ch'ŏn'gun chinbo" (Heavenly Troops Advance), *Shinhak wŏlbo* (July 1901): 315–16.

14. See "Taehwangje t'anshin ch'ukha ham" (Celebrating the Great Emperor's Birthday), *Shinhak wŏlbo* (September 1901): 400–02. He writes: "The glorious virtue of our great emperor shines like the sun and the moon to awaken the darkened mind of our ignorant subjects. It is only proper that we as the subjects of his majesty fulfill our obligations and celebrate the national event."

15. *Shinhak wŏlbo* (October 1901): 479.

16. *Shinhak wŏlbo* (September 1902): 435–37. The monument committee members include Ch'oe Pyŏng-hŏn, Min Ch'an-ho, No Pyŏng-sŏn, Kang Min, Yun Ch'ang-yŏl, Im Chong-myŏn, Song Ki-yong, Chŏng Kyo, Cho Man-su, Yŏ Pyŏng-hyŏn, Kang Cho-wŏn, Mun Kyŏng-ho, and Chu Sang-ho.

17. Hyŏn Sun gives two different accounts on his trip in his autobiography and his Korean work *P'owa yuram ki*. In the former, he writes that his group of 120 men and women arrived in Honolulu on February 20, 1903, but in the latter, his group was sixty in number and arrived on March 2.

18. Shin Hŭng-shik, *Inch'ŏn Naeri Kyohoe Yŏksa*, 16.

19. *Annual Report of the Board of Foreign Missions of the M.E.C., Korea Mission, 1884–1943*, in Han'guk kidokkyo yŏksa yŏn'guso, *saryo ch'ongsŏ* 16 (1993): 239; *Annual Report of the Board of Foreign Missions of M.E.C., 1904*, 311.

20. *Annual Report of the Women's Foreign Missionary Society of the M.E.C., 1903–1904*, 158.

21. *Annual Report of the Women's Foreign Missionary Society of the M.E.C., 1904–1905*, 188.

22. *Shinhak wŏlbo* (February 1903): 57–59.

23. *Shinhak wŏlbo* (October 1903): 437–39. This report confirms that Hong Sŭng-ha was in Korea until the end of 1903. Accordingly, *Naeri 50-nyŏn sa*'s account that "Preacher Hong Sŭng-ha led the founding of Sinminhoe (New People's Association) in Honolulu on August 7, 1903 and became its president" appears to be mistaken in date.

24. Hyŏn Sun, *P'owa yuram ki*, 8. If Hyŏn is correct on this, the claim made in *Naeri 95-nyŏn sa* that the first Korean church work was started by Hong Sŭng-ha needs to be reexamined.

25. Soon Hyun [Hyŏn Sun], "My Autobiography," 65; Hyŏn Sun, *P'owa yuram ki*, 8–10.

26. *Annual Report of the Women's Foreign Missionary Society of the M.E.C.,* *1903–1904,* 190.

27. *Naeri 95-nyŏn sa,* 110.

28. Yi Sŭng-man [Syngman Rhee], "Sangdong Ch'ŏngnyŏnhoe ŭi hakkyo rŭl sŏlch'i ham" (A New School is Founded by the Youth Group of Sangdong Church), *Shinhak wŏlbo* (November 1904): 440–50.

29. *Chosŏn kŭrisŭ hoebo* (Korean Christian Bulletin), vol. 3 (Han'guk Kamri Kyohoe Sahakhoe, 1986), May 30, 1911, 67.

3

Syngman Rhee in Hawai'i
His Activities in the Early Years, 1913–1915

O NE OF THE most important leaders of modern Korea, Syngman Rhee (Yi
Sŭng-man) used Hawai'i as his home base for his nationalist activities during his long years of exile abroad before Korea was freed from Japanese colonial rule. This chapter examines his activities in Hawai'i from 1913 to 1915.

RHEE'S ACTIVITIES BEFORE ARRIVING IN HAWAI'I

Born in 1875 into a family that traced its lineage back to King T'aejo, the
founder of the Chosŏn dynasty (he was an eighteenth-generation descendant of
Yi Sŏng-gye), Rhee had already had a colorful and turbulent career as a young
radical and maverick diplomat before going to Hawai'i. A graduate of Paejae
School, the first modern school in Korea, run by American missionaries, he
joined the Independence Club (Tongnip Hyŏphoe), the foremost reform-minded
political organization in Korea in the last decade of the nineteenth century, and
soon came to be known as an effective agitator for political and social reform.
For his radical views and activities, he was thrown into prison and received a life
sentence in 1899. After serving five years, he was released in 1904 in an amnesty.
While incarcerated, he wrote his famous book *Tongnip Chŏngshin* (Spirit of
Independence), in which he appealed to his fellow Koreans to transform the
country by accepting Western ideas and technology in order to enable Korea to
survive as an independent nation.[1] While serving his prison term, he accepted
Christianity and befriended a fellow inmate named Pak Yong-man (also known
as Young-Man Park), and they became "sworn brothers," pledging eternal
brotherly friendship and collaboration.

   In 1904, Rhee went to the United States and was soon swept into the whirl-
wind of international diplomacy. As Russia and Japan tried to negotiate a peace
treaty under the mediation of President Theodore Roosevelt to conclude the
Russo-Japanese war of 1904–5, the fate of Korea as an independent state was
at stake. The young Rhee, assuming the role of representing Korea, tried des-
perately to seek the assistance of Roosevelt and the U.S. government in preserv-

ing Korea's independence, invoking the official treaty the United States had signed with Korea a little over two decades earlier in 1882, in which the two countries pledged to render assistance if one party was treated "unjustly or oppressively" by a third power. When the United States ignored his appeal, and Russia and Japan went on to sign the Portsmouth Treaty in 1905, surrendering Korea to Japan, the young Rhee learned a valuable lesson about the cold reality of international politics.

Frustrated in his diplomatic efforts, Rhee decided to pursue academic programs in the United States. In 1907, he graduated from George Washington University and moved on to Harvard University, where he received an M.A. degree in 1910. But before receiving his degree from Harvard, he went to Princeton University to study for a Ph.D. degree, which he earned in 1910,[2] thus becoming the first Korean to receive the highest academic degree from a Western university. While at Princeton, he became a protégé of Woodrow Wilson, who often called him "the future redeemer of Korean independence."[3]

Upon completion of his studies, Rhee returned to Korea in 1910 to take the position of chief Korean secretary of the Seoul Young Men's Christian Association (YMCA). The year 1910, however, was a fateful year for Korea, as Japan put an end to Korean independence, reducing it to a colony. Unwilling to yield to Japanese pressure to cooperate and realizing the difficulties of pursuing his goals under Japanese rule, Rhee left Korea and went to the United States in 1912. He was able to leave his beloved country only because of the help he received from Merriman C. Harris, missionary bishop of Japan and Korea of the Methodist Church, who obtained the needed documents for Rhee.[4] After attending the Quadrennial General Conference of the Methodist Episcopal Church at Minneapolis as a lay delegate of Korean churches, Rhee went to Hastings, Nebraska, to meet his old friend Pak Yong-man, who was running a Korean military school there. After discussing their future plans, the two young nationalists decided that Hawai'i would be the best place to work toward the redemption of Korea—that is, to regain independence—as the Pacific islands had the largest concentration of Koreans in North America.[5] Rhee's decision to go to Hawai'i may also have been influenced by an invitation from the Methodist Mission in Hawai'i.[6]

RHEE'S ARRIVAL IN HAWAI'I

As they had agreed in Nebraska, the two Korean nationalists (who had pledged sworn brotherhood) went to Hawai'i. Pak Yong-man reached Hawai'i first, arriving in December 1912. While in the mainland United States, Pak had contributed greatly to nurturing the Korean National Association (KNA), which was founded in 1909 as a representative organization for all Koreans living abroad with central headquarters located in San Francisco and a Hawai'i branch located in Honolulu. (It also organized a branch in Mexico and envisioned doing the same in the Far East and elsewhere.[7]) Soon after his arrival in Hawai'i, Pak Yong-man, who had once worked as the editor of *Shinhan minbo* (The New Korea), an organ of the KNA in San Francisco, exercised a dominant influence over the KNA and prepared for the arrival of his friend, Syngman Rhee.[8]

Three months after Pak's arrival, Rhee reached Hawai'i in February 1913. Hungry for strong leadership and in need of guidance from well-educated leaders, the Koreans in Hawai'i enthusiastically welcomed the two prominent nationalist leaders. But in the case of Rhee, unlike Pak, the welcome reception came from the powerful *haole* community as well. In particular, the Methodist Episcopal Mission of Hawai'i was anxiously waiting for him. Rhee was not a

6   Korean National Association and its first officers in 1909: *left to right: front,* Kim Sang-Ha, Chung Won-Myung, Kang Yong-Soo; *standing,* Ahn Won-Kiu, Hong In-Pyo, Lee Nae-Soo, Seung Yong-Hwan, Chung Chillay.

total stranger to Hawai'i. In 1904, on his way to the mainland United States, Rhee stayed overnight at Honolulu, and during his twenty-four-hour stay, he met Rev. John D. Wadman, the superintendent of the Methodist Mission, who introduced Rhee to the enthusiastic Korean church members at Nu'uanu and Ewa and announced his desire to have Rhee work in Hawai'i with him upon completion of Rhee's mission on the mainland.[9] Also, Rhee must have had strong support from Bishop Merriman C. Harris,[10] Methodist missionary bishop of Japan and Korea, who was responsible for taking Rhee out of Korea to keep him out of harm at the hands of Japan.[11] On his departure from Korea in 1912, "Bishop Harris," to quote Rhee's own words, "did everything he could to get me the permission from the Japanese Government." Harris and Rhee traveled together aboard the same ship across the Pacific Ocean, during which they discussed many issues, including the current Japanese-Korean relationship; Harris unsuccessfully but insistently tried to persuade Rhee to accept Japanese rule in Korea.[12] Since Harris knew about Rhee and his works, it is likely that he had strongly recommended Rhee to the Hawai'i Mission.

Rhee received a big welcome in Hawai'i from both the Korean community and white leaders. Within a week of his arrival, the *Honolulu Star-Bulletin,* one of the two major newspapers in Hawai'i, carried on February 8, 1913, an article with a heading in bold letters stating "Dr. Rhee is Great Leader of Koreans" along with a photo of him in a Ph.D. gown. The opening sentence reads: "There is perhaps no greater religious leader in Korea today than Dr. Syng Man Rhee, Ph.D., who is now visiting in Honolulu at the request of Dr. John W. Wadman, head of the Korean and Japanese works of the First Methodist Church." It then gives an account of Rhee's activities as a young reformer, his subsequent imprisonment, and his academic achievements in the United States. In a separate article reporting on forthcoming activities at Central Union Church, it announced Rhee's planned talk on Sunday, the next day, as follows: "The Rev. Syngman Rhee, Ph.D., the most prominent Korean in the world, who served seven years in prison and for two years was general secretary of the Y.M.C.A. for all Korea, will give an interesting talk on his experiences, at the morning service. It is hoped that a large attendance will greet Mr. Rhee."[13] From these *Star-Bulletin* articles, we learn that Rhee was introduced to Hawai'i as "the most prominent Korean in the world" and that he was invited to speak within a week after his arrival at one of the most influential churches in Hawai'i, a reception no other Korean could have expected.

A few months later, on September 29, 1913, *The Pacific Commercial Advertiser,* the other major paper in Honolulu, introduced Rhee in a big, bold headline in its Sunday edition, "Korea's Pioneer Editor and Publisher / A Honolulu School Teacher," with three photographs—one, Rhee's portrait; the second, a photo of Rhee in prison garb along with his friends and relatives; and the third, a photo of an 1898 issue of *Hyŏpsŏnghoe hoebo* (Bulletin of Hyŏpsŏnghoe), which Rhee edited. The *Advertiser* article gave an account of Rhee's life as a young revolutionary fighting for reform in Korea, ending up in prison, whose scene the *Advertiser* described: "Seven years in foul-smelling jail, with his neck lodged in a wooden collar, with his hands manacled behind his back, and his feet in irons; all this merely because he had attempted to educate his fellow-country-men in the rudiments of Western civilization; and because he had courage to start a newspaper, the first that had ever been published in Korea." It also dis-cussed extensively Rhee's work as a publisher and editor of the weekly magazine to educate Koreans and his conversion to Christianity while in prison. Upon his release from incarceration, he came to the United States to obtain three degrees from the prestigious universities and became a friend of many prominent Amer-icans. The *Advertiser* wrote:

> With what success his efforts were attended may be judged by the fact that he has obtained degrees from Harvard, Princeton and George Wash-ington Universities; that he numbers such men as President Wilson and Colonel [Theodore] Roosevelt among his intimate friends. These and other great celebrities all over the United States have enjoyed the friend-ship of the great little doctor.

This "great little doctor" now established his residence in Hawai'i, having been invited to take charge of the education of the Koreans in Hawai'i, according to the *Advertiser*. The article concluded: "In Honolulu, on American soil, he is bending his energies to train young Koreans to be able to step into their places as leaders in the New Korea of his hopes. He is not to be classed as a conspir-ator, but as a patriot, working towards high ideals and that for Korea that will help her most."[14]

With such an introduction by the two major English-language newspapers, Rhee entered the Hawaiian stage with a big splash not just in the Korean com-munity but also in the powerful white community as well. Even among the white elites in Hawai'i, few could boast the prestigious academic degrees that Rhee had earned or claim an intimate friendship with the popular incumbent president as well as the colorful former president, as Rhee did. In other words, Rhee entered the Hawaiian scene as a figure recognized instantly by the white elites as a major personality who boasted prestigious academic achievements and elitist social ties that virtually no one even among the Caucasians in Hawai'i at the time could match, and this at a time when whites completely dominated politics, the econ-omy, and culture of Hawai'i and when Asians were still severely discriminated against as semi-civilized. Finding a fellow countryman who could speak directly with the white elites, the Koreans in Hawai'i must have been awed and at the same time encouraged by the arrival of Rhee in Hawai'i.

THE METHODIST MISSION AND THE KOREAN COMMUNITY
ON THE EVE OF RHEE'S ARRIVAL

The Hawaiian Mission of the Methodist Episcopal Church was in charge of ministering to Korean immigrants in Hawai'i. At the time Rhee arrived, the Methodist Mission was in serious trouble with the Korean community in Hawai'i. Koreans were seething in anger because remarks some of the Methodist Mission leaders had made publicly were seen as downright hostile to the nationalistic sentiment of most Koreans.

In April 1908, Bishop Merriman C. Harris—the same bishop who would help Rhee get the necessary documents from the Japanese government to go to Minneapolis in 1912—spoke on Korean issues while passing through Hawai'i. A longtime missionary in Japan, Bishop Harris strongly favored the Japanese domination of Korea. While speaking at a Japanese church in Hawai'i, he unabashedly supported Japanese actions toward gaining dominance in Korea. He stated, according to the *Advertiser:* "I will make it a part of my duty to call upon President Roosevelt and Secretary [of State] Root while I am in Washington and tell them that from my own knowledge I am convinced that Prince Ito and Hayashi[15] are in earnest in Korea and are working patiently and earnestly for the good of that country." He went on to say that "the general sentiment among the mass of the Korean people is not hostile to the Japanese, the people generally favoring the system inaugurated." As if this were not enough, the good bishop even invoked the will of Providence in justifying the Japanese domination of Korea. He summarized his own assessment of the situation: "The occupation of the country [Korea] by the Japanese seems to be the hand of Providence working for the good of Korea."[16] These remarks stirred up a hornet's nest among the Koreans in Hawai'i.

It is to be understood, however, that Bishop Harris's remarks were made against the backdrop of the assassination of Durham W. Stevens, which had taken place only a month before. An American employed by the Japanese government in Korea as an advisor to the Foreign Ministry, Stevens was embarking on a tour in the United States to win the support of the American government and public for the acceptance of Japanese policy in Korea. Following the appearance in the *San Francisco Chronicle* of his remarks praising the Japanese domination of Korea, Stevens was shot to death by a Korean nationalist in San Francisco on March 23, 1908. The Stevens assassination was justified and even extolled by Korean nationalists as a supreme act of patriotism.[17] The American press, however, did not see it that way, condemning the assassination as an act of lawlessness, if not anarchy.

It was against this background that the *Advertiser* editorialized in support of Harris and warned Koreans who might do harm to the bishop: "Bishop Harris was quoted as saying that the hand of God could be seen in the Japanese occupation of Korea" and that "this natural and reasonable statement has awakened profound resentment among the Koreans, and their expressions have been so bitter as to alarm local friends of Bishop Harris as to his personal safety." What apparently happened was that "a committee of Koreans" was formed and went about investigating whether Harris had truly made such remarks, and these inquiries appeared so serious that the newspaper detected clear hostility toward the bishop. The editorial continued:

> It is well for these Koreans to understand that if a hair of the head of Bishop Harris is injured, there will be an investigation here which will not be to their taste. So much can be predicated of the Federal power. But apart from that, it is time for these semi-civilized Orientals to understand that the Territory of Hawaii is not a place for them unless they are here to obey the laws. We have seen too much of their semi-political intriguing. . . . If anything like an Oriental Mafia is set up here, or any Mollie Maguiredom instituted, those who are responsible for it will find that American law has a keen eye, a long arm and mailed hand.[18]

Was the *Advertiser*'s fear of violence against Bishop Harris justifiable? There is no evidence that any Korean had contemplated doing harm to the bishop. To be sure, there is no doubt that most Koreans in Hawai'i were angry at and resentful of the statement attributed to Harris. Who would not be incensed when hearing a hostile remark justifying foreign domination of his or her motherland as the work of God? Korea at this particular juncture was waging a last desperate struggle to resist Japanese penetration, and the Koreans in Hawai'i were closely watching the ultimate outcome of their fellow countrymen's last-minute resistance. (Some of them, perhaps as many as nearly two hundred, had even joined the famed Righteous Armies in Korea to fight the Japanese militarily before escaping to Hawai'i.) It was in this particular situation that Bishop Harris, who had worked as a missionary in Korea, called the Japanese domination a work of God.[19] Utterly insensitive to Korean sentiment, the *Advertiser* not only supported Bishop Harris's remarks but went on to characterize the Koreans in Hawai'i, without any justifiable ground, as "semi-civilized Oriental[s]" and an "Oriental Mafia," equating them with the Molly Maguires, a notorious terrorist group in the Pennsylvania coal mines.

Bitter sentiment lingered even after the departure of Harris, and this resentment was transferred to Rev. John Wadman, the superintendent of Methodist Mission in Hawai'i, who was in charge of ministering to Koreans and Japanese. When Bishop Harris made his controversial speech hostile to Korea at a Japanese church in Honolulu, Wadman was also on the podium and made a remark that was not friendly to Korea. When Harris spoke to the audience, he started, according to B. H. Nhee, the editor of the *United Korean News*, by saying "The Koreans—oh, no, I mean the Chosen." Chōsen is the Japanese reading of the name of the old dynasty that had ruled Korea, Chosŏn, and this Japanese reading suggests the acceptance of the Japanese domination. Whereupon, Rev. Wadman is quoted to have said: "They are Japanese now." Moreover, Wadman called a former editor of the Korean newspaper "a fool."[20] These remarks infuriated the Koreans, and Wadman was not in good graces with at least certain members of the Korean community in Hawai'i.

Two years later in February 1913, on the day when Rhee arrived in Honolulu, the *Advertiser* reported that Wadman was again in trouble with the Koreans. In running schools and doing other work assisting Koreans, Rev. Wadman accepted $750 from the Japanese consul general as an aid for educating Korean youths without prior consultation with Koreans, and this once again caused a furor in the Korean community. Having lost their country to Japan with the 1910 annexation, the Koreans in Hawai'i regarded Japan and the Japanese as their mortal enemies, against whom they were determined to fight to the last man in order to recover the independence of their homeland. They had previously rejected all offers by the Japanese consul general in Honolulu to act as their representative. They did not want to have anything to do with the Japanese government representatives. Acceptance of money from the Japanese consul general was seen by the Koreans as an act of betraying their beloved country. They could not tolerate Wadman's acceptance of money from Japan on behalf of the Koreans in Hawai'i. The angry Koreans asked Wadman to return the money to the Japanese, and some even went so far as to demand that Wadman leave Hawai'i. The *Advertiser* reported: "Members of the Korean colony stated yesterday the bitter feeling between influential factions among them and the Rev. John Wadman, head of the Methodist Korean and Japanese missionary work, is increasing to such an extent that the minister has been asked to sever his connection with the Korean association, and to leave the Islands."[21] In other words, Rev. Wadman, the man in charge of ministering to Koreans in Hawai'i, was persona non grata in the Korean community.

It was in this situation that Rhee arrived in Hawai'i. It is an ironic coincidence that the *Advertiser*'s article, "Angry Koreans Threaten Wadman: Members of Hermit Colony Said to Have Ordered Minister to Leave the Islands," was carried on the very day that Rhee disembarked in Honolulu. For the Methodist Mission, Rhee must have been seen as a godsend who could rescue the missionaries from the messy situation they had created in dealing with the Koreans.

RHEE'S EDUCATIONAL WORK UNDER THE METHODIST MISSION

The first work Rhee assumed after his arrival in Hawai'i was to take charge of the education of Korean youth under the Methodist Mission. Since September 1906, the Methodist Mission had operated a boarding school for Korean boys, and Rhee was entrusted to run this school. The school was initiated, according to Hyŏn Sun (Soon Hyun), in July 1905, when Song Hŏn-ju, Pak Yun-sŏp, and others formed an educational society and elected Rev. Wadman to chair the society. These Koreans then met at Wadman's home to set up a formal organization with the "objective being the building of a school, dormitory, and hospital here in Honolulu with a Korean-speaking resident Missionary in charge." They decided the school was to be a boarding school to accommodate Korean youths from various plantations throughout the Islands. Koreans raised $2,000 for this purpose right away. The Methodist Mission purchased land in downtown Honolulu for $18,000 and built necessary facilities for school and church services.[22] Located on the corner of Punchbowl and Beretania streets in downtown Honolulu, this group of buildings came to be known as the Korean Compound.

Wadman reported that "the total enrollment the first year was 65, with classes in all grades up to the eighth, three American teachers and two Korean, with a dormitory superintendent" and that "early in 1907 the school was officially recognized as a private government school and several boys were received as boarders and allowed to attend elsewhere if they chose." Most of these students worked to pay their expenses. "The annual expense for food only is $40 for the smaller and $50 for the larger boys" and the students were able to earn enough to pay such costs "during the vacation periods by labor on the plantations or in pineapple factories." Many of them also worked "as household servants before and after school session." The school also maintained a printing press and a shoemaker's shop where students worked. There were students without parents who received scholarship aid. "They all make good students, being quick to learn and eager to advance," according to Wadman. The official interdenominational ties with the Mid-Pacific Institute allowed graduates to be placed "freely in either the Kawaiahao Seminary or Mills School" and "the largest number of Korean students in Mills School at one time has been 32 boys and in the seminary 10 young ladies." Because students could advance to these schools, the Korean Boarding School taught only up to the sixth grade. Besides the two schools just mentioned, graduates also moved on to McKinley High School and some even went to mainland schools. The school also ran athletic programs, in which "our students excel both in football and baseball" and "no day in the school session lends more interest to the student body than a match, either at the bat or with the 'kickers.'"[23]

Upon assuming control of the education of Korean youths in 1913, Rhee changed the name of this school from Korean Boarding School to Korean Central School (Han'in Chungang Hagwŏn). In his report to the Methodist Mission within a few months after becoming the school principal, he wrote:

> The Korean [Central] School, as a part of our Mission, has done more
> effective and more faithful work for the Koreans and for the Korean
> Church on these Islands than any other agency that I know of. Training
> young men and young women for Christian leadership is the most neces-
> sary part of missionary work in Korea today. A strong desire for Christ-
> ian education is growing among our young people both at home and
> abroad. Hawaii is so peculiarly situated that we can meet this need more
> satisfactorily and more economically here than anywhere else.[24]

From the opening paragraph of this report, we can detect at least two aspects of Rhee's personality at the time. One is his strong personal belief in Christianity and in Christian education as a way of redeeming his homeland. The other is self-assuredness. With his typical self-confidence, Rhee claimed that he had "done more effective and more faithful work for the Koreans and for the Korean Church . . . than any other agency that I know of." Regarding the training of the future leadership of Korea as the most important task he could do while in Hawai'i, Rhee pursued his task seriously and effectively.

Within six months after Rhee took control of the school, the number of students enrolled increased from thirty-six to 120, more than a threefold increase. The sharp increase in the enrollment was most probably due to the fame Rhee commanded among the Koreans, and Korean parents did not hesitate to send their children to the school where Rhee was the principal. The school was divided into four classes with four American and three Korean teachers, who, according to Rhee, worked for "their own love for work" in spite of "inadequate compensation." In addition to English, students were taught both Korean and the Chinese classics *(hanmun)*. There was strong emphasis on Christian education.[25]

At the Korean Central School, Rhee introduced a revolutionary practice with the adoption of coeducational schooling. When we examine the background leading to Rhee's adoption of the coeducational system, we can learn how innovative and pragmatic Rhee's approach to the education was. In the summer of 1913, only a few months after his arrival in Honolulu, he visited various islands as a part of his mission work and looked into the conditions of Koreans living there. One surprising discovery Rhee made, according to the *Star-Bulletin*, was that "there were a number of young girls who were either not attending school or who stood likely to be taken from school by their parents and forced to become married against their wishes."[26] When Rhee became the school principal, nineteen girls came forward and said they too wished to be educated. Although Rhee had no difficulty in finding a place for these girls to stay, it was not easy to find separate classrooms and teachers for them. Rhee therefore decided to allow the girls to study along with boys in the same classes.

This was an earth-shaking move that went directly against centuries-old practice in Korea. Steeped in the Confucian tradition, Korean society had for centuries followed the adage "men and women above the age of seven must never sit together." To have boys and girls together in the same classroom would have caused a huge scandal in Korea. Disregarding this tradition, Rhee started coeducation in his Korean Central School at first as an experiment, and when he found it to be successful, he adopted it fully. The *Advertiser* gives the following account:

> The present co-educational arrangement of the school, commenced
> this year as an experiment, has so far proved a success. Doubts were
> expressed at first as to the advisability or inadvisability of the new
> proposition. According to the Confucian ethics, boys and girls "above
> seven years of age must not even sit together." Strictly observing this
> ancient teaching of the great sage as "the laws of heaven and earth," the
> Korean conservative parents had never dreamed of the possibility of a
> co-educational institution for their children. Some of their leaders, how-
> ever, getting hold of modern ideas boldly recommended the adoption of
> a new system. Although heartily approved by the leading members of the
> Mission, both Korean and American, such a radical change in the educa-
> tional system met at first with no little opposition. But the novel experi-
> ment has already given such a gratifying result that no question has been
> raised concerning the practicability of this plan. The co-educational plan,
> advantageous to other races, is equally advantageous to the Korean chil-
> dren, morally, socially and otherwise.[27]

Under Rhee's leadership, the Korean Central School made significant advances in both the number of students enrolled and curriculum improvement. The first big task that confronted Rhee as the principal was the problem of dormitory facilities. Because most of the students were children of poor sugar plantation workers from various islands, there was no way for them to commute from home, so they had to be accommodated in a dormitory. To resolve the pressing need of housing facilities, a new dormitory building for boys was built at a cost of $4,900. In addition, a girls' dormitory was built in the Puunui area, from where students commuted on foot a distance of about 2 miles. As a result, the average daily attendance of the school numbered 139. Of these, 73 boys resided in the dormitory, but only a half of them were able to pay the tuition of $60 per year. Rhee reported: "These figures, combined with our experience proves the fact that one half of these students could not come to school were they required to pay their tuition in advance."[28]

After Rhee took over the school, there were those who could not advance to high school when they finished the Korean Central School. Some of them were too old to be accepted in McKinley High School, the only public high school in Honolulu at the time, or McKinley did not have enough space. Since they had no money to enroll in private schools, they asked to continue to receive more education at the Korean Central School. To meet these students' needs, Rhee started a high school program, employing qualified teachers.[29] Under the able leadership of Rhee, the Korean Central School made great advances within a very short period of time, and the Korean community was strongly supportive of this school, opening their purses very generously.

The American missionaries were even more enthusiastic about Rhee's work. With his arrival, there was very little criticism of the missionaries from the Korean community. Moreover, the Methodist Mission was greatly impressed by Rhee's strong and effective leadership and offered the highest praise possible. In February 1914, less than a year after Rhee took over the school, Rev. John Wadman reported at the annual mission conference: "Dr. Rhee has been a tower of strength during the year. We wonder now how we succeeded in any measure without his services in the past, and we cherish the hope that he will tarry in Hawai'i for many and many years."[30] In the following year, Rev. William Henry Fry, the new superintendent who succeeded Wadman, reported: "Too much cannot be said in praise of the splendid work Dr. Rhee has rendered our mission thru [sic] his work as principal of this school. His have been the struggles of a real man of God. Many have been his heart-aches and heavy has been his burden, his valuable services have been given without pay."[31]

In spite of such accolades, Rhee's relationship with the Methodist Mission did not last long. Within three years after becoming the principal, Rhee resigned from the Korean Central School. The immediate circumstances surrounding his resignation are not clear. Without any advance inkling, Rev. Fry reported in the 1916 annual report that "after three years of efficient and voluntary service in connection with the Korean Boys' School, Dr. Syngman Rhee retired from the principalship and Mrs. Ross Page was sent out to take his place." There is no reference to what prompted him to give up the principal's post. But the fact that Methodist Superintendent Fry, at a dinner gathering of Koreans on February 18, 1916, presented Rhee a desk with a clock and a study lamp along with giving a speech praising Rhee's selfless services indicates Rhee's departure from the American mission took place in a friendly atmosphere. But as we now know, following the resignation from the principal's position, Rhee became completely independent of the Methodist Mission and went on to establish his own independent church and schools.

What were the reasons for Rhee's sudden resignation from the Korean Central School? There is no explanation from the Methodist Mission, nor from Rhee himself. The available documents of the Methodist Mission only express regret for Rhee's resignation without clarifying why he retired. But from other sources, we can detect that there were at least two fundamental differences between Rhee and the Methodist Mission on educating the Korean youths in Hawai'i.

First, there was a big difference in the fundamental approach to and objective of the education of Korean youths. Dr. Robert T. Oliver, who was long a close lieutenant and confidant of Rhee, offers us a good account of the reason behind Rhee's separation from the Methodist Mission in his book, *Syngman Rhee: The Man Behind the Myth*, which reads like an autobiography of Rhee. In a nutshell, the Methodist Mission wished to Americanize the Korean immigrants by offering an American curriculum, while Rhee wanted to train Korean youths so that they could later work for the Korean independence movement by teaching them the Korean language, history, traditions, and so forth, as well as the American curriculum. Rhee felt strongly, according to Oliver, "that the Koreans should continue to speak their own language, should be educated in history and customs of their own country, and should dedicate themselves to the resurrection of their fallen nation. The Methodist Church officials were strongly opposed to the idea."[32] There was, in other words, a fundamental difference between the two in the basic philosophy of educating Korean youths.

The whole philosophy behind setting up schools and churches for the Koreans and other ethnic groups in Hawai'i was to wrench out any vestige of Asian characteristics and to make them Americanized. Such a view was expressed in no uncertain terms by the leaders of the mission in their annual reports and elsewhere. For example, in the annual report of the Methodist Mission in 1912, Superintendent Wadman emphasized the importance of "more Americanization" of the Asian immigrants.[33] Similarly in 1916, in emphasizing the need to educate Hawai'i-born Asian children in American ways, Superintendent Fry stated at the annual conference that "if these young people are untaught in the hours of their awakening and left to themselves in the hours of their superstition and prejudice, the results are not far to speak." He then added:

> What I want to emphasize here is: Honolulu is an American city just as surely as Chicago is, and Hawaii is American soil just as surely as California is. If the Oriental in Hawaii is to reach the position which the integrity of our American institutions and the safety of our government here demands, *he must do it through his children.*[34]

He then called for the church to prepare for the day when its Sunday services would be conducted wholly in English: "If the Hawaiian-born Asiatic is to be Americanized we must prepare for the time when religious services will be conducted in English."[35]

With recovery of the sovereign nationhood of his beloved country foremost in his mind, Rhee could not accept or follow the educational objectives of the American missionaries. His strong sense of nationalism led him to part with the Methodist Mission so that he could pursue his nationalistic goals more independently.

The second reason for Rhee's departure was the conflict arising from the centralism of the Methodist Church versus Rhee's strong sense of independence. To begin with, there was tension over the management of the Korean Central School. According to Rev. Kingsley K. Lyu, who collided with Rhee at one time in the 1940s and later wrote an important study on the Koreans in Hawai'i, Superintendent Fry, hearing a rumor of financial irregularities within the Methodist Mission, tried to tighten financial controls so that the Mission would become more business-like and "ambitiously supervised every detail of the mission, making no exception for the school administration" of the Korean Central School. Fry "especially wanted to know the financial matters of the school in detail. Moreover, Fry objected to the use of the school as a training ground for politicians or for political activities." Rhee, according to Lyu, did not like Fry's "meddling" with school affairs on the ground of "academic freedom." "Rhee wanted to teach Korean nationalism and train Korean political leaders and would not take orders from Superintendent Fry for, he declared, the Chungang Hagwon [Central School] was built for Koreans, and not for Americans." Moreover, Rhee demanded, according to Lyu, self-governance of the two Korean institutions—the church and the school—since they were "almost entirely supported with money contributed by Koreans in Hawaii." Fry's flat refusal of this demand led Rhee to resign.[36]

Bernice B. H. Kim, who wrote an invaluable M.A. thesis in 1937, gives a similar account, but her report is more authoritative since it is based on her interview with Rhee himself. Rhee and his followers felt, according to Kim, that the Koreans needed a more independent educational institution free of interference from the Methodist Mission, as they came to think that "the Methodist people had hindered the educational progress of" Rhee. "To carry on his work he had to ask financial help from the Korean people and to this end he accepted the donations. At this juncture it was pointed out to him that he was violating a rule of Methodism in collecting such funds without due authorization," according to Kim. Rhee, however, "felt that he had promised the Koreans to do educational work for the young people and it was a promise he felt bound to keep." This, according to Kim, led Rhee to leave the Methodist Mission and go on to establish his own independent church and school. Kim then offers us Rhee's thinking behind forming his own church, based on her interview with Rhee:

> The idea of independence having such dominant position in his mind, he stood for complete independence and self-support of the Korean church and with that was his main objective in establishing the Korean Christian Church. He intended to lay a solid foundation so that after many years the Korean people could say that "this is really our church which rests upon our land."

The Methodist Church's central control left little room for the Koreans to have their own way concerning the control of land, property, and others. Kim wrote:

> When Dr. Rhee and others came to the realization that within the Methodist Church, everything material and tangible belonged to the Methodist mission board—land, building, etc. and that the Koreans could claim no ownership and no prospect of ever being able to say that all such are theirs. The principle as he saw it that the well-being and security of the Koreans depended upon the wishes and disposition of the Mission Board was what he and his followers fundamentally objected to.[37]

Within three years after he had begun to work for the Methodist Mission, Rhee came to the realization that as long as he remained under the Methodist Mission, he would have to abide by Methodist Church rules. A man of strong independence, Rhee simply could not accept a position that did not permit him to act freely in pursuing his goals, especially in the quest to restore Korean independence.

RHEE'S INDEPENDENT EDUCATIONAL WORK

After resigning the principalship of the Korean Central School and freeing himself from Methodist rules, Rhee embarked on educational work for Korean youths independently, relying on support largely from the Korean community. The first school he started on his own was the Korean Girls' Seminary. Shortly after he had assumed the principal's position, he toured different islands in the summer of 1913 to survey the conditions of Korean life on various sugar plantations. One of the most striking situations he found was the plight of young Korean girls. Growing up in poor plantation workers' families, not only were these girls unable to attend school but also they were about to be married off, often in return for money, before they even reached their teens (still following Korea's old practice of early marriage). Deploring this situation, Rhee inquired into the matter and learned that many of the girls wished to attend school if only they were allowed to do so. Whereupon, Rhee brought fourteen girls to Honolulu and placed them in the Susanna Wesley Home. Five of them were allowed to attend the Korean Central School.[38]

Hearing this news, twenty-seven more girls came to Rhee for education the following year, and there were forty additional girls who wished to study under Rhee in 1915. Since these girls could not be accommodated in the boys' dormitory, Rhee secured a dormitory for them in the Puunui area, from where they commuted on foot about two miles to their school twice or three times a day. To spare the students the trouble of walking that distance, Rhee decided it would be better to set up a separate school for these girls. Thus, the Korean Girls' Seminary was started in 1916 in the Puunui area with the purchase of three and a half acres of land. Buildings and a dormitory were built at a cost of $10,000. Of this sum, all but $200 was raised from contributions made by Koreans.[39]

Most of the students in the Korean Girls' Seminary are believed to have come from sugar plantations. A story in the *Advertiser* in 1916 draws our particular attention. In Puna on the island of Hawai'i, Rhee appealed to Judge C. K. Quinn to place a ten-year-old girl in the Korean Girls' Seminary. After inspecting the girl's home at the Korean camp at Kapoho with Rhee, the judge ordered the girl to be placed in Rhee's custody, as he was "impressed with the necessity of saving the girl from being sold by the time she was twelve years old." With this decision, the girl, "delighted at having a chance for education and good care,"

7   Korean Girls' Seminary at Puunui, Honolulu, ca. 1914. Syngman Rhee standing in the center of the back row.

accompanied Rhee to Honolulu. There are no other details concerning the girl's condition other than that this unnamed "little girl, who is bright and intelligent, is an Oriental beauty for her age."[40] It is believed that many of the students at the Korean Girls' Seminary were from similar poor family backgrounds. Because of the extreme shortage of Korean women, Korean girls were married off at an early age, sometimes with monetary exchanges, following old Korean practices.[41]

The second task Rhee undertook after he became an independent educator was to found the Korean Christian Institute. When he resigned from the Korean Central School, an unknown number of boys also left the school so that they could continue to study under Rhee. In September 1918, Rhee started a new school named the Korean Christian Institute (Han'in Kidok Hagwŏn) by reorganizing the Korean Girls' Seminary as a coeducational school. Rhee moved the campus to a newly purchased nine-acre tract in Kaimuki, where new school buildings such as classrooms and a dormitory were constructed.[42] (This campus is now occupied by Aliiolani Elementary School.)

With the founding of the Korean Christian Institute, Rhee started an all-out effort to educate the Korean youths in Hawai'i. He set up a new board of directors, of which he became the chairman, and selected R. O. Matheson, the editor of the *Advertiser;* Rev. John P. Erdman; and Mrs. Roofberg, the wife of the pastor of the First Methodist Church, as board members.[43] The board members were all prominent individuals who represented Hawai'i's powerful Caucasian elites. The selection of such board members suggests at least two things. First, it shows Rhee's seriousness about his educational program. It indicates his determination to set up and run his school in such a way that it could be recognized by the white elites. He wanted to make sure that his school would successfully meet the standards set by the white community. Second, by bringing influential individuals of the white community onto his school board, Rhee demonstrated the extent of the recognition he was receiving from the white elites in Hawai'i. At a time when white dominance was unchallenged, Rhee's recognized stature in Hawai'i must have made a powerful impression on Koreans, who were suffering from a severe sense of racial inferiority and outright discrimination.

In order to meet American standards, most of the teachers were Americans who instructed the students in English. The curricula for all grades followed the public school system in Hawai'i, meeting the approval and encouragement of the territorial school superintendent, and graduation from the school was equivalent to graduation from any English grade school. In addition, as the name of the school indicates, Christian education was strongly emphasized with daily study of the Bible, and by the time of graduation, all students had become "familiar with the life of Christ, and all the great truths of the Bible." Many graduates advanced to McKinley High School and others, and some even attended colleges. The *Advertiser*, which carried a lengthy article on the school in 1920, was full of praise, extolling how well and effectively Rhee, whom it called "a man of discernment and wise forethought," was running the Korean institution.[44]

Since most of the students came from poor plantation workers' families, meticulous care was taken to make sure that monetary reasons would not preclude students from attending. Tuition, according to the *Advertiser*, was free, and dormitory and laundry charges and the like were nominal. Those who were unable to pay the dormitory fee were allowed to stay free of charge, and "no distinction or discrimination of any kind is made between these and the ones that are being paid for regularly." Part-time work was also available for students, allowing them to pay for their school expenses. On parents' willingness to sacrifice for the education of their children, the *Advertiser* commented:

> Korean parents, the great majority being poor laborers, no matter how willing they might be, are utterly unable to teach their children anything in English about the Bible or the Christian religion, but they are nevertheless willing to stint themselves in order to raise the small sum necessary to enable them to send their children to a Christian school. This shows an admirable spirit of self-sacrifice on the part of the parents, whose earnings are meager. In many instances both parents are working hard in the fields in order to give their offspring a decent education. Is not this a worthy cause?[45]

Although the *Advertiser* article emphasized "Americanization and Christianization" as an important part of the school, Rhee never neglected his other important objective: to train the future leaders of Korea. According to Salome Han, who was a student at both the Korean Girls' Seminary and the Korean Christian Institute, the students studied, in addition to the English curricula, the Korean language and Korean history as well as the traditional Sino-Korean classics *(hanmun)*. She remembered studying the *Ch'ŏnjamun* (a Sino-Korean primer), reciting each character in the traditional way, under a Korean instructor. In addition to physical education as a part of the regular school program, there were extracurricular activities, such as Boy Scouts, sports, band music, and the like. For band music, Captain Heinrich Berger, the famous leader of the Royal Hawaiian Band, volunteered his services for Rhee's students, and Mrs. Han proudly reminisced about the training she received personally from Berger. Above all, according to Mrs. Han, Rhee emphasized to the students the importance of maintaining their Korean identity and of working to regain Korean independence.[46]

One noteworthy fact is that the Korean Christian Institute set up a publishing house, which published *Taehan tongnip hyŏlchŏn ki* (A Record of the Bloody Struggle for Korean Independence), edited by Kim Yŏng-u. Published in August

1919, soon after the outbreak of the March First Movement in Korea, this book records various declarations of independence issued by Korean nationalists in different regions, activities of the Korean nationalists in Korea and the United States, and various reports on the March First Movement carried in newspapers in different parts of the world. This book is a valuable source for understanding the great March First Movement.

As the Korean Christian Institute became greatly successful as an educational center for Korean youths, Rhee decided to expand the school. Unable to accommodate all those who wished to attend his school at the Aliiolani campus, the ambitious Rhee decided to move the school to a new location with more space. In February 1921, the Aliiolani campus was sold for $13,600 and Rhee acquired a thirty-seven-acre parcel in Kalihi[47] (the area around the present Kalihi Elementary School) for $15,000. The new school facilities built there included two dormitory buildings accommodating sixty boys and girls. Each building had a dining room, study hall, and bedrooms, including teachers' living quarters. Roads were also constructed leading to the school from the street. The total cost as of June 1923 was estimated to have been $45,883, according to Rhee. To pay for this, Rhee was hoping to sell the Puunui property (Korean Girls' Seminary) for $12,000 and obtain donations, including $10,000 from Koreans and $1,000 from Rev. W. D. Westervelt. When expenses and income were balanced, there

8   Korean Christian Institute faculty and students in front of "Aliiolani" dormitory, at Kaimuki, Honolulu, ca. 1919. Syngman Rhee standing fourth from the left.

was still a shortage of $28,683, which was further reduced to $15,000 when the contractor (City Mill Co.) agreed to work at a reduced cost.[48]

Money had always been a problem, and Rhee needed continuous financial support to run the school. In order to raise money, Rhee came up with the novel idea of sending a group of his students to Korea to solicit contributions, aiming to raise $30,000. The group, consisting of twelve boys and eight girls, led by three adults (Rev. Min Ch'an-ho, Kim Yŏng-u, and Nodie Kim), left in May and returned in September 1923. Dispatching students to Korea was very controversial from the beginning, and Rhee received strong criticism from his opponents. In order to travel to Korea, one had to obtain travel documents from the Japanese Consulate General. Because Koreans in Hawai'i and elsewhere were waging a boycott campaign against Japan (after the March First Movement of 1919), a big question arose regarding the appropriateness of approaching the Japanese authorities to obtain passports and other permissions. Rhee in particular came under severe criticism in view of his special position as the president of the newly founded Provisional Government of Korea in exile, whose main objective was to wage an all-out struggle against Japan. Ignoring such criticism, Rhee sent the students to Korea.[49]

The itinerary for the Korean Christian Institute students included, in addition to Seoul, fifteen cities in both the northern and southern parts of Korea, where the boys played an exhibition baseball game while the girls performed music and dance. The student delegates from Hawai'i, it is reported, were warmly received by large and sympathetic crowds wherever they visited and received generous donations.[50] Mrs. Salome Han, who was a member of the student delegation at the age of seventeen, recalled specific instructions given by Rhee that the main objective of visiting Korea was for the students to learn as much as possible about their motherland through firsthand experience and observations. During their travel in Korea, they were given good care by such prominent men as Yi Sang-jae and stayed with well-to-do families in various localities, and curious people flocked to see their performances, according to Salome Han. The whole trip was greatly instructive regarding conditions in Korea, and the student group in turn helped Koreans understand America better, in the view of Mrs. Han.[51] The contributions received in Korea totaled 25,770 yen, but after the deduction of expenditures, a sum of $3,600 was raised from the trip—a far cry from Rhee's original expectation.[52]

Monetary problems apparently continued to dog the school. In a letter dated June 27, 1922, Rhee wrote from Washington, D.C., to Rev. Min Ch'an-ho, the school superintendent, expressing his strong disappointment at the school's piling up a debt of more than $6,900 over the previous several years. This letter is revealing in that it shows how careful Rhee was in handling money matters. He wrote:

We must remember that we are handling public funds. Whatever we do, we can not afford to betray the confidence of our people. For any amount of fund they put into our trust for certain purposes, you and I are responsible. We can not be too careful in handling any of these funds. But sometimes, we make mistakes and often we discover them too late. In such a case, the best thing to do is to lay the facts before the people and let them decide so that they may criticise us justly for the mistakes we made but never for betraying their trust.[53]

As the financial problem became serious, the school found it necessary to sell ten acres of land to pay off its debt. It is, however, not clear when this sale took place.[54] A report on the Korean Christian Institute included in the Hawai'i Newspaper Morgue at the University of Hawai'i Library with no date (presumably made in the 1930s) gives the monthly budget of the school. According to this report, the total receipts that month (exact date unknown) were $801.66 while expenditures amounted to $776.92. This budget indicates that there was an annual grant of $500 from the Samuel N. and Mary Castle Foundation, allowing a monthly income of $41.66 from the foundation. Also, a total of $150 was contributed by Koreans. The income from board and tuition paid by the students was $450. Among disbursements, $350 was spent on groceries, and three American teachers were paid a combined amount of $150, while one Korean teacher and one superintendent were given $30 and $75, respectively. There were also four helpers who received a combined amount of $85.[55]

While the school was operating at the Kalihi campus, most of the students were from different islands and had no homes on the island of O'ahu. As they became "more or less orphans, the Institute has been, not only a school, but also a home" for the students, according to a report. There were seventy-five students in attendance at the time the report on the "Korean Christian Institute" was written. Most of these students worked in the kitchen, the dormitory, or elsewhere,[56] and others worked off campus. One former student at the Kalihi campus in the 1930s confided to me her personal experiences. Having come from an impoverished family, she was able to finish elementary school only because she was allowed to stay at the Korean Christian Institute. After school (when she was in the fourth grade), she worked as a maid in a Caucasian household in the upper Liliha area. Late one afternoon, upon completion of her work, as she was returning to the Institute dormitory, she encountered a sudden heavy storm, which halted the city bus services and disrupted electricity. Helpless and terror-stricken, she had to wait at a bus stop all alone in pitch darkness. Several hours later, she heard the voice of Rhee calling her name, which she said was "an angelic voice." He had come to rescue her. She later learned that when Rhee did not find her at the dinner table, he inquired about her whereabouts all over the town and that when he could not locate her, Rhee walked a distance of about four miles in the storm along the bus route to find her. Rhee, according to this woman, treated his students warmly and with meticulous care.[57]

With improvements in the living conditions of Koreans in Hawai'i and due to generational changes, the Korean Christian Institute closed its doors in the late 1940s. The land was sold in 1950 for $138,500, which was in turn donated to the founding of Inha Institute of Technology, now Inha University in Inch'ŏn.[58] Throughout its existence, the Korean Christian Institute was an important educational center for the Koreans in Hawai'i, allowing hundreds who otherwise would not have been able to attend school to receive an education. It fulfilled Rhee's dream of training the future leaders of Korea and the Korean community in Hawai'i, as school graduates included such men as You-Chang Yang (Yang Yu-ch'ang), a noted physician in Honolulu who later became Korean ambassador to the United States; Kwan-Doo Park (Pak Kwan-du), a well-known architect and a civic leader; and Chan-Jai Kim (Kim Ch'an-je), an engineer and civic leader, among others.

FEUD OVER THE KOREAN NATIONAL ASSOCIATION IN 1915

In the field of education, Rhee achieved great success, but one cannot say the same in the area of politics. In 1915, only two years after his arrival, a major feud erupted in Hawai'i over the control of the Korean National Association (KNA), and Rhee was at the center of this storm. Since there are already other detailed studies on this incident,[59] I will give only a brief outline of what happened and then deal with the role Rhee played and its impact upon the Hawai'i community.

Before the feud broke out, tension was growing between Rhee and the KNA over the funding of the school Rhee was running. According to Kim Wŏn-yong, whose writing is not always evenhanded, Rhee asked the KNA to donate a site on Emma Street to be used for Rhee's Korean Girls' Seminary, to which the KNA was willing to accede. But, as the KNA was planning to donate the land to the school, Rhee, according to Kim Wŏn-yong, demanded that the land be ceded to him in his name. This the KNA refused to do, insisting that the site could be given only to a public institution, not to an individual. Angry over this dispute, Rhee found an opportunity to take over the KNA when financial irregularities were discovered in the organization's budget.[60]

When the Korean National Association (Kuk Min Hur or Kungminhoe) was first organized on February 1, 1909, by bringing various organizations under its unitary wing, it was soon recognized by all the Koreans in Hawai'i as their representative organization. In 1915, soon after Kim Chong-hak was elected as president for a second term, financial irregularities were discovered in which certain individuals used or borrowed money belonging to the KNA without proper authorization. The individuals involved in the irregularities, when confronted, promised to return the money. In dealing with the restitution of the missing funds, a split occurred within the KNA. One group, which supported Rhee, accused KNA President Kim Chong-hak and his staff of mishandling the issue, demanded an immediate return of the money, and wanted to pursue the issue by taking the case to court. Faced with this demand, the KNA called an emergency meeting of the KNA delegates, which, contrary to Rhee's group's demand, agreed to ask those involved in the irregularities to return the money within a certain time and to handle the issue within the framework of the KNA without taking it to an outside agency. Angry over this decision, the supporters of Rhee made more accusations against the KNA leadership, forcing the KNA to call for another meeting of delegates. Although there was a serious question of the presence of a quorum, the new meeting of the delegates dismissed Kim Chong-hak and elected Hong Han-sik as the new president. The new officers, after looking into the financial records of the KNA, accused Kim Chong-hak of embezzling $1,365, for which Kim was arrested and released on $1,000 bond.[61] With these moves, the KNA came under the control of Rhee.

There was considerable violence during the feud between what the Honolulu newspapers called the new faction, which supported Rhee, and the old faction, which followed Pak Yong-man. Yee Hong Kee (Yi Hong-gi) was badly beaten by followers of Rhee and "looked as though a threshing machine had run over him," according to a police report; based on his complaint, the police issued an arrest warrant for nineteen Koreans, including An Hyŏn-gyŏng and Ko Sŏk-chu, Rhee's supporters. The *Star-Bulletin* also reported that, according to a detective's report, the new KNA under the followers of Rhee, the so-called new faction, adopted a resolution to "kill all leaders of Y. M. Pak's party."[62] (Y. M. Pak refers to Pak Yong-man.) The new faction leaders, however, denied having made such a resolution. But in a strange twist, according to the *Star-Bulletin,* another resolution stating that no resolution to kill Pak Yong-man's followers had been adopted was rejected by a vote of 191 to 209 at an emergency session of the delegates. If this account is true, a resolution to "kill" all the leaders of Pak Yong-man's faction had indeed been adopted.[63] Insisting on its own righteousness, each faction accused the other faction and took the case to the U.S. courts.[64]

As the feud raged on, Rhee issued the following statement:

> I believe that Y. M. Pak, editor of the Korean National Herald [Kungminbo] has no connection with the embezzlement of the association's funds. . . . I have no direct connection with the Korean National Association and the statement that I am the leader of a new faction is entirely

untrue. All the Koreans in these islands are united in an effort to clean up the financial corruption which has undermined the association and to make such corruption impossible in the future. . . . All the present trouble is due only to a handful of men who have been running the association for their own ends and who want to continue to do so. The charge of Yee Hong Kee is prompted by this faction and is aimed to bring prominent members of the new faction into disrepute.[65]

Rhee insisted that he was not involved in the fighting and claimed that he remained a good friend of Pak Yong-man, "whom," he said, "I always feel proud to claim as one of my best friends."[66] As a result of the 1915 dispute, the KNA in the end came under the control of those who supported Rhee.

In spite of his denial, Rhee was in fact deeply involved in the feud and was able to gain control of the KNA when the dust of the dispute settled. What may have been the reasons for Rhee's going to so much trouble? One can cite at least four. First is that Rhee wanted to gain control of the KNA. Since its founding in 1909, the KNA had become a truly representative organization of all the Koreans in the United States and Hawai'i. In Hawai'i, the KNA acted as a virtual government of the Koreans, and most Koreans accepted its semi-governmental role. The preamble of the by-laws of the Hawai'i Regional General Assembly of the KNA, adopted in February 1913, states:

> In order to secure our safety and orderly life, to promote our common interest, to nurture the strength of the organization of our people, and to fulfill our duties as the citizens of our motherland, we, the Koreans in the islands of Hawaii, having selected our delegates from our compatriots in different areas, hereby solemnly adopt the By-Laws in the name of the Almighty and Holy God.[67]

One of the objectives of the KNA was "to fulfill our duties as the citizens of our motherland," and the "motherland" here of course means Korea. In other words, the KNA was assuming the role of a government on behalf of the Koreans in Hawai'i, as its by-laws stipulated.

Not only did the KNA claim governmental authority, but it also exercised actual police and judicial power over Koreans to a considerable extent. Articles 58 through 76 of the by-laws deal with the Judicial Department (Sabŏpbu), stipulating the authority of police and justice officers in matters dealing with laws. Not just on paper but in reality as well, the KNA did exercise its judicial authority, as minor crimes and illegal acts by Koreans were adjudicated by the KNA police and justice officers. The Hawai'i government, according to Kim Wŏn-yong, permitted the KNA to exercise police power among the Koreans, and many cases involving Koreans were investigated and disposed of by the police and justice officers of the KNA.[68] Also, as we have seen above, the so-called old faction of the KNA got into trouble with the new faction as it tried to deal with the missing-funds issue of 1915 within the KNA judicial authority.

In this way, the KNA was acting as "a government within the government" in the territory of Hawai'i. It is only natural that anyone with political ambition would want to gain dominance of this powerful organization. Rhee, whose political ambition was extraordinary to say the least, must have realized that control of the KNA was essential in furthering his political goals in the future.

The second reason may have been Rhee's wish to secure a constant source of money. In order to continue his educational work and to carry out other activities to regain Korean independence, Rhee needed secure and steady sources of revenue. The KNA in Hawai'i met Rhee's financial expectations, as it commanded formidable financial power and had good potential to become a continuous source of money for a long time to come. As of 1915, there were about 5,000 Koreans, mostly male adults, from whom the KNA collected $5.00 each in the name of a toll tax *(induse)* every year. In 1914, according to Kim Wŏn-yong, the toll tax collected exceeded $10,000.[69] But according to one Korean who was active in the KNA in its early years, the KNA "had a sum of about $35,000 coming in every year."[70] In addition to the toll tax, the Koreans in Hawai'i frequently contributed money to the KNA whenever the need arose. In other words, the KNA was in control of a large sum of money, and the source of such funds seemed to be secure as long as the KNA remained a viable representative organization. In order to fulfill his grandiose nationalistic and political goals, Rhee must have felt that securing this vital financial resource was important and necessary.

The third reason had to do with the strategy of the Korean independence movement. The philosophical difference in what strategies Koreans should pursue in efforts to regain Korean independence was one of the most serious issues that divided Korean nationalists abroad. One such divide surfaced in 1915 between the two most important nationalist leaders in Hawai'i, and this division would plague the Korean community most of the first half of the twentieth century. Pak Yong-man believed that only military struggle against Japan would enable Korea to win its independence, while Rhee advocated diplomacy and public relations to win the support of world opinion in favor of the Korean cause.

Pak Yong-man's orientation toward military preparation had deep roots. Before he moved to Hawai'i in late 1912, Pak ran a military school in Nebraska. Advocating the idea that "all Koreans should be soldiers" (Kungmin kaebyŏng sŏl), he even wrote a book titled *Kunin suji* (Soldier's Manual). Having worked for the KNA in the mainland United States and having arrived in Hawai'i a few months before Rhee, Pak Yong-man was able to establish his influence over the

KNA in Hawai'i by the time Rhee joined him there. Pak's first major activity after arriving in Hawai'i was to organize the Korean National Independence Army (Tae Chosŏn Kungmin Kundan) in 1914. The formation of the Korean National Independence Army was the brainchild of three men—Pak Yong-man, An Wŏn-gyu (Won-Kiu Ahn), and Pak Chong-su. In 1913, Pak Chong-su obtained a lease for 1,660 acres of land in the Kahaluu area on the island of O'ahu for sugar cultivation, for which An Wŏn-gyu was willing to provide financing. They then learned that Pak Yong-man, having arrived recently in Honolulu, was interested in setting up a military school. These three men met one Sunday night at a Honolulu hotel and agreed to set up a military camp where Koreans would work on the plantation as laborers during the day and would receive military training after work. For this, Pak Chong-su would provide his leased land and An Wŏn-gyu would contribute $1,200 to set up the camp. Following this agreement, the military camp opened formally on April 8, 1914.[71] For his military program, Pak Yong-man set up his headquarters at Ahuimanu and also established a military academy. When its barracks were dedicated on August 30, 1914, some 150 Korean cadets paraded before a crowd of more than 500 Koreans. At the end of the dedication ceremony, Rhee deliv-

9   Korean National Independence Army at Ahuimanu, O'ahu, ca. 1914 (founded by Pak Yong-man).

ered a sermon with the title of "faith" *(midŭm).*[72] There were probably as many as 200 former Korean soldiers in Hawai'i—that is, persons who had served in the old Korean army, calling themselves "Kwangmu kun'in" (Emperor Kojong's Soldiers)—and it is likely that they constituted the core members of the Korean National Independence Army.[73]

According to Robert T. Oliver, a longtime associate of Rhee, Pak "wanted Rhee to support this [i.e., military] program publicly and to incorporate it in his Hawaiian school."[74] Rhee, however, believed that Pak's military program was dangerous and risky. Considering Japan's position as one of the world's leading powers, Rhee thought that a military confrontation would only provoke Japan into further military action that would surely cause needless bloodshed, and he wished to avoid this. Moreover, violent action would be counterproductive, he believed, as it might give the impression to the world that the Koreans were a lawless people. "Rhee's own conviction," according to Oliver, "was that no such revolution could possibly succeed, and that the Koreans must strive above all to merit and to win the diplomatic support of the Western powers and the sympathy of the American public. These differences of policy proved irreconcilable."[75]

In order to win Korean independence, Rhee believed that the support of

world powers such as the United States and the European countries was most important, and he wanted to pursue diplomatic efforts to win their endorsement. To gain Western backing, Rhee also wished to mobilize world public opinion, especially that of Americans, by appealing to the conscience of humanity by exposing the oppressive and inhuman treatment of Koreans by Japan. Toward this end, Rhee felt that it was important for Koreans to demonstrate that they were good, law-abiding citizens deserving sympathy. Thus, on the strategy for winning Korean independence, the differences between Rhee and Pak Yong-man were irreconcilable.

A fourth factor was Rhee's dissatisfaction over the KNA. In the eyes of Rhee, the KNA, with its large resources, had failed to meet his expectations. Despite collecting the toll tax and other donations, the KNA, in Rhee's view, was not doing anything useful for Koreans. When the KNA was spending a large sum of money to build its headquarters office on Miller Street, he criticized the organization in his newspaper by asking, "Will the building of the KNA hall give us great learning or greater revenue?" Rhee felt that the KNA was wasting money on useless projects. When the issue of the KNA's missing funds was exposed, he wrote an editorial in his weekly magazine, *T'aep'yŏngyang chapchi* (Pacific Magazine), challenging the KNA: "For what purpose did the KNA use the money it collected as the due payment from the people in the past two years? What has it done with the money that the laborers earned with their sweat in the sugar plantations?" He wanted the KNA to give full support to his educational programs, as he claimed: "If the money had been given to Syngman Rhee, a student dormitory would have been completed by now; and the KNA may have been affected favorably or unfavorably as a result, but the student dormitory would have served well permanently in educating our children." He accused the KNA leadership of ignoring the public will and of failing to give sufficient support to his programs. Giving money to the KNA, he claimed, was like "pouring water into a bottomless jar." Criticizing the organization's leaders, he wrote: "The current leadership is ignoring the public will, and such a deed will only bring ruin to the KNA. If they are allowed to rule continuously, the KNA will eventually face a dangerous dilemma."[76]

Rhee's criticism of the KNA was valid to some extent. Although it collected no small amount of money every year, the KNA did not use its resources effectively or wisely and thus was not in a strong position to rebut Rhee's criticism. The real estate and facilities Rhee bought and built for his educational programs all became in the end valuable assets for the Koreans in Hawai'i. Above all, Rhee's educational programs produced a number of individuals who went on to make significant contributions to the Hawaiian community as well as to Korean causes.

In addition, Rhee may have been outraged by KNA's misuse of public funds.

Having witnessed in his youth how rampant corruption and embezzlement within the Korean court and government contributed to the tragic downfall of his motherland, Rhee may have developed extra sensibilities in dispensing public funds, as evidenced by much of his personal correspondence. Simply, he could not tolerate the KNA abusing the precious funds that had been collected from the struggling plantation workers. Rhee once told Robert T. Oliver about himself: "I am an agitator all my life, not a good administrator."[77] Perhaps Rhee's sense of justice stirred up his "agitator" personality.

It is believed that Rhee provoked the feud within the KNA in 1915 for these reasons and succeeded in the end in gaining control of the KNA. It was, however, a Pyrrhic victory. The KNA that Rhee's followers took over was a ruined house. In the process of the takeover, the KNA was torn apart by the conflict and was irreparably damaged: it was no longer a representative organization that could embrace the entire Korean community in Hawaiʻi. The events of 1915 left a bitter legacy: never again were the Koreans in Hawaiʻi able to enjoy the harmony and unity that had previously prevailed. The seeds of rancor sown at this time continued to grow, poisoning the politics of the Korean community ever since. In 1919, the Methodist Mission stated in its annual report on its work for Koreans: "The one outstanding difficulty in the development of our Korean work in Hawaiʻi is their inability to agree among themselves." On Rev. Kim Yu-sun's work among the Koreans, it reported that "the minds of the people were so distracted with political agitation that it would be unwise for him to continue [any] longer in that work."[78]

10   Headquarters of Korean National Association in Hawaiʻi at Miller Street, Honolulu, 1914 to 1947.

Exchanges of violence and the bitter court fights cast a dark shadow over the image of the Koreans in Hawai'i. The Honolulu police and other law enforcement authorities were mobilized to restore order and to restrain mobs from inflicting further violence. These were of course reported in big headlines by the Honolulu newspapers, both in English and in Japanese. The events of 1915 and other feuds that followed contributed significantly to creating a negative image of Koreans as an ethnic group who constantly bickered without harmony and unity. Such a negative image (coupled with Korea's colonial status with prevalent poverty) discouraged second-generation Koreans in Hawai'i from identifying themselves with Korea. In a survey conducted in the early 1940s, Andrew Lind, a sociology professor at the University of Hawai'i, found among second-generation Koreans "a distinct lack of interest in the nationalistic aspirations and quarrels of the first generation."[79] One second-generation Korean (apparently in his sixties) I met in Honolulu in the mid-1980s told me unabashedly that he was ashamed of being a Korean without giving any reason.

CONCLUSION

For Rhee, Hawai'i was the "virgin land" where he first exhibited his political leadership as a totally independent person unencumbered by old personal or social ties. His earlier political activities in the 1890s in Korea were carried out as a neophyte largely under the shadow of the old order and of his seniors. After Rhee obtained the highest Western education, Hawai'i was the first place where he began to pursue his political goals as a mature adult. In view of his subsequent rise to the head of a nation (the Republic of Korea), it behooves us to reflect upon the nature of his political leadership during his initial years in Hawai'i.

In Hawai'i, Rhee identified himself largely with poor and illiterate Koreans, rejecting those who were relatively well-educated and economically more secure. Those with certain degrees of education and money had established themselves within the power structure of the KNA before Rhee arrived in 1913, and Rhee, with the fight he initiated, threw them out in 1915, branding them as "a handful of men who have been running the association for their own ends."[80] Learning of the prevalence of poverty and dysfunctional families among Koreans in Hawai'i, Rhee worked tirelessly for the education of their children, many of whom otherwise would have wound up maladjusted in Hawaiian society. Grateful for Rhee's dedicated service, many of these poor Koreans became his strong and firmly loyal supporters.

One noticeable characteristic we find is that Rhee either did not know how to compromise or did not believe in compromise. Differences in opinions and views are bound to happen in any society, and in order to maintain social harmony, it is imperative that people make mutual concessions to reach a compromise. For Rhee, there was very little room for compromise. He could not recognize, let alone accommodate, views that were different from his. Perhaps such an attitude might have come from his self-confidence in his own intellectual superiority. In terms of intellectual and educational achievements, no one in Hawai'i at the time even came close to him. Several Koreans who knew Rhee in Hawai'i told me that Rhee often urged Korean audiences to make more generous contributions to the work he was undertaking, claiming "I [Rhee] alone can give independence to Korea." This sense of superiority and self-righteousness might have led him to reject views that diverged from his own. His inability to compromise with those who disagreed with him was a source of constant tension within the Korean community in Hawai'i, which flared up from time to time in the form of feuds and altercations, causing serious damage to the reputation of Koreans in general.

Rhee's unwillingness to compromise might also have been derived from his early upbringing. Raised as the only surviving son of a family that had barely sustained its lineage by a single son for five previous successive generations in a society that placed a prime importance in continuing male lineages, Rhee must have been brought up with indulgence, if not pampered. As he grew up, it was very likely that he was allowed to do things in his own ways in almost anything, as had typically been the case in similar situations in traditional Korea. His early childhood personality formation may have contributed to his inclination not to compromise.

Another characteristic one can detect in Rhee's conduct is his two-handed approach in dealing with critical situations. In the 1915 crisis, as his henchmen used physical violence to take over the KNA, Rhee publicly maintained a posture of aloofness, disclaiming any responsibility, as he stated to the *Advertiser*: "I have no direct connection with the Korean National Association and the statement that I am the leader of the new faction is entirely untrue."[81] He may have had no direct connection with the KNA as he claims, but it is unthinkable that the so-called new faction did what it did without the personal knowledge of Rhee himself. Although it is difficult to ascertain whether Rhee actually agitated his followers to take the kind of action they did, as many of his critics have charged,[82] it is most likely that he knew what they were doing. More important, however, while the altercations were taking place, which were widely publicized in the Honolulu news media, Rhee as *the* most prominent Korean leader did not utter a word of discouragement against the use of violence or lawless acts. His conspicuous silence can only be interpreted as tacit approval, if not open encouragement, of unruly conduct by his followers. One can detect an element of duplicity in the conduct of Rhee, at least with regard to his handling of the infamous 1915 incident.

In the area of education, Rhee achieved great success through his selfless sacrifice and dedication. But we cannot say the same for his early activities in the arena of politics. His action—or inaction—during the 1915 feud over the KNA contributed significantly to the division of the Korean community, seriously undermining the morale and spirit of the Koreans in Hawai'i. The rancor created in 1915 did not dissipate until many years after his return to Korea in 1945, preventing the Korean community from enjoying the harmony and unity it so eagerly sought. Rhee should share the bulk of blame—certainly more than any other individual—for this unhappy outcome.

NOTES

This is a revised and expanded version of the original written in Korean and published in *Yi Sŭngman yŏn'gu: Tonnip undong kwa Taehan Min'guk kŏn'guk,* ed. Yu Yŏng-ik (Seoul: Yonsei University Press, 2000), 63–97.

1. This book has recently been translated into English; see Syngman Rhee, *The Spirit of Independence: A Primer of Korean Modernization and Reform,* trans. Han-Kyo Kim (Honolulu: University of Hawai'i Press, 2001).

2. Yu Yŏng-ik, *Yi Sŭng-man ŭi sarm kwa kkum* (Life and Dreams of Syngman Rhee) (Seoul, 1996), 54–60.

3. Robert T. Oliver, *Syngman Rhee: The Man Behind the Myth* (New York: Dodd Mead and Co., 1960), 111.

4. Ibid., 118–20.

5. Yu Yŏng-ik, ed., *Yi Sŭng-man yŏn'gu,* 100.

6. The *Honolulu Star-Bulletin* reported on February 8, 1913, that Rhee "is now visiting in Honolulu at the request of Dr. John W. Wadman, head of the Korean and Japanese work of the First Methodist Church."

7. A similar organization was also established in Pyongyang, North Korea, in 1917, which North Korean leader Kim Il-sung's father, Kim Hyŏng-jik, joined as a founding member. See Yŏng-ho Ch'oe, "Christian Background in the Early Life of Kim Il-sŏng," *Asian Survey* 26, no. 10 (October 1986). Born to a devout Christian family, Kim Il-sung had strong roots in the church.

8. Kim Wŏn-yong, *Chae-Mi Hanin 50-nyŏnsa* (50-year History of Koreans in America) (Reedley, Calif., 1959), 136–37.

9. Yi Chŏng-sik, trans., "Ch'ŏngnyŏn Yi Sŭng-man chasŏjŏn" (Autobiography of Young Syngman Rhee) *Shin Tong* (September 1979): 442. See also Son Se-il, "Yi Sŭng-man kwa Kim Ku" (Syngman Rhee and Kim Ku) *Wŏlgan Chosŏn* (October 2002): 548–50.

10. Harris Memorial Church in Honolulu is named after him.

11. Yu Yŏng-ik, *Yi Sŭng-man ŭi sarm kwa kkum,* 86–92.

12. Chong-Sik Lee, *Syngman Rhee: The Prison Years of a Young Radical* (Seoul: Yonsei University Press, 2001), 179–80.

13. *Honolulu Star-Bulletin,* February 8, 1913.

14. *Pacific Commercial Advertiser,* September 29, 1913.

15. A former prime minister of Japan, Ito Hirobumi forced the Korean government to sign the Protectorate Treaty of 1905 subverting Korean independence and became the first Japanese resident general in Korea. Hayashi Gonsuke was the Japanese minister stationed in Korea and played a key role in depriving Korea of its sovereign rights.

16. *Advertiser,* April 25, 1908.

17. At the murder trial of the assassin, Rhee, then a graduate student, was invited but refused to act as an interpreter on the grounds that his Christian faith did not allow him to defend murderers, for which he was criticized by many Korean nationalists. See Kim Wŏn-yong, *Chae-Mi Hanin 50-nyŏnsa,* 326. For other possible motivations for Rhee, see Oliver, *Syngman Rhee,* 105–6.

18. *Advertiser,* April 28, 1908 (editorial).

19. Having obtained Japanese permission for Rhee to leave Korea in 1912, Bishop Harris even tried to convince Rhee to accept Japanese rule during the voyage to Minneapolis. Rhee wrote: "Bishop Harris and I often spoke on the boat; each time led by the Bishop. I was trying to convince him and he to win me over. I was the first one to give up but he kept on trying." Lee, *Syngman Rhee,* 180. See also Oliver, *Syngman Rhee,* 119–20.

20. *Advertiser,* May 4, 1911. The *Advertiser* erred in spelling the name of the editor of the *United Korean News.* His correct name is Victor Hung Nhee (Yi Hang-u). Born in 1885, he had studied in England (at Oxford, according to one unconfirmed source) before going to Hawai'i to take up the position of editorship of the *United Korean News (Kungminbo).* With his excellent command of English and broad knowledge, he was regarded as a rising star of the Korean community in Hawai'i until 1911, when he committed suicide near Waikiki beach at the youthful age of twenty-six (apparently driven by what he regarded to be slanderous accusations against him).

21. *Advertiser,* February 3, 1913.

22. *Journal of the First Session of the Hawaiian Mission of the Methodist Episcopal, 1906,* 25; *Journal, 1912,* 146–48; Hyŏn Sun, *P'owa yuram ki* (Seoul, 1909), 10–11.

23. John W. Wadman, "Educational Work Among the Koreans," *Journal, 1912,* 146–50.

24. Syngman Rhee, "Report of the Korean Boarding School," *Journal, 1914,* 21.

25. Ibid.

26. *Star-Bulletin,* October 25, 1913.

27. *Advertiser,* December 14, 1913.

28. *Journal,* 1915, 23.

29. Ibid.

30. *Journal,* 1914, 16.

31. *Journal,* 1915, 17–18.

32. Oliver, *Syngman Rhee,* 123.

33. *Journal,* 1912, 13.

34. *Journal,* 1916, 21–22.

35. Ibid., 23.

36. Kingsley K. Lyu, "Korean Nationalist Activities in Hawaii and the Continental United States, 1900–1945, Part I, 1900–1919," *Amerasia Journal* 4, no. 1 (1977): 77–78.

37. Bernice B. H. Kim, "The Koreans in Hawaii" (unpublished M.A. thesis, University of Hawai'i, 1937), 143–45.

38. *Star-Bulletin,* October 25, 1913.

39. *Advertiser,* February 29, 1916; *Journal,* 1914; *Journal,* 1915; Kim Wŏn-yong, *Chae-Mi Hanin 50-nyŏnsa,* 244–45; Lyu, "Korean Nationalist Activities in Hawaii and the Continental United States, 1900–1945, Part I, 1900–1919," 77.

40. *Advertiser,* December 6, 1917.

41. See Brandon Palmer's chapter (Chapter 4) in this book.

42. Kim Wŏn-yong, *Chae-Mi Hanin 50-nyŏnsa,* 244–45; Lyu, "Korean Nationalist Activities in Hawaii and the Continental United States, 1900–1945, Part I, 1900–1919," 77–79.

43. "Korean Christian Institute," a report in the University of Hawai'i Special Collection.

44. *Advertiser,* December 19, 1920.

45. Ibid.

46. My interview with Mrs. Salome Han on August 7, 1997, in Honolulu.

47. "Korean Christian Institute," Hawai'i Newspaper Morgue, University of Hawai'i. Kim Wŏn-yong wrote that the land purchased was four thousand acres, but this is wrong. See also *Star-Bulletin,* September 26, 1950.

48. A letter of the Korean Christian Institute, dated June 9, 1923, soliciting donations from friends (copy in possession of the author). Kim Wŏn-yong gives a different account, however. The total cost of moving into the new campus was $84,815, and Rhee, according to Kim Wŏn-yong, anticipated donations of $50,000 from American friends and of $35,000 from Koreans. But the contributions that came failed to meet Rhee's expectations, leaving a shortage of $30,000. (See Kim Wŏn-yong, *Chae-Mi Hanin 50-nyŏnsa,* 244–45.)

49. Ibid.

50. According to *Shinhan minbo,* July 19, 1923, the cities they planned to visit

were Seoul, Inchŏn, Taegu, Kyŏngju, Pusan, Chinju, Kwangju, Chŏnju, Iri, Kaesŏng, Haeju, Pyongyang, Chinnamp'o, Sŏnch'ŏn, Wŏnsan, and Hamhŭng. See also ibid., August 30, 1923.

51. My interview with Mrs. Salome Han on August 7, 1997.

52. Kim Wŏn-yong, *Chae-Mi Hanin 50-nyŏnsa*, 245–46.

53. Box 3, Folder 9, in the Hei-Sop Chin Collection, Special Collection, University of California, Los Angeles.

54. "Korean Christian Institute," Hawai'i Newspaper Morgue, Hamilton Library, University of Hawai'i.

55. Ibid.

56. Ibid.

57. My conversation with an unnamed woman in September 1985 at the apartment of Mrs. Kay Chung.

58. *Star-Bulletin*, October 12, 1950; October 5, 1953.

59. Kim Wŏn-yong, *Chae-Mi Hanin 50-nyŏnsa*, 137–49; Pang Sŏn-ju, *Chae-Mi Han'in tongnip undong* (Independence Movement of Koreans in the United States) (Ch'unch'ŏn: Hallyum University Press, 1989), 82–92; Hong Sŏn-p'yo, "1910-nyŏndae huban Hawaii Han'in sahoe ŭi tonghyang kwa Taehan'in Kunminghoe ŭi hwaldong," *Han'guk tongnip undongsa yŏn'gu* 8 (1994).

60. Kim Wŏn-yong, *Chae-Mi Hanin 50-nyŏnsa*, 138–39. See also *Shinhan minbo*, May 27, 1925.

61. *Star-Bulletin*, May 15, 1915. The bond was provided by Won-Kiu Ahn (An Wŏn-gyu), "the merchant tailor, who is said to be the richest Korean in Hawaii," according to the *Star-Bulletin*. Kim Chong-hak was acquitted in the end. (See Kim Wŏn-yong, *Chae-Mi Hanin 50-nyŏnsa*, 146.)

62. Ibid., June 7, 1915.

63. *Star-Bulletin*, May 15, May 18, June 7, June 8, June 25, July 20, and July 30, 1915; *Advertiser*, June 8, 1915.

64. *Taehan'in Kungminhoe wa Yi Sŭng-man: 1915-36 nyŏn kan Hawaii pŏpchŏng charyo* (The KNA and Syngman Rhee: Hawai'i Court Documents, 1915–1936) (Seoul: Kuksa p'yŏnch'an wiwŏnhoe, 1999) (Han'guk hyŏndaesa charyo chipsŏng No. 45), 1–8. To prove his innocence, Kim Chong-hak attempted suicide unsuccessfully and was acquitted by the court in the end.

65. *Star-Bulletin*, June 8, 1915.

66. Ibid., June 21, 1915.

67. *Taehan'in Kunminghoe Hawaii chibang ch'onghoe chach'i kyujŏng* (Bylaws of the KNA Hawai'i General Assembly), February 1, 1913, 1.

68. Kim Wŏn-yong, *Chae-Mi Hanin 50-nyŏnsa*, 136.

69. Ibid., 138. See also the imperial Japanese consul general in Honolulu, "Hawaii Chosenjin chijo" (Conditions of Koreans in Hawai'i), in *Chosen tochi shiryo*, ed. Kim Chŏng-myŏng (Tokyo: Chosen shiryo kenkyujo, 1971), 7:952.

70. "Political—Korean National Association," a survey conducted by University of Hawai'i students (apparently in the 1930s), in the Special Collection Department, University of Hawai'i Library.

71. Handwritten memoir (in Korean) by Pak Chong-su in the author's possession. In sacrificing his vast economic stake, Pak Chong-su wrote: "How can I not sacrifice my personal interest for the sake of my fatherland."

72. *Shinhan minbo*, September 24, 1914. See also Pang Sŏn-ju, *Chae-Mi Han'in tongnip undong*, 80.

73. T'ae Pyŏng-sŏn (Byung-Sun Tai) was a captain in the Queen's Guards in Korea and fought against the Japanese before escaping to Hawai'i in 1905. (My telephone interview with Mr. Arthur Tai of Manhattan Beach, Calif., on August 28, 2002, who is a ninety-five-year-old son of Captain T'ae.) Captain T'ae served as an adjutant officer in the Independence Army in Hawai'i (Pak Chong-su memoir).

74. Oliver, *Syngman Rhee*, 129.

75. Ibid., 128–29.

76. Kim Wŏn-yong, *Chae-Mi Hanin 50-nyŏnsa*, 139–41.

77. Robert T. Oliver lecture at my Korean history seminar at the University of Hawai'i on February 15, 1973, reflecting on Rhee's presidency under the Republic of Korea.

78. *Journal*, 1919, 27.

79. Andrew Lind, "Some Types of Social Movements in Hawaii," *Social Process in Hawaii* (November 1941): 13.

80. *Advertiser*, June 8, 1915.

81. Ibid.

82. Chŏng Tu-ok, "Chae-Mi Hanjok tongnip undong shilgi" (True Record of the Korean Independence Movement in the United States) in *Han'gukhak yŏn'gu*, No. 3 (1991) Pyŏlchip, 62–63; Kim Wŏn-yong, *Chae-Mi Hanin 50-nyŏnsa*, 137–48.

4

Images and Crimes of Koreans in Hawai'i
Media Portrayals, 1903–1925

UPON QUESTIONING THEM *as to their knowledge of our laws and customs they are found to be densely ignorant. Indeed, these poor fellows represent a class of Orientals not so desperate and dangerous . . . but wretchedly ignorant and depraved—more to be pitied in a way than to be actually blamed.*
—REV. JOHN WADMAN, *Pacific Advertiser,* APRIL 17, 1906

Among the noteworthy qualities which they [Koreans] possess may be mentioned thrift, industry, desire to . . . become Americanized. That they are a thrifty people is shown by the many successful business men in the territory today.
—*Honolulu Star-Bulletin,* OCTOBER 10, 1921

In 1905 Pak Han-no stole $56 and a passport from another Korean and then gambled the money away before the crime was discovered. The victim suspected Pak to be the perpetrator and gathered six friends and tortured Pak until he confessed. His confession resulted in two days of hanging, beatings, and other "Oriental tortures" (a term used by the newspaper). The seven men immediately surrendered themselves to the police. After a single two-day trial, the court sentenced five of the seven to death.[1] This sentence aroused intense debate in Honolulu because many people, especially Rev. John Wadman, the superintendent of the Methodist Mission in Hawai'i, felt the seven Koreans, as well as all Koreans, were ignorant folk who deserved paternalistic mercy. On the other hand, others thought the Koreans were uncivilized barbarians deserving of a full measure of justice to keep them in line. In the end, Wadman's efforts resulted in two death sentences being reduced to fifteen years' hard labor; the other three men were hanged.

This bygone debate offers a glimpse into American perceptions of Korean migrants as well as American racial thought in Hawai'i during the early 1900s. During the Korean community's first decade in Hawai'i the daily newspapers portrayed Koreans in a myriad of ways, ranging from criminals who relied on mob justice and superstitious heathens to Christian nationalists. By the early 1920s, the Christian nationalist image, as typified by the opening quotation, was the dominant one. This chapter examines the public image of the Korean community in Hawai'i as it evolved from a plurality of largely negative perceptions to that of Christian nationalists. Furthermore, I argue that the concerted efforts of Korean community leaders and participation in civic activities of those Koreans living in Honolulu were the driving force of this evolution.

BACKGROUND

The United States annexed Hawai'i in 1898, five years before Korean immigration commenced. At the time, sugar production was the foundation of Hawai'i's economy. Five companies, all related to the sugar industry, controlled Hawai'i's economy. One scholar noted that eighty individuals owned almost half the land in Hawai'i and the American government owned much of the rest; thus there was little economic opportunity for those who left the plantations.[2] The plantation economy created two social classes in Hawai'i: the "haves," namely, the whites, and the "have nots," all other races. As a result, there was no sizable middle class.[3] An April 17, 1903, *Advertiser* article noted that Hawai'i had no strong middle or farming class and was, therefore, economically and socially un-American.

Prior to the Koreans' arrival in Hawai'i in 1903, 27,000 Chinese and 76,000 Japanese had been imported to work on the plantations. Japanese laborers constituted a majority of the plantation workforce and began to agitate for higher wages. The plantation owners sought to counterbalance the power of Japanese labor by importing other ethnic groups. To this end, they brought 5,000 Puerto Ricans in 1900 and around 7,200 Koreans to Hawai'i between 1903 and 1905. As a consequence, the Korean community was dwarfed by the other ethnic groups and therefore somewhat shielded from the discrimination and tensions between Americans and the larger ethnic groups.[4]

Nonetheless, the Koreans faced harsh social conditions in Hawai'i. Racial prejudice was clearly visible throughout the United States between 1900 and 1924, and Hawai'i was not immune.[5] In Hawai'i, plantations brought in Asian laborers as a means of production to increase their profits. There was no effort on the part of plantation owners to assist the social or cultural adjustment of the migrants. Instead, the white social elites used their economic power to assume and maintain cultural, political, and economic hegemony over the Asian and Hawaiian ethnic groups that outnumbered them. Racial issues were at the root of political and social inequality. Many Caucasians thought that Asian peoples were racially and culturally inferior. Henry B. Restarick, an *Advertiser* journalist, stated, "The white race has never consented to be governed by those of a different racial stock." Commenting on the Japanese, he continued, "They do not want to assimilate us, and we do not want to assimilate them. . . . it is a question of the essential difference in racial stock."[6] This quotation highlights the racial prejudice of the white elites during the period under consideration.

The two largest daily newspapers in Hawai'i, the *Pacific Commercial Advertiser* and the *Hawaiian Star* (which merged with another paper in 1912 to become the *Honolulu Star-Bulletin*), were printed in Honolulu, home to Hawai'i's white social and political elites. Both dailies were establishment papers that represented the interests of the government and big business. The two papers differed little in their coverage of racial minorities, although Riley Allen, the editor of the *Honolulu Star-Bulletin* from 1912 to 1960, was a known supporter of Korean independence and a friend to the Korean nationalists.[7] Nonetheless, neither paper advocated economic or social equality during the time under consideration.

Given these issues, it is important to address the relationship between newspaper coverage of the Korean population in Hawai'i and public opinion. The *Advertiser* and *Star-Bulletin* were representative of the Caucasian elites' opinions of the Koreans. In the absence of scholarly works, diaries, and other resources, inquiring minds are left with only the printed press. Very few whites had contact with Koreans and relied on word of mouth and the newspapers for information about minorities. Thus, three points should be made. First, up to the early 1910s blatant racism was evident in the newspapers. An example of this openly hostile social environment was an *Advertiser* article carried on February 10, 1908, that printed a letter written by several Koreans who were looking for work. The article mocked the grammatical and spelling mistakes and titled the article, "Pathetic Plea From Koreans For Work." By the early 1920s racial discrimination became more subtle, but beneath the tranquil surface, institutional discrimination remained.

Second, there "is little evidence that Caucasians . . . distinguished Koreans from the more numerous Chinese and Japanese."[8] East Asians, as members of the Mongol family, were discriminated against as racially and culturally inferior. Few whites took the time to differentiate between the various ethnic groups. On top of this, the Korean state had been annexed by Japan in 1910, which contributed to the Koreans' being identified as Japanese subjects. This issue came to the forefront soon after the Japanese attack on Pearl Harbor, and the Koreans were recognized as enemy aliens (see Lili M. Kim's chapter in this book). Only a handful of individuals familiar with Korean affairs made any distinction between the Koreans and other Asian ethnic groups.

A third point, not related to media coverage, is that Koreans faced discrimination from the Japanese community. The fact that Japan rapidly modernized while Korea's international position deteriorated and the peninsula became a Japanese colony contributed to what the Koreans felt was Japanese haughtiness toward Koreans. The plethora of historical, political, and cultural factors contributing to the animosity between the two nations continued in Hawai'i.

Koreans faced dismal economic opportunities during their early years in Hawai'i. Most Koreans relied on the sugar plantations for their livelihood during their first decade in Hawai'i. In 1905, 4,946 Koreans worked on the plantations, but the number quickly declined and then stabilized between 1,299 and 1,771 between 1910 and 1920.[9] Living and working conditions on the plantations were harsh. Housing consisted of barrack-style accommodations that made one's private life public information. Personal space was negligible, exacerbating already shortened tempers. Wages averaged sixty-five cents a day (plus potential attendance bonuses) from 1903 to 1909 and seventy-five cents a day from 1909 to 1914. The low social status of the average plantation worker was due to the predominance of immigrant workers on the plantations, the odious nature of plantation labor, the relatively low wages, and the lack of opportunity to rise in the industry. These factors resulted in large numbers of workers from all racial groups leaving the plantations as rapidly as they could find more agreeable employment. Those who remained on the plantations were accorded little social respect.

The Koreans' desire to leave the plantations was influenced by the occupational background of the immigrants. It is widely assumed that the predominant occupations of the Korean immigrants prior to arrival contributed to their desire to leave the plantations. The most common occupations were manual laborers, followed by ex-soldiers, government clerks, refugees, and at least one counterfeiter. According to Bernice Kim, only one-seventh were farmers, the occupation most suited for plantation work.[10] The majority chose to immigrate to Hawai'i due to a combination of push (nationwide famine in 1901) and pull (promise of a better life) factors. Whatever their reasons for migrating to Hawai'i, most Koreans assumed that they would be able to save money and return to Korea within a few years.[11]

In summary, the economic and social atmosphere in Hawai'i when Koreans arrived was closed to non-Caucasians. Discrimination, both blatant and subtle, remained a constant factor during this period. It should be noted that Koreans were rarely singled out for discrimination. The media portrayed each ethnic group in a slightly distinctive, but nonetheless negative, manner. The aim of this chapter is to analyze the media and popular images of the Korean community.

EARLY IMAGES, 1903–1915

Before looking at the various images of the Korean community, it is instructive to note several factors that influenced Hawai'i's Caucasian elites' initial images of the Korean population. Newspaper images of the Koreans stemmed in large measure from the prevalent American opinions of Korea as the weakest nation in East Asia. A *Hawaiian Star* article stated that "after a thousand years of effort the Koreans have shown no fitness for self-government."[12] During this time, theories of evolution and Social Darwinism were prevalent. Such logic maintained that Korea, the weakest nation in Asia, was inhabited by an inferior race of people. Americans in Hawai'i and the mainland accorded Korean immigrants respect on a par with that of their nation: very little. In a report that compared the Koreans and the Japanese, the *Advertiser* stated that "the two people have absolutely nothing in common. The Koreans are slovenly and unmethodical, while the Japanese are orderly and precise. The Korean has rude manners and the Japanese is punctilious. The Korean is dirty and the Japanese is clean."[13] These images were fueled by authors such as George Kennan during the early 1900s. Kennan portrayed the Koreans in Korea as filthy, disorganized, and lazy.[14] The Koreans in Hawai'i were not viewed any more favorably.

Caucasians considered Korean legal practice to be barbaric and semi-civilized, and one newspaper even carried an article titled "Korea's Draconian Law."[15] This must be noted because the Koreans continued to act according to Korean laws for several years after their arrival and received negative publicity as a result. Korean legal practice differed from Western legal practice in that Koreans (in Korea) preferred to avoid courts to resolve criminal cases because they, as peasants, had to pay the judge's and his servants' travel and lodging expenses. Additionally, court officials resorted to torture, extortion, and other forms of corruption during the legal process.[16] Thus, lacking formal knowledge of American legal practice, the Koreans continued to adjudicate their problems according to Korean practice.

The social background of the Korean laborers in Hawai'i was also an unflattering topic of discussion in the Honolulu papers, which considered them from the lower social classes. A manager of the American Mining Company, who was passing through Hawai'i, commented that the "Korean laborers in Hawai'i are drafted from the seaport scum."[17] Judge William J. Robinson said that Portuguese, Puerto Ricans, and Koreans, "in many instances social pariahs, moral lepers and religious fanatics in the country from which they hail . . . possessing no intellectuality and but little intelligence, furnish a poor foundation for an intelligent American citizenship during the present generation and offer but little hope for many generations to come."[18] In response to these unsavory accusations, Christian missionaries attempted to minimize the impact of negative media images by accentuating favorable attributes of the Korean community. Rev. G. L. Pearson, for example, stated that "the [Koreans] are intellectually inclined. They take readily to instruction and are easily awakened to ambition for self-improvement." He continued, "It is natural that they should bring their fear, superstition, and customs with them on coming to Hawaii."[19]

The Korean community enjoyed a brief period of favorable press during their first year in Hawai'i. Plantation managers noted the Koreans' hard work and diligence; however, these positive images were short lived, and from 1904 to the early 1910s the majority of news reports were negative. The predominant image presented to the public was of a shiftless and superstitious group who relied on mob justice to resolve their problems and, consequently, deserved harsh legal punishment to teach them to obey American laws. In fact, between 1903 and 1916 the *Pacific Commercial Advertiser* carried 435 articles related to the Koreans in Hawai'i. Of these, 231 were related to Korean criminals and other unlawful conduct.[20] Furthermore, many articles labeled the Korean community as a radical nationalist group that deserved the suspicion of the wider community. On the other hand, not all news reports were negative. Methodist missionaries tried to combat these images by portraying the Koreans as docile Christians. Rev. W. A. Noble, a missionary to Korea, wrote a letter to the superintendent of the Methodist Mission in Hawai'i that was published in the *Advertiser*. He stated that any Korean in Hawai'i was "the same ready convert and enthusiastic Christian that he is in his own country."[21] Noble claimed that the Koreans were superior to Japanese and Chinese and prophesied "of the great blessing that will flow from the conversion of this people upon our Western Coast to the solution of the great racial problem there." This topic will be addressed in greater detail below.

Another way to examine these images is through Orientalism.[22] A basic tenet of Orientalism is that the relationship between two groups is based on power. In this case, the more powerful Caucasians adopted stereotypes of the Koreans in order to define the Koreans. News reports stereotyped the Koreans as infantile yet dangerous; feminine yet sexually threatening; organizationally incompetent yet capable of international conspiracies. An essential measure of Orientalism is the dehumanization of others in order to alienate the weaker race psychologically. This facilitated the insularity of the white elites from other races. The images utilized by the social elites will be analyzed in the wider context of white-Korean relations. It should be noted that each of the following stereotypes was based on elements of truth, no matter how thin or veiled. More often than not, however, these images were based on simplistic, yet incorrect, assumptions. The validity of each image is addressed below.

The following section provides a summary of the eight most dominant media images utilized by whites to define the Korean community in Hawai'i from 1904 to 1915. The Koreans were labeled as shiftless, an ignorant lot, given to vigilantism, uncivilized, a criminal minority, anarchical nationalists, incapable of self-government, and also Christians. There was no single dominant image; each image existed in congruence with the others. It should be noted that during this period, the Koreans did not actively publish newspaper reports for public relations; instead, they appear to have been unversed in the nature of news coverage and public relations.

KOREANS AS SHIFTLESS

Plantation managers viewed the Koreans as a mobile group that would leave one job in favor of another at the slightest rumor of better wages. One article noted that if "one of their number suddenly departs, perhaps to another plantation, soon it is surmised that he has been spirited away. Then it is known that he is confined in some dungeon. Fear does its work and some morning the manager finds that many or all have fled."[23] Another article reported that gambling and drinking, which were associated with shiftlessness, were common. Considering their low wages and harsh living conditions, this is understandable behavior. Nonetheless, newspaper coverage did not account for these factors.

The Koreans had a "very bad" reputation among plantation managers.[24] In 1906 W. G. Walker, manager of the Ookala Plantation, was quoted saying, "The Koreans are not worth a great deal as laborers . . . they are a very tricky race and are more bother than they are worth."[25] From the plantation managers' point of view, the Koreans were a shiftless lot who could not be trusted.[26] To curb laborer desertion and fight crime, city police departments and plantations worked together to round up vagrants and give them the choice of going to work on the plantations or working for the public (chain-gang style).[27]

KOREANS AS IGNORANT OF AMERICAN PRACTICES

A second theme, the suspicious and ignorant Korean, derived from the fact that Koreans were suspicious, if not completely ignorant, of American medical and legal practices. Korean immigrants on the plantations, like other ethnic groups, were not tutored by the plantations as to Western legal or medical practices. On top of this, plantation doctors were rarely trusted by plantation workers because the doctors looked after the well-being of the plantation, not the patient. Occasionally, the Koreans, out of frustration, lashed out in violence. The newspapers saw these as the actions of a barbaric and ignorant people. One reporter noted that "they are a benighted and superstitious lot, believing in signs, omens and ghosts and they are deeply suspicious of the white man" and "these translated hermits believe anything against the strange men of the West."[28] Distrust of Western medicine often led to more serious problems. A Korean couple removed a plantation doctor's dressings from their child because they reportedly distrusted Western medicine. The parents proceeded to apply traditional Korean remedies that included pricking the toes, violent slapping and shaking, and scalding with hot water, likely causing the child's untimely death.[29]

On a separate occasion, in 1904, a group of Koreans attempted to seize the corpse of a dead comrade to prevent an autopsy, claiming that such a practice was not a Korean custom. After the police told the Koreans that autopsies were Western practice, the Koreans dispersed. The autopsy found that the Korean had died of natural causes, but this did not satisfy the Koreans because of various cuts and bruises on the dead man's body. Adding to the charged atmosphere, the Koreans claimed that the dead man had been kicked to death by a plantation doctor. The Koreans then resorted to the laws they knew best and assaulted the doctor, whom they claimed had kicked the man to death.[30] This problem was largely the result of the plantations making no effort to educate new immigrants about American medical or legal practices, thereby contributing to practices that Americans found superstitious and barbaric. Newspaper coverage did not examine the causes, however, just the results.

KOREANS AS GIVEN TO VIGILANTISM

The third image, vigilantism, is closely related to the legal ignorance of the Koreans. Newspapers reported that the Koreans' "mob justice" was a traditional Korean practice. One plantation manager noted that "Japs, Chinese, and, Koreans alike are disposed to take the law into their own hands."[31] The most tragic and sensationalized case of vigilantism, discussed above, was when seven Koreans killed a fellow countryman who had stolen money. A tragicomic case similar to one mentioned above arose in 1905, when a Korean who worked at the Makaweli plantation was found dead near the plantation railroad tracks. Despite the presence of bruises, the coroner ruled that the Korean had died of natural causes. Not satisfied with the ruling, three hundred Korean migrants gathered at the coroner's office and rioted in protest. The mob attacked a policeman and then seized the corpse and buried it according to Korean tradition.[32] Finally, in 1905 a Korean who murdered his wife was "fastened, up and down the rough boards of the store veranda" by a crowd of excited Koreans who had taken it upon themselves to punish the murderer.[33]

From the Korean standpoint, American justice was slow and ineffective. An article by Choi Sang-Ek in the April 22, 1905, *Hawaiian Star* exemplifies this. Choi expressed earnest cynicism of the American legal system. Speaking of an assault case in which Choi Young-Man was bedridden for six months while his assailant, Song Hing-Chew, remained free, he wrote, "If criminals are permitted to live and associate with the good citizens, the citizens will be compelled to take the law into their own hands and protect themselves."

KOREANS AS BARBARIC AND CHILDISH

These incidents reinforced the fourth stereotype: that Koreans were a less civilized and childish group. Early reports frequently noted that Koreans needed harsh legal control and punishment to prevent greater disorder. Government authorities were swift to mete out punishment to Koreans who resorted to vigilantism. Hawai'i authorities wanted all Koreans to recognize the judicial system as the ultimate authority of the land. As mentioned above, five Koreans were sentenced to die for the murder of a single fellow citizen.

In one case in 1912, Seung Sung-Chin, the editor of the *Korea Times*, fell in love with Mary Lim and obtained her parents' permission to marry her. Lim demanded a courtship along Western lines and Seung went along with her wishes for a Western-style engagement until she changed her mind about marrying him. "Right there he balked at the occidental mode. He had had her parents' consent and he wanted her." Seung claimed that her parents' consent for their marriage was sufficient grounds to make her his wife and *"deliberately stripped himself of any semblance of a Main Street gallant* and seized his lady love by the hair of her head."[34] He took her to "their" home and spent the next four hours trying to convince her that she was his wife because her parents consented. The police soon saved her from the ordeal.[35]

On another occasion, in 1904, A. W. Taylor, a debt collector for a Korean bank, was attacked by a group of Koreans who had outstanding loans that were used to pay for passage to Hawai'i. He had gathered about forty Koreans who owed money to the bank into a room and attempted to make arrangements to have their meager plantation wages garnered to settle their accounts. The newspaper reported that several Koreans agreed, but "a rough element among the laborers thought it would be a good thing to kill Taylor . . . [and] wipe out the debt."[36] The "rough element" held a traditional Korean court and decided that Taylor "must die—and according to the traditions of some of the lower classes of Korea."[37] The judge sentenced eight Koreans to three months' hard labor. He expressed "hope that this would be a warning to other Koreans that the laws of the country must be respected and that if they thought themselves injured they should visit the proper authorities and make their complaints instead of attempting to carry out their own revenge in a blood thirsty manner."[38] The sentence and media coverage typified Caucasian racial opinions of the Koreans during this period.

KOREANS AS CRIMINALS

Koreans as criminals and social deviants constitute the fifth, and largest, realm of *haole* stereotyping of Koreans. The newspapers' obsession with crime stories by nonwhites is the most engaging and insightful, yet ignored, topic related to the Koreans in Hawai'i and deserves considerable attention. The media portrayal of the Korean migrants as a criminal minority had statistical foundation. On the island of Hawai'i, the Hilo prison received 463 prisoners between July 1905 and May 1915. Of this total, 55 (11.9 percent) were Koreans—far higher than their percentage in the population. In 1908 Koreans had the third highest number of convictions among all ethnic groups for gambling (114 of 2,252); third highest in offenses against property (32 of 238); and fourth highest in offenses against the peace (73 of 809); they were tied for third highest in drunkenness (99 of 1,231), but were seventh highest in offenses against chastity (4 of 171) and had no convictions for violations of the liquor laws.[39] Between 1915 and 1924 Koreans had the highest average number of convictions per 1,000 people in fraud; second highest in narcotic and liquor violations, robbery, forgery, and gambling; and third highest in murder, burglary, and drunkenness. If all offenses for this period are totaled, Koreans had the third highest conviction ratio (behind the Filipinos and Puerto Ricans).[40] Statistics do not present the full story, but they suggest that the media portrayal of the Korean immigrants as a criminal minority was not wholly unfounded.

Well into the twentieth century the newspapers generally portrayed minorities as criminal groups that dominated most categories of island crime. For example, the media unjustly labeled Puerto Ricans as a criminal minority that was "dangerous to the community."[41] One journalist noted that doors and windows were seldom locked prior to the Puerto Ricans' arrival.[42] The Chinese had the highest number of convictions in narcotics, gambling, and smuggling inadmissible aliens into Hawai'i. Countless articles from 1900 to 1915 associated the Japanese with wife selling, violent crimes, and, during Prohibition, bootlegging.[43]

The Koreans' portrayal as criminals developed under several distinct categories. On gender issues, the newspapers followed popular opinion that the legal system should be used to control the "dangerous sexual proclivities of the nonwhites' underclass."[44] In other words, whites viewed minorities as having uncontrollable sexual tendencies that posed a threat to the community and the Caucasian-dominated courts helped prevent social disorder.[45] For example, the newspapers frequently reported stories of Japanese selling their wives and children. While there were no reports that Koreans participated in this "oriental custom," there is evidence that it did exist.[46] On a number of occasions news articles reported that Korean men kidnapped women in hopes that the women would accept the relationship as a fait accompli.[47] These actions were likely the result of the disproportionate sex ratio that existed in Hawai'i. The sex distribution of men to women of marriageable age (20 and 49 years old) in 1910 was 3,378 Korean men and only 261 Korean women—or 13 men per woman. By 1920 the ratio was 3 men per woman.[48]

One Korean in a cross-cultural encounter paid a fee to a sixteen-year-old Russian girl's stepfather for a four-day "trial marriage." The stepfather claimed that such marriages were according to Russian tradition. The stepfather ended the "marriage" after two days because the Korean had failed to pay. The young woman was later married to a Japanese man who paid on schedule.[49] In another case, Mai Choon Yong claimed that five men had kidnapped his wife, who happened to be divorcing him for ill-treatment. He then "sued out a writ of habeas corpuses." Weary of the slow legal process, he attempted to rescue his estranged wife by kidnapping her from her lawyer's office.[50] The previous two cases were acts of desperate men seeking companionship, but this did not matter to the media. The acts were interpreted and publicized in the media as the deeds of a less civilized race.

Other coverage was equally derogatory. The April 26, 1905, *Hawaiian Star* carried an article titled, "Some Koreans Are Bad Sneak Thieves." News coverage reinforced this image for years to come as article after article mentioned the arrests and convictions of Korean thieves. A September 28, 1907, *Advertiser* article read: "At the present time the Puerto Rican citizens of the country are losing their great point of distinction . . . that of furnishing the biggest proportion of criminals of any race in the city. And they are now allowing the Koreans to grasp the banner of distinction away from them." It then added:

> Police find the Korean a harder proposition to handle, too, than the
> Puerto Rican. The latter, once he is caught, will immediately look for
> police favor by preaching on all the other of his countrymen that he
> knows anything about. The Korean, on the other hand, will affect a
> stupidity that resists all efforts to extract information and when induced
> to speak, if he does, he will lie plenteously and unnecessarily, even when
> the truth might help him.

Of the 231 articles related to criminal activity in the *Advertiser* from 1903 to 1916, sixty articles were devoted to three well-known intractable criminals who blotted the image of the Korean community. The heyday of these three fit loosely between 1908 and 1917. The three were: con artist Moon-sung Kim, erstwhile thief and escape artist Chun Duck Soon, and the volatile Yee Yo Keuk. Analysis of the press coverage of these three criminals provides a subsection to the criminal image because it serves as a valuable medium to explore how the newspapers viewed the Korean community. In other words, the actions of these three nefarious Koreans, in the Caucasians' opinion, cast a dark shadow on the rest of the Korean community. The Honolulu Police Department said of Korean criminal cases: "A Korean case gathers trouble like a rolling snowball gathers snow."[51] It may well have been true of these three men.

Soon after Moon-sung Kim arrived in Hawai'i in 1905, he secured employment in a law office in Hilo on the pretense that he spoke Korean, English, and Chinese. The lawyer subsequently fired Kim after he sold business cards to Koreans for $1, claiming that the card entitled the holder to a lifetime of legal service from the lawyer.[52] After that, Kim was frequently in trouble with the law for counterfeiting, passing bad checks, and extracting money from the needy and naive. One time he impersonated a marshal and demanded $100 bail money from a Spanish woman to effect the release of her husband, who was in jail.[53] In a separate swindle, he collected money from prominent Japanese, including the consul general, claiming to be a Christian seeking to start an education bureau. Of course, this endeavor never took form.[54] Kim was even able to con people out of money while in prison. During his longest incarceration (1911–13), he convinced a jailer that he was a legitimate businessman and got an unsuspecting guard to drive him around as he swindled $2,300 from victims.[55] At one point his monthly expenses reached $3,890—a tremendous amount considering the average annual wage in Honolulu was $446.[56]

Media coverage of Kim was anecdotal, though not sympathetic. For example, he drove to one of his trials in a carriage secured under the false pretense that he worked for the Korean National Association (KNA). The media acknowledged Kim's intelligence, particularly when he acted as his own lawyer during his trials. One time his defense oration was so moving that he brought all in the courtroom to tears.[57] Between 1905 and 1916 Kim was free for a total of two months; he was incarcerated the remainder of the time.[58] In 1916 he escaped to Japan while awaiting trial. The newspapers were so fond of him that they continued coverage of him even after he left Hawai'i. Within several months the Japanese government literally branded him a criminal and in 1922 executed him for his nationalistic activities.[59]

Chun Duck Soon, Japanese alias Ishi (he spoke Japanese fluently), was a well known petty thief and escape artist. He escaped from prison a total of five times. He claimed that his crimes, largely theft and burglary, were designed to accumulate enough money for him to pay for his passage back to Korea. His first known arrest, prison escape, and recapture occurred in 1907. The Honolulu police chief said of him, "Duck Soon is never happy out of jail."[60] One time he used the fifty-pound steel ball chained to his leg to break the floor boards and used the boards as a spade and ladder to escape.[61] The police eventually gave Chun rust- and saw-proof shackles and placed him in a new cell that had solid iron bars and a three-layered hardwood floor.

The newspapers portrayed members of the Korean community as aiding their countrymen who were criminals. For example, during Chun's time as a fugitive, news articles claimed that members of the Korean community supplied him with food and information that enabled him to stay out of prison. Several times, Chun used his Korean friends to convey the message that he derived no pleasure from escaping and discomforting the police and cited poor prison food as the reason for his escape. Chun offered to turn himself in if the prison would make him a "trusty" (being allowed greater freedom within the prison)—a bargain the police chief refused.[62] Because Chun's exploits were so well known, he became a hero to young boys. American boys imitated criminals like Jesse James and Butch Cassidy, but Korean youths imitated Chun Duck Soon.[63]

Many of Chun's victims were Japanese; one paper noted that "[Duck-] Soon made a record for himself and terrorized Japanese about Honolulu."[64] Once he attempted to rob a Japanese hotel, but failed and took off on foot. Employees of the hotel pursued him for four hours in order to capture him themselves and turn him over to the police.[65] In 1916 the police released Chun from prison with $100 in reward money for providing information that led to the arrest of Yee Yo-Keuk (see below), but, alas, within a day of his release Chun was arrested for stealing the cash register from a Japanese store.[66] In 1917, the Korean community in Hawai'i decided to purge itself of Chun by donating money to send him back to Korea. The "authorities granted freedom [to Chun] on the understanding that he leave the Territory."[67]

The most notorious and feared Korean criminal was Yee Yo-Keuk. Although history has forgotten his name and deeds, his exploits shared headlines with World War I. Yee came to Hawai'i after being banished from Korea by the Japanese for his efforts to overthrow the Japanese in Korea. He weighed 180 pounds and was larger than most Asians of his day. His size helped him hold the Japanese wrestling championship for "some time." Yee was initially employed as a laborer by a man who docked Yee's pay for each petty mistake. This experience embittered Yee, who turned to a life of crime in 1912 and declared a nationalistic war of vengeance on the Japanese for having colonized Korea.[68]

Yee was a thief known for his violent nature and preference of Japanese as victims. According to the press, Yee's nationalistic philosophy was that the "Japanese were the enemies of the Koreans." Even though Yee singled out the Japanese, Koreans and the police alike feared him. Yee was first arrested in 1912 and remained in prison until he escaped in May 1915. On June 21, 1915, he shot a Honolulu Japanese shopkeeper in the back during an attempted robbery.

Within a week the police had a lead on him, and the police chief asked the police force for volunteers to help catch Yee. But, in light of the fact that the officers had no insurance (the Workers Compensation Law was to take effect two weeks later), no officers volunteered, so the lead was lost.[69] At one point, Yee became so bold that he even broke into a detective's home and stole a watch.

Eventually a Korean named Chee Won-Yer cooperated with the police to drug Yee's beer. After Yee drank the spiked beverage, he realized Chee had drugged him, so he jumped out the window of the apartment. He landed among the hiding police, who were caught off guard, and Yee got away. He ran to a laundromat to pick up his laundry and shot the Japanese clerk for providing slow service. Later that night the police captured Yee as he slept.

Within two months Yee escaped from prison for the second time, promising to kill those involved in his capture. During Yee's freedom, the Japanese community blamed Yee for a crime wave that erupted around the time of his escape, although the police credited opportunists instead. The Japanese press and merchants berated the police's half-hearted efforts to capture Yee, and the Japanese and English newspapers ran stories of the police's fear of Yee. The December 2 *Advertiser* printed the detectives' song: "We'd like to corner Yee Yo Keuk, but we confess we're fearful; he packs a dirty thirty-eight, and you bet your life we're careful." The police thought that several Koreans who looked similar to Yee were acting as doubles to lead police on wild goose chases so Yee could commit crimes elsewhere.[70] On two separate occasions police had legitimate leads, but he got away in a fusillade of bullets. Another time, Yee escaped from a police raid while the detectives drew straws to decide who would lead the assault.

The Japanese community was so scared that it debated whether to evoke the Japanese-American treaty that guaranteed their safety. Other Japanese advocated using the National Guard for protection, while others wanted to bring in detectives from Tokyo to catch Yee.[71] The *Hawaii Hochi,* a Japanese-language newspaper, organized a gang of detectives to hunt down Yee and other Korean criminals. The would-be detective captured one known Korean thief, but not Yee.[72] The Japanese Merchants Association offered a $300 reward for Yee's capture: dead or alive.[73] In fact, during Yee's flight, Japanese firearms purchases increased 1,000 percent.[74]

The Korean community also feared Yee because he vowed to kill anyone who participated in his arrest; thus, most law-abiding Koreans would not cooperate with the police. Despite the atmosphere of fear, nineteen members of the KNA signed a petition on December 7 calling for Yee's capture. That night Yee pinned a reply on the door of the KNA headquarters threatening to kill all nineteen who had signed the petition. He began his intended killing spree by killing Chee Won Yer, who had drugged Yee for the police. The police captured Yee the next day with the assistance of Chun Duck Soon, Yee's one-time partner in crime. Chun agreed to lead the police to Yee's hiding place in exchange for a pardon. On December 8, 1915, the police surrounded Yee's hiding place and amid a rainstorm of bullets captured Yee, who was shot in the neck and leg. Yee's capture was highly publicized, taking up half the front page in the *Star*; it made the front page of the December 9, 1915, *Nippu Jiji* and headlined section two of the December 9 *Advertiser*. The court convicted Yee for the murder of Chee and pronounced the death sentence, which was carried out in January 1916. Shortly after Yee's arrest, the Japanese Actors' Society produced a two-part play based on Yee's life that drew a crowd of more than five hundred people.[75] Chun ended up back in jail within a week for theft.

These three criminals achieved greater fame than any other Korean, possibly excepting Syngman Rhee. In fact, the August 8, 1913, *Advertiser* dubbed Chun the "most famous Korean in Hawai'i." Analysis of Yee's media coverage yields interesting observations. Most notable is the racial tension that Yee caused. The Japanese businessmen felt that Korean thieves, particularly Yee, favored Japanese victims for nationalistic reasons. The Caucasian community felt that the Korean community was willing to harbor Korean fugitives at the expense of justice and resented the Japanese-Korean racial tensions created by Chun and Yee. This is especially true in Chun's case because it was widely believed that Koreans were aiding and abetting him.[76] Additionally, police suspected Yee used Korean body doubles to distract them.[77] Yee exacerbated racial tensions but did not have the support of the Korean community. The KNA public call for Yee's arrest indicated that the KNA wanted to distance the Korean community from the criminal.

KOREANS AS NATIONALISTS

The sixth theme, Koreans as nationalists, was first raised in 1904 by a Methodist missionary, who stated that one Korean "on hearing the first news of the [Russo-Japanese] wars . . . left his camp and spent three days and three nights in solitude on the mountains praying for the welfare of his country."[78] Another 1904 article that covered a fight between two Koreans over politics stated that "surely, when Koreans start to become reformers and revolutionists there is no limit to what may be expected."[79] Yet, Korean nationalism received scant press coverage until 1908. The nationalist image became a stigma because nationalist Koreans were viewed as radicals and anarchists. Specifically, onetime Hawai'i resident Chang In-hwan assassinated Durham Stevens, a Japanese-sponsored advisor to the Korean government, on March 23, 1908, in San Francisco for making comments in support of the Japanese position in Korea. News coverage claimed Koreans in Hawai'i knew of the plot beforehand and that had Stevens not been killed in San Francisco, he would have been killed in Hawai'i, a report the Koreans denied. One report stated, "The reputation of the [Korean] society in official circles is decidedly that of a body of anarchists."[80] These contradictory images should be highlighted: the Koreans were childish and incapable of self-government, yet were capable of maintaining secret societies that plotted international conspiracies.

Part of the Korean and Chinese communities in Hawai'i hailed the Stevens assassination as a legitimate method to fight Japanese imperialism; some went as far as to donate money to help pay for Chang's defense. That same month, rumors abounded that the Koreans intended to attack Bishop M. C. Harris, head of the Methodist Mission for Korea and Japan, for making comments similar to Stevens's. Koreans again denied the validity of these rumors and blamed the Japanese community for fabricating these falsehoods.[81] These rumors were fed by the numerous secret meetings that the Koreans supposedly held.[82] In response to these incidents, an April 28, 1908, *Advertiser* article read, "The Federal government, which is keeping a sharp eye on anarchists here, would do well to include the political Koreans of Hawai'i within its sphere of observation. . . . It is time for these semi-civilized Orientals to understand that the Territory of Hawai'i is no place for them unless they are here to obey the laws. We have seen too much of their semi-political intriguing." Tensions between the Japanese and Koreans remained high, and in August 1908 a group of drunken Koreans on Kaua'i, after celebrating the Korean emperor's birthday, descended on a nearby Japanese camp and started a riot. This resulted in the arrest of nineteen Koreans.[83] These actions, namely, the vocal support for "terrorist actions," contributed to the image that the Koreans were revolutionary nationalists who were dangerous to the wider community.

The image of Koreans as anarchists revived in 1909 after the assassination of Ito Hirobumi, the former Japanese resident general of Korea. Several Koreans in Hawai'i spread leaflets commending the assassination. Some Chinese joined the Koreans in praise of the assassination, leading to their being called anarchists.[84] Members of the KNA sought to protect their image, however, by printing an article that read in part: "[the] better class of the Koreans in the community can not mourn over the death of Ito, [but we] do not believe in acts of individual violence."[85] This response to bad public relations is important because it showed that the Korean community under the leadership of the KNA was working to build a positive public image of the Koreans in Hawai'i.

In 1910 Japan annexed Korea, leading to increased tensions between the Korean and Japanese ethnic groups in Hawai'i. The tension reached a breaking point after the attempted murder of a Korean reporter for a Japanese newspaper by a Korean patriot. The victim, Choy Yong Jo, also happened to be half-Japanese. On three occasions Choy leaked secret KNA minutes to the Japanese-run *Nippu Jiji*. The KNA warned Choy to refrain from collaborating with the Japanese, but these cautions went unheeded. After a fourth warning, Lee Song-in denounced Choy as a menace to the Korean community and, in a failed attempt to kill him, Lee slashed Choy's stomach open in broad daylight on a busy street.[86] Racial enmity escalated to the point that the police prepared for riots between the two groups.[87] The above examples, all well-publicized in the daily papers, served to reinforce the image within the wider community that the Koreans were radical nationalists.

In response to the annexation of Korea, a large number of Korean men turned to military drills. The September 12, 1910, *Advertiser* took an alarmist tone:

> The character of the Korean as a fatalist has been shown in many cases, such as the Count Ito and Stevens murders and the recent attack on Choy Young Jo in Honolulu, and unless some measures are taken to prevent the association of Koreans in this Territory from conspiracies, etc. it will seem likely that further crimes of similar character to those mentioned above may develop.

In response to this accusation, Koreans, in what the *Advertiser* called "a pathetic note," contended that "we are not anarchists . . . our aim is to educate the young and take care of the sick, inculcate morality and industry among the Korean people, only this and nothing more."[88]

KOREANS AS INCOMPETENT AT SELF-GOVERNANCE

A seventh image fostered by the newspapers was that Koreans were incapable of self-government. The frequent factional rifts were seen as a sign of incompetence and lack of capacity for self-government; following this line of reasoning, the white elites thought the Japanese colonization of Korea was necessary. The KNA, organized in 1909, suffered from chronic factional infighting that hurt its public image and credibility. In fact, for its first decade, infighting was the most widely reported negative image of the KNA.

For example, in the weeks after Japan annexed Korea in 1910, the KNA was so embroiled in factional strife that the Association provided no public response to the newspapers in Hawai'i. The Korean community was torn in two over a dispute relating to the adoption of a young girl. The case began in mid-1909, when Cho Pyŏng-yo and his wife adopted the two-week-old daughter of a Korean man who supposedly sold his wife and returned to Korea. The Cho family adopted the infant according to Korean tradition. A year later, the natural mother, who had remarried, claimed that the child was illegitimate and her new husband, Chai H. Y., was the child's natural father, and since Korean law was not recognized in the United States, the child should be returned to the custody of her natural parents.[89] This feud between the two families blossomed into a full-blown fracas between two factions within the KNA.

The KNA was so distracted by the infighting that it did not seek to plead for Korea's independence in the press. The only press the KNA received at the time were articles covering stories relating to fistfights between the two factions. The Chai adoption issue led to a free-for-all fistfight among the Korean factions at Palama Junction in downtown Honolulu. The police saw the growing crowd and expected a brawl between the Japanese and Koreans. A squad of police was quickly dispatched to the area, where the police found the Koreans battling each other over the Chai adoption case while the Japanese enjoyed the show.[90] The *Advertiser* noted that "the Korean convention to discuss the Korean absorption by Japan got sidetracked in its patriotic exuberance and split on this same Yong [Chai] matter." It also noted, "The patience of the police authorities is being sorely tried by the factional fights among the Koreans."[91]

In the aftermath of the 1910 riots, the KNA banned all lawyers, or those employed by lawyers, from being members. The press noted that the KNA ostracized the people most useful to its cause.[92] The *Hawaiian Star* and *Pacific Commercial Advertiser* had far more coverage of the assassination attempt of the pro-Japanese Choy Yong-jo (discussed above) and the Chai case than the annexation of Korea. The Korean community had missed a golden opportunity to publicize criticism of Japanese imperialism and exalt their patriotism; instead, they contributed to the stereotypical image that Koreans were unfit for self-government.

Factionalism within the KNA was a recurring media image that was pervasive for decades. The above incident was the first of many. Factionalism reared its ugly head again in 1915. Syngman Rhee's faction gained control of the KNA through levying charges of embezzlement against the leaders of the organization. Rhee seized control of the KNA during an irregular meeting in which 350 members of Rhee's faction passed a resolution to "kill all the leaders of Y.M. Pak's party." Three men even offered to lay down their lives to remodel the organization through assassination. Pak had fled prior to the meeting, but Rhee's cronies were able to kidnap two members of Pak's faction. One escaped by jumping out of a speeding car, while the other received a solid beating that resulted in the arrest of nineteen members of Rhee's faction.[93] The Honolulu police, tiring of Korean factionalism, placed officers at the door of the meeting hall for a short time after to prevent further violence. In an article in the *Honolulu Star-Bulletin*, Rhee attempted to downplay the incident and ameliorate the KNA's image. He wrote:

> By this election the former leaders of the association, who have been running the association for years, were completely ousted and with no hope

of getting back their former position again. . . . It may seem strange how these few Koreans in Honolulu could expect to win the fight against the entire Korean population in these islands. . . . It is therefore not a "factional fight" as some persons would represent it, but a struggle of a few politicians against the general mass of the people who demand a "clean government" in the association.[94]

This incident resulted in the permanent split of the Korean nationalist movement and decade-long court battles over landownership.

KOREANS AS CHRISTIANS

The eighth, and only positive, recurring newspaper theme of the Koreans from 1903 to 1924 was that they were a Christian group. For the first decade, however, this image was overshadowed by the aforementioned seven images. This image was to become the dominant newspaper, and public, opinion from the 1920s onward. Christian and nationalistic themes dominate the historiography of Koreans in Hawai'i, but this characterization was clearly in the minority for the first two decades. It was only through the early work of Methodist missionaries and later work by the Koreans that the derogatory images were replaced by the Korean Christian image.

For several years after the Koreans' arrival, Methodist missionaries who defended Koreans conceded that the Koreans brought superstitions and mob justice with them, but defended them on the ground that the Koreans were becoming Christians and overcoming their ignorance of American laws. Early accounts of the Koreans written by the Methodist missionaries noted that many Koreans were Christian before coming to Hawai'i. The Koreans' tendency toward religious zeal was noted early on. One journalist noted that "they [Koreans] are an unusually devoted race in regard to religion."[95] These articles stated that the Koreans were more likely to convert to Christianity than other Asian minorities. The Methodist missions devoted great energy toward the general welfare and acculturation of the Korean community. A July 31, 1904, article in the *Advertiser* noted that the "Methodist church is trying hard to disabuse them of their fantastic notions and make them see civilization as it is, but the task is often discouraging."

The media acknowledged the Methodists' efforts to help Koreans adjust to life in Hawai'i, but they often contrasted it with more negative images. One reporter wrote that Koreans were the most susceptible to religion and morally the most needy. Another article noted that "the Methodist church is trying hard to disabuse them of their fantastic notions and make them see civilization as it is, but the task is often discouraging."[96] One missionary stated in the February

2, 1904, *Advertiser*: "Efforts are being made to enlighten them regarding the essentials of our government. It is confidently expected that they will be law-abiding."

Other accounts reported the amounts Koreans donated toward building churches and when those new churches had opened. One *Advertiser* article noted that Koreans were donating $4,000 a year for evangelical work, and another claimed that up to two thousand Koreans were members or probationary members of the Methodist faith.[97] For many years, the Methodist Church was the main contact point between the white and Korean communities, which is why nearly all Korean Christians were Methodist.

The theme of Koreans as a Christian minority was soon to become the most dominant and enduring one. In time, the majority of the Korean population settled in Honolulu and focused on economic and social advancement. By the 1920s, criminal activity by Koreans was portrayed as the acts of individuals and did not reflect on the Korean community. Having addressed the more common newspaper portrayals of the Koreans, I now turn to how the Korean community was able to erase the negative images of itself and promote the positive image of a Christian nationalist.

EMERGENCE OF THE CHRISTIAN NATIONALIST IMAGE

Hyung June Moon's dissertation, "The Korean Immigrants In America: The Quest For Identity In The Formative Years, 1903–1918," offers insights into the Korean community's creation of its own identity. Moon reveals the rapid occupational adjustment of the Koreans, their puritanical society through self-government and Christianization, and the emergence of a purely political society— all relevant points for this study. Moon's study, however, is insular because it focuses on self-identity, thereby ignoring the Koreans' identity within the wider community, which is the focus of this chapter. In other words, how did this self-identity translate into positive news reports? I argue that the Korean community polished its tarnished image through acculturation and aligning itself with the Caucasian community (religiously and socially), reducing crime levels, educating its young, and establishing the KNA as an informal consul. In each of these realms the Korean community took the initiative and created opportunities for positive newspaper coverage, thereby creating a Christian nationalist image in place of the negative reports.

It must be noted, however, that media portrayals slowly adjusted to conform to more credible representations of nonwhites and images evolved into less threatening characterizations. The basic attitudes held by whites toward other ethnic groups did not significantly change, however. In other words, racism became less blatant during this period. On occasion, as with the Massie rape case in 1932, racism came to the forefront, showing that the white elites had not reconciled themselves to the idea of social equality. During this latter period it is more difficult to gauge the relationship between news reports and public opinion concerning race issues. No detailed study has been done on newspapers and racism in Hawai'i during this period, and this chapter is merely an exploratory survey.

By 1909 the Korean community appears to have decided to pursue Americanization in order to escape the discrimination that the insular and non-American Chinese and Japanese groups experienced. The Korean community leaders, by distancing themselves from the "un-American" Japanese, sought to gain social recognition. They also hoped that acculturation would translate into American support for Korea's independence. This decision had two attributes: first, the Koreans voiced anti-Japanese rhetoric at each opportunity, which often aligned the Koreans with the white social elites; second, acculturation meant adopting American culture. Essentially, the Korean community attached itself to the coattails of the Caucasian elite and big business.

ANTI-JAPANESE ACTIVITIES

The Caucasians in Hawai'i had tense, but not violent, relations with the Japanese. International tension between the United States and Japan, largely due to immigration, influenced race relations in Hawai'i. Additionally, the plantation owners, who were white, and Japanese were regularly at odds over plantation wages and living conditions. With this short background we can better understand why the KNA sought to align the Korean community with the whites against the Japanese.

The main method by which Koreans struck at the Japanese was by working as strikebreakers. In 1909 roughly seven thousand Japanese plantation workers went on strike for higher wages. The Koreans seized this opportunity to work for twice the normal wage and "threaten the Japanese."[98] During a Japanese stevedore strike in 1911, Koreans again sided with the interests of Hawai'i's elites by working as strikebreakers. During a 1920 strike by Japanese and Filipino workers, Koreans disclaimed any support of the strike and again worked as strikebreakers. During the 1920 strike, the Koreans pledged their loyalty to the planters. Early in the strike, several KNA officers claimed that the Koreans were uninterested in the wage movement and were focused on independence—highlighting the nationalistic motives of the Koreans.[99] The Korean community even founded the Association of Strike Breakers, which had one hundred members, most of whom were available only on Sundays.[100]

Early in the 1920 plantation strike, Japanese household workers (cooks and gardeners) in Honolulu joined the plantation strike by asking for higher wages.

Koreans responded by going door to door offering to replace Japanese servants at a lower wage.[101] These strikebreaking activities were ineffective because there were too few Koreans, but the Koreans did receive generous press for their efforts. Strikebreaking was a manifestation of anti-Japanese emotions that coincided with the planters' interests but did little to improve Koreans' public image since plantation work was considered menial labor reserved for the lower ethnic classes.

Boycotts were another activity that Koreans utilized to highlight their anti-Japanese political statement. Soon after the March 1, 1919, independence movement in Korea, the Koreans in Hawai'i called for a general boycott of Japanese goods. Koreans and Chinese in Honolulu, in an effort to boycott Japanese soy sauce, began a soy sauce factory with $20,000 of overhead.[102] The boycott was taken to a new level when the KNA urged Koreans not to work for any company, except the plantations, that employed Japanese.[103] The strikebreaking and boycotts of 1920 were the KNA's response to the Japanese government's bloody suppression of the Korean March First Movement. The KNA's decisive response in 1919 and 1920 contrasts with the ambivalent response to the annexation of Korea in 1910.

ACCULTURATION EFFORTS

On a social level, Honolulu Koreans became increasingly active. Many activities paralleled the social scene of the Caucasian elites and created an opportunity for positive news coverage. It should be noted that these activities were not designed to promote media coverage but served this end. Examples of this include the organization of a Korean Boy Scout troop, Troop 19, in 1922;[104] a baseball team as early as 1911;[105] and a Korean branch of the Young Men's Christian Association (YMCA) in 1914.[106] Participation in social activism and civic duty provided positive news reports that were lacking during the Koreans' first decade in Hawai'i. Additionally, this civic activity gave Koreans the opportunity to mingle with whites on a social level.

Another way that Korean community leaders sought positive publicity was to align themselves with socially popular themes. Syngman Rhee publicly announced that the Korean community favored Prohibition.[107] Koreans were also involved in multiethnic organizations such as the Hands-around-the-Pacific and the popular Pan-Pacific Club.[108] These groups offered Koreans a forum through which they could showcase Korean culture and mingle with other ethnic groups.

In addition to social activities, Koreans were active in America's war efforts during World War I. Newspapers noted the Koreans' willingness to serve in the military and on the home front. Koreans showed their patriotism by sending 163 young men into the military.[109] In Hawai'i, young women canned pineapples for the war effort and the Korean Seminary offered musical presentations for the servicemen stationed in Hawai'i.[110]

To appreciate fully the social activism of Koreans, discussion must turn to the role of the church in Koreans' Hawai'i experience. Christian churches were the center of Koreans' social and educational activities in Hawai'i. Church attendance was socially beneficial on several fronts. First, Christian churches were one of the few regular points of contact between whites and Asians—an important tie that provided Koreans with protagonists, usually Methodist missionaries (as in the case in the introduction). Statistically, one scholar has claimed that upward of 40 percent of the Koreans who came to Hawai'i were Christians, and this number continued to grow until most Koreans were at least nominally Christians.[111]

The Christianization of Koreans is significant because Korean churches and missions became the leading proponents of Korean schools. These schools, in turn, became key instruments in the Americanization of the second generation. The media highlighted the fact that Korean laborers were the main source of revenue for the schools. For example, a January 9, 1918, *Advertiser* article commented that Korean plantation workers met up to 91 percent of the Korean Girls' Seminary expenses and that this was a source of great pride for Koreans.

There were no turning points or defining moments that led to the ascension of the Koreans as Christians image. I posit that regular news articles on the establishment of new Korean churches and seminaries, active participation in the YMCA, and conforming to American social norms gradually heightened the awareness of the media to the Koreans as Christians. Korean Christians, most notably Syngman Rhee and Hyŏn Sun, led Korean nationalist and social activities, solidifying close ties between Korean churches and the nationalist movement.[112]

The first news coverage of Korean educational activities was related to the Korean Mission School organized and conducted by Methodist Rev. John Wadman. Founded in or before 1908, it was designed to make Korean boys into evangelists or interpreters.[113] But the most popular Korean educational facility was the Korean Christian Institute. Syngman Rhee founded it in 1918 to promote Americanization and train Korean boys to cherish "Christian and patriotic [American] ideals."[114] The Korean community devoted great energy and monies to the education of their children. The Korean Girls' School, which formally opened in 1916, was initially financed by donations totaling $10,000 from Korean workers.[115] These Korean schools provided the Korean community with a medium through which to acculturate and receive beneficial news coverage.

The first generation's initial inability to communicate in English hindered the

Koreans' rapid acculturation to the American legal system and ability to find regular employment off the plantations—crucial steps to improving their image as a civilized people. In 1910 only 18.2 percent of Koreans over the age of ten could speak English; by 1920 close to half the Koreans could speak English.[116] Despite Koreans' success with acculturation and building an image as Christian nationalists, they remained outside the intimate circles of the social elites because of their race.

In the legal sphere, many Korean migrants had a difficult experience. Adapting to the codified laws of the United States meant altering some deeply ingrained aspects of their lives and values. But with time and hard-earned experience, Koreans acculturated to the American legal system. By 1908 newspapers carried fewer stories of mob justice and devoted more attention to Koreans' employment of the American legal system to meet their legal ends. In the midst of the Chai adoption row, mentioned above, the September 12, 1910, *Advertiser* commented, "The Koreans have discovered that peculiar thing of ancient extraction called The Law and are using it to beat the band. It makes a great deal more noise than a knife or even a bullet." The Korean community found merit in the American legal system.

Jealous husbands used American laws to protect their marriages and to ward off unscrupulous bachelors. At the time the Edmunds Act, originally designed to end Mormon polygamy, outlawed adultery. In one case, a wife was fined $30 and her lover was fined $100 and imprisoned for three months as a result of a suit brought by a husband. Apparently, the male lover received a heavier punishment because he "was alleged to have lured the woman away from her husband . . . and [took] her to Honolulu."[117] Two other men were unsuccessful in applying the law to their wives and resorted to murder. In 1909 Yi Hai Dam's girlfriend left him for another man. Yi attempted to have them imprisoned under the Edmunds Act "but was cheated of his revenge by the couple getting married." In a rage, he attempted to kill the newlyweds. In the other case, Cho Yee Sau was released from prison after serving a nine-year sentence. He charged his wife with adultery, but the charges were dismissed. Feeling that justice had not been served, he killed his wife.[118]

Korean women also used Western laws to protect themselves by divorcing abusive husbands. In 1914 Elizabeth Choy, a Chinese woman married to a Korean, obtained a divorce on the grounds that her husband had brought three men to her for "immoral purposes" several times.[119] In 1915 Kim Ching Hee, a picture bride, divorced her husband for nonsupport and abuse.[120] In 1922 another woman filed for divorce, citing her husband's infidelity and gambling.[121]

Nonetheless, adaptation led to manipulation. Less scrupulous Koreans abused American law for personal reasons, often to remove a competing suitor. Such actions brought negative news coverage. In a 1915 case, Park Young Sur was infatuated with sixteen-year-old Dorothy Kim, but she rejected his advances and decided to marry Yee Sung Chill, the man her parents "recommended." Dejected, Park attempted to use the law to prevent the marriage. He told the police that Dorothy's grandmother had sold Dorothy, then thirteen, to Yee for $5. He further alleged that Yee was trying to sell Dorothy for $150. The police delayed the wedding but soon discovered Park was merely a suitor whose advances the young woman had refused.[122] In another case, a wife and her "paramour" lied in court, claiming that the woman's husband, Yi Hang Kui, had murdered a Chinese man, thereby effecting Yi's imprisonment and clearing the way for their love affair.[123] The newspapers treated these incidents anecdotally, however, not as the acts of a depraved race.

As for their image as radical nationalists who were incapable of self-government, Koreans were initially stymied because they lacked a Korean consul to mediate legal and public relations problems for them. The Chinese and Japanese had consuls to combat negative media portrayals, mitigate harsh legal sentences, and serve as a connection to their homelands. Additionally, Americans and Koreans viewed the absence of a Korean consul in Honolulu as an example of Korea's backwardness. The Koreans in Hawai'i had requested, and even offered to finance, a consul from the native Korean government in 1904, but instead, the Korean government appointed the Japanese consul in Hawai'i as an honorary consul in 1905.[124] The Korean community spurned the very thought of relying on the Japanese consul. As a result, until 1907, the Koreans relied on the Methodist Church and socially conscious individuals to act as their social representatives.

The absence of a Korean national consul worked against the Korean community at many levels. Above I discussed five Koreans who were sentenced to hang for murder in 1906 after a single two-day trial. Even though the five voluntarily confessed to the crime, many Caucasians in Honolulu felt that they did not receive a fair trial. Those who criticized the trial noted that Carl Smith, the single lawyer who defended the five at their trial, betrayed his clients' confidence by openly favoring the death penalty for them.[125] The questionable conduct of the lawyer and harsh sentence were issues that a consul might well have addressed for the Koreans. As a result, Rev. John Wadman and the Social Science Club (a club for social elites) took it upon themselves to advocate more lenient sentences. Japanese Vice Consul Kazuo Matsubara took no active role in this situation. Wadman called on the Japanese consul to attend a meeting with the acting governor to discuss reducing the sentences. At the meeting, Matsubara explained that he was not present in any official capacity and had no complaint as to the enforcement of the law. He stated he was attending the meeting because Wadman asked him to be present.[126] In the end, the governor reduced two sentences only after considerable social debate. It would be speculation to suggest that the sentences could have been further reduced had there been a Korean consul to take an active role.

The Koreans' efforts for legal protection, self-improvement, and social well-being found fruition in self-governing bodies called *tong-hoe* (community associations). These bodies, a continuation of Korean traditional practice, were designed to preserve law and order among the Koreans, as they had in Korea, and were thereby an (indirect) attempt to improve the image of the Koreans. Plantation authorities tacitly accepted the *tong-hoe*'s rulings as long as there were no problems. For example, the fines for one camp were as follows: "drunkenness, $1.00; drunken brawling, $5.00; gambling in Japanese or Chinese camps, $5.00."[127] Other punishments included banishing offenders or flogging.[128] But these organizations were limited to the plantations and were useless against the American legal system.

The vulnerability of the Koreans to harsh legal and social treatment was one reason that the Hawaiian *tong-hoe* united into a single body in 1907 and eventually joined with its mainland counterpart in 1909 to become the Korean National Association (KNA). Within several years the KNA had seventy-three local chapters with 2,351 members in Hawai'i alone.[129] One of its regular functions was to act as a consul-like organ to protect Koreans. In its role as a consul and legal mediator for the Korean community, the KNA conducted preliminary investigations into allegations made by Korean victims, helped Koreans secure legal counsel, at times paying all legal expenses, and in many other ways acted as a legal guardian for Koreans from 1909 to 1915. These acts show that the Korean community took steps to rein in errant members and provide one source of legal assistance that consuls usually provided. The KNA provided a host of other services that are beyond the scope of this chapter. The consequence was that the KNA was able to unite the Korean community in Hawai'i and serve in the capacity of an informal Korean consul. It also reduced negative media coverage of the Korean community by conducting investigations, providing care for the ill, and offering news releases advocating Korean independence.

In an effort to rectify the Koreans' image, the KNA sent out a circular to plantations in 1910. The KNA stated that it was seeking to lower Koreans' use of alcohol and opium, promote goodwill with the plantations, and stop Koreans from wandering from plantation to plantation. To effect this, the KNA would vouch for any Korean who was a card-carrying member. Gauging the impact the KNA's anti-vice movement had on improving the media image of the Koreans is difficult, but it is revealing that the organization undertook such an endeavor.

The KNA legal activities included supporting or denouncing the claims made by Korean victims. In one case in 1913 a Korean claimed several Portuguese robbed and shot him. After a brief investigation by the KNA, the organization told the police that the Korean was a bunco steerer (con man) who embezzled the money and shot himself to cover up his crime.[130] In 1911 the KNA complained that interpreter "Townsend could not make himself intelligible to them, and that he did not grasp the meaning of what they said."[131] In a separate episode a police officer needlessly abused Ko Sung Won. The KNA retained a lawyer on Ko's behalf and succeeded in having the officer temporarily dismissed.[132] Finally, in 1919 the KNA offered a $50 reward for the capture of a Japanese who had needlessly killed a Korean.[133] These are but a few examples of how the KNA performed an invaluable service to Korean immigrants by protecting their legal well-being.

As mentioned previously, the KNA also was the hub of occasional partisan battles that contributed to the stereotyping of Koreans as factionalists. In 1920 tempers flared when nationalist factions issued death threats against each other. Fortunately, the Koreans resorted to civil, not physical, action.[134] But in 1931 tempers and fists exploded so much that the police threatened to deport the KNA leadership if they did not resolve their differences in court.[135] Factional strife remained fodder for news from the late 1910s well into the 1950s.

Nonetheless, the continued efforts of the KNA and its leaders were indispensable to the overall improvement of the Korean community's media image. Syngman Rhee, more than any other individual, helped to shape the image of Koreans in Hawai'i. The media devoted wide-ranging coverage to his efforts among the Koreans. Rhee was credited with many educational accomplishments, most notably the establishment of the Korean Christian Institute, the Korean Central School, the Korean Girls' Seminary, the Korean Care Home, and an orphanage.

Rhee's graduation from Harvard, Princeton, and George Washington University gave him stature that no other Korean, and few Americans, could tout. He became the media's chosen representative of the Korean community. With the likes of Yee Yo-keuk and Chun Duck Soon out of the picture, the media needed a new representative of the Korean community. The *Star-Bulletin* called him "the Korean widely known as a student, thinker and Christian worker, a personal friend of President Wilson and a laborer in the Christian educational field here." A 1920 article added, "His story is well known to most people in Hawai'i, and his career has been little short of remarkable."[136] The *Advertiser* commented: "Dr. Rhee's perseverance, and his faithful self-sacrificing work among the Koreans in this community, are too well-known to require any explanation. . . . He saw the need of educating the youthful Koreans, in order to bring out the best that is in the race."[137]

Finally, Rhee was among the first to call on the Koreans to celebrate March First as a Korean holiday.[138] Rhee's public image remained unscathed during the factional struggles even though many were of his own making. In short, Rhee was an articulate leader who efficiently used the press to present the Koreans as Christian nationalists.

Koreans played an active role in forming their own public image. To accomplish this, they aligned themselves with the American community, often in contrast to the Japanese. Many Koreans, especially the second generation, were educated and Christian—two conditions essential to Americanization. The Korean community also benefited from the activities of the KNA, which acted as an informal consul. Despite factional infighting among the Korean rank and file, astute leaders such as Rhee received positive publicity that reflected well on the Korean community as a whole.

CONCLUSION

We come back to the opening question: "How did the newspaper image of the Koreans as Christian nationalists emerge from a field of earlier negative images?" The 7,200 Korean immigrants who arrived in Hawai'i between 1903 and 1905 were sent directly to the sugar plantations. The majority of Koreans remained on the plantations for roughly a decade. The Korean community's relationship with the Caucasian community during the years under review was stratified; the Caucasians owned and ran the plantations the Koreans worked on. This unequal relationship, based on social, political, and economic power, resulted in open racial prejudice and discrimination. This phenomenon is currently recognized as Orientalist stereotyping of the other.

This chapter is an analysis of how the Koreans were portrayed in the Honolulu newspapers. News reports of the Koreans during their first decade in Hawai'i can be grouped into eight loose categories. One group of images presented the Koreans as a superstitious and semi-civilized people who distrusted American laws and medicine. In lieu of "enlightened American legal practice" Koreans resorted to mob justice and vigilantism to resolve their problems. Tragicomic incidents and a high level of criminal activity reinforced the whites' belief that Koreans were an infantile class who needed stern lessons to force them to live according to American laws. News articles on Korean nationalist activities highlighted the radical and anarchist tendencies of the Korean community. To restate this point in Orientalist terms, Koreans were infants who needed stern guidance; a feminine group capable of sexual proclivities; and an incompetent migrant community that was radical. Initially, Koreans relied on the Methodist missions and the rare intervention of social groups to mitigate harsh legal justice and unfavorable public images. But these images soon gave way to that of the Christian nationalist.

How did the Korean Christian nationalist newspaper image emerge from these largely negative images? One factor was the increasing subtleness of racial discrimination. This factor played a role in the decrease of the negative reports, but had little impact on the number of articles highlighting the Christian and nationalist activities of the Korean community. The Korean community had altered its image by Americanizing and acting as a socially progressive minority.

I credit the Koreans' efforts of acculturation, Christianization, and utilizing the KNA as a consul for the rise of the Korean Christian nationalist image. The Koreans aligned with the Caucasian community and in the process contrasted themselves to the larger Japanese community, whose loyalty was questioned. For example, the Koreans readily established American-style organizations, such as the Boy Scouts, in an attempt to acculturate. An even more important factor is the Christianization of the Koreans.

The Korean churches acted as one of the few contact points between the Koreans and Caucasian community. Through the churches, the Koreans founded schools and a Korean branch of the YMCA. The churches, schools, and YMCA provided the bulk of news reports of the Koreans during their second decade in Hawai'i—slowly replacing criminal activity and radical nationalism.

It should be noted that Koreans as blundering nationalists remained a reoccurring theme in the newspapers, but, by and large, the KNA gained an air of respectability by acting as a consul for the Korean community. The KNA was reported to intervene on behalf of Koreans who needed legal assistance or medical assistance. In short, the KNA, along with Syngman Rhee, created a buffer between Koreans and the American justice system and local news media.

Analyzing newspaper images is a break from current historiography, which is dominated by Korean nationalism. By focusing on the newspaper images of the Koreans in Hawai'i, I hope to illuminate an ignored topic related to the Korean-American experience. I hope that this chapter will spark additional research on the Koreans' antisocial behavior, interracial relations, and other neglected subjects.

NOTES

1. *Pacific Commercial Advertiser*, March 27, 1906.

2. Gary Y. Okihiro, *Cane Fires: The Anti-Japanese Movement in Hawaii, 1865–1945* (Philadelphia: Temple University Press, 1991), 14–15.

3. Bong-youn Choy, *Koreans in America* (Chicago: Nelson-Hall, 1979), 91.

4. Hyung June Moon, "The Korean Immigrants In America: The Quest For Identity In The Formative Years, 1903–1918" (Ph.D. diss., University of Nevada at Reno, 1976), 12.

5. Yŏng-ho Ch'oe, "The Early Immigrants to Hawaii: A Background History," in *Koreans in Hawaii: A Symposium on Their Background History, Acculturation and Public Policy Issues,* ed. Myongsup Shin and Daniel B. Lee (Honolulu: University of Hawai'i Press, 1978), 13.

6. *Honolulu Advertiser,* July 13, 1922.

7. Arthur L. Gardner, *The Koreans in Hawaii: An Annotated Bibliography* (Honolulu: University of Hawai'i Press, 1970), 24.

8. Wayne Patterson, *The Ilse: First Generation Korean Immigrants in Hawaii, 1903–1973* (Honolulu: University of Hawai'i Press, 2000), 153–54.

9. Romanzo C. Adams et al., *The Peoples of Hawaii: A Statistical Study* (Honolulu: Institute of Pacific Relations, 1925), 26.

10. Bernice B. H. Kim, "The Koreans in Hawaii" (M.A. thesis, University of Hawai'i, 1937), 85–86; *Hawaiian Star*, August 3, 1907.

11. Choy, *Koreans in America*, 77.

12. *Hawaiian Star*, September 17, 1905.

13. *Pacific Commercial Advertiser*, December 24, 1905.

14. Patterson, *The Ilse*, 31–32.

15. *Pacific Commercial Advertiser*, April 25, 1904.

16. William Shaw, "Social and Intellectual Aspects of Traditional Korean Law, 1392–1910," in *Traditional Korean Legal Attitudes*, ed. Bong Duck Chun et al., Korea Research Monograph 2 (Berkeley: University of California Press, 1980), 41–43.

17. *Pacific Commercial Advertiser*, July 28, 1906.

18. *Pacific Commercial Advertiser*, August 13, 1906. A religious fanatic seemed to equate to a pagan.

19. *Pacific Commercial Advertiser*, February 23, 1904.

20. Unlawful conduct is defined as fights, riots, vagrancy, possible connections to the assassination of Ito Hirobumi at Harbin, China, in 1909 and Durham W. Stevens at San Francisco, in 1908, and so forth. I also included follow-up coverage to arrests, namely, trials, jail escapes, and executions.

21. *Pacific Commercial Advertiser*, September 18, 1905.

22. Edward W. Said, *Orientalism* (New York: Pantheon, 1978), 15–31.

23. *Pacific Commercial Advertiser*, February 23, 1904.

24. *Pacific Commercial Advertiser*, January 1, 1906.

25. *Hawaiian Star*, May 19, 1906.

26. Hawaii Sugar Plantation Archives, PSC 18/3; Patterson, *The Ilse*, 24–27, 35, 38–40.

27. *Pacific Commercial Advertiser*, March 16, 1906; September 25, 1905.

28. *Pacific Commercial Advertiser*, July 31, 1904.

29. *Pacific Commercial Advertiser*, November 18, 1907.

30. *Pacific Commercial Advertiser*, August 2 and 3, 1904; *Hawaiian Star*, August 2 and 15, 1904.

31. *Hawaiian Star*, May 21, 1906.

32. *Hawaiian Star*, October 2, 1905.

33. *Hawaiian Star*, October 18, 1905.

34. *Pacific Commercial Advertiser*, September 2, 1912. Italics mine.

35. *Pacific Commercial Advertiser,* November 20, 1912.

36. *Pacific Commercial Advertiser,* August 19, 1904.

37. Ibid.

38. Ibid.

39. *Report to the Legislature of the Chief Justice of the Supreme Court for 1907 and 1908* (Honolulu: Gazette, 1908), ix.

40. Adams et al., *The Peoples of Hawaii,* 36–37.

41. *Pacific Commercial Advertiser,* April 17, 1906; October 11, 1906. Expounded in Norma Carr's "The Puerto Ricans in Hawaii, 1900–1958" (Ph.D. diss., University of Hawai'i, 1989).

42. *Pacific Commercial Advertiser,* June 11, 1903. A February 17, 1904, article blamed high crime rates on the Japanese, Chinese, and Negroes.

43. This is based on my observations of the news coverage of the period.

44. Helen Geracimos Chapin, *Shaping History: The Role of Newspapers in Hawaii* (Honolulu: University of Hawai'i Press, 1996), 154.

45. The Massie case exemplifies this point. In 1932 five young men were accused of raping Thalia Massie, the wife of a navy officer. After a hung jury her husband, her mother, and two sailors kidnapped and murdered one of the accused men. The four were arrested and convicted of murder, but Territorial Governor Lawrence Judd commuted the sentences to one hour to be served in his office.

46. The December 6, 1916, *Pacific Commercial Advertiser* stated that Syngman Rhee was able to place a ten-year-old Korean girl in school, thereby saving her from being sold before she turned twelve. Also, there were reports in the September 3, 1910, *Hawaiian Star* that Chai H. Yong had bought his wife.

47. For examples, see *Pacific Commercial Advertiser,* October 2, 1911; September 2, 1912; *Star-Bulletin,* July 11, 1917.

48. See Yŏng-ho Ch'oe, "The Early Korean Immigration: An Overview," in this book (Chapter 1).

49. *Pacific Commercial Advertiser,* August 7, 1910.

50. *Pacific Commercial Advertiser,* October 2, 1911.

51. Ibid.

52. *Pacific Commercial Advertiser,* September 14, 1913.

53. *Honolulu Star-Bulletin,* May 29, 1914.

54. *Pacific Commercial Advertiser,* July 22, 1916.

55. *Honolulu Star-Bulletin,* September 6, 1913; *Pacific Commercial Advertiser,* September 13, 14, 1913.

56. Robert C. Schmitt, *Historical Statistics of Hawaii* (Honolulu: University of Hawai'i Press, 1977), 128.

57. *Pacific Commercial Advertiser,* September 24, 1913.

58. *Pacific Commercial Advertiser,* June 24, 1916.

59. *Pacific Commercial Advertiser,* July 22, 1916; January 11, 1922.

60. *Honolulu Star-Bulletin,* May 10, 1910.

61. *Honolulu Star-Bulletin,* March 21, 1913.

62. *Honolulu Star-Bulletin,* September 8, 1913.

63. *Pacific Commercial Advertiser,* April 4, 1913. The boys in this case had shot a number of animals. This incident led to state legislation prohibiting the sale of guns to minors.

64. *Honolulu Star-Bulletin,* February 19, 1916.

65. *Pacific Commercial Advertiser,* September 13, 1913.

66. *Honolulu Star-Bulletin,* February 19, 1916.

67. *Pacific Commercial Advertiser,* January 25, 1917.

68. *Pacific Commercial Advertiser,* January 13, 1917.

69. *Pacific Commercial Advertiser,* June 22, 1915.

70. *Pacific Commercial Advertiser,* November 29, 1915.

71. *Pacific Commercial Advertiser,* November 24, 1915.

72. *Pacific Commercial Advertiser,* November 27, 1915.

73. *Honolulu Star-Bulletin,* December 2, 1915.

74. *Star-Bulletin,* January 22, 1916. *Advertiser,* December 15, 1915: 147 individuals sought firearm permits.

75. *Pacific Commercial Advertiser,* December 21, 1915; *Honolulu Star-Bulletin,* December 20, 1915.

76. *Honolulu Star-Bulletin,* September 8, 1913.

77. *Pacific Commercial Advertiser,* November 29, 1915.

78. *Pacific Commercial Advertiser,* February 23, 1904.

79. *Hawaiian Star,* December 6, 1904.

80. *Hawaiian Star,* March 23 and 30, 1908. Also see *Pacific Commercial Advertiser,* March 31, 1908; April 11–12, 1908; September 12, 1910.

81. *Pacific Commercial Advertiser,* May 11, 1908.

82. *Hawaiian Star,* April 29 and 30, 1908. Also see *Pacific Commercial Advertiser,* April 28–30, 1908.

83. *Hawaiian Star,* August 24, 1908.

84. *Hawaiian Star,* October 27, 1909.

85. *Pacific Commercial Advertiser,* November 2, 1909.

86. *Hawaiian Star* and *Pacific Commercial Advertiser,* September 1 and 2, 1910.

87. *Pacific Commercial Advertiser,* September 19, 1910.

88. *Pacific Commercial Advertiser,* September 15, 1910.

89. *Hawaiian Star,* September 3, 1910.

90. *Pacific Commercial Advertiser,* September 12–13, 1910; *Hawaiian Star,* September 3 and 6, 1910. Unfortunately, the newspapers did not report the outcome of the trial.

91. *Pacific Commercial Advertiser,* September 13, 1910.

92. *Pacific Commercial Advertiser,* September 5, 1910. This resolution may have been aimed at Chai, who worked for a lawyer.

93. *Honolulu Star-Bulletin,* June 7, 8, 17, 1915. See also Yŏng-ho Ch'oe's chapter on Syngman Rhee in this book (Chapter 3).

94. *Honolulu Star-Bulletin,* June 21, 1915.

95. *Pacific Commercial Advertiser,* July 10, 1905.

96. August 13, 1906, and November 20, 1905. More modest reports put membership at three hundred (*Pacific Commercial Advertiser,* February 23, 1904). Also see *Hawaiian Star,* July 10, 1905.

97. *Pacific Commercial Advertiser,* February 6, 1908; July 31, 1904.

98. Okihiro, *Cane Fires,* 51–53.

99. *Pacific Commercial Advertiser,* September 4, 1919; *Honolulu Star-Bulletin,* September 4, 1919.

100. *Honolulu Star-Bulletin,* August 24, 1920; *Pacific Commercial Advertiser,* September 5, 1919; January 30, 1920.

101. *Pacific Commercial Advertiser,* February 8, 1920.

102. *Pacific Commercial Advertiser,* April 23 and August 6, 1919.

103. *Pacific Commercial Advertiser,* November 25, 1919; *Honolulu Star-Bulletin,* November 24, 1919.

104. *Pacific Commercial Advertiser,* April 7, 1922.

105. *Pacific Commercial Advertiser,* January 2, 1912. This article relates a game between Koreans and Japanese that ended in a riot between the two teams.

106. *Pacific Commercial Advertiser,* January 9, 1914.

107. *Pacific Commercial Advertiser,* February 7–9, 1918; *Honolulu Star-Bulletin,* February 6, 1918.

108. *Honolulu Star-Bulletin,* September 2, 1916; *Pacific Commercial Advertiser,* December 21, 1918.

109. *Honolulu Star-Bulletin,* January 11, 1919.

110. *Pacific Commercial Advertiser,* April 19, 1918; May 10, 1918.

111. Choy, *Koreans in America,* 77. This may be an overstatement, yet a healthy percentage of the Korean population was Christian.

112. So Hee Bae, "The Education and Social Functions of Korean Churches that Contribute to the Cultural Adaptation of Korean Immigrants on O'ahu" (M.A. thesis, University of Hawai'i, 1996), 10–14.

113. *Pacific Commercial Advertiser,* January 14, 1908. It had a staff of six with forty-five pupils.

114. Hawaiian Sugar Plantation Archives. May 1920. KAU 19/1. Circular letter to Hawaiian Agriculture Co.

115. *Pacific Commercial Advertiser,* October 31, 1915; February 28, 1916.

116. Romanzo Adams, *Interracial Marriage in Hawaii: A Study of the Mutually Conditioned Processes of Acculturation and Amalgamation* (New York: Macmillan Company, 1937), 112.

117. *Honolulu Star-Bulletin*, January 13, 1919.

118. *Honolulu Star-Bulletin*, June 21, 1909; May 22, 1914.

119. *Pacific Commercial Advertiser*, June 18, 1914.

120. *Pacific Commercial Advertiser*, May 25, 1915.

121. *Pacific Commercial Advertiser*, March 22, 1922.

122. *Honolulu Star-Bulletin*, November 10, 11, 15, 1915.

123. *Honolulu Star-Bulletin*, December 27, 1918.

124. In 1905 the Korean government had dispatched Yun Ch'i-ho to review the conditions of the Koreans in Hawai'i, but this mission lasted less than a month.

125. *Pacific Commercial Advertiser*, May, 31, 1905. He was later called on by the Bar to explain his actions.

126. *Pacific Commercial Advertiser*, April 17, 1906.

127. Kim, "The Koreans in Hawaii," 110.

128. Kingsley Lyu, "Korean Nationalist Activities in the U.S.," *Amerasia Journal* 4, no. 1 (1977): 45.

129. Warren Y. Kim, *Koreans In America* (Seoul: Po Chin Chai, 1971), 54.

130. *Pacific Commercial Advertiser*, August 16, 1913.

131. *Pacific Commercial Advertiser*, January 17, 1911.

132. *Pacific Commercial Advertiser*, October 16, 1913.

133. *Honolulu Star-Bulletin*, April 28, 1919.

134. *Honolulu Star-Bulletin*, February 3, 1920.

135. *Pacific Commercial Advertiser*, January 30, 1931.

136. *Honolulu Star-Bulletin*, June 21, 1915, and June 29, 1920.

137. *Pacific Commercial Advertiser*, December 19, 1920.

138. *Honolulu Star-Bulletin*, March 2, 1921.

5

The March First Movement of 1919 and Koreans in Hawai'i

THE YEAR 1919 was historically significant in Hawai'i for two reasons. First, it marked the centennial of the death of King Kamehameha I and the succession of Kamehameha II. Second, the outbreak of the great March First Movement in Korea galvanized Koreans in Hawai'i to work for the independence of their homeland in Korea. On March 1, 1919, following the declaration of Korean independence, virtually the entire population of Korea rose up in what has subsequently been known as the March First Movement. The Koreans were inspired by President Woodrow Wilson's Fourteen Points proposal for peace in Europe to bring an end to World War I, which included a clause calling for self-determination of those people under alien rule. Believing the principle of self-determination should also be applied to Korea in determining its future destiny, a group of Koreans secretly planned to issue a declaration of Korean independence to be followed by a nationwide demonstration. On March 1, 1919, a large crowd gathered in central Seoul and proclaimed Korean independence. The proclamation was soon followed by peaceful demonstrations that reached every corner of the country. Upholding a nonviolent principle, the Koreans shouted "Taehan tongnip manse!" (Long Live Korean Independence!), waving their national flag as if Korea had achieved independence. This nationwide uprising, however, was brutally suppressed in the end by the Japanese authorities, who used extreme measures to quell the uprisings, leading to the deaths of thousands of Koreans and the arrests of even a larger number. The March First Movement marks an important watershed in Korea's modern history, as it ushered in a new phase in the Korean nationalist movement and inspired all Koreans, including future generations, to work for the lofty goal of national regeneration.

This chapter examines how the Koreans in Hawai'i reacted to the outbreak of the March First Movement and how it affected the Korean community in Hawai'i.

NEWS OF THE MARCH FIRST MOVEMENT AND THE
KOREAN COMMUNITY IN HAWAI'I

Upon learning the contents of Wilson's peace proposals, Koreans in North America began to work toward gaining international recognition for Korean independence. Their aspirations, however, were soon frustrated as the "Big Powers" at the Paris Peace Conference sacrificed the desires and grievances of those peoples under alien rule to satisfy their imperial and colonial interests around the globe. Disappointed, representatives of those countries that were under foreign rule held a meeting of the League of Small and Subject Nationalities in New York in 1918, in which the Koreans in the United States also participated. Kim Hŏn-sik represented Shinhanhoe (New Korea Society) while Min Ch'an-ho (Chan-Ho Min) and Chŏng Han-gyŏng (Henry Chung) did so for the Korean National Association (KNA).[1]

U.S. President Wilson's Fourteen Points proposal also prompted Syngman Rhee (Yi Sŭng-man), who was residing in Hawai'i at the time, and other individuals and organizations to engage in a flurry of activity. At the news of the Paris Peace Conference, the central headquarters of the KNA in San Francisco[2] formally adopted a resolution to send Rhee and Chŏng Han-gyŏng to Paris to appeal for Korean causes. Even before the adoption of this resolution, Rhee left Hawai'i for the mainland United States to work for Korean independence.[3] In February 1919, when it became clear that Rhee would be unable to obtain needed travel documents (from the State Department) in order to travel to Paris and that the self-determination proposal would not be applied to Korea, Rhee and Chŏng Han-gyŏng came up with a controversial idea, which they submitted to President Wilson in the form of a petition. In the hope of removing the Japanese grip on Korea, the petition called for placing Korea under a trusteeship under the mandate of the League of Nations until such a time when the international environment would become more favorable for Korea to regain complete independence.[4] The Koreans in the United States and elsewhere were divided over this proposal. In Hawai'i, the followers of Pak Yong-man (also known as Young-Man Park), who had advocated armed struggle against Japan, strongly opposed the idea of Korea going through a trusteeship under a foreign power and tried to gain ground for his political stand in Hawai'i, which this group had lost in an earlier feud with Rhee, by exploiting the unpopularity of Rhee's proposal.[5] It was amid these activities in the United States and Hawai'i that the news of the declaration of independence issued by the Korean students in Tokyo in February 1919 reached the United States. Soon thereafter the great popular uprising within Korea for independence took place on March 1, 1919. With this breathtaking news, the controversy surrounding the trusteeship issue disappeared among the Koreans.[6]

What was the situation in the Korean community in Hawai'i on the eve of the March First Movement? The Koreans in Hawai'i were basically divided into two groups largely as a result of a power struggle between the two most powerful individuals in Hawai'i—Syngman Rhee and Pak Yong-man. What separated the two men was their disagreement over the basic strategy to achieve Korean independence from Japan's colonial rule. Pak Yong-man and his followers advocated an armed struggle against Japan as the only weapon, and toward this, they had at one time even run a military camp in the Kahaluu area on O'ahu. Rhee, on the other hand, criticized Pak's plan as dangerous, believing it would only cause needless bloodshed. Instead, he called for diplomatic and public relations efforts to win support from the U.S. government as well as turn world public opinion in favor of Korean independence by appealing to humanity and justice. After a bitter feud in 1915, Rhee secured a stronghold on the Korean community by gaining the control of the KNA in Hawai'i, which had hitherto been under the influence of Pak Yong-man, who suffered a serious setback.[7] (See Chapter 3.)

In February 1919, the KNA, now under the domination of Rhee, chose its new officers. Yi Chong-gwan and Son Ch'ang-hŭi were elected as president and vice president, respectively, while An Hyŏn-gyŏng, Yun Kye-sang, and Yu Sang-gi were chosen as representatives of the general assembly. As for the staff, Kim Kwang-jae became the executive officer, while Kim Yŏng-u was appointed as both secretary and finance officer. Other appointments included Rhee to head the education department, Sŏ Sang-hun the legal department, Chŏng Yong-p'il the relief department, Son Tŏk-in the military department, and Shin Sŏng-il the agriculture and commerce department.[8]

Having lost control of the KNA to Rhee, Pak Yong-man and his followers set up a new organization called the Hawai'i Branch of the Korean National Independence League (Tae Chosŏn Tongnipdan Hawaii Chibu) on March 3, 1919, before the news of the outbreak of the March First Movement in Korea reached Hawai'i. It claimed a membership of more than 353. Its by-laws stated that the Independence League should consist of various organizations that included those within Korea as well as in the Far East with the headquarters located in Hawai'i. The by-laws also outlined the two-fold objectives in articles 4 and 5. Article 4 called for the improvement of the livelihood of Korean people through broadening knowledge, democracy, and freedom, while article 5 pledged to "concentrate all its energy and efforts for the independence movement of the Korean people." Article 7 called for severing all ties with Japan and rejection of Japanese culture.[9] We do not know whether the Independence League set up its organizations in Korea or elsewhere in the Far East or whether they had ever attempted to do so. It is, however, clear that its main objective was to carry out activities for Korean independence in conjunction with other organizations in the Far East through such measures as raising funds, military action, and others. Although it also called for diplomatic efforts, publications, and so on, it was organized largely to emphasize military struggle as the best means for achieving its ultimate objective—Korean independence.

In the meantime, the news of the death of Emperor Kwangmu (Kojong) reached the United States by the end of January 1919. *Shinhan Minbo*, the official newspaper of the Central KNA in San Francisco, carried the news of "the Death of the Former Emperor Kwangmu on January 20" along with the emperor's photo on January 30, 1919.[10] We believe that this news also reached Hawai'i through the *Kungmingbo* (Korean National Herald), the organ of the KNA in Hawai'i, although no issues dating from these days are available. *Nippu Jiji*, a Japanese newspaper in Hawai'i, on the other hand, reported on March 3, 1919, the death of the Korean emperor. The Japanese paper, apparently failing to detect the significant connection between the emperor's death and the outbreak of the March First Movement that followed in Korea, carried the news only as "an unfortunate death of an emperor."[11]

The news of the outbreak of the March First Movement in Korea first reached the Koreans in the United States when Hyŏn Sun (also known as Soon Hyun) disseminated the information from Shanghai. Having been entrusted on February 22 as a special diplomatic envoy by the clandestine committee in Seoul that was planning the March First Movement, Hyŏn Sun slipped out of Korea and arrived in Shanghai on March 1; he immediately embarked on the task of publicizing the March First Movement to the outside world.[12] He dispatched a telegram to An Ch'ang-ho, the president of the KNA of North America, which reached San Francisco at around 11:00 a.m. on March 9. The message reported the proclamation of the declaration of independence as having taken place and the subsequent outbreak of demonstrations in Korea.[13] He also sent a similar telegram to the KNA in Hawai'i, which arrived in the morning on March 9 (local time).[14] The *Pacific Commercial Advertiser* in Honolulu gives the following report on the outbreak of the March First Movement in Korea under the headline, "Koreans Assert Independence":[15]

> On March 1 at 1 p.m., the independence of Korea was proclaimed in Seoul, Pyongyang, and other cities by the Korean National Independence Union, comprised of 3,000,000 people and including 3,000 Christian churches, 5,000 Church of Heaven [Ch'ŏndogyo] worshipers, all colleges, schools, and other bodies, according to a cablegram received Sunday morning by the Korean National Association of Hawaii from Dr. Hy Unsoon [Hyŏn Sun]. Special representatives of the new government were named. They are Sen Pyunghi [Son Pyŏng-hŭi], Rhee Sangchai [Yi Sang-jae], Kil Sunchu [Kil Sŏn-ju], all leaders of Christian denominations in Korea representing millions of the Korean people.

The paper then went on to give a brief history of how Korea had come to be dominated by Japan.

The Koreans in Hawai'i greeted the news of the March First Movement with excitement, although they knew very little about the details or magnitude of the uprising. Because March 9 was a Sunday, the news was publicized through church services. That afternoon, a "National Convention" (Kungmin Kong-donghoe) was convened in the name of the KNA at its headquarters located in downtown Honolulu, at which more than six hundred excited Koreans participated at short notice.[16] After discussing the issue of winning international recognition for the newly organized Korean government, the Convention adopted a resolution to transmit a petition to Washington, D.C., requesting American cooperation in Korea's attempts to free itself from Japanese rule.[17] President Yi Chong-gwan of the KNA in Hawai'i sent a telegram to An Ch'ang-ho, the president of the KNA of North America, entrusting him with full diplomatic authority in the work of realizing Korean independence.[18]

On March 10, the *Honolulu Star-Bulletin* reported that "Young M. Park [Pak Yong-man], the editor of the *Pacific Times*, the Korean paper of Honolulu, received a letter last week confirming the cable news of the movement for independence."[19] This report raises an interesting question because if it is true, it means that someone had already informed Pak Yong-man of the impending uprising in Korea before anyone else in Hawai'i knew about it. The report, however, gives no information on the identity of the person who wrote the letter and from where. Chŏng Tu-ok (Chung Doo-Ock), a loyal supporter of Pak Yong-man, likewise wrote in his memoir as follows: "Before the outbreak of the independence movement in Korea on March 1, 1919, Rev. Hyŏn Sun had written a letter to Pak Yong-man informing him that an independence movement would break out within the country [Korea] in the near future and that I [Rev. Hyŏn] am planning to go to the Paris Peace Conference, and you [Pak] should also go to Paris. This was the first news of the [March First] independence movement [that reached Hawai'i]."[20] Here, Chŏng Tu-ok suggested that Pak Yong-man had been informed of the impending outbreak of the March First Movement beforehand. We have no clear evidence at this time to verify Chŏng's contention. It certainly raises an intriguing question, however, about Pak Yong-man's activities in Hawai'i before March 1. On March 3, two days after the outbreak of the March First Movement in Korea but a few days before its news reached Hawai'i, Pak organized the Korean National Independence Corps in Hawai'i. Was the formation of the Independence League in Hawai'i related to the March First Movement? Or, was it merely a coincidence in timing? It is indeed an intriguing question, to which we do not yet have a clear answer.

SUPPORT FOR THE MARCH FIRST MOVEMENT AMONG
KOREANS IN HAWAI'I

The outbreak of the March First Movement became widely known in Hawai'i
on March 10, when the *Advertiser* first carried the news. Two days later, on
March 12, *Nippu Jiji*, a Japanese newspaper in Honolulu, reported on its front
page that Koreans residing in Beijing (China) had presented a petition to the U.S.
embassy there, requesting American assistance to bring about Korean independence at the forthcoming Paris Peace Conference. Thereafter, a cablegram from
Hyŏn Sun in Shanghai to the KNA in Hawai'i gave a more detailed report:

> The followers of Christianity and Ch'ŏndo-gyo, having formed a grand
> unity with the representatives of the independence movement, have been
> engaged in the independence activities with daily occurrence of demon-
> stration at more than 100 locations throughout the country. More than
> 500 people have already been killed cruelly by the Japanese and as many
> as 5,000 have been arrested. The country as a whole is now paralyzed
> because of a general strike.[21]

Two English newspapers in Hawai'i also carried daily the news of large demonstrations taking place in Korea.

As the news from Korea spread, the Koreans in Hawai'i suddenly became
busy in responding to the development in their homeland. Japanese newspapers
in Hawai'i reacted to such Korean activities with derision and cynicism. *Nippu
Jiji*, for example, wrote the headline, "Heck! It Will Only Fatten Greedy Politicians' Stomachs." The accompanying story read in part, "Ever since the English
newspaper *Advertiser* reported under a big headline on the Korean declaration
of independence, Koreans in [Hawai'i] have been holding meetings at many
places from five o'clock in the morning every day."[22] From this report, we learn
that the Koreans in Hawai'i gathered together daily from early in the morning
to discuss various measures for future actions to be taken for the promotion of
Korean independence. The Japanese consul general of Honolulu gave a similar
report: "Koreans in various islands assembled at such places as the KNA offices,
churches, and parks, and listened to speeches, and their agitations exceeded even
what happened at the time of the annexation [in 1910]." This report went on
to state that the Koreans collected money for independence funds and that there
were cases where violence was inflicted upon Japanese.[23]

At the center of these activities in Hawai'i was the KNA, which assumed a
leadership role to consider various measures that would assist the independence
movement. Among the measures taken at the initiative of the KNA were the
decision to support the newly organized provisional government in Shanghai
and making a formal request to the U.S. government for assistance in emancipat-

ing Korea from Japanese oppression.[24] *Hawaii Hochi,* another Japanese news-paper, gave the following account of a meeting held on March 10:

> Koreans have been holding meetings frequently for their independence. At a meeting held last Monday [March 10], a resolution was adopted to collect funds for [Korean] independence from all 5,000 Koreans living in Hawaii islands. Moreover, all those who attended this particular meeting contributed all in their possession at the spot. Some women gave their gold rings.[25]

Nippu Jiji, on the other hand, tried to downplay Korean activism by depicting it as the work of a small minority:

> A total number of Koreans residing in Hawaii is 2,000. Those who are active in the independence movement are only about 200 or 300. Under such a circumstance, they forcibly collected five dollars each from every Korean except children, and a total amount they raised is about $3,000. There are some who made extra donations.[26]

In spite of the attempt to tone down the Korean reaction, we learn from these accounts that the Koreans in Hawai'i, encouraged by the declaration of independence in Korea, held many meetings and collected $5 from each adult in the Korean population to support the nationalist activities.

Fundraising was an important part of the nationalist activities in Hawai'i following the March First Movement, but there is no report on the total amount of money collected. *Nippu Jiji,* as stated above, gave a figure of $3,000, but this is not reliable for various reasons. We can, however, make deductions on the possible amount raised that would be closer to reality based on the available figures of Koreans in Hawai'i. First, it is reasonable to assume that every Korean adult contributed at least $5 each. This is the amount the KNA collected as a "poll tax" *(induse)* from each adult before 1915 and thus most Koreans were accustomed to paying that amount. *Nippu Jiji* reports, as we have just seen, that $5 was the amount collected from each Korean adult to help fund nationalist activities. Second, according to a U.S. Army report, the total Korean population in Hawai'i as of June 1920 was 4,950.[27] Based on this data, we can make the following calculations. Assuming each Korean family consisted of 4 members with 2 adults who donated $5 each, we come up with a figure of $12,500 as the possible amount collected. In addition, there were those who made extra donations. A contribution of $10 from each household may have amounted to one-third of the monthly income for these Korean families, as their monthly living expenses at the time may have been around $30. According to another report given by a Korean newspaper on November 23, 1919, the Koreans in Hawai'i actually contributed even more than the amount calculated above. As of October 1919, a sum of $35,034 had been raised from 2,907 individuals. This means each individual contributed $20.[28] Dr. Pang Sŏn-ju, on the other hand, estimates the total amount of the contributions made by Koreans in Hawai'i to be around $60,000, in which case, we can say that 3,000 Koreans donated an average of $20 each. If so, this means they gave more than their monthly living expenses.[29] Although the estimations of the total amount collected varies, it is clear that a large sum of donations was collected for nationalist causes in Hawai'i.

Characteristically, Korean women also reacted strongly to the news of the March First Movement. In addition to participating in various community activities, more than three hundred Korean women in Hawai'i organized a Red Cross society to provide assistance to those who were wounded or in need of aid in Korea when the Associated Press reported the occurrence of a large number of human casualties in Korea caused by the brutal suppression by the Japanese authorities.[30] Mrs. Mary Song was elected as the president of the society and Mrs. Ahn Won-Kiu (An Wŏn-gyu) became its manager.[31] Also, on March 15, representatives for Korean women from various regions held a "Women's Convention," and, based on an agreement reached there, the Korean Women's Relief Society was formally established on April 1, bringing together delegates from all women's organizations in Hawai'i under its wing with Ch'oe Sun-in as its president and Mary Shin as general secretary. (It later went on to become one of the most important and influential women's organizations in Hawai'i.) The Korean Women's Relief Society printed copies of the declaration of independence, which were sold to collect funds for the nationalist struggle.[32] According to one witness, "many members of the society skipped a meal a day to save rice, which they made into Korean rice cakes to be sold for the purpose of fund raising. They also made Korean national flags which they displayed in their houses. In addition, they made handkerchiefs for sale, and all the money they raised was given to [the independence movement]."[33] The Korean Women's Relief Society also sent a petition to various women's organizations in the United States, Great Britain, and France, appealing for their assistance for Korean independence. A similar letter was also sent to Mrs. Woodrow Wilson in Paris, where the Peace Conference was being convened.[34] Female high school students organized the Korean Girls High School Students Association on April 20 and chose Ch'oe Sun-hŭi as its president. Their desire was to continue the spirit of the Korean declaration of independence. They even raised $60, which they sent to Kim Kyu-shik, who was engaged in diplomatic activities in Paris to win Korean independence.[35]

While the Koreans in Hawai'i were busy supporting the independence movement, the English newspapers in Hawai'i carried news almost daily reporting atrocities committed by Japan in Korea. There was a report of an American missionary being beaten up by Japanese military police officers with rifle butts. Under the headline "Missionary Returning to China from Korea Reveals Indignities Heaped Upon Americans by Japanese Military Officials," the *Advertiser* carried an eyewitness account of how Koreans were beaten up and stabbed by Japanese officials in Korea.[36] In reaction to such reports, the KNA started a campaign to condemn Japanese brutalities while at the same time working toward winning sympathy from the American public for Korean causes. As a result, local newspapers carried articles that were clearly sympathetic to Korea. For example, on March 28, the *Advertiser* printed the whole text of the English version of the declaration of Korean independence and reported that the situation in Korea had become so serious that martial law was declared there and that as many as 11,000 Koreans had been arrested, many of whom were being tortured severely by the Japanese authorities.[37] The two English papers in Honolulu also carried the testimony of Mr. and Mrs. V. S. McClatchy, the publisher of the *Sacramento Bee* and his wife, who stopped over in Honolulu while returning from a trip to Korea, where they had personally witnessed Japanese atrocities against Korean demonstrators.[38] On April 2, the *Star-Bulletin* then carried the article "Korean Envoy in Paris has Difficult Job," which reported on the difficult task of Korean representatives in winning support of the big powers at the peace negotiations.

The Koreans in Hawai'i then decided to hold a large celebration for the Korean independence declared during the March First Movement. On April 5, Pang Hwa-jung, Chŏng Yun-p'il, and Shin Sŏng-il, representing the KNA, formally requested the mayor of Honolulu to give permission for them to use Kapiolani Park for the occasion.[39] Fearing controversy, the mayor referred the case to the board of supervisors. The board, however, rejected the request on the grounds that the celebration might turn into an anti-Japanese demonstration,[40] whereupon the KNA changed the site to the Korean Christian Institute located in Kaimuki (the present Aliiolani Elementary School). Thus, on April 12, the Koreans gathered at the KNA headquarters in downtown Honolulu[41] and paraded through the city streets all the way to Kaimuki with colorful floats, carrying Korean and American flags.[42] As many as 1,200 Koreans—one-quarter of the total Korean population in Hawai'i—took part in the parade.[43] The *Advertiser*, dated April 13, offers the following account of the rally:

> Very early in the morning men and women, boys and girls started to
> come into the city from all parts of the island to take part in the meeting.
> Each one carried the beautiful flag and national emblem of his or her
> adopted country, the Stars and Stripes, and they moved toward the
> Korean National Association Headquarters on Miller Street. . . . On the

platform [at the Korean Christian Institute at Kaimuki], which was also decorated with the flag of Korea and America, there were more than twenty leaders who were selected and sent from other islands to make addresses or sing. As soon as the meeting was called to order by the president of the Korean National Association, C. K. Lee [Yi Chong-gwan], and the band played the national air of both Korea and America. Following the reading of the Korean Declaration of Independence in English by Mrs. Mary Song and in Korean by Y. W. Kim, prayer by Mr. K. S. Yoon and the presentation of Korean and American flags by girl students, appropriate addresses were made by prominent men of the Korean colony in Hawaii and American friends, among them being H. K. Ahn [An Hyŏn-gyŏng], a former president of the Korean National Association; Dr. H. J. Song [Song Hŏn-ju], W. K. Ahn [An Wŏn-gyu], Editor Y. W. Seung [Sŭng Yong-hwan], Rev. W. C. Pang [Pang Hwa-jung], and Dr. Y. M. Park [most probably Pak Yong-man], Edward P. Irwin, the editor of the *Advertiser.*

At this meeting, a resolution was adopted requesting the State Department to issue necessary documents that would allow a Korean delegation to proceed to the Paris Peace Conference. The resolution also called for the United States to let the world know of the barbaric deeds Japan had committed in Korea.[44]

In the meantime, in Asia the March First Movement prompted the Korean nationalists to form a provisional government that would represent Korea and would direct and coordinate future nationalist activities. The Korean nationalists active in the far eastern region of Russia were the first to announce the formation of a provisional government, whose leadership included Son Pyŏng-hŭi as president, Pak Yŏng-hyo as vice president, Syngman Rhee as prime minister, and An Ch'ang-ho as interior minister. This news arrived in the mainland United States on March 17[45] and reached Hawai'i in late March through a report in the *Kungminbo.*[46] A similar government formed within Korea as well a short while later; on April 23, representatives from all thirteen provinces within Korea held a clandestine convention and announced the formation of their own provisional government, which came to be known as the Hansŏng (Seoul) government, with Syngman Rhee as "the chief executive-general" and Pak Yong-man as foreign minister, among others.[47] (In the end, the Hansŏng government was reorganized in Shanghai, China, bringing together diverse elements of Korean nationalists and was recognized as the Provisional Government of the Republic of Korea.) This news reached Hawai'i around June 13, when the *Advertiser* reported that the leaders of the Korean independence movement organized in secrecy a Provisional Government with Syngman Rhee as its president.

Upon hearing the news of Rhee being chosen as the president of the new provisional government, the KNA of North America directed all its regional offices to hold a celebration on August 16. In Hawai'i, however, a ceremony "celebrating the election of Syngman Rhee as the president" was held on August 17 (Sunday), instead of August 16, and at the ceremony a resolution was adopted to support the new Korean government.[48] There was also a movement among Koreans in the mainland United States, Mexico, and Hawai'i to boycott Japanese goods until Japan recognized Korean independence. Before the March First Movement, the Koreans in Hawai'i in general had bought their groceries from Japanese merchants. At this time, however, without any instruction from the KNA or any other organization, the Koreans in Hawai'i voluntarily refused to buy Japanese goods.[49] For example, Ch'a Yŏng-ok, a member of the Korean Women's Relief Society, recollected many years later that "we did not buy Japanese soy sauce or other food items in order to boycott Japan."[50] As the Korean boycott of Japanese goods spread widely among the Koreans in Hawai'i, the KNA decided to endorse it formally.[51]

Upon hearing the news that a large number of Koreans were being killed or wounded in Korea by the Japanese authorities in the course of the brutal suppression of the March First Movement, a "national convention" *(kungmin taehoe)* was convened at the KNA headquarters on June 5 with the participation of about eight hundred Koreans, representing all the Korean organizations in Hawai'i.[52] At this meeting, Hwang Sa-yong and Kang Yŏng-so from the KNA Central Office at San Francisco gave rousing speeches exhorting that "every single Korean should make a pledge to assist the independence movement."[53] On June 11, when Hawai'i observed the centennial of King Kamehameha's death, several Korean organizations participated in the commemoration. Students of the Korean Christian Institute took part in the parade and members of the KNA performed Korean dances, while people representing *T'aepŏngyang sisa (Pacific Time)* paraded with national flags and banners.[54] One of the banners carried a proclamation "Long Live Korean Independence!" at which one Japanese newspaper expressed its displeasure at the parade organizers for permitting banners that were offensive to the Japanese.[55] The *Star-Bulletin* in its editorial under the heading of "A Tactless Blunder" defended the Koreans: "Koreans have just as much right to work for the freedom of their brothers and sisters at home, or to put their cause before the civilized world, as Irishmen have to proclaim their wrath against England." The editorial then went on to rebuke the Japanese:

> The Japanese in Hawaii, if they be American citizens, should know that such discrimination is foreign to our ideals. And until they accept our ideas and become part of us, they are lacking in the essentials of genuine Americanism. The Japanese, as aliens, must expect rebuff, if, in their misguided propaganda, they seek to infuse Americans with Japanese militaristic ideas. We do not tolerate them.[56]

It was clear that Koreans in Hawai'i were gaining sympathy from the Hawai'i community as a whole.

On June 15, another meeting was held at the KNA headquarters with about 1,500 Koreans in attendance. They discussed how best to carry out their activities for the independence movement, while at the same time they reiterated their determination to boycott Japanese goods. They also took issue with *Nippu Jiji* for what they considered to be distorted coverage of news on Korea and warned that they would not tolerate unfair reporting on Korea. In addition, they resolved to coordinate their activities with those Koreans in the mainland United States and Mexico and to fight until Korea became independent. On June 17, there was another meeting where many, including women's representatives, gave speeches reiterating their determination to fight for the independence of their motherland.[57]

In the meantime, a diplomatic liaison office that had been established in Philadelphia was reorganized into the Communication Department of the Republic of Korea on April 25, 1919, in order to collect funds for transmission to the provisional government in China. The provisional government had requested Koreans in North America to contribute $10,000, but the Koreans in Hawai'i did not send any money to China. This is because most of the money raised in Hawai'i went to Syngman Rhee to support his activities in Washington, D.C.[58]

Encouraged by the March First Movement, the KNA and the Korean National Independence League merged on July 18, 1919. Their unity, however, lasted only two months and the two organizations broke apart in September and began to act separately for the independence movement. The Korean National Independence League dispatched its leader Pak Yong-man to the Far East and continued to offer assistance for his activities there. Margaret K. Pai, whose parents were loyal supporters of Pak Yong-man, gives the following testimony: "They [her parents] also continued to support Yongman Park [Pak Yong-man] by sending him funds regularly through party channels to Shanghai, where he was known to be training a military army."[59] The Korean Independence League afterward sent Yi Sang-ho and Kim Su-sŏng to China to work with Pak Yong-man,[60] while the KNA dispatched An Hyŏn-gyŏng and Yu Kye-sang to Shanghai to coordinate its activities with the provisional government that had recently been formed there.[61]

PRESS REPORTING IN HAWAI'I ON THE MARCH FIRST MOVEMENT

The March First Movement aroused international attention from the world media on the general issue of colonial rule. There are some important studies on media reaction within the United States to the March First Movement.[62] In this section, however, we examine how newspapers in Hawai'i—English and Japanese—covered the news and what impact their coverage had upon the Korean community.

Both the *Advertiser* and the *Star-Bulletin* showed considerable interest in Korea and the Koreans in Hawai'i even before the outbreak of the March First Movement. For example, on January 11, 1919, the *Star-Bulletin* carried an article with the bold-letter headline, "Koreans Have 163 Stars in Service Flag: Make Splendid Contribution to U. S. Army," with a large photo, showing a parade scene in which Koreans were carrying the service flag of the KNA. The 163 stars represented "young men of Korean blood who have gone into the service of the United States since July 1, 1918." It praised the Korean contribution to World War I: "Young Koreans of Hawaii have made a record during the period of the war of which they are justly proud." It was the end of this war that prompted the Koreans in Korea to rise up and demand their independence and freedom from Japanese rule.

Once the March First Movement broke out, the Koreans in Hawai'i were eager for news from their homeland, but the strict press censorship by the Japanese authorities and the mysterious silence on the part of the Japanese media offered them very little access to information on the great historical event unfolding in Korea. Under such circumstances, the English newspapers in Honolulu provided much-needed information for the news-hungry Koreans in Hawai'i. Both the *Advertiser* and the *Star-Bulletin* gave rather extensive coverage to the development of the March First Movement and Korean reactions, and, as we have seen above, the March First Movement galvanized Koreans in Hawai'i to renew their nationalist activities. The sympathetic reports by the local newspapers also played an important role in stimulating Korean activism.

The English papers used reports from Beijing to cover the uprising in Korea from the beginning, including Japan's brutal suppression that led to the arrest of thousands of Koreans. They also reported clearly that the Korean demonstrators resorted to nonviolent means as specified in their declaration of independence.[63] Ironically, Japan had just presented to the Paris Peace Conference a proposal to end racial discrimination, but its own colonial policy and conduct in Korea contradicted its demand for racial equality. Both the *Advertiser* and *Star-Bulletin,* quoting reports from the Korean border region, described the nationalist uprising in Korea as far more serious than had been reported by the Japanese news media. The newspapers in Hawai'i characterized the uprising as a nationwide movement in which all ranks of the Korean population participated. They also reported that in the course of the brutal suppression, a large number of Koreans were killed or wounded and that more than a thousand of the arrested were being subjected to inhuman treatment by the Japanese authorities. They reported that at a place called Sungohun, 30 people were killed and 40 others were wounded on March 14, and at a place called Suheung, 4 Japanese gendarmes killed 41 Koreans as the Japanese set fire to a building in which the Koreans were reading their declaration of independence.[64] Quoting an American missionary who had just returned from Korea, the *Star-Bulletin* reported that the March First Movement was one of the most noble examples of nonviolent resistance in history and that many churches in Korea had been forced to close and their ministers were being imprisoned by the Japanese.[65] The Honolulu papers carried many other reports that were critical of the Japanese authorities in Korea.

One of the most telling examples of such coverage was a photo showing a gruesome scene of execution with the headline, "How the Japanese Executed Korean Revolutionists," in the *Star-Bulletin*. It was explained as follows:

> This photo shows Korean revolutionists a minute after their execution by Japanese soldiers. The victims were placed in a kneeling position, their arms extended straight out and attached to the arms of rudely constructed crosses. With their eyes bandaged and their heads and bodies securely tied to the upright of the cross they awaited the firing squad.

It went on to report: "On March 1, three million Koreans, men, women and students, started the independence demonstration simultaneously throughout the ancient kingdom of Korea. The public squares of every large city throughout the country were crowded with people whose only weapon was the manifesto, declaring the independence of Korea from Japan." It then characterized the demonstration as "passive in nature, forbidding any act of violence."[66] Anyone who sees this picture of execution even now cannot but be struck by the cruelty committed by the Japanese authorities and the pain and suffering the Koreans experienced.

In editorials, the Honolulu newspapers openly criticized Japanese colonial policy in Korea. On June 17, the *Star-Bulletin,* in an editorial titled "The Truth About Korea," wrote: "Japan has never justified her stern measures in Korea except on the foundation of political expediency. And such expediency, as we have reason to know, is usually a cloak to illicit empire building. In pursuance of her determination to keep a stranglehold on Korea, Japan has diligently and studiously sought by all means at her command to keep back the truth from the world about Korea." It then cites a report made by Moriya Konosuke, a member of the Japanese House of Representatives who belonged to an opposition party. In the report, Moriya offered his reasons why the Koreans rose in revolt against Japanese rule based on his investigation of the situation in Korea. Moriya cited the following reasons according to the *Star-Bulletin* editorial: "discriminatory treatment given to the Korean subjects," "complicated and impractical administrative measures," "extreme oppression of public speeches," "forcible adoption of the assimilation system," and "spread of the principle of the self-determination of nations." The *Star-Bulletin* went on to say that "Korea today is a seething furnace. Repression and coercion are not measures calculated to popularize Japanese rule." The editorial then concluded: "But her [Japanese] ruthlessness is speeding the day whose dawn will usher in the parting of the ways."[67] This editorial is a good example of how the English papers in Hawai'i treated the Korean issue.

Perhaps most thought-provoking was an October 1919 report from Tokyo by H. H. Kinyon, special Far East correspondent for the *Star-Bulletin*. Kinyon noted that the general public in Japan was kept ignorant of developments in Korea largely because of "the silence of the Japanese press." He went on to state that this "silence" was at last broken with reports and commentaries carried initially by an English paper, the *Japan Advertiser,* and then followed by other Japanese papers in Tokyo. He then recounts the analysis of the Korean situation offered by the Japanese newspaper *Jiji:* "The fundamental mistake in Korea," according to *Jiji*, "is militarist rule—government by saber. Military rule is simply government by gendarmes." This militarism pervaded even in the education imposed in Korea by Japan, as Kinyon quotes: "MOST OF THE SCHOOL TEACHERS ARE EX-SOLDIERS. THEY WEAR SWORDS IN THE SCHOOL ROOM—A PRACTICE UNKNOWN IN ANY OTHER COUNTRY" (capitalization in the original). On the discriminatory treatment the Koreans were subjected to, Kinyon gave an example of disparity in the Japanese salary payment in Korea: "out of [a total amount of] 10,000,000 yen paid in salaries to officials of the government-general a few Japanese officials receive 80 or 90 per cent; the remainder serves to pay a large number of Korean officials." As for Korean farmers, in addition to being subjected to government extortion, they were compelled to provide all sorts of labor work such as road construction. Defrauding also was widely practiced in Korea by the Japanese: "Not only is the administration of the law severe, but private Japanese are guilty of fraud and cruelty," he writes. The common practice of lending a small amount of money on valuable security and then seizing it was a case where "Japanese money lenders are in league with officials to defraud Koreans," according to Kinyon. He wrote: "In one case quoted by the newspaper [*Jiji*] a loan fell due at noon on a certain day. The Korean borrower showed up promptly at the hour, but the Japanese money lender coolly turned the hands of his own watch to one o'clock and refused to surrender the security." In such cases, Koreans would have no legal recourse to take since the Japanese courts were partial to Japanese, according to Kinyon. He then concluded: "If this [Japanese policy] goes on . . . Japan will be regarded by foreign countries as a nation of people whose moral ideas are low, who bow down to militarism and are likely to follow in the footsteps of Germany."[68] Such reporting and commentary must have aroused indignation among the Koreans in Hawai'i and made them even more determined to fight for the nationalistic cause.

Japanese newspapers in Hawai'i, on the other hand, saw the Korean nationalist movement in quite a different light. There were more than ten Japanese-language newspapers in Hawai'i around this time, including *Nippu Jiji, Hawaii Hochi, Hawaii Shimpo,* and *Hawaii Mainichi.*[69] Both *Hawaii Hochi* and *Nippu Jiji,* the two major Japanese newspapers in Honolulu, carried the news of the March First Movement and the Korean reactions in Hawai'i quite frequently, but their reporting in general characterized the March First Movement as an act of lawlessness perpetrated by hooligans, using such terms as *bokudō* (riot) or *sōjō* (violent disturbance). The editorial tone of the Japanese newspapers in general was disdainful of the Korean nationalists. There is, however, a significant difference between the two major newspapers, *Nippu Jiji* and *Hawaii Hochi,* in their dealings with the March First Movement and the reactions of the Koreans in Hawai'i. Whereas *Nippu Jiji* exhibited an unabashed contempt and dislike for the Korean resistance against Japanese rule, *Hawaii Hochi,* while remaining generally critical of the Korean opposition to Japanese rule, showed remarkable restraint in censuring the Koreans and even carried an article urging the Japanese to try to understand why the Koreans were rebelling against Japanese rule.

On March 5, 1919, a few days before the news of the March First Movement reached Hawai'i, *Nippu Jiji* carried a large article on the activities among the Koreans in Hawai'i to send a delegation headed by Syngman Rhee to the Paris Peace Conference in order to appeal for Korean independence by invoking President Wilson's principle of self-determination. After denigrating Korea as incapable of becoming an independent nation, *Jiji* characterized the Korean campaign to gain independence as the work of professional troublemakers who were trying to fleece money from innocent people to satisfy their selfish greed. It wrote:

> The Independence movement is being carried out by a small group of Koreans living in the mainland United States and Hawaii, and in Hawaii alone there are several dozens of them who regard their work in the movement as a [full-time] profession. For them, the independence movement is a professional job, and hence, in the name of Korean independence, they squeeze the blood of the innocent laborers to raise money only to enjoy their own hedonistic life. . . . What is truly pitiful is that the innocent Koreans are now allowing themselves to be utilized by the men of greed and agitation, not knowing that the [Wilsonian] self-determination clause is irrelevant to Korean independence.[70]

Such a derisive tone continued after news of the March First Movement had reached Hawai'i. On March 12, 1919, *Nippu Jiji* reported on daily meetings

Koreans in Hawai'i were holding with the headline "Hey! It will only fatten greedy men's bellies: pathetic sight of Koreans being corralled for money every night: masters of trickery in the name of independence movement." In this article, *Nippu Jiji* claims that all the funds collected at the meetings were pocketed by men of unprincipled greed, who in turn produced more falsified telegrams and letters to squeeze even more money from the innocent workers. In the view of *Nippu Jiji*, the Koreans in Hawai'i were largely mobilized against their will by their leaders in the name of Korean independence, and Korean leaders were nothing more than charlatans, whose sole objective was to satisfy their selfish interests.

Another object of criticism by *Nippu Jiji* was American missionaries in Korea. The Japanese paper followed closely the official line of the Japanese government in reporting the development of the March First Movement in Korea. According to the official Japanese position, there was really no reason for the Koreans to revolt against Japan because since Japan had taken control of Korea tremendous improvements had been made in all aspects of life. Because Koreans were happy under Japan's benevolent rule, why would the Koreans protest on their own volition? In the view of the Japanese government, if there were demonstrations against Japan, they must have been caused by outside agitators. Who were these outside agitators? They were American missionaries, who, according to Japanese officials, worked behind the scenes to instigate the innocent and ignorant Koreans to start the March First Movement. Perhaps the Japanese reasoning was based on the fact that virtually the entire Protestant church in Korea participated in the March First Movement in unison and with fervor. Unable to control the Korean demonstrations, the Japanese blamed American missionaries for the trouble in Korea.

Reflecting such a view, both *Hawaii Hochi* and *Nippu Jiji* carried news critical of American missionaries, but *Nippu Jiji* made far more serious accusations against them. On March 14, *Nippu Jiji* carried a short news dispatch from Tokyo, dated March 7, with the heading, "Riots in Korea instigated by foreign missionaries." Its full text reads: "The riot that started in Seoul on March 1 was caused by instigation of the foreign missionaries, who stirred up girl students as well as children. The demonstration spread in many parts of the country and clashed with the [Japanese] gendarmes, and the disturbance is spreading in all parts of Korea."[71] As Japan made its claim that the American missionaries were behind the March First Movement, *Nippu Jiji*, echoing Japan's official line, even wrote an editorial on this issue in its English section under the title "Korean Uprising and American Missionaries." Although the editorial admitted "political blunders" made by the Japanese government in Korea, it quotes in length from *North China Daily News* the great progress achieved under the Japanese rule. It then asks: "What is the real cause which led to the sudden uprising of the Korean people?" It admits "a portion of the responsibility may rest with the Japanese government." But, it goes on to say that "the responsibility of those agitators who uselessly foment troubles where harmony exists is much greater. Unfortunately, a portion of the agitators are American missionaries, to our greatest regret."[72]

We now know that such a charge against the American missionaries was totally unfounded. It is true that the Protestant church in Korea was the main force that initiated and sustained the March First Movement. But all the evidence so far indicates that the American missionaries were kept in the dark when the uprising was being prepared and that the foreign missionaries played no role in this great Korean nationalist movement. In fact, most of the Western missionaries in Korea had advised the Korean Christians to cooperate with Japan. When the March First Movement broke out, the missionaries were caught by complete surprise, having underestimated the depth of the nationalistic sentiment among the Korean Christians.

Another aspect of the Japanese propaganda in dealing with the March First Movement was to depict the Koreans as innocent and ignorant people who were easily misled and manipulated by charlatans who spread wild rumors. We have seen above how the Japanese newspapers in Hawai'i characterized the leadership of the Korean community in Hawai'i as swindlers who manipulated innocent people. On March 29, *Nippu Jiji* carried a special cable from Tokyo in both the Japanese and the English sections with the large headline: "JAPANESE OFFICE IN KOREA WILL BE BOMBED? False Rumor that Wilson Comes to Korea Is Cause of New Outbreak in Seoul." According to this dispatch from Tokyo, which was started by the false rumor that President Wilson would come to Korea, the Koreans once again started the uprising. One rumor that aroused the Koreans was that Wilson would bomb the Japanese Government-General's office in Seoul. A part of this text in English reads:

> President Wilson comes to Korea not by ordinary means, but in an aeroplane so that he could dodge the Japanese authorities. Immediately after his arrival in Seoul, the American president will engage in bombing the Japanese governor-general's office and residence from his aeroplane high up in the air. He will be the only man who can assist the Korean people. Such is the gist of a rumor which is spread by the irresponsible agitators among the Koreans in Seoul and other large cities where some disturbances occurred recently. The ignorant mass is thus misled and is incited against the Japanese.[73]

One cannot but be struck by the outrageous nature of this news dispatch. It alleges that irresponsible Korean leaders had spread a rumor about President Wilson planning to bomb Japanese government offices in Seoul and that the foolish Korean public fell victim to such a vicious rumor. Are there any grounds for such a report from Tokyo? It seems to be a false rumor that was manufactured by the desperate Japanese to discredit the Korean nationalists and their honest calls for independence. The Japanese newspapers such as *Nippu Jiji* blindly followed the official line of the Japanese government in reporting the March First Movement. Unfortunately, the news coverage and editorial comments on Korea by *Nippu Jiji* were often biased and distorted. Their prejudicial reporting further inflamed the anger of the Koreans in Hawai'i toward Japan.[74]

Hawaii Hochi, on the other hand, was more moderate in dealing with the Korean issue and even suggested the Japanese in Hawai'i show sympathy for the Korean plight. For instance, in an article with the heading "Do Not Attack Koreans: Japanese Should All Sympathize with Koreans and Should Try to Maintain Good Relations with Them," *Hawaii Hochi* quoted an unnamed passenger who had just arrived in Honolulu from Japan aboard the S.S. *Korea:*[75]

> The Japanese residents [in Hawai'i] should never show hostility against or attack Koreans. Even though there may be some among the Koreans who, under the pretext of the independence movement, work to satisfy their own selfish greed, we cannot absolutely say that there is none among them who desire independence for Korea with a sincere heart. From the standpoint of the Koreans, it is not unreasonable for them to launch an independence movement taking advantage of the World [Paris] Peace Conference. For the hostility shown by the Koreans toward the Japanese, Japan is guilty. . . . The Japanese in Hawaii should maintain an attitude of kindness in dealing with the Koreans and should try to preserve friendly ties with them.

Although *Hawaii Hochi* showed an unmistakable tone of condescension toward the Koreans and justified Japanese rule over Korea, it is nevertheless remarkable that *Hochi* carried such a moderate view expressed by an anonymous passenger from Japan. This gentleman even urged his compatriots in Hawai'i to sympathize with the Koreans in their struggle for national independence. Although we do not know the identity of this man, we can say that he is truly a man with a humanitarian vision.[76]

SPLIT WITHIN THE KOREAN COMMUNITY AFTER THE MARCH FIRST MOVEMENT

The Korean community in Hawai'i was beset by internal feuds on the eve of the March First Movement. After its establishment in Hawai'i in 1909, the KNA was largely recognized and accepted by most Koreans in Hawai'i as their representative organization. A feud, however, developed when the two most important leaders of the Korean community fought over the control of the KNA. In 1915, the followers of Syngman Rhee challenged the KNA leadership then under the influence of Pak Yong-man and gained control of the organization, causing a serious split within the Korean community.[77] Having lost control of the KNA, Pak Yong-man formed his own organization called Kalihi Yŏnhaphoe (Kalihi Alliance) to promote his political goals.[78] This situation led to a split within the Korean church as well. Korean churchgoers in Hawai'i had largely been under the Methodist Mission until 1915, when Rhee broke away from the American missionaries to establish his own church.[79] Amid such an unsettling situation, Pak Yong-man organized, as was indicated above, Tae Chosŏn Tongnipdan (Korean National Independence League) on March 3, seven days before the news of the March First Movement reached Hawai'i.

Such a division within the Korean community posed serious problems among the Koreans in Hawai'i, making it difficult for them to pursue united action for the common goal of winning Korean independence. Concerned with this situation, Yun Pyŏng-gu, the president of the KNA of North America, wrote an article in *Shinhan Minbo* titled "A warning to the compatriots in Hawaii," urging the Koreans in Hawai'i to put an end to their internal squabbles and to unite for a common end. Similar advice and admonitions were offered by concerned Koreans in the mainland United States requesting unity of the Koreans in Hawai'i.[80] Although we cannot determine whether this advice had an effect or not, the Koreans in Hawai'i did unite, putting aside their differences upon hearing the news of the March First Movement. Faced with a critical situation developing in Korea following the March First Movement, Koreans in Hawai'i came together and acted as one body to support the independence movement, overcoming their past animosity.

From March 9, when news of the outbreak of the March First Movement first reached Hawai'i, various organizations in Hawai'i, such as the KNA and other social, educational, and church groups, began to work together toward supporting the nationalist movement. A "convention" was called immediately after news of the March First Movement that brought together more than six hundred Koreans at the KNA headquarters, where they shouted "Long Live Korean Independence!" with a great emotional excitement. Again, we do not know whether those who attended were all members of the KNA, but the fact that such a large number assembled at such short notice suggests that many of them must have been nonmembers of the KNA, who attended the meeting at the exciting news of possible Korean independence. Thereafter, these Koreans met daily in the early morning to discuss further measures that might be needed for the cause of independence. Koreans on the other islands also held meetings at regional KNA offices, churches, and parks to discuss and support further activities for the cause of Korean independence. The news of the March First Movement brought back the unity of the Korean community that had been lacking after the split in 1915. Also, according to the *Advertiser,* at "the celebration of the Korean independence" on April 12 (mentioned above), Dr. Y. M. Park was one of the speakers at the podium. This Dr. Y. M. Park is most likely Pak Yong-man, from whom Rhee had taken away the leadership of the KNA only a few years earlier. If he is indeed Pak Yong-man, it indicates that the Koreans in Hawai'i did put aside their differences and join together in the aftermath of the March First Movement.

In order to better coordinate nationalist activities in the wake of the March First Movement, the KNA of North America sent Kang Yŏng-so and Hwang Sa-yong to Hawai'i. Both Kang and Hwang gave speeches at the rally held on June 4 and worked toward bringing unity to the Korean community in Hawai'i. Their efforts were fruitful: the KNA and the Korean National Independence League agreed to merge and an official ceremony took place on July 18.[81] This unity, however, did not last long. After Pak Yong-man left Hawai'i in May 1919 to carry on his activities in China, his followers gradually lost their influence in Hawai'i and the two organizations split once again in September 1919. Chŏng Tu-ok, a loyal supporter of Pak Yong-man who took over the leadership of the Independence League following Pak's departure, blamed the KNA leadership for the split. He claims in his memoir that after the League's regional offices voted in favor of merging with the KNA, Yi Chong-gwan, who then headed the KNA, rejected the League's proposal to unite.[82] Although Chŏng's memoir is often very useful, we need more information to have a better understanding of the short-lived merger and split that took place at the time.

After the unity of the two major organizations broke apart, the rivalry between the two intensified. The KNA directed its efforts largely toward supporting Syngman Rhee, who was now active in Washington, D.C., working with the Korean Commission he organized to lobby for the Korean cause. The Independence League, on the other hand, was not happy with the fact that all the funds raised in Hawai'i were being sent only to Rhee, and tried to regain control of the KNA. Then, at the annual general meeting held on January 8, 1920, Yi Chong-gwan was reelected to the presidency for another term. The KNA then made the fateful decision that it would no longer abide by the prior agreement with the Central KNA of North America, whereby the KNA of Hawai'i would not send a delegation to the Central KNA, nor would it transmit its annual dues it had previously submitted based on an agreement between the two KNA organizations. This decision severed the ties between two KNA organizations.[83] The KNA of Hawai'i, under the influence of Syngman Rhee, did not send any money to the Provisional Government in Shanghai or to the KNA of North America. The funds it collected were largely sent to Rhee. Thus there was really no need on the part of the KNA in Hawai'i to continue its ties with its mainland counterpart. The split posed a grave problem for all Koreans in North America and Hawai'i.

Then on the night of January 22, 1920, more than a hundred Koreans led by Sŭng Yong-hwan, Yi Nae-su, An Yŏng-ch'ŏl, and Kim Chin-ho, all of whom were unhappy with the KNA decision to sever ties with the mainland KNA, held a meeting at the KNA headquarters. Calling itself Han'in Kongdonghoe (Joint Convention of Koreans), it elected Sŭng Yong-hwan as chairman and Kim Chin-ho as secretary and adopted a resolution opposing the separation of the Hawai'i KNA from the Central KNA.[84] Sŭng Yong-hwan, who was the editor of *Kungminbo*, and Kim Chin-ho sent a joint telegram to the KNA of North America in which they reported on their attempts to bring about change to the Hawai'i KNA and requested the Central KNA to dismiss the Hawai'i KNA leadership. This was clearly an attempt on the part of the Korean National Independence League to take control of the KNA by taking advantage of the absence of Syngman Rhee from Hawai'i.[85] Claiming to be "reformers," members of the Independence League tried to expose irregularities committed by Rhee. A bitter struggle ensued as both sides tried to gain an upper hand for control of the KNA.

The feud continued until April 1920, when a compromise was reached through the mediation of the KNA of North America. But until a compromise could be reached, there was bitter fighting, including litigation, which cost both sides considerable time and money. Briefly, the following occurred. Members of the Joint Convention accused the KNA leadership of violating the by-laws on fifteen different occasions. On January 29, 1920, the Joint Convention sent a letter to the Central KNA requesting dismissal of the current executive members of the Hawai'i KNA. The Central KNA responded on January 31 by issuing a directive to the KNA in Hawai'i, in which it announced the appointment of nine men who would form a special committee with the duties of reorganizing new executive members of the KNA in Hawai'i on the grounds that the Hawai'i KNA had violated the by-laws and failed to live up to its obligations to the Central KNA. It also ordered the dismissal of the current executive members of the KNA in Hawai'i. The nine men included Hwang Sa-yong, Chŏng Ch'il-lae, An Wŏn-gyu, Chŏng Wŏn-myŏng, Yi Nae-su, Yun Kye-sang, Sŭng Yong-hwan, Kim Chin-ho, and An Yŏng-ch'ŏl. All but Yun Kye-sang had maintained ties with the Independence League.

Upon receiving the directive from the Central KNA, in order to reorganize the Hawai'i KNA, the Joint Convention group decided to occupy the KNA building and proceeded to do so at 7:00 p.m. on February 2, 1920. According to the *Star-Bulletin*, Sŭng Yong-hwan and his followers forcibly entered the building, bound KNA President Yi Chong-gwan, and demanded he turn over KNA documents and the key to the cashbox.[86] When other KNA members heard this news they rushed to KNA headquarters, where an altercation took place. Cho

Yong-ha, the president of *T'aep'yŏngyang sisa* (Pacific Magazine) and a member of the Joint Convention, was taken by ambulance for emergency treatment after receiving a blow to his face with an iron stick. About ten men from the KNA were arrested by the Honolulu police for inflicting physical violence. Both sides accused the other of starting the violence, which in turn led to the arrest of a number of people and lawsuits from both sides.[87]

Amid such conflict, the Joint Convention group proceeded to select its own leadership to take control of the KNA, electing Song Ch'ang-hŭi as president, Chŏng Wan-sŏ as vice president, Yi Ch'ang-hun as secretary, Chŏng Wŏn-myŏng as finance chief, and Sŭng Yong-hwan as director. Angered by this action, the KNA leadership under Yi Chong-gwan, insisting it alone possessed legitimate authority over KNA, countered with a lawsuit against the Joint Convention group on February 25.[88]

As the dispute over control of the KNA led to a court battle, the Central KNA headquartered in San Francisco became seriously concerned with the ultimate fate of its counterpart in Hawai'i. In fact, however, the Central KNA was at least partly responsible for the cause of the controversy. In a desperate attempt to resolve the dispute, Central KNA president Yun Pyŏng-gu sent a letter to Rev. Min Ch'an-ho, a well-respected church and community leader in Hawai'i. In the letter, after explaining the reasons why he had dismissed the old KNA leadership, Yun emphasized the importance of unity among Koreans and the need to sacrifice individual interests for the sake of national interests. He wrote: "We must put our foremost priority to the business of our nation, and to do so, we must not fight over our private interests." He then offered a new proposal with two points. First, he proposed to make a new slate of the executive committee of the Hawai'i KNA that would embrace both sides. Second, the new KNA should be obliged to abide by the existing by-laws.[89]

On March 12 the circuit court ruled in favor of the KNA. It decided that the KNA leadership that had been elected at the annual meeting on January 8 was legitimate, dealing a defeat to the followers of the Joint Convention. The Joint Convention group, however, refused to accept this ruling and appealed the case to a higher court. In the meantime, the Central KNA in San Francisco called a special session of the board of directors on April 8 to find a resolution to the Hawai'i disputes. After deliberating, the board sent out a directive to the parties in dispute as well as to all KNA regional offices urging both parties to withdraw their lawsuits. In addition, the board wrote letters to all the attorneys and judges involved explaining its position. Persuaded by the mediation efforts of the Central KNA, both parties in the dispute eventually withdrew their lawsuits, thus bringing an end to the feud.[90] On the surface, the dispute appears to have been resolved amicably, but in reality it was a victory for the KNA; the old KNA leadership (who followed Syngman Rhee) remained intact, reassumed control of the KNA building on April 26, 1920, and proceeded with business as usual.[91] Meanwhile, having lost its fight, the Independence League continued to harbor resentment toward Rhee and his followers.

As indicated above, the March First Movement brought the fractured Korean community in Hawai'i together once again as a united group. This unity, however, did not last long. The animosity of the 1915 split was still too strong to overcome. Once the excitement of the March First Movement faded away, a power struggle over the control of the KNA resurfaced in 1920. Although the KNA won the battle against the Independence League, it was a Pyrrhic victory. The stature of the KNA as an organization to represent the Koreans in Hawai'i as a whole diminished significantly as a result. Margaret K. Pai, whose mother was imprisoned in Korea for participating in the March First Movement and was active in the Korean community in Hawai'i, recounts her mother's observations about the changes in the KNA after returning from Korea: "She was puzzled. She heard that the once-powerful Korean National Association, which was the headquarters for all independence activities, had lost its influence. Its paid membership of 2,300 at the height of the independence fervor had plummeted to about 150 supporters by 1921, the year of our return."[92] The KNA no longer represented the entire Korean community in Hawai'i. It was reduced to merely one of many organizations that sprang up among the Koreans in Hawai'i. This of course had a debilitating effect upon the Korean community as a whole as well as upon the future of the independence movement in Hawai'i.

CONCLUSION

In the end, the March First Movement in Korea failed to achieve its desired goal —Korean independence. It was, however, a magnificent expression of the aspiration of all Korean people to be free, especially from alien rule, and to become the master of their own destiny. As such, the movement became a constant source of inspiration for future Korean nationalism.

In Hawai'i, the March First Movement reenergized the nationalistic spirit of the Koreans, who rallied to help the independence movement. They tried to send a delegation to the Paris Peace Conference to appeal for the Korean cause, but were unsuccessful because of the lack of cooperation from the U.S. State Department. They raised a large sum of money to be used for independence activities, to which many Koreans in Hawai'i willingly contributed a large portion of their meager earnings. They worked energetically with considerable success to win public support in Hawai'i as well as in the United States for Korean independence. They appealed and publicized to the United States and the world the need for Korean independence as an indispensable ingredient in promoting peace in East Asia.

For the Koreans in Hawai'i, the two major English newspapers were important sources of information. As the Japanese authorities in Korea had imposed strict censorship on all means of communication, the Koreans in Hawai'i had virtually no access to news from Korea. Thus the occasional coverage of the Korean news by the English-language newspapers was sweet rain to Koreans thirsty for information on what was happening in their motherland. The Koreans in Hawai'i came to believe that these papers were sympathetic to the plight of Korea. They were also heartened by the forthright reports critical of Japan's brutal suppression of the peaceful nonviolent demonstrations. Whereas the local Japanese newspapers tried to belittle what the Koreans were trying to do, often with cynical and distorted remarks, the English papers exposed the injustice of Japanese colonial rule and the suffering of the Koreans. Above all, the English newspapers' editorials calling for self-determination and justice on the Korean Peninsula were important sources of moral encouragement for the Koreans in Hawai'i.

The March First Movement brought the fractured Korean community in Hawai'i together, albeit only briefly. The excitement that Korea might finally free itself from the Japanese yoke and might regain national sovereignty with the proclamation of Korean independence in the March First Movement made the Koreans in Hawai'i forget their past differences and unite. They worked together with great enthusiasm and offered countless hours of self-sacrifice for the cause of Korean independence. As the hope of achieving Korean independence faded under the brutal power of imperial Japan, feuds within the Korean community resurfaced. The struggle to win control of the KNA in Hawai'i in 1920 degraded into a nasty brawl necessitating police and court interventions. When the issue was settled by a court decision and Central KNA mediation, it was nevertheless clear that Syngman Rhee and his followers had now gained a dominant position in the KNA. The KNA, however, was never able to regain the claim that it represented all Koreans in Hawai'i. Instead, it was reduced to just one organization among many and its influence was significantly eroded.

The division and feuding within the Korean community did not weaken the spirit and determination of an independent Korea among the Koreans. It is true, however, that the feuding undermined the morale and spirit of the Koreans in Hawai'i and that, more significantly, it brought dishonor to the Korean community as a whole. In the long run, however, their spirit and determination for regaining Korean independence never wavered. The rivalry that developed among various organizations later became a competition to do more for the Korean community in Hawai'i and to support the cause of Korean independence. Hawai'i thus became one of the most important bastions of Korean nationalism in the first half of the twentieth century.

NOTES

1. See "Min Ch'an-ho ssi rŭl hwanyŏng" (Welcoming Mr. Min Ch'an-ho) *Shinhan Minbo,* January 16, 1919, 3; Pang Sŏn-ju, "3-1 undong kwa chaemi Han'in" (The March First Movement and Koreans in the United States), in *Hanminjok tongnip undong sa* (Seoul: Kuksa p'yŏnch'an wiwŏnhoe, 1988), 490.

2. When the Korean National Association (KNA) was first organized in 1909, there were two coequal organizations. One was the KNA of North America with headquarters located in San Francisco (also known as the Central KNA). The other was the KNA in Hawai'i headquartered in Honolulu. The organizers had hoped to establish a similar organization in Korea and in various regions in the Far East. One was organized in Pyongyang, North Korea, in 1917 with Kim Hyŏng-jik as a founding member. Kim is the father of Kim Il-sung, the former leader of North Korea.

3. *Shinhan Minbo,* January 16, 1919, 3; No Chae-yŏn, *Chae-Mi Han'in saryak* (Abbreviated History of Koreans in the United States) (Los Angeles, 1951), 134.

4. Pang Sŏn-ju, *Chaemi Han'in ŭi tongnip undong* (Independence Activities of Koreans in the United States) (Ch'unch'on: Hallim Taehakkyo, 1989), 214–21.

5. See Chŏng Tu-ok, *Chaemin Hanjok tongnip undong shilgi* (True Record of the Korean Independence Movement in the United States), in *Han'gukhak yŏn'gu* 3 (Inchŏn: Inha Taehakkyo, 1991), "pyŏlchip," 68.

6. Pak Ch'an-sŭng, "3-1 undong ŭi sasang-chŏk kiban" (Ideological Basis of the March First Movement), in *3-1 minjok haebang undong yŏn'gu* (Seoul: Ch'ŏngnyŏnsa, 1989), 417.

7. For the feud in 1915 and its impact, see Yŏng-ho Ch'oe, "Syngman Rhee in Hawaii: His Activities in Early Years, 1913–1915," Chapter 3 of this book.

8. *Shinhan Minbo,* February 13, 1919, 3.

9. For the full Korean text, see Kim Wŏn-yong, *Chae-Mi Han'in 50-nyŏn sa,* 187–89.

10. The death of the former emperor Kojong played an important role in the March First Movement. The Movement organizers chose the date (March 1) to take advantage of the anticipated large gathering of people who would want to take part in the emperor's funeral in Seoul, which was scheduled on March 3, 1919. There was also widespread rumor (unconfirmed) that the emperor's death might have been caused by poisoning by the Japanese.

Shinhan Minbo gives an erroneous date for the emperor's death. The correct date is January 22.

11. The leaders of the March First Movement planned the date of the uprising to coincide with the date of the emperor's funeral scheduled on March 3, for which a larger crowd would assemble in Seoul.

12. For the activities of Hyŏn Sun in Shanghai, see Peter Hyun, *Mansei!* (Honolulu: University of Hawai'i Press, 1986), 93–96.

13. *Shinhan Minbo*, March 13, 1919, "extra."

14. Pang Sŏn-ju, "3-1 undong kwa che-Mi Han'in," 503. Hyŏn Sun has special ties with Hawai'i, where he worked both as a plantation and missionary worker from 1903 until 1907, when he returned to Korea. For his activities, see Hyŏn Sun, *P'owa yuram ki* (1909); Hyun, *Mansei!*; and Han Kyu-mu, "Hyŏn Sun (1878–1968) ŭi inmul kwa hwaltong" (Hyŏn Sun's Personality and Activities), *Kuksagwan nonch'ong* 40 (1992).

15. *Pacific Commercial Advertiser*, March 10, 1919, 1.

16. Ibid.

17. Kim Yŏng-u, *Taehan tongnip hyŏlchŏn ki* (A Record of the Bloody Struggle for Korean Independence) (Honolulu, 1919), 32.

18. *Shinhan Minbo*, March 13, 1919, "extra."

19. *Honolulu Star-Bulletin*, March 10, 1919. See also Pang Sŏn-ju, "3-1 undong kwa chaemi Han'in," 498.

20. Chŏng Tu-ok, *Chaemin Hanjok tongnip undong shilgi*, 67.

21. Kim Yŏng-u, *Taehan tongnip hyŏlchŏn ki*, 34.

22. *Nippu Jiji*, March 12, 1919, "Hen! Yashinka no hara o futosu nomida."

23. Japanese consul general of Honolulu, "Hawaii Chosenjin jijo," (1925) in *Chosen tochi shiryo* 7 (1971): 976.

24. Kim Yŏng-u, *Taehan tongnip hyŏlchŏn ki*, 32.

25. *Hawaii Hochi*, March 13, 1919, "Fund Raising for Independence Movement: Koreans contribute their gold rings." The report of Korean women giving up gold rings in 1919 is a reminder of a similar nationwide campaign that took place in Korea several decades later in 1998, when many Koreans contributed their gold rings to help their nation recover from a severe financial crisis.

26. *Nippu Jiji*, April 4, 1919.

27. U.S. Army, Hawai'i Department, Office of the Assistance Chief of Staff for Military Intelligence, "A Survey of the Koreans in the Territory of Hawai'i," January 1930 (Microfilm, National Archive, Washington, D.C., 1985), 3.

28. *Shinhan Minbo*, December 16, 1919, 3. There is another report that they collected $70,000 in Hawai'i, which is twice the amount of the official report, but this cannot be verified. (See *Shinhan Minbo*, October 11, 1919, 3.)

29. Pang Sŏn-ju, "3-1 undong kwa chaemin Han'in," 511–13.

30. *Hawaii Hochi*, March 17, 1919, 1, "Chosenjin sekijuji o soshiki seri to."

31. *Pacific Commercial Advertiser*, March 17, 1919, 1, "Honolulu Koreans Organize Red Cross Society to Help Member of Race in Korea."

32. John K. Hyun, *A Condensed History of the Kungminhoe: The Korean National Association, 1903–1945* (Seoul: Koryŏ Taehakko, Minjok munhwa yŏnguso, 1986), 21.

33. Kang Shin-p'yo, *Tansan sahoe wa Han'guk ijumin* (Hawaiian Society and Korean Immigrants) (Seoul: Han'guk yŏn'guwŏn, 1980), "Purok" 44.

34. *Shinhan Minbo*, July 5, 1919; *Honolulu Star-Bulletin*, May 23, 1919. See also Kuksa P'yŏnch'an Wiwŏnhoe, *Han'guk tongnip undong sa: charyo* (History of the Korean Independence Movement: Sources) (Seoul, 1975), 5:211.

35. *Shinhan Minbo*, May 15, 1919; June 19, 1919.

36. *Pacific Commercial Advertiser*, March 19, 1919; *Honolulu Star-Bulletin*, March 19, 1919.

37. See *Shinhan Minbo*, April 5 and 8, 1919.

38. *Star-Bulletin*, March 26, 1919, "Japanese Torture Korean Girls in Suppressing Riot"; *Advertiser*, March 28, 1919, "McClathy sees Koreans Clubbed as Revolts Open."

39. *Star-Bulletin*, April 5, 1919, "Koreans Want to Celebrate: Mayor Wavers." See also *Nippu Jiji*, April 9, 1919.

40. *Advertiser*, April 9, 1919, "Koreans' Appeal for Celebration Spurned by Board."

41. 1306 Miller Street.

42. *Nippu Jiji*, April 12, 1919.

43. *Shinhan Minbo*, April 15, 1919. The *Star-Bulletin* (April 14, 1919), however, reported the number to be around eight hundred.

44. *Star-Bulletin*, April 14, 1919.

45. No Chae-yŏn, *Chae-Mi Han'in saryak* (Abridged History of Koreans in the United States), 146; Kim Yŏng-u, *Taehan hyŏlchŏn ki*, 40.

46. *Hawaii Hochi*, March 31, 1919.

47. There were two or three more similar governments formed at different regions, but the Korean nationalists soon realized the urgency to have only one representative government and agreed to recognize the reconstituted Hansŏng government as the legitimate Provisional Government of the Republic of Korea, which set up its headquarters in Shanghai, China, with Syngman Rhee as the first president.

48. *Shinhan Minbo*, August 21, 1919; *Nippu Jiji*, June 21, 1919; Kim Chŏng-myŏng, ed., *Chosen tokuritsu undo* (Korean Independence Movement) (Tokyo: Hara shobo, 1967), 1:737–38.

49. *Shinhan Minbo*, May 1, 1919; *Nippu Jiji*, April 25, 1919.

50. Kang Shin-p'yo, *Tansan sahoe wa Han'guk ijumin*, 24.

51. *Star-Bulletin*, April 24, 1919, "6000 Koreans Start Boycott against Japan."

52. *Nippu Jiji*, June 7, 1919.

53. *Nippu Jiji*, June 5, 1919.

54. *Shinhan Minbo*, June 24, 1919.

55. *Nippu Jiji*, June 12, 1919.

56. *Star-Bulletin,* June 16, 1919. *Shinhan Minbo* carried a full Korean translation of this in the July 1, 1919, issue.

57. *Shinhan Minbo,* June 26, 1919, 1; *Nippu Jiji,* June 16, 1919, 2; *Star-Bulletin,* June 14, 1919, 2.

58. *Shinhan Minbo,* October 11, 1919, 3.

59. Margaret K. Pai, *The Dreams of Two Yi-min* (Honolulu: University of Hawai'i Press, 1989), 41.

60. Chŏng Tu-ok, *Chae-Mi Hanjok tongnip undong shilgi,* 68.

61. *Shinhan Minbo,* August 28, 1919, 3.

62. For the reactions in foreign countries to the outbreak of the March First Movement, see Ma Sam-rak, "3-1 undong kwa oeguki sŏn'gyosa" (The March First Movement and Western Missionaries), in *3-1 undong 50-junyŏn kinyŏm nonjip* (1969); Son Po-gi, "3-1 undong e taehan Miguk ŭi panhyang" (American Reaction to the March First Movement), ibid.; Yu Pyŏng-yong, "3-1 undong kwa Han'guk tongnip munje e taehan Miguk ŏllon ŭi panghyang" (The March First Movement and the American Press toward Korean Independence), in *Kim Ch'ŏl-chun paksa hwagap kinyŏm sahak nonch'ong* (Seoul: Chishik sanŏpsa, 1983).

63. *Advertiser,* March 13, 1919, 1; *Star-Bulletin,* March 13, 1919, 1.

64. *Advertiser,* March 17, 1919, 1, "Independence Movement Increase: Many Dead and Wounded in Riots"; *Star-Bulletin,* March 17, 1919, 1, "Korean Uprising Against Japanese Becomes General." Two place names mentioned in the report cannot be identified because of the confusion in spelling.

65. *Star-Bulletin,* March 19, 1919, 1, "Americans in Korea Beaten by Japanese."

66. *Star-Bulletin,* June 18, 1919, 7, "How the Japanese Executed Korean Revolutionaries."

67. *Star-Bulletin,* June 17, 1919, "The Truth About Korea."

68. *Star-Bulletin,* October 9, 1919.

69. See Shunzo Sakamaki, "A History of the Japanese Press in Hawaii" (M.A. thesis, University of Hawai'i, 1928).

70. *Nippu Jiji,* March 5, 1919.

71. See also *Hawaii Hochi,* March 14, 1919.

72. *Nippu Jiji,* March 29, 1919 (English section).

73. Ibid.

74. Incensed at the prejudicial reporting by Japanese newspapers, a Korean named Kim Han-bŏm broke into the office of *Hawaii Shimpo* and overturned boxes containing printing fonts. After the incident, the KNA issued a statement that Kim had no ties to its organization. See *Nippu Jiji,* March 18, 1919.

75. *Hawaii Hochi,* March 14, 1919.

76. Among the passengers arriving in Honolulu were Goto Shimpei and Nitobe Inazo. See ibid.

77. These two men met each other while serving prison terms as political pris-

oners in Korea and became sworn brothers pledging eternal brotherly ties. They came to Hawai'i after they had agreed that Hawai'i would be the best place to work for their nationalistic goals. Within a few years after their arrival, however, their political differences led them to become sworn foes, causing incalculable damage to the Korean community in Hawai'i. For the historical significance of the 1915 feud, see Chapter 3 of this book.

78. See Hong Sŏn-p'yo, "1910-nyŏndae huban Hawaii Han'in sahoe ŭi tonghyang kwa Taehanin kunminghoe ŭi hwaldong" (Trend of the Korean Community in Hawaii and Activities of the KNA in the Late 1910s), *Han'guk tongnip undongsa yŏn'gu* (Tongnip kinyŏmgwan) 8 (1994).

79. Yu Tong-shik, *Hawai'i ŭi Han'in kwa kyohoe* (Honolulu: Christ United Methodist Church, 1985), 109; Yong-ho Choe, "A Brief History of the Christ United Methodist Church, 1903–2003," in *Christ United Methodist Church, 1903–2003: A Pictorial History* (Honolulu: Christ United Methodist Church, 2003), 39–40.

80. *Shinhan Minbo,* April 29, 1919, 1.

81. Japanese consul general of Honolulu, "Hawaii ni okeru konichi dokuritsu undo ni kansuru ken" (A Report on the Anti-Japanese Independence Movement in Hawaii), in *Chosen dokuritsu undo,* Kim Chŏng-myŏng (Tokyo, 1967), vol. 1, bunsatsu, 734.

82. Chŏng Tu-ok, *Chaemin Hanjok tongnip undong shilgi,* 68.

83. *Shinhan Minbo,* March 19, 1920, 2, "Chungang ch'onghoe po."

84. *Shinhan Minbo,* February 24, 1920, 3, "Hawai Kungminhoe hyŏngmyŏng ŭi humun."

85. *Shinhan Minbo,* February 5, 1920, "extra."

86. *Star-Bulletin,* February 2, 1920, 1, "Police Quell Rival Factions of Koreans."

87. *Shinhan Minbo,* February 26, 1920, 3.

88. Circuit Court, First Judicial Circuit, Territory of Hawai'i, Docket No. 008132, Type Criminal: C. K. Lee, K.K.J. Kim, Choi Sun Choo, W. K. Ahn, N. K. Pike, Kim Chung Chip, Min Han Ok, and Yang Hung Yup (Plaintiffs) vs. Song Chang Hee, Chung Wan Ser, Lee Chang Hoon, Chung Won Myung, and Seung Yong Whan (Defendants).

89. *Shinhan Minbo,* March 19, 1920, 4.

90. *Shinhan Minbo,* April 16, 1929, 1; No Chae-yŏn, *Chae-Mi Han'in saryak,* 158.

91. Japanese consul general of Honolulu, "Hawaii Chosenjin jijo," in *Chosen tochi shiryo,* 956–57; *Shinhan Minbo,* May 11, 1920, 3.

92. Pai, *The Dreams of Two Yi-min,* 36.

Richard S. Kim

6

Local Struggles and Diasporic Politics
The 1931 Court Cases of the Korean National Association of Hawai'i

THIS CHAPTER EXAMINES the highly contentious legal battles within the Korean National Association (KNA) of Hawai'i during 1931. The battles grew out of complicated struggles for community leadership among various groups of Koreans in Hawai'i. Accordingly, this chapter concerns itself with the factional strife that consumed much of the Korean community of Hawai'i in 1931. These factional disputes are often cast as meaningless episodes of frivolous community bickering. They are written off as "dead moments" in the history of the Korean independence movement. As a result, the complexities and significance of such factional disputes are greatly diminished. This chapter seeks to demonstrate that the factional strife exhibited within the Korean community of Hawai'i during the protracted court cases of 1931 was not a meaningless dead moment in history. Rather, these disputes reveal that the struggle to create and maintain a community in exile was inextricably linked to the struggle for national independence. As such, perhaps a more appropriate title for this chapter might be "Local Struggles are Diasporic Politics." In order to understand more fully these close linkages between local-level community dynamics and larger diasporic processes at the global level, this chapter opens with an account of events that occurred at the KNA headquarters in Honolulu during January 1931, events that would become the source of heated legal contention between factions within the Korean community of Hawai'i.

THE OPENING SCENE: MAYHEM AT THE KOREAN NATIONAL ASSOCIATION OF HAWAI'I HEADQUARTERS

On January 5, 1931, the KNA of Hawai'i proceeded to hold its annual delegate convention to determine its activities and budget for the coming year. A group of twenty-one delegates from various localities arrived at the KNA headquarters in Honolulu to take part in the annual meeting. Officials at the door refused to let them enter the KNA building, however. Citing provisions from the KNA by-laws, officials claimed that the delegates were not qualified to participate in the convention due to their failure to pay their membership dues from the previous year. A boisterous argument quickly ensued, which soon erupted into a physical altercation. The unexpected ruckus forced KNA officials to postpone the convention until the following week.[1]

One week later, on January 12, KNA officers tried to reconvene the annual delegate assembly meeting. During the adjournment, officials had distributed admission badges to delegates who were determined to be duly qualified to participate in the convention. Additionally, officials posted guards at the entrance of the KNA building in anticipation of another altercation. When the disqualified delegates returned to seek admittance to the meeting, the guards would not allow them to enter without the mandatory admission passes. The delegates protested vehemently, prompting the guards to expel them from the premises. After the minor scuffle, the delegates inside proceeded to hold their annual convention.[2] At the end of the meeting, KNA President Duk-Yin Shon (Son Tŏk-in) was notified that the excluded delegates had threatened to take over the KNA building by force.[3] In response, Shon continued to employ guards at the entrance of the building.

The following day, January 13, the excluded delegates, with a group of some forty supporters, returned to the KNA headquarters on Miller Street. Without warning, they stormed the building during the assembly meeting in session and forcefully expelled the members inside the building. The disgruntled delegates and their supporters then barricaded themselves inside the building and refused admittance to the ousted members.[4] A large part of the Honolulu police force was called in to restore order.[5]

The delegates who had taken over the KNA headquarters refused to give up possession of the building for two weeks. During that time, they conducted their own delegate assembly, appointing Tai-Wha Chung (Chŏng T'ae-hwa) as the new chairman to preside over the annual convention. In the meantime, the police maintained watch over the KNA premises to prevent the ousted members from reentering the building while those inside continued with their assembly meeting.[6]

The violent altercation and subsequent police action received widespread local press coverage in Honolulu. Tai-Wha Chung informed reporters that the delegates holding the present convention believed that President Shon and his officers had misappropriated KNA funds. This constituted a serious violation of the KNA constitution and by-laws. More specifically, Chung stated that the ousted officers had transacted a mortgage of KNA property to the Bishop Trust Co. on December 24, 1930, for $1,050 without proper authorization from the KNA membership. According to Chung, Henry Kim (Kim Hyŏn-gu), treasurer of KNA, had refused repeated requests to release the organization's financial records for an official audit, which prompted the seizure of the building. Chung declared that the delegates inside the convention were now deliberating on whether to take legal action against Henry Kim and the other officers in order to gain access to the financial records of the KNA, which Kim and other officers had removed from the headquarters to an unknown location just days earlier.[7]

Chung also informed the press that President Shon's refusal to admit qualified delegates who were entitled to participate in the annual convention constituted yet another violation of the KNA's constitution and by-laws.[8] As such, the meeting held on January 12 under Shon's leadership was unlawful and any decisions passed during the meeting should have been nullified. According to Chung, the assembly in progress had voted to impeach and discharge KNA President Shon and his officers for violations of the KNA constitution and by-laws. Chung announced that new elections to replace the dismissed officers would take place on January 31, 1931. Pending the results of the elections, the delegates appointed Chung Hyun Kim (Kim Chŏng-hyŏn) as temporary president, Baik Yurl Choy (Ch'oe Paek-yŏl) as secretary, and Tai-Wha Chung as manager, all of whom were in attendance at the convention in question. Chung also notified the press that the temporary officers had decided to retain the legal services of Honolulu attorney Fred Patterson in order to force Henry Kim and the other ousted officers to release the KNA financial records for an official audit. Further legal action, according to Chung, depended on the outcome of the audit.[9]

On January 24, the ousted officers and delegates, who described themselves in the local Honolulu press as the "regular" faction, filed charges in police court against those involved in the takeover of the KNA building. The regular faction declared that they were the lawful owners of the KNA building and proclaimed that the "irregular" group had illegally trespassed upon and seized private property. The ousted delegates also charged their opponents with assault and battery committed during the forcible seizure of the building.[10]

Later that day, Judge Francis Brooks of the police court ruled that his court was not the proper place to settle internal factional disputes among the Koreans. The judge dismissed the charges and ordered the disputants to take their grievances to circuit court. He stated that "pulling down doors, rushing halls, and flourishing firearms was not the recognized method of settling factional disputes in this country" and that any decision on his part "would merely fan the flames again."[11]

Informed that another violent altercation at the KNA building between the two feuding factions was set to occur on January 26 Honolulu Sheriff Patrick Gleason closed the KNA building indefinitely and maintained a police watch over the premises. Despite his efforts, the two factions opened hostilities elsewhere in the city on the night of the 26th. According to police reports, the newly appointed officers of the KNA were conducting a meeting near Liliha and School streets when members of the ousted faction arrived. Both sides engaged in a clamorous argument, which quickly escalated into violence. A Japanese man, who was an innocent bystander, suffered a gunshot wound to the leg from a revolver fired during the melee. A Korean man sustained a deep laceration on the head after being hit with a wrench by two assailants. Both men were taken to the hospital. Responding to a riot call, the police arrested fourteen men and one woman, who were booked for investigation and taken to county jail for the night.[12]

The next day the combatants once again faced Judge Francis Brooks in police court. Brooks denounced the fights as "utterly alien to the spirit of American lawfulness," stating that the violent acts committed the night before constituted a felony of unlawful assembly.[13] He strongly recommended that the district attorney investigate the matter, asserting that the factional strife "has become too serious to be tolerated any further. The police court is no longer the place to bring these bickerings. While I have no knowledge one way or the other as to which side is responsible, the manner in which the dispute is being conducted has become a criminal matter and should be investigated by our prosecuting authorities."[14]

A few days later, Sheriff Gleason brought together members from both factions for a meeting. Gleason accused the disputants of unlawful assembly and inciting a riot. He said that his office had gathered sufficient evidence to request federal authorities to deport the parties responsible for the recent rash of violence. He demanded the feuding factions end their attacks on each other and instead seek to settle their differences in the court of law. Gleason told those present, "I warn you not to hold any more meetings, to stop gathering around street corners and in homes, and to cease threatening to 'get' certain members of the opposing factions . . . You are living in an American community, are bringing your children up to American standards, and must abide by the laws of the United States."[15] He further warned the group at the meeting that if the police had to respond to any more incidents of violence between the two factions, he would take the necessary steps to deport all those involved. Tai-Wha Chung explained to the sheriff that the dispute could be settled peacefully without resorting to legal action if only the leaders of the other faction were willing to negotiate a compromise. Members of the opposing faction immediately denied Chung's claims and accused his group of fomenting the violence and current troubles.[16] The meeting ended with both sides arguing over who was to blame for the present problems afflicting the Korean community.

On February 3, 1931, the "irregular" group, comprised of Yil Chin Pai, Char Moon Choo, and Bong Cho Choi, filed a writ of mandamus against KNA officers Duk-Yin Shon, Young Chan Ahn (An Yŏng-ch'an), Henry Kim, and Warren Y. Kim (Kim Wŏn-yong) in the first circuit court of Hawai'i.[17] The petition sought to gain access to the financial records of the KNA in order to determine whether Shon et al. had committed any financial wrongdoing. The plaintiffs charged Shon and his officers with committing "gross irregularities in the books of account" by raising large amounts of money from members of the Association and then deliberately failing to deposit the funds into the KNA bank account and to record properly the amounts received in the accounting books of the KNA.[18] The plaintiffs also accused Shon et al. of covertly mortgaging KNA property on December 24, 1930, and using the resultant funds for their own personal use or "for purposes other than contemplated by the by-laws and charter of the Society [KNA]."[19] Pai et al. further charged the defendants of repeatedly refusing their requests to submit the financial records of the KNA for an official audit, which constituted a conspiracy to keep the books concealed from KNA members. Lastly, the plaintiffs accused the defendants of failing to hold the annual delegate meeting in accordance with the KNA constitution and by-laws as demonstrated in their refusal to recognize legitimate members and allow delegates to participate in the meeting. The plaintiffs concluded that the charges against Pai et al. constituted grievous violations of the by-laws and constitution of the KNA and provided sufficient grounds for their removal from office.[20] The presiding judge, Albert M. Cristy, ordered Shon et al. to appear in court on February 17, 1931, to argue why the contents of the books should remain undisclosed to the plaintiffs.[21]

On February 17, 1931, Shon et al. responded to the charges by denying all allegations of wrongdoing and declaring that they had not violated any by-laws of the KNA. Referring to section 9 of the KNA by-laws, the respondents acknowledged that the delegate assembly had the power and authority "to make the annual budget, to audit and examine accounts of the past year, to appropriate expenditures for the year and the sole power to examine and inspect the books, records and accounts of said Society at any time upon request."[22] The respondents continued that they had abided by this provision in a meeting on or about January 10, 1931. At this meeting, the delegate assembly had examined and audited the financial records from 1930 and determined that all the information was correct and true. The respondents emphasized that the assembly did not voice a single complaint about any inconsistencies or errors in the bookkeeping. Based on these facts, the respondents requested that the writ of mandamus be dismissed by the court.[23]

After hearing both sides, Judge Albert Cristy issued a decision on February 28, 1931, in favor of the petitioners, Pai et al. Judge Cristy ordered that the respondents deposit all the financial records of the KNA for 1930 with the court and that the petitioners could examine and audit them at the courthouse from March 4 to 6, 1931.[24]

Despite the ruling, the case was far from over. A few days later, on March 2, attorney Ray J. O'Brien, representing Shon et al., filed an appeal contesting the ruling.[25] The court accepted the appeal, and the case would be continually drawn out by both sides for much of the year.

DIASPORIC DILEMMAS—THE DIALECTICS OF THE LOCAL AND THE GLOBAL

The judicial proceedings in early February 1931 marked the beginning of a highly contested Rashomon-like legal battle between the "regular" and "irregular" factions within the KNA. Lasting for most of the year, the case would involve heated testimonials and compelling evidence presented by both sides. As indicated in the initial proceedings in February, the conflict between the two groups of litigants ostensibly involved disputes over the administrative affairs of the KNA. The disputes also exposed a more fundamental conflict between the opposing factions that revolved around multiple and irreconcilable differences in interpretations of the constitution and by-laws of the KNA of Hawai'i. Unable to resolve these differences among themselves, the two groups turned to a third party, the U.S. judicial system, to determine which interpretation was "correct."[26]

As the litigation continued over the next several months, both sides would bombard the court with multiple and often repetitive charges and allegations against each other as they told and retold their own versions of the events that had transpired at the KNA building in January 1931. Upon first glance, the piles of the extant court records documenting the maddening legal minutia presented over the course of nearly one year seem to indicate nothing more than a meaningless factional feud about procedures, by-laws, and charters. The dispute was devoid of any significant ideological differences such as the ones that had dismantled the united front within the Korean Provisional Government (KPG) some ten years earlier. Upon closer examination, however, the conflicts and debates emanating from the court case appear to be much more than just the incidental legal rantings of a politically vacuous factional feud. The testimony, evidence, and legal arguments presented by both sides throughout the duration of the case was cumulative in that each successive hearing before the court added a new layer of complexity to the issues and facts under dispute. I argue that these local disputes were intricately linked to a larger chain of events within the Korean independence movement. Thus, the protracted legal battle of 1931 was in fact a series of complex stratagems in the struggle for local leadership to determine the right of governance and the control of organizational resources in representing Koreans of Hawai'i in the diaspora.

Splintered into an array of opposing factions, the Korean nationalist movement was in a state of dormancy and disillusionment by the end of the 1920s. In contrast, the nationalist movement entered the decade of the 1920s on a more hopeful note with the establishment of the KPG in Shanghai in April 1919. The creation of the KPG came in the wake of the nationwide nonviolent demonstrations of the March First Movement in 1919. Inspired by the doctrine of self-determination set forth in Woodrow Wilson's Fourteen Points, demonstrators throughout the Korean Peninsula called for Korea's independence and right to national self-determination. On March 1, organizers of the demonstration presented a copy of the newly drafted Korean declaration of independence to Japanese officials in Seoul. Simultaneously, the declaration was read publicly in downtown Seoul, sparking waves of nonviolent protests against Japanese rule throughout Korea. Millions of Koreans from all walks of life took to the streets, repeatedly chanting "Mansei!" (Long Live Korean Independence). The Japanese, alarmed by the massive scale of the demonstrations, brutally squashed the protests with its powerful military police force, which indiscriminately arrested, imprisoned, tortured, and killed thousands of Koreans.

The nationalist sentiments generated by the March First Movement and its violent suppression led to the formation of the KPG in April 1919. As a government in exile, the KPG represented the organizational embodiment of a new sovereign Korean nation-state, the Republic of Korea. In creating the KPG, nationalist leaders sought to establish a centralized organization to unify the widely dispersed Korean exile community. Japan's declaration of Korea as a protectorate in 1905 and subsequent annexation in 1910 spawned a number of organized protest groups among Koreans living abroad in the United States, China, Manchuria, and Siberia. For the most part, these exile groups conducted their activities independent of each other. The creation of the KPG, headquartered in Shanghai, China, served to bring together this loose network of exiled activists into a more tightly knit structure.[27]

Japan's brutal repression of the March First Movement protests clearly demonstrated that organized resistance against the Japanese within Korea would be nearly impossible to sustain. As a result, the independence movement had to be organized and maintained in the diaspora. The KPG was a direct product of the transnational, diasporic activities of the Korean independence movement. The transnational nature of the newly formed Republic of Korea presented a fundamental paradox, however. The nation-state demands loyalty to the single territorial unit of the nation-state. Formed entirely within the diaspora, the new Korean nation-state had no actual geographically bounded territory to govern. As a deterritorialized unit, the Korean nation-state had, in effect, transcended itself upon its birth.

Given these diasporic foundations, the Republic of Korea lacked a true political center. Instead, several centers existed simultaneously. As a result, the locus of power in the diaspora was scattered throughout a matrix of sites, creating multiple and often conflicting attachments and loyalties. The KPG faced the formidable challenge of trying to centralize a national authority that could unite dozens of local communities spread all over the world and develop a focused policy toward a homeland. The diffusion of power inherent in organizing across the diaspora also produced bitter political and cultural contestations over who rightfully represented the national constituency of Koreans at home and abroad.

These types of conflicts plagued the KPG from the onset as factional feuding greatly strained relations within the government. Within less than two years, the KPG fell apart under the pressure of this factional strife. In seeking to unify the disparate elements of the nationalist movement scattered throughout the Korean diaspora, the KPG represented a fragile united front of nationalist and communist groups, each adhering to vastly different ideological and strategic approaches in the struggle for Korean independence. One contemporary observer described these opposing ideological camps as the "American group" and the "Siberian-Manchurian group."[28] In the end, KPG leaders were never able to overcome these differences. In January 1921, the withdrawal of the Korean Socialist Party from the KPG, precipitating mass resignations of important cabinet members, signaled the official dissolution of the united front. With this event, the KPG could no longer claim to be the center of the independence movement.

In the months and years after January 1921, factional strife remained a great hindrance to the Korean nationalist movement. After the withdrawal of the Korean Socialist Party from the KPG at the beginning of 1921, Korean communist groups in Siberia and Manchuria soon found themselves at odds with each other, leading to deep factional rifts within the Korean communist movement. Although only a shell of a government after 1921, the KPG continued primarily as a vehicle for Syngman Rhee's supporters. Rhee's support within the KPG rapidly waned, however, as the KPG fell into severe financial and administrative troubles. In a state of disarray, the KPG impeached Rhee as president in 1925. This rampant factionalism throughout the diaspora left the Korean independence movement deeply divided and dispersed by the end of the 1920s.[29]

Conflicts within the KNA of Hawai'i in 1931 emerged from this period of retrenchment and division within the Korean independence movement. As an important ancillary of the KPG in China, the KNA of Hawai'i had been a vital part of the diasporic movement to restore Korea's national independence. The social and political identities of Koreans in Hawai'i were firmly rooted in their connections to their homeland as individuals and social groups were deeply invested in preserving and maintaining a national Korean identity outside of Korea. Themes of displacement and the cause for the independence of Korea were mobilized into various forms of collective action.[30] Organizational activities of the KNA, for instance, focused on aspects unique to Korean history and culture. The KNA also played an important role in the mobilization of financial resources for the nationalist movement. From its inception, the KPG was almost entirely dependent on funds contributed by the KNA from its members in Hawai'i and the U.S. mainland.

Besides active involvement in the Korean independence movement, the KNA of Hawai'i also functioned as a self-governing body to protect and advance the interests of Koreans in Hawai'i. Adhering to democratic principles, the organization purported "to transcend all differences of religion, occupation or class" and to unify Koreans residing throughout the Hawaiian Islands into a single self-governing collective body.[31] Toward these ends, the KNA of Hawai'i was structured much like a centralized national government with intricate bureaucracies at the central, district, and local levels, each empowered with various state functions, which were outlined in the KNA constitution.[32]

With the collapse of the KPG and subsequent period of retrenchment, there was no longer a supreme authority to coordinate activities within the diaspora. Nevertheless, questions of state power and its uses continued to dominate the political concerns of all Koreans abroad. By 1931, however, these questions assumed a greater local significance rather than a global, diasporic one. The diasporic dilemma of who represented the national will of Koreans at home and abroad was now played out at the local level. Under these circumstances, the importance of the self-governing functions of the KNA were greatly heightened and soon became a source of heated contention among factions competing over who had the legitimate claim of authority to lead the KNA and its membership. The remainder of this chapter examines these complex political dynamics among Korean immigrants living in Hawai'i by focusing on the bitterly contested court case of 1931 involving the KNA of Hawai'i.

SUBJECTIVE TRUTHS, MULTIPLE REALITIES

The petition submitted by Pai et al. on February 3, 1931, would be the first of numerous pretrial motions filed by both sides during the next several months. On the same day, members of the "regular" faction, comprised of Shon and other KNA officers, filed their own court action against their antagonists. Shon et al. petitioned Judge Albert M. Cristy of the first circuit court for a writ of quo warranto against Chung-Hyun Kim and Baik-Yurl Choy, who had been appointed temporary president and secretary, respectively, during the delegate assembly conducted by the "irregulars."[33]

The trial quickly escalated from charges of financial mismanagement to much more contentious issues involving which group had the legal mandate to lead the KNA of Hawai'i. For the next several months, the case revolved around multiple and contending interpretations of the "takeover" of the KNA building in January. In a Rashomon-like manner, both sides repeatedly recounted to

Judge Cristy their own accounts of the events in January, attaching completely different meaning and significance to the events in question. Ultimately, the judge had to sift through these multiple perspectives to determine which interpretation was the most credible to decide the case.

Shon et al. claimed that they had been lawfully elected to their respective offices for two-year terms based on the results of KNA elections held on December 18, 1929. They listed their elected posts as Duk-Yin Shon—president, Young-Chan Ahn—vice president, Kyung Choon Kim (Kim Kyŏng-jun)—manager, and Henry Kim—secretary/treasurer. Yernsho Park, Shinho Char (Ch'a Shin-ho), Chun Kun Lee (Yi Chŏng-kŏn), Sung Koon Park, and Moon Chil Cho, who had all been appointed directors by President Shon, were also listed as plaintiffs in the suit.[34]

The plaintiffs charged that the defendants, Kim and Choy, had no legal authority to their claims of leadership in the KNA. In support of their allegations, Shon et al. recounted their version of the chain of events that had occurred at the KNA building during the month of January 1931. On January 12, 1931, the KNA had convened its annual meeting in accordance with the Association's by-laws. After being refused entry from this legitimately organized meeting, the defendants, Chung-Hyung Kim and Baik-Yurl Choi, along with other members of their group, returned the following day and broke into the KNA building through the use of force and violence. After ousting the legal officers, Kim and Choy unlawfully usurped the offices of president and secretary/treasurer.[35] From that day on, the defendants had "unlawfully and without right and contrary to law and contrary to the rights and interests of plaintiffs herein attempted to exercise and hold the aforesaid office of said corporation and association and withhold the same from the plaintiffs herein who are duly elected and qualified officers of said corporation and association."[36] When informed that further violence would ensue at the KNA headquarters, Sheriff Patrick Gleason ordered the KNA building to be closed indefinitely. As a result, the plaintiffs maintained that they had been unable to enter the KNA building to fulfill their duties and responsibilities as the legitimate officers of the KNA.[37]

The plaintiffs requested a writ of quo warranto, requiring the defendants to appear before the court to demonstrate "by what authority and right they and each of them attempt to claim, hold, or usurp offices in said corporation and association and by what authority to exercise and exercised the functions, duties, and powers of any office of said association."[38] Judge Christy granted their request and ordered Chung-Hyun Kim and Baik-Yurl Choy to appear before the court on February 14, 1931, to respond to the complaint filed against them.[39]

Citing legal technicalities, attorney Fred Patterson managed to delay the appearance of his clients, Kim and Choy, before Judge Cristy for several weeks. On March 6, the defendants finally submitted an answer to the court, denying the charges that they had usurped offices held by the plaintiffs. The litigants provided their own version of the events in January to demonstrate their lawful and rightful leadership in the KNA. The defendants presented a copy of the minutes of their delegate assembly meeting held at the KNA building in January. While their account did not dispute the actual "takeover" of the KNA building, their interpretation of the events at the KNA headquarters departed significantly from the one presented by their adversaries.[40]

The defendants claimed that twenty-one delegates from nineteen local associations arrived at KNA headquarters on January 5, 1931, to participate in the annual delegate assembly convention. They were unlawfully refused entry to the meeting. Due to the confusion, KNA officials decided to postpone the meeting for one week. When the defendants came back a week later on January 12, they were again turned away and eventually chased off the KNA premises. On the following day, they returned, occupied the KNA building, and opened the proceedings of the convention among themselves. They first collected $526 in membership dues from those in attendance and then elected Tai-Wha Chung as chairman, Chong Kwan Lee (Yi Chong-gwan) as vice chairman, Choong Shin as secretary, Do Won Chung as correspondent secretary, and Kio Hyun Kim as assistant secretary to preside over the convention. On the first day, the assembly voted to issue an order for KNA President Duk-Yin Shon to turn over the financial records of the KNA for the entire year of 1930. They then formed a committee to inspect and audit the records. For these purposes, the delegate assembly hired the legal counsel of Fred Patterson to obtain through legal means the financial books of the KNA from Shon et al.[41]

During the next several days, the delegates voted to impeach and expel President Shon and his officers from the Central Association of the KNA on five counts of violating KNA by-laws. They nominated the following individuals to replace the ousted officers: Chong-Kwan Lee and Kwang Chai Kim for president of KNA Central Association and Yin Soo Chung (Chŏng In-su) and Hyun Kyung Ahn (An Hyŏn-gyŏng) as vice president. Until the new officers were officially elected by the KNA membership at large, the delegate assembly appointed Chung-Hyun Kim, Baik-Yurl Choy, and Tai-Wha Chung as temporary president, secretary, and manager, respectively. These temporary officers announced news of the impeachment and dismissal of President Shon and his cabinet to all chapters of the KNA throughout the Hawaiian Islands and that new elections would be conducted on January 31, 1931.[42] The respondents answered that the petitioners had been impeached through legitimate means and were thus no longer qualified to represent themselves as KNA leaders.[43]

Dissatisfied with the arguments and evidence provided by both sides, Judge Cristy moved to continue pretrial hearings. On April 28, 1931, Yil Chin Pai, Cha Moon Choo, and Kun Koo Lee filed a new petition against KNA President

Duk-Yin Shon and his officers, emphasizing charges of financial wrongdoing. Represented by new attorneys from the firm of Thompson, Beebe, & Winn, Pai et al. requested the court to issue a temporary restraining order that directed the respondents to deposit all KNA financial records for 1930 with the court. They also petitioned the court to find Duk-Yin Shon and Young-Chan Ahn unfit to preside over their respective offices as president and vice president and requested the court to appoint two new members in good standing to replace them.[44]

Pai et al. brought forth a number of specific complaints against Shon et al. They alleged that Shon and his cabinet had (1) spent money other than that provided for in the budget; (2) failed to spend money as called for in the budget; (3) mortgaged KNA property without authority; (4) excluded accredited members from the right to participate and vote in the annual delegate assembly; and (5) allowed nonmembers to participate in KNA affairs. The petitioners claimed that each charge constituted a violation of the KNA by-laws and constitution, each providing sufficient grounds for dismissal from office. The petitioners declared they were seeking these legal measures against Shon et al. not only to recover damages for themselves, but more significantly, for the general good and benefit of the KNA.[45]

The petitioners once again provided a descriptive account of the events that had led directly to the forcible takeover of the KNA building. On January 13, 1931, KNA officers held their annual delegates meeting. The petitioners claimed that the meeting was unlawful because Shon and his officers deliberately denied the admission and participation of qualified members and delegates. In doing so, Shon et al. had committed a gross violation of the KNA by-laws and the meeting should, therefore, be invalidated. According to the petitioners, only those who supported President Shon were issued admission passes and permitted to enter while all others were excluded through the use of force and violence. Pai et al. contended that some of those allowed to enter the meeting were not even members or delegates of the KNA and were therefore ineligible to participate and vote in an assembly convention. If the meeting had been lawfully organized with all eligible members and delegates permitted to enter, Shon and his officers surely would have been ousted from office due to widespread discontent among the membership concerning their misappropriation of KNA funds.[46]

According to the petition, Shon et al. were well aware of this discontent among the delegate body and were currently in the process of preparing a new set of financial books that would absolve them of any wrongdoing.[47] Pai et al. believed that the respondents were planning to complete this new set of books by April 29, 1931, after which the old books and records, containing the "true state of the corporation [KNA] either as to its financial condition, its membership or in any other important detail" would be destroyed.[48] The petition declared that these actions constituted a conspiracy to deceive the KNA membership so that the respondents could retain control and authority over the KNA. They concluded that the constitution of the KNA stated that officers who committed "actions deliberately contrary to the Constitution and by-laws and embezzlement of public money" were to be discharged from office.[49]

On April 29, 1931, Judge Cristy ordered Shon et al. to "restrain from destroying, concealing, or tampering with the books, data and records of the Korean National Association of Hawai'i" and required them to turn over all the financial records in question to the court.[50] The judge also issued a court summons for all the defendants to appear before him on May 2, 1931, to answer to the charges contained in the petition.[51]

On April 30, KNA Secretary/Treasurer Henry Kim complied with Cristy's order and submitted the following financial records to the court clerk:

1   Stubs from fifteen receipt books for the year 1930.
2   Cancelled checks from the Bank of Hawai'i for the months February through November.
3   A complete file, consisting of twenty-four folders, of paid bills of the KNA.
4   Two accounting books, one documenting KNA income and the other recording KNA expenses.
5   Two accounting books, one documenting the income of the *Korean National Herald* and the other recording expenses of the *Korean National Herald*.
6   An accounting book for funds collected for the Korean Commission.
7   An accounting book for Korean Independence Funds.
8   Stubs for receipt books #5701 and #7474 for 1930.
9   Independence Fund bills and receipts (expenses).[52]

As for their appearance before the court, Ray O'Brien, representing Shon et al., successfully motioned the judge to order the petitioners to amend and resubmit their lengthy petition on grounds of improper legal procedures. After nearly three months of haranguing over legal technicalities, the respondents finally submitted an extensive answer on July 21, 1931.[53]

In their response, Shon et al. denied that they had misappropriated any funds by mortgaging KNA property without proper authority. As officers of the KNA, they claimed that they had the power to mortgage any property belonging to the KNA under Sections 16–45 and 56 of the KNA by-laws. Nevertheless, the property in question was already under a mortgage transacted by their predecessors in office, which had been approved at the annual delegates convention in January 1914. Moreover, the respondents claimed that all funds collected through mortgage were spent for and on behalf of the KNA.[54]

Shon et al. also refuted charges that the annual meeting held on January 12 was unlawful. In accordance with KNA by-laws, all delegates qualified to participate were admitted and those ineligible were rightfully refused admission. Moreover, the respondents asserted that petitioners Pai Yil Chin and Choo Cha Moon had been determined to be qualified delegates and were accordingly admitted to the annual convention. The two men left the meeting on their own volition shortly after the commencement of the convention, however. According to Shon et al., this fact demonstrated indisputably that they did not refuse admission to any qualified delegate or prevent the entry of any qualified member by using force.[55]

Shon et al. admitted that they had issued admission passes to qualified delegates in order to keep out nonmembers and ineligible delegates. More specifically, the respondents charged that

> Syngman Rhee, who was not a member of the KNA, but seems to have had influence among certain Koreans living in the Territory of Hawaiʻi, had laid plans to commit violence against the officers of the Korean National Association, take possession by force the books and property of said association, cause said meeting to be interrupted, and endeavor to secure control of said Korean National Association for his personal gain.[56]

According to Shon et al., this precarious situation necessitated a formal method to identify those delegates who were duly qualified to attend the annual convention. Despite this slight departure from normal procedural processes, they asserted that the meeting was lawfully organized under the by-laws of the KNA and attended by only those qualified to participate and vote in accordance to the by-laws of the Association.[57] Lastly, the respondents denied charges that they had either tampered with the financial records or prepared new ones. Shon et al. wrote off these accusations as "absurd, without foundation and an endeavor by the petitioners to create some ground upon which to bring respondents into court and to harass and annoy them."[58] In all instances, the respondents claimed that they acted lawfully within the bounds of the KNA constitution and by-laws and asked the court to dismiss all the charges filed against them.[59]

The July 21 answer by Shon et al. was the first mention of Syngman Rhee in the proceedings of the case. Other sources, however, indicated that Shon and his officers had believed for some time that Rhee was directly responsible for instigating the violence at the KNA building and the recent deluge of "unfounded" legal suits against the KNA filed with the district courts in Hawaiʻi. The present legal case was a direct carryover of this factional strife between the Tongjihoe (Dong Ji Hoi) and the KNA that had begun a year earlier in 1930. According to Henry Kim, nearly ninety legal cases involving Koreans were pending in the courts; seventy had been filed by the Tongjihoe, Rhee's personal organ, and the rest by the KNA.[60] In many respects, the highly contested case of *Pai et al. v. Shon et al.* represented the culmination of the numerous legal battles between the two groups.

Shon et al. maintained that the current legal case was a last-ditch effort by Rhee to gain control over the KNA, which he had been plotting since 1930. That year witnessed a rejuvenation in nationalist activities among Koreans in Hawai'i as Japanese military expansion into China had become a cause of growing concern among world powers. Up to that point, the international political front had been relatively peaceful and stable. In the aftermath of World War I, the decade of the 1920s was largely a period of global pacification as manifested in the expansive influence of the League of Nations. With Japan firmly situated as a world power, Japan's dominion over Korea went unchecked by the international community throughout most of the 1920s. Moreover, mass protests against the Japanese within Korea had tapered off sharply after the repression of the March First demonstrations and the institution of colonial reforms by the Japanese to minimize potential dissent within Korea.[61] Given the rather quiescent state of affairs within Korea, the Korean nationalist movement fell into a period of deep retrenchment and disillusionment during the 1920s as many nationalists throughout the diaspora became frustrated with their inability to induce any significant changes to the political situation in Korea. In 1930, the international community's growing disapproval of increased Japanese military activities into areas controlled by China, which would eventually lead to complete occupation of Manchuria in 1931, provided a spark of hope for Korean nationalists, who began to seek ways of revitalizing the movement against the Japanese. In Hawai'i, the KNA of Hawai'i decided in January 1930 to initiate a large-scale publicity campaign to raise independence funds.[62]

Rhee, who had returned to Hawai'i indefinitely in 1929, also saw an opportunity to resume his diplomatic activities and regain his ascendancy within the nationalist movement. He sought to revive his personal organization, the Tongjihoe, which had been languishing in dormancy for several years. Wishing to project an image of unity to attract international support, Rhee convened a Tongjihoe Delegates Conference in Honolulu in the summer of 1930, which resolved to initiate a movement for the merger or unification of Korean organizations in Hawai'i under the single authority of the Tongjihoe.[63] In reality this plan was a ploy for Rhee to gain control over all Korean political activities in Hawai'i. To accomplish his goal, Rhee initiated a series of calculated steps to undermine and abolish the authority of the KNA of Hawai'i, which carried the support of the majority of Koreans residing throughout the Hawaiian Islands. According to Shon and his officers, the current hostilities between the Tongjihoe and the KNA, which had caused so much havoc for Koreans in Hawai'i, were rooted in Rhee's ploy to sabotage the functions of the KNA.

Even though he was not a member of the KNA, Rhee first tried to sell off the KNA building in August 1930 under false pretexts and without authorization of KNA officers. Rhee's attempts to sell the building were thwarted by the newly elected KNA president Duk-Yin Shon, who asserted that Rhee had no authority to make such arrangements.[64] Rhee then tried to oust Shon from office but failed.[65] Rhee finally turned to Henry Kim, secretary/treasurer of the KNA and editor of the *Korean National Herald,* the official organ of the KNA. Rhee repeatedly requested Kim to support a publicity campaign on behalf of the Tongjihoe, which entailed publishing exclusive endorsements of the Tongjihoe plan for unification while repudiating the KNA. Henry Kim refused to comply with Rhee's requests. Unable to persuade Kim, under his self-proclaimed authority as president of the KPG, Rhee ordered Kim to resign from his posts in the KNA. Kim, wishing to avoid further conflict with Rhee, tendered his resignation to the KNA board of directors. Meanwhile, Rhee issued public statements asking the Koreans of Hawai'i to accept Kim's resignation and to turn over the secretary/treasurer and editor positions to him. The situation created a stir within the KNA when members claimed that a nonmember could not dismiss a regular member from office. The local chapters of the KNA took a vote on the matter and overwhelmingly voted to retain Henry Kim, who promptly returned to his posts.[66]

Unable to sway KNA majority opinion in his favor, Rhee resorted to more aggressive methods. Claiming that the KNA was the "common property" of all Koreans in Hawai'i, regardless of whether they were due paying members or not, Rhee publicly called for the "forceful occupation" of the KNA.[67] According to Shon and his officers, Rhee then invited to the 1931 annual delegate assembly in January "all sorts of delegates from where there are no local associations, from local associations which have no required number of members for their own legal status, from local associations deprived of a delegation, from local associations of which no member paid a membership fee, from local associations installed by the worst methods of Gambetta—all contrary to customs and by-laws of the Association."[68]

These "unqualified" delegates demanded entrance to the annual conference on January 4, 1931. Their demands created mass confusion, causing a postponement of the meeting. KNA officials issued admission passes to identify those delegates who were qualified in accordance with the by-laws. The following week Rhee's supporters, accompanied by a group of "roughnecks" hired by Rhee, returned to the KNA headquarters and took over the KNA building by force.[69] They refused to vacate, arguing that they were the rightful proprietors and that they had reoccupied the building, which had been illegally taken from them.[70] According to Henry Kim and others, the legal suits to determine the legitimate leaders of the KNA began soon afterward. Because Rhee was not a member of the KNA, the suits were filed by KNA members Pai and others, who supported Rhee's plan to abolish the KNA in favor of the Tongjihoe. Shon et al. maintained that these suits brought upon by members of the KNA were intended to benefit Rhee and the Tongjihoe, not the KNA, and were ultimately part of an extensive plot for the Tongjihoe to gain control of the KNA. According to Henry Kim, he presented "in detail the whole history of the factional strife and tactics employed by Rhee" in his court testimony before Judge Cristy.[71]

Naturally, the other side had their own interpretation of the origins of the disturbances that had left the Korean community of Hawai'i "paralyzed and helpless for a while."[72] In a press statement shortly after the court proceedings had begun in February 1931, the faction in support of Pai et al. stated that they were baffled by the sudden occurrence of violence among Koreans in Hawai'i, explaining that the present troubles were neither a renewal of old hostilities nor the beginnings of a new factional rift. In fact, they felt that internal divisions among Koreans in Hawai'i had been rapidly declining in recent years as all organizations were working toward the common goal of unification. They claimed that the Koreans of Hawai'i had been successful in creating a prosperous and self-reliant community since their arrival as plantation laborers. They listed the following properties and institutions owned by the Korean community in Hawai'i: the KNA on Miller Street worth $20,000; the Korean Old Men's Home on School Street near Liliha worth $10,000; the Korean Christian Church near Palama Settlement with a one acre lot worth at least $17,000; the Korean Christian Institute in Kalihi Valley, which owned 27.5 acres of land worth about $100,000; and the Dongji Investment Co., which held some 90 acres of farm land in Olaa, worth another $100,000.

These institutions, in all worth nearly $250,000, were collectively owned and maintained by the Korean community of Hawai'i.[73] A group of "educated" Koreans from the mainland had sought control over these valuable community resources for their own purposes, however. The press singled out four men in particular, Henry Kim, Warren Kim (Kim Wŏn-yong), Young Ki Choy (Ch'oe Yŏng-gi), and Rev. William Y. Lee (Yi Yong-jik), all of whom had managed to acquire positions of authority in the KNA and the Korean Christian Church.[74] From their positions of power and with the support of a few local Koreans, Pai's group claimed that these men "declared war on us with the weapons which we placed in their hands . . . endeavoring to get rid of some of our outstanding leaders, who they believe to be standing in their way."[75] When the twenty delegates representing various local associations arrived in Honolulu in early January for the annual convention, they discovered that their entrance to the KNA building had been blocked by these "outsiders." The statement to the press declared that this moment signaled the beginning of the "Korean riots" and how they came to be known unfairly as the "irregular" faction.[76]

All these facts proclaimed by each side emerged from two very different realities for the actors involved. These two contradictory realities were the subject of heated debate in the legal case that consumed much of the year 1931. The court of law could only recognize one as the "objective truth."

THE VERDICT

Judge Cristy finally set a trial date for October 3, 1931. Rather than a trial by jury, however, Judge Cristy would decide the verdict himself. Filing a bill of equity against Shon et al., Pai et al. presented their arguments and evidence to Judge Cristy, which were outlined in a brief presented on behalf of Pai et al. by their attorneys, Thompson, Beebe, and Winn, on October 31, 1931. Their suit against Shon and his officers revolved around two basic issues: "have the respondents, the officers and directors of KNA, exceeded their authority, not under honest mistake, or have they been guilty of fraud and negligence in management of the affairs of the corporation, threatening or causing loss to the corporation?"[77]

On the first issue of exceeding their authority, Pai et al. reviewed the previously presented allegations against Shon et al. Referencing specific clauses in the constitution and by-laws, the petitioners accused Shon et al. of violating multiple provisions of the KNA constitution and by-laws in organizing the annual delegates convention in January 1931. They argued that the respondents had deliberately waived or amended certain provisions of the by-laws so that they could hold the annual convention with only delegates who favored their policies. Many of these delegates were delinquent in their membership dues and thus ineligible to attend and vote in the assembly. The petitioners asserted that these "handpicked" delegates participated at the expense of qualified members and delegates who were denied entry to the meeting. For these reasons, the annual delegates convention organized by Shon et al. was unlawful and invalid.[78]

Pai et al. then turned to charges of financial wrongdoing, singling out KNA Secretary/Treasurer Henry Kim. The petitioners claimed that Kim had unlawfully transferred the KNA bank account into his own name.[79] In addressing the issue of fraud and negligence, attorneys for Pai et al. discussed in detail numerous discrepancies in the financial records of the KNA, which had been submitted to the court earlier in April and subsequently audited by the petitioners. The attorneys for the petitioners dwelled on expenses that exceeded the KNA annual budget and the questionable bookkeeping practices of Henry Kim, pointing out his failure to record accurately and honestly the expenses in question. The petitioners concluded that Henry Kim and the other respondents were guilty of concealing their unauthorized use of the public funds of the KNA for their own personal use and advantage.[80]

Pai et al. determined that the evidence overwhelmingly indicated that the respondents were guilty of both exceeding their authority without honest mistake and fraud and negligence in the management of administrative affairs, thereby threatening or causing loss to the KNA. Citing a well-known legal precedent, the petitioners' attorneys argued that officers of a corporation found guilty of the aforementioned offenses were subject to immediate removal from office and could be sued by individual members of the corporation, on behalf of the majority, to recover any financial losses. Given the evidence, Pai et al. argued that they were entitled to relief on both.[81]

The respondents, Shon et al., took their turn responding to the charges contained in the petition against them. Once again, their testimony and arguments provided a completely different interpretation of the chain of events that led to what they perceived as their illegal ouster. On November 21, 1931, their attorney, Ray J. O'Brien, submitted a brief of their case to Judge Cristy.

The brief was extremely lengthy. It not only refuted each and every fact alleged by the petitioners, but also drew upon an exhaustive docket of legal precedents to challenge the legal reasoning of their opponents. The testimony and arguments of Shon et al. revolved around several assertions. First, they claimed that the petitioners had failed to establish the allegations of financial wrongdoing contained in their bill of equity. Second, there was no proof that the petitioners had sought or gained the consent and support of the KNA membership at large to file their case on behalf of the majority. Lastly, the petitioners could not bring suit upon the respondents on behalf of the KNA because Pai et al. were not members of the KNA in good standing at the time of the trial.[82]

On the charges of financial misappropriation, Shon et al. challenged the validity of the audit that yielded the alleged discrepancies stated by the petitioners. On cross examination, the individual responsible for the audit testified that he was not a certified public accountant and was an employee of an accountant firm hired by Syngman Rhee, whom O'Brien described as "the enemy of the respondents."[83] As such, the results of the audit could not be considered reliable or objective. O'Brien brought Henry Kim to the witness stand to account for each of the alleged discrepancies in the bookkeeping records of the KNA with O'Brien noting most as errors committed by the auditor.[84]

Henry Kim also testified that he put the KNA account under his own name due to widely circulating rumors that Rhee intended to appropriate KNA funds as his own. As a result, Kim explained that he had been authorized by the KNA board of directors to transfer the account to safeguard the assets of the KNA. Given the multiple disturbances caused by Rhee dating back to September 1930, Shon et al. argued that such measures were reasonable and necessary.[85]

The respondents then turned to the charges of holding an unlawful delegate assembly on January 12, 1931, one day before the "ouster." O'Brien asserted that there was no evidence that showed his clients had refused admission to any duly qualified delegate or that they prevented anyone's entry by force. He called to attention that petitioners Yil Chin Pai and Cha Moon Choo were both admitted to the assembly as qualified delegates, but they left the meeting on their own volition. As such, legal precedent stated that they could not "invoke the aid of the court for the purpose of contesting the delegates meeting, from which they voluntarily withdrew."[86] Petitioner Lee Eun Koo was denied entry because KNA records revealed that his district association from Maui was no longer eligible for representation at the annual convention.[87]

Given the confusion caused by the factional disputes at the time Shon et al. explained that admission passes were required to identify qualified members. The respondents asserted that in no way did they deny admission to any qualified delegate, even if they were unfavorably inclined toward the respondents and their policies. O'Brien stated that petitioners Pai Yil Chin and Choo Cha Moon were indisputably opposed to the actions and policies of President Shon and his cabinet. Yet, O'Brien pointed out, both men had testified to the court that the respondents had issued each of them admission passes to participate in the annual convention.[88] For those denied entry to the meeting O'Brien provided detailed records showing that the individuals had either failed to pay their member dues for 1930 at the time of the meeting or represented local associations that were no longer eligible to participate in the annual convention. On the latter, O'Brien cited specific provisions from the KNA by-laws that authorized the president and his cabinet to determine the status of local associations for representation at the annual delegates assembly.[89] In all, O'Brien concluded that KNA records indisputably demonstrated "all persons who were entitled to admission as delegates were permitted to attend and those who did not meet the requirements of the constitution and by-laws were correctly disqualified."[90]

Moreover, records indicated clearly that the petitioners had failed to pay their dues for 1931 and were therefore no longer members in good standing. Again invoking legal precedent, O'Brien argued that only members in good standing of a corporation at the time of the trial could file a bill of equity in the court of law. As a result, the petitioners had no legitimate standing in court and thus could not sue the respondents for damages.[91]

Based on the conclusive evidence presented, O'Brien concluded that Shon and his officers were fully entitled to complete their two-year terms, which were set to end in January 1932. As such, there was no need for new elections or new appointments as requested by the petitioners. According to O'Brien, Shon et al. had properly upheld the KNA constitution and by-laws in all incidences and therefore should be granted a ruling in their favor.[92]

After hearing the exhaustive testimony and arguments from both sides, Judge Cristy issued a decision on December 19, 1931. The judge ruled in favor of the respondents, Shon et al., clearing them of all the charges involving the embezzlement and misappropriation of public funds, organizing and holding an unlawful delegate convention, and tampering with KNA financial records. Judge Cristy based his decision on a close reading of the KNA constitution and by-laws, which he cited quite extensively in rendering his verdict. He found that the plaintiffs, Pai et al., had failed to provide conclusive proof to support their multiple allegations against Shon et al.[93] Dismissing the case on the grounds of lack of evidence, Judge Cristy declared:

> The record in this case shows that the officers have been through a very trying period, beset by hasty and unfounded accusations and by the efforts of persons who apparently were either misinformed or who were seeking to disrupt the organization. The record shows that the officers have made a bona fide effort to carry on the association within the spirit of the Constitution and By-laws. Whatever temporary enlargement of the By-laws may be indicated by the evidence appears from the record to have been reasonable and for the purpose of *preserving the corporation* [emphasis added in original text], rather than preserving the power of the respondents.[94]

In the end, Judge Cristy found the respondents' version of the facts in dispute to be most credible. In particular, Cristy's decision afforded credence to the respondents' claims and testimony that accused the petitioners of acting as part of a faction led by Syngman Rhee. Cristy concluded that the respondents' reading and interpretation of the KNA constitution and by-laws were correct and appropriate given the tense and hostile environment caused by the factional strife within the Korean community.[95]

CONCLUSION

The outcome of the 1931 court case had significant consequences for Koreans living in Hawai'i. Judge Cristy's verdict in favor of Shon et al., in essence, had indicted Syngman Rhee as the primary instigator of the disruptions within the KNA and the overall Korean community in Hawai'i. The widely publicized court decision severely damaged Rhee's reputation and position in and outside of the Korean community. Within six months, Rhee would leave Hawai'i in ignominy. New developments on the international stage also contributed to Rhee's sudden departure from Hawai'i. Japan's full-scale occupation of Manchuria in 1931, which elicited immediate international condemnation, renewed the activities of the Korean nationalist movement, including most notably the reorganization of the Korean Provisional Government with Kim Ku as president. Rhee also sought to resume his diplomatic activities by hastily departing

Hawai'i under duress for Geneva to petition the Korean cause before the League of Nations. Consequently, international concerns and issues would once again dominate the political activities of the Korean diaspora. These new circumstances ushered in significant changes for the Korean community of Hawai'i as new voices, new alliances, new leaders, and new strategies emerged throughout the 1930s.

While organizing across the diaspora expanded the resources available for the nationalist movement, it also broadened the scope and nature of factional disputes within the movement as clearly demonstrated in the legal battle of *Pai et al. v. Shon et al.* in 1931. The lengthy trial and final verdict of 1931 centered around contending interpretations over which side failed to comply with and uphold the by-laws of the KNA. At the same time, these local disputes were emblematic of larger struggles within the diaspora in determining the right to leadership. The battle over the interpretation of the KNA constitution and by-laws was in essence a battle over which group had properly upheld the laws of the state and was thus entitled to the right of governance. The KNA faced the challenge of trying to validate and perpetuate its legal status within the diaspora without a central authority such as the KPG to arbitrate over such disputes. As a result, the KNA appealed to another sovereign authority, the U.S. state, to help determine which group's interpretation of, and compliance with, the laws of the KNA were the most accurate and faithful.

Each side sincerely believed that they were correct and truthful in their legal claims. Yet, the court could only recognize one side of the facts and interpretations as the "objective truth." One cannot assume that only one point of view categorically represents the single objective truth, however. Multiple subjectivities create multiple realities, each "true" on its own terms. This was in large part the dilemma that continually confronted the Korean nationalist movement. As a diasporic political movement, the matrix of sites within the transnational network of the independence movement provided conditions for the emergence of multiple and at times contradictory subject positions, as a host of exile organizations each claimed to represent legitimately the national will of Koreans at home and abroad. Ultimately, however, this dilemma, endemic to diasporic politics, was one that could never be fully resolved.

NOTES

1. "Police Guard Korean Hall to Keep Peace," *Honolulu Advertiser,* January 15, 1931; "Korean Faction May Resort to Court Action," *Honolulu Advertiser,* January 16, 1931; "Outline from Their Own Record (Minutes) of the Irregulars' Convention of Delegate Assembly," Box 4, Folder 1, Hei Sop Chin Collection, Korean American Research Project, Department of Special Collections, University

of California, Los Angeles; D. Y. Shon et al., "The Case of the Korean National Association" (March 27, 1931), State Archives of Hawai'i, History and Miscellaneous.

2. "Korean Faction May Resort to Court Action," *Honolulu Advertiser,* January 16, 1931.

3. The original primary source materials are inconsistent in recording the personal names of Korean individuals. To maintain consistency throughout the text of this chapter, I use the transliteration of Korean personal names as written in the bulk of the original sources, which place the family surname of individuals at the end of the full name rather than the standard Korean practice of listing the family surname first. Whenever possible, the McCune-Reischauer system of romanizing Korean personal names is also provided and used thereafter.

4. "Outline from Their Own Record (Minutes) of the Irregulars' Convention of Delegate Assembly" and "The Case of the Korean National Association."

5. "Koreans Battle to Determine Official Staff," *Honolulu Advertiser,* January 14, 1931; "Police Guard Korean Hall to Keep Peace," *Honolulu Advertiser,* January 15, 1931.

6. "Korean Faction May Resort to Court Action," *Honolulu Advertiser,* January 16, 1931.

7. Ibid.

8. Ibid.

9. Ibid.

10. "Korean Row Coming Into Court Today," *Honolulu Advertiser,* January 24, 1931.

11. "Koreans' Private War No Concern of Judge Brooks," *Honolulu Advertiser,* January 26, 1931.

12. "Gun, Wrench Used as Rival Camps Battle," *Honolulu Advertiser,* January 28, 1931.

13. "Judge Scores Korean Feud Disorders," *Honolulu Advertiser,* January 28, 1931.

14. Ibid.

15. "Deportation of Rioters Threatened," *Honolulu Advertiser,* January 30, 1931.

16. Ibid.

17. Petition for Writ of Mandamus to the Circuit Court, First Judicial Circuit, Territory of Hawai'i, *Pai Yil Chin et al. v. D. Y. Shon et al.,* S.P. 170-1-170 (1931).

18. Ibid., 2–3.

19. Ibid., 3.

20. Ibid., 4–7.

21. Alternative Writ of Mandamus, ibid., 7–8.

22. Return to Alternative Writ of Mandamus, ibid., 2.

23. Ibid., 2–3.

24. Peremptory Writ of Mandamus, ibid.

25. Appeal and Notice of Appeal, ibid.

26. Korean immigrant appeals to U.S. state entities were not a new development. The diasporic dimensions of the Korean nationalist movement created opportunities for Koreans in the United States to participate in various political arenas within the U.S. polity. Further discussion of this point, however, is beyond the scope of this chapter. For more, see Richard S. Kim, "Korean Immigrant (Trans)Nationalism: Diaspora, Ethnicity, And State-Making, 1903–1945" (Ph.D. diss., University of Michigan, 2002).

27. Carter J. Eckert et al., *Korea Old and New: A History* (Seoul: Ilchokak Publishers and Korea Institute, Harvard University, 1990), 279–80; Ki-baik Lee, *A New History of Korea* (Cambridge, Mass.: Harvard University Press, 1984), 344.

28. Nym Wales and Kim San, *Song of Ariran: A Korean Communist in the Chinese Revolution* (San Francisco: Ramparts Press, 1941), 113–14.

29. For more on the complicated array of factional disputes within the KPG and their debilitating effect on the Korean independence movement, see Kim, "Korean Immigrant (Trans)Nationalism"; Byung Yool Ban, "Korean Nationalist Activities in the Russian Far East and North Chientao (1905–1921)" (Ph.D. diss., University of Hawai'i, 1996); Chong-sik Lee, *The Politics of Korean Nationalism* (Berkeley: University of California Press, 1963); Robert A. Scalapino and Chong-sik Lee, *Communism in Korea, Part I: The Movement* (Berkeley: University of California Press, 1972); Dae-Sook Suh, *The Korean Communist Movement, 1918–1948* (Princeton: Princeton University Press, 1967).

30. This is one of the defining characteristics of a diaspora. I draw upon the work of William Safran in my formulations of diaspora. Safran identifies several defining characteristics in discussing the concept of diaspora as it pertains to expatriate minority communities. Among those characteristics, he cites dispersal from an original homeland to at least two or more foreign regions; a collective sense of shared memories, cultural values, and historical experiences in relation to their original homeland; a collective commitment to the restoration of their homeland; and an ethnic group consciousness and solidarity based on real and/or imagined ties to their homeland. Safran argues that group experiences must incorporate all these aspects to some degree in distinguishing diasporas from other forms of migration. William Safran, "Diasporas in Modern Societies: Myths of Homeland and Return," *Diaspora* 1, no. 1 (Spring 1991): 83–99. For another useful and more extensive discussion of diaspora, see Robin Cohen, *Global Diasporas: An Introduction* (Seattle: University of Washington Press, 1997).

31. "Constitution and By-laws of the Korean National Association of Hawaii," 1, Box 4, Folder 1, Hei Sop Chin Collection, Korean American Research Project, Department of Special Collections, University of California, Los Angeles.

32. Ibid.

33. Petition on Writ of Quo Warranto to Circuit Court, First Judicial Circuit, Territory of Hawai'i, *Shon Duk Yin et al. v. Kim Chung Hyun and Choy Baik Yurl*, S.P. 171-1-171, (1931).

34. Ibid., 2–3.

35. Ibid., 4.

36. Ibid.

37. Ibid., 5.

38. Ibid.

39. Ibid.

40. Answer, *Shon Duk Yin et al. v. Kim Chung Hyun and Choy Baik Yurl.*

41. "Outline from Their Own Record (Minutes) of the Irregulars' Convention of Delegate Assembly," Box 4, Folder 1, Hei Sop Chin Collection, Korean American Research Project, Department of Special Collections, University of California, Los Angeles.

42. Ibid.

43. Answer, *Shon Duk Yin et al. v. Kim Chung Hyun and Choy Baik Yurl.*

44. Petition to Circuit Court, First Judicial Circuit, Territory of Hawai'i, *Pai Yil Chin et al. v. Shon Kuk Yin et al.* E3171, (1931), 1–2.

45. Ibid., 5–7.

46. Ibid., 2–3.

47. Ibid., 3–4.

48. Ibid., 4.

49. Ibid., 5.

50. Restraining Order, ibid.

51. Chambers Summons, ibid.

52. Receipts, ibid.

53. Answer, ibid.

54. Ibid., 2–3.

55. Ibid., 3.

56. Ibid., 4.

57. Ibid.

58. Ibid., 5.

59. Ibid., 6–10.

60. Henry Cu Kim, *The Writings of Henry Cu Kim: Autobiography with Commentaries on Syngman Rhee, Pak Yong-man, and Chong Sun-man*, ed. and trans. Dae-Sook Suh (Honolulu: University of Hawai'i Press, 1987), 230.

61. For more on the impact of these reforms on the political situation in Korea, see Michael Edson Robinson, *Cultural Nationalism in Colonial Korea, 1920–1925* (Seattle: University of Washington Press, 1988).

62. Kim, *The Writings of Henry Cu Kim,* 214.

63. Ibid., 215–18.

64. Ibid., 223.

65. D. Y. Shon et al., "The Case of the Korean National Association" (March 27, 1931), State Archives of Hawai'i, History and Miscellaneous.

66. Ibid., 5–6.

67. Ibid. and "Conflict of Theories," Hei Sop Chin Collection, Box 4: Folder 1.

68. "The Case of the Korean National Association," 6.

69. Ibid.

70. Kim, *The Writings of Henry Cu Kim*, 233–34.

71. Ibid., 235.

72. "Koreans Tell Their Story of Disorders," *Honolulu Advertiser*, February 23, 1931.

73. Ibid.

74. Ibid.; "The Case of the Korean National Association," 1.

75. Ibid.

76. Ibid.

77. Brief on Behalf of the Petitioners to Circuit Court, First Judicial Circuit, Territory of Hawai'i, *Pai Yil Chin et al. v. Shon Kuk Yin et al.* E3171, (1931), 1.

78. Ibid., 1–3.

79. Ibid., 2–3.

80. Ibid., 3–7.

81. Ibid., 7–8.

82. "Brief on Behalf of Respondents," ibid., 4–5.

83. Ibid., 7.

84. Ibid., 5–10.

85. Ibid., 29.

86. Ibid., 20.

87. Ibid., 11.

88. Ibid., 11–12.

89. Ibid., 19–22.

90. Ibid., 19.

91. Ibid., 26–27.

92. Ibid., 40–41.

93. Decision, ibid., 1–9.

94. Ibid., 9.

95. Ibid.

7

The Unification Movement of the Hawai'i Korean Community in the 1930s

To overcome national pain and humiliation, Koreans under Japanese colonial rule continued their struggle for independence. Along with efforts toward national independence, Koreans also struggled to establish internal harmony and solidarity among the various independence movements both in Korea and overseas. These efforts by the Korean independence movement toward establishing internal harmony are important, for such solidarity and unity of purpose were necessary for a more effective struggle toward achieving national independence.

With this in mind, this chapter examines the unification efforts of Koreans in Hawai'i during the 1930s. This chapter focuses on the decade of the 1930s, as it was during this period in particular that Koreans in Hawai'i struggled to consolidate the potential energy the national independence movement demanded.

Unification efforts by Korean nationalist groups during the 1930s were taking place not only in Hawai'i, but in China and North America as well.[1] Therefore, the nature and meaning of the Hawai'i Korean community's unification movement should be examined not simply as the efforts of an isolated local community, but in the context of an internationally led national independence movement. The primary focus of this chapter, however, will be on the unification movement of Koreans in Hawai'i.

Background To The Unification Movement

Situation of the Hawai'i Korean Community in the 1920s

As the enthusiasm of the March First Movement (1919) cooled, the Korean community in America in the 1920s began to splinter. In an attempt to bolster his own political base, Rhee, after returning from Shanghai, organized the Tongji-hoe (Dong Ji Hoi) with Min Ch'an-ho, An Hyǒn-gyǒng, and Yi Chong-gwan on July 21, 1921. On March 22, 1922, Rhee dissolved the Hawai'i branch of the Korean National Association (KNA) (Kungminhoe), in accordance with the "Declaration of the Law of Overseas Compatriots" of the Korean Provisional

Government (KPG) in Shanghai. In its place, Rhee organized the Korean Residents Association (Taehan'in Kyomindan; hereafter Kyomindan). In January 1923 Rhee formulated the by-laws of this new organization to favor himself, placing it under his personal authority. According to the new by-laws, the president and the vice president of the Kyomindan were to be chosen with the approval of the chairman of the Korean Commission (Kumi Wiwŏnhoe), which Rhee created and led in Washington, D.C., thus placing it effectively under Rhee's control. As a result, the Koreans in America, who had previously been united under the influence of the KNA, were now divided into two groups—those in Hawai'i under the Kyomindan and those in the mainland United States under the KNA with the national headquarters located in San Francisco.

The Hawai'i Korean community in the 1920s was itself divided into two groups—that of Rhee, which controlled both the Tongjihoe and Kyomindan, and that of Pak Yong-man (Young-Man Park), which was composed of members of the Korean National Independence League (KNIL) (Tae Chosŏn Tongnipdan). These two groups had been fighting with one another since 1915 and their reconciliation proved difficult. While visiting Hawai'i on July 8, 1925, Sŏ Chae-p'il (Philip Jaisohn) brought together leaders of the Korean community, including Pak Yong-man, Rhee, An Wŏn-gyu (Won-Kiu Ahn), Hyŏn Sun (Soon Hyun), Min Ch'an-ho (Chan-Ho Min), Kim Yŏng-gi (Kim Young-ki), and Hwang Sa-yong, at an informal meeting in Honolulu where they discussed the establishment of unity among Korean community leaders in Hawai'i. The meeting, however, did not go well, as those at the meeting could not come to a consensus,[2] indicating the extent of distrust among the Korean leaders in Hawai'i.

In the meantime, there were certain parties that belonged to neither of these two groups, and they began efforts at reconciliation. The mediating influence of these neutral parties grew greater in the late 1920s.

Formation of the Korean National Unification Promotion Association

It was in the 1920s that Koreans in Hawai'i first began to exert efforts to heal the divisions and disunity within the Korean independence movement in Hawai'i. As a direct result of these efforts, on February 16, 1928, twenty-nine leaders representing the Korean independence movement gathered and organized the Korean National Unification Promotion Association (Taehan Minjok T'ongil Ch'okchinhoe).[3] In March 1928, the association announced a statement of three general principles for the establishment of unity among Koreans, to which 166 signatories affixed their names. These three principles were:

1   To set a unified course in the independence movement by establishing unity among Koreans

2   To share responsibility for the accomplishment of national independence through the concentration of the resources and energy of all Koreans

3   To pursue the rebuilding of Korea with the ideals of all Koreans in mind[4]

The key point of the declaration was the call for unity among all Koreans toward the common goal of national independence.

The association appointed Ch'oe Ch'ang-dŏk as the administrative officer, Min Ch'an-ho to head the publicity office, and Yi Pok-ki as the parliamentarian. For the establishment of this unified front, the association elected its officers from among the members of all three representative groups: four from the KNIL,[5] six from the Kyomindan,[6] and ten from the third, unaffiliated group.[7] The association included the key leaders of the Korean community in Hawai'i —evidence that Hawai'i Koreans endeavored hard to establish unity among themselves.

The association disbanded, however, without accomplishing any meaningful activities not long after its first conference was held in Honolulu on May 21, 1928. There were two primary reasons for this. First, concerned largely with idealistic principles, it failed to develop any realistic activities or strategies for the accomplishment of unity. Second, with the sudden death of Park Yong-man in October 1928 (he was assassinated in China) members of the KNIL lost the leader around whom they had been united and thus the position of the KNIL became significantly weakened. Nevertheless, this association became a useful basis for Rhee's unity-building activities of the 1930s.

Formation of the Korean Association (Han'in Hyŏphoe)

Koreans in Hawai'i regained their zeal for the establishment of community solidarity in 1930. The Kwangju Student Demonstration against Japanese rule that took place in Korea on November 3, 1929, served as a catalyst that galvanized Koreans in America and elsewhere to reactivate their efforts at unity.[8]

In this atmosphere, former members of the KNIL, along with certain non-aligned parties, founded the Korean Association (Han'in Hyŏphoe) on January 13, 1930, for the purpose of exerting unified activities for regaining Korean independence. The founding members declared the following three principles, emphasizing the importance of "supporting the KPG as a true spirit of independence and as a way for unity":

1   To exert all efforts toward supporting the KPG in Shanghai

2   To fight to the last person

3   To accomplish the unity of the Independence Party[9]

These principles demonstrate that the Korean activists attempted to place all groups active in the struggle for national independence under the single direction of the KPG.

The Korean Association began with forty members with Cho Yong-ha as the chairman, Kim Yun-bae in charge of finance, and Kim Chin-ho as the secretary. Within two months its membership had grown from forty to more than eighty. Due to Rhee's personal activities, however, this new association was soon divided and disabled. Nevertheless, the founding of the Korean Association is significant in that it stimulated the Hawai'i Korean community of the 1930s to come together to promote unity among all the Koreans struggling for national independence.

Syngman Rhee's Activities in the Unification Movement

Revival of the Tongjihoe (Dong Ji Hoi) and its Unification Efforts

Upon Rhee's return to Hawai'i from a North American trip (from September 1929 to January 1930), he committed himself to the unity movement of the Korean community. During his trip, Rhee had hoped for strong financial support for the Tongjihoe, which was then going through a difficult time, but his expectations did not materialize due to the poor economic conditions of the Koreans, who were affected by the Great Depression.[10] This economic situation along with the Kwangju Student Demonstration galvanized the Korean community in Hawai'i to form the Korean Association in order to work for united action for Korean nationalistic causes. Rhee simply wanted to utilize such a development for his own political purposes. As previously mentioned, former members of the KNIL along with nonaffiliated parties had organized the Korean Association. Rhee, however, did not join them, wishing instead to establish his own political party and to place members under his personal control.

To this end, Rhee began to move actively to revive the Tongjihoe and at the same time tried to bring unity among Koreans centering around the Tongjihoe. Although the Tongjihoe was a private organization formed largely to support Rhee's activities, most of its work was being carried out through the Kyomindan, which had been reorganized under the statutes of the KPG in Shanghai. In fact, it was difficult to make a distinction in membership between the Tongjijoe and the Kyomindan, as they were both under the control of Rhee. For example, the Tongjihoe did not even have its own office until July 1930. Also founded by Rhee in 1913 the *Korean Pacific Magazine* (T'aep'yŏngyang chapchi) later became an organ of the Tongjihoe, but suspended its publication for a few years due to financial difficulties until February 1930, when it resumed again. Moreover, the Tongjihoe did not even have central organization. That Rhee decided to revitalize the Tongjihoe at the expense of the Kyomindan seems to suggest that Rhee might have thought the Tongjihoe was more useful for his personal activities than the Kyodmindan.

In order to revive the Tongjihoe, Rhee drew up the organization's governing statutes and platforms and used them as guidelines for its subsequent activities. In addition to justice, humanitarianism, and nonviolence (as manifested in the March First Movement), the Tongjihoe platforms subscribed to obedience to the organization and economic self-sufficiency.[11] Obedience to the organization of course meant loyalty to Rhee himself. For practical strategies, the revived organization asked first to achieve unity with an ambitious goal of recruiting one million Tongjihoe members; second, to recruit members with diverse ideas who would not cause conflict; third, to accept as members anyone who would agree with the goals of the Tongjihoe, regardless of social status, religion, or regional background; and fourth, to actually practice in rendering material support for Koreans so as to promote better living standards.[12]

With these objectives, Rhee continued to gather followers under the Tongjihoe. He worked on Kim Hyŏn-gu (Henry Cu Kim) and other key members of the Kyomindan to recognize the necessity of unity among Koreans, and used them for his own political ends. At first, he tried to attract former KNIL members into the Tongjihoe by professing his deep regret for the negative remarks and conduct he had previously committed against them and their leader Pak Yong-man. Rhee also expressed his sadness at the untimely and unfortunate death of Pak. Debunking rumor that Pak might have betrayed the Korean nationalists, Rhee strongly defended Pak as a man of great patriotism and integrity who would not sell his soul to the Japanese even for a huge sum of money. Rhee also expressed his personal regret that he had failed to amend his soured friendship with Pak before his death. Insisting there was no difference in the ultimate goals and ideals between himself and Pak, Rhee called for the joining of forces of the two organizations into one.[13] This gesture persuaded the core members of the KNIL such as Yi Sang-ho, Kim Yun-bae, Yi Wŏn-sun, and several others to join the Tongjihoe in the name of grand unity for Korean independence.

There was an impetus for unity under the Tongjihoe banner. In April 1930, two representatives each from the Kyomindan, KNIL, the Korean Association, and the Tongjihoe met and reached an agreement to bring unity to the Hawai'i Korean community under the Tongjihoe organization.[14] A social gathering held in June 1930 further enhanced the air of unity as some members of KNIL and others who maintained a neutral position attended this Tongjihoe meeting.[15] As a result, the Tongjihoe became more active and its membership began to grow.

As the influence of the Tongjihoe grew, Rhee called a Hawaii Tongjihoe Representative Conference from July 15 to 21, 1930, in an attempt to spur the movement for greater unity. Chicago representative Kim Wŏn-yong (Warren Y.

Kim) and Los Angeles representative Ch'oe Yŏng-gi attended the Conference, along with about eight hundred others. This Conference accepted the constitution of the Tongjihoe and clarified the legal relationship between the KPG and the Korean Commission by deciding to support the activities of the Korean Commission. It also confirmed the platform of the Tongjihoe, and recognized the Tongjihoe as the sole political organization of the Korean national independence movement in America.[16] Moreover, at the Conference it was decided to strengthen the Tongjihoe organization by creating a central board of directors, for which Rev. Yi Yong-jik (William Y. Lee) was chosen as the chairman, Kim Wŏn-yong as a standing member of the board and also in charge of finance, and Kim Hyŏn-gu, Kim Kyŏng-jun, Son Tŏk-in, and nine others as board members. The selection of these men indicates that on the surface there was a fair and even distribution among the board members of the Tongjihoe, the mainland U.S. representatives, the Kyomindan, KNIL, and the nonaligned.[17] It also demonstrates that the central board of the Tongjihoe represented the highest organ of both the Korean community in Hawai'i and the mainland United States.

With the reorganization that embraced diverse Korean groups, the Tongjihoe tried to represent itself as the sole legitimate organization for the Korean independence movement, which in turn stimulated the unity movement of the Koreans centering around the Tongjihoe. Rhee and the Tongjihoe must have been greatly encouraged by the success they achieved in their effort toward bringing unity to the Korean community.

Conflicts and Division

Contrary to its surface appearance of success in unifying the Korean community, in reality the Representative Conference failed to attain any substantial success. For one thing, the Tongjihoe initiated no new program to follow up the Conference. The list of the central board members was withheld for public announcement until September 26, a full two months after the Conference ended.[18] These facts suggest that there was discord during the Conference over Rhee's attempt to revive the Tongjihoe and his efforts at unification. In fact, before the Representative Conference was held, Rhee had collided with Yi Yong-jik over certain issues concerning the Korean Christian Church (Yi was a minister of the church that Rhee had founded in 1918) and had also begun a conflict with Kim Hyŏn-gu, who harbored suspicions that Rhee might be trying to disband the Kyomindan. Also, there were certain members within the Korean community and the KNIL who came to believe that the three platforms of the Tongjihoe might not be an appropriate guide for the independence movement. In addition, there was fear among members of the Kyomindan that Rhee's attempt to revitalize the Tongjihoe might lead to the dissolution of the Kyomindan.

Dissatisfaction with the Kyomindan exploded when the Representative Conference adopted a resolution to allow the Tongjihoe to take over work with Korean youth. The president of the Kyomindan, Son Tŏk-in, openly denounced such a move. Son declared that the youth program properly belonged to the Kyomindan, and Tongjihoe's attempt to develop its own youth program could only be regarded as an effort to emasculate the Kyomindan. Son then resigned his membership from the central board of directors of the Tongjihoe.[19]

The issue of the youth program was not the only cause for Kyomindan's unhappiness. It was hard for the Kyomindan to accept the claim by the Tongjihoe to be the sole representative organization of Koreans after it had been inactive for so long. The Kyomindan claimed that it alone was the true representative organization of all Koreans, as it had been chartered under the KPG, whereas the Tongjihoe was a mere private organization. The Kyomindan thus could not accept the decision of the Representative Conference on the position of the Tongjihoe as the sole representative of the Koreans. The Kyomindan regarded Rhee's move as an attempt to enhance the Tongjihoe position at the expense of the Kyomindan, which it viewed as violating the proper authority of the KPG. As conflict with Rhee increased, the Kyomindan criticized Rhee on the grounds of legitimacy under the laws of the KPG.

As Rhee became aware of the conflict he blamed Kim Hyŏn-gu as the source of all the troubles. At first Rhee tried to negotiate with Kim, but when things did not turn out as Rhee had wished, Rhee tried to force Kim to resign from his position as the Kyomindan's secretary and finance chief. Rhee mistakenly believed that by removing Kim his trouble with the Kyomindan would diminish. The Kyomindan, however, strongly opposed Rhee's move against Kim Hyŏn-gu and rallied behind Kim with an anti-Rhee campaign. This situation in turn led to a full-scale conflict between the Tongjihoe (who supported Rhee) and the Kyomindan (who opposed Rhee). The open conflict was fought over the issue of who truly represented the Koreans in Hawai'i; the conflict even led to court battles. After expensive litigation, the Kyomindan won the trial in the end. (For a detailed study of this court case, see Richard S. Kim's chapter in this book.) As a direct result of this conflict, the Kyomindan and the Tongjihoe became bitter rivals, and rancor between the two organizations remained deep, further polarizing the Korean community in Hawai'i.

The Nature and Significance of Syngman Rhee's Unification Movement

As mentioned previously, Rhee's attempts to unify the Korean community in Hawai'i failed. Moreover, rather than contributing to the cause of unity, they exacerbated differences and division. There are several reasons for this. First, Rhee neither suggested clear strategies toward unity nor defined his goals clearly. Second, his efforts to gain the public support of Koreans in Hawai'i were inadequate. Third, Rhee tried to use his unity movement largely to benefit his own interests and made no attempts to coordinate his work with that of the KPG, under whose authority the Kyomindan was organized. Fourth, Rhee demonstrated no serious willingness to embrace his opponents.

From these conflicts, Koreans in Hawai'i learned just how challenging and difficult it would be to accomplish unity. At the same time, they also learned that unity was needed for more effective struggle toward national independence. Even though Syngman Rhee's self-centered unity movement failed and caused deeper rifts within the Korean community, it nevertheless became a useful educational experience for the second unification movement that came in the late 1930s.

The Unification Movement of the KNA and the Tongjihoe

The failure of Rhee's efforts toward unification led to deep divisions within the Korean community, and new smaller organizations began to appear in Hawai'i. Koreans on the island of Kauai organized the Korean Unity Association (Han'in tanhaphoe) in April 1931.[20] The Federation of Young Koreans was organized in October 1931 to coordinate the activities of Korean youth in Hawai'i.[21] A secret organization called the Hawai'i Aeguktan (Hawai'i Patriotic Society) was set up, and the Society to Support the KPG (Imsi chŏngbu huwŏnhoe) was formed in the Wahiawa area in the same year.[22]

With the appearance of these new organizations the Kyomindan and the Tongjihoe tried to resume their independence activities. The Tongjihoe began to support the KPG[23] actively and committed itself to diplomatic activities of the Korean Commission in the aftermath of the "Manchurian Incident" of September 1931.[24] At the same time the Tongjihoe attempted to unite the varying independence groups. As a result, on April 9, 1933, the Tongjihoe was able to found the United Korean Association (Han'in yŏnhap hyŏbŭihoe) in cooperation with the Association to Support the KPG, the KNIL, the Tongsaenghoe (Mutual Livelihood Society), the Korean-American Club (Cho-Mi kurakbu), and the Wahiawa Kongdonghoe.[25] This newly organized Association set as its goal the harnessing of the Korean people's energy toward the goal of national independence and the joint discussion of strategies of such a movement. It also published a newsletter called the *Hyŏbŭi hoebo*.[26]

There is no documentation that tells us what activities the United Korean Association might have undertaken. It is, however, believed that with the merger of the KNIL and the Korean National Association (KNA) in 1934 the United Korean Association was dissolved. Even so, this Association helped the Tongjihoe recover its strength from the damage it had previously suffered due to its conflict with the Kyomindan. It also allowed it to become a central organization of the Korean community in Hawai'i.

The Kyomindan, on the other hand, had been suffering from deep financial difficulty, but in spite of its hardship it launched a series of diplomatic initiatives in the aftermath of the 1931 Manchurian Incident. The Kyomindan set up the Korean National Information Bureau (Sŏnjŏnbu) in October 1931 and appointed Chŏng Tu-ok (Doo-Ock Chung) as its director, Kim Hyŏn-gu as secretary, Ch'a Shin-ho as financial director, and Han Kil-su (Kilsoo Haan) as the public relations person.[27] The Information Bureau actively engaged in various diplomatic activities for the cause of Korean independence, including sending a petition for Korean independence to President Herbert Hoover and the League of Nations.[28]

Mobilized into action by the unity movement of Koreans in the mainland United States that began in January 1931, the Kyomindan reformed itself and tried to revitalize the KNA.[29] On January 16, 1933, the Kyomindan formally changed its name to the KNA, thereby officially resurrecting its old title on February 1, 1933. With the recovery of the original name, the KNA in fact freed itself from the influence of Syngman Rhee. Subsequently, the KNA suggested a merger with the KNIL. On October 15, 1934, with the exception of a small number of KNIL members, the two organizations formally came together.[30] Following this unification, the KNA also became an organization that played a central role in the Hawai'i Korean community.

From 1935 the Korean community in Hawai'i began to discuss the consolidation of the Tongjihoe and the KNA. In October 1935, Kim Sŏng-ok, Ch'oe Sŏn-ju, Cho Pyŏng-yo, and An Ch'ang-ho volunteered to serve as mediators for the reconciliation and eventual unification of the two associations, but their efforts came to naught, and antagonism between the two groups persisted.

First Unification Movement

In July 1937, the outbreak of the Sino-Japanese war prompted Hawai'i Koreans to unite their energies effectively toward achieving national independence. On July 15, 1937, the KPG in Shanghai announced the formation of a "Committee for Military Action." Following this, on August 1, 1937, the KPG promulgated its "Declaration for the Unification of the Overseas Korean Independence Movements," wherein it urged the unification of all Korean groups struggling for national independence. Through these efforts, the KPG greatly invigorated the independence movement, and the energy so displayed by the Korean independence movement in China also stimulated the Hawai'i Korean community as well.

Thereafter, the Korean community in Hawai'i threw their full material and spiritual support behind the KPG's independence efforts. In support of the KPG, the KNA collected money in the names of the "Blood Donation Fund" *(hyŏlsŏnggŭm)* and the "Patriotic Fund" *(aegukgŭm),*[31] while the Tongjihoe started a donation campaign for the "Independence Movement Fund" *(tongnip undonggŭm).*[32]

The KPG urged all independence movement organizations to cooperate and submit to its overall direction. The Korean community in Hawai'i responded positively to this request and gradually began to feel the necessity of more effectively supporting the KPG's independence efforts.[33] Korean public opinion also pushed the leaders of Hawai'i groups toward a united effort for the independence movement, prompting the KNA and the Tongjihoe to work for a unity campaign. In August 1937, the KNA proposed a unification of all Korean organizations without any precondition with the common goal of supporting the KPG and carrying out more effective efforts to obtain Korean independence. The Tongjihoe, on the other hand, initially called for greater coordination with the KNA, but upon learning of the KNA's position in favor of a merger, responded favorably to the KNA proposal. The two organizations selected a negotiating committee, whose efforts brought about the following agreement:

1   Under the mandate of bringing the two organizations together, the two organizations shall disband.

2   The two organizations shall work under their respective by-laws toward securing consent from various local organizations for the merger of the two organizations.

3   After securing consent from the local organizations, the two organizations shall take proper action toward doing away with their respective charters.

4   After taking the three steps mentioned above, the two organizations shall select five persons each who will then negotiate with various regional representatives to form a new united organization that will satisfy the desire of the Korean people for unity.[34]

After these agreements were reached, the KNA belatedly proposed an amendment on article 3, which called for doing away with the organizational charter. The KNA claimed that under its by-laws it could not remove the charter, which had been formally registered with the governmental authorities in Hawai'i. The Tongjihoe, however, opposed the KNA proposal: it insisted that the agreements should not be altered. The negotiations ended in failure and brought no result. Nevertheless, despite the failure to unify their efforts, open conflict between the two groups was avoided. Instead, the meaningful dialogues and debates they had exchanged provided an opportunity for the two groups to come to a better understanding of one another and helped alleviate lingering antagonism and anger between them. It was this experience of working together that laid the foundation for the next stage of efforts to unify the two rival organizations.

SECOND UNIFICATION MOVEMENT

After the failure of the first unification effort, there was no talk of unity for a while. The Korean community in Hawai'i now realized just how difficult the task of unification was, and yet there was little doubt in the community that unity was necessary for the success of their independence activities. Kim Ku, the president of the KPG, dispatched letters to the Korean communities in America and elsewhere, urging them to unite for national liberation from the Japanese. In a letter to Hwang In-hwan, the editor of the *Kungminbo (Korean National Herald)* dated June 20, 1938, Kim Ku urged all Koreans to unite to maximize their strength in the independence struggle. This letter had the effect of arousing the Hawai'i Korean community. Min Ch'an-ho, Ch'oe Ch'ang-dŏk, and Ch'oe Sŏn-ju, who belonged to the nonaffiliated group, invited the leaders of the KNA and the Tongjihoe to an informal gathering to discuss the unity of the two organizations (in July 1937).[35] After three informal meetings, the leaders of the KNA and the Tongjihoe agreed on the need to consolidate.

On August 14, 1938, the KNA then sent a formal letter to the Tongjihoe proposing they hold a meeting to discuss unification. The KNA and the Tongjihoe appointed three delegates from their respective organizations to form a taskforce to meet and discuss unification. A few from the nonaffiliate group were also included in the taskforce, suggesting this time the move embraced the entire Korean community. Beginning on August 23, 1938, five meetings were held to prepare the way for consolidation. The meetings produced the following agreement:

> The KNA and the Tongjihoe agree to unite while keeping their respective charters and statutes as legal institutions. In accordance with the agreement, a new name shall be selected based on public participation, by-laws shall be adopted, and officers of the new organization shall be chosen in open election. Members of the new organization shall enjoy equal rights and duties. If either organization needs to cancel its charter, it must obtain the approval of the officers of that organization who are incumbent as of 1938.[36]

After accepting this resolution, the two organizations agreed to a joint conference to discuss in more detail the process of consolidation. They held thirteen meetings from November 18 through December 7, 1938. In the hope of forming a united organization that would embrace not just the KNA and the Tonghijoe but all Korean organizations, the joint conference invited the Kauai Tanhaphoe (Kauai United Society) and the KNIL to take part in the discussions. On the pretext of difficulty in dispatching a delegation from Kauai, the Kauai Tanhaphoe refused to join while the KNIL attended only four sessions before abandoning the joint conference.[37] The KNIL refused to take part because KNIL members felt they were being left out of the unity movement being undertaken largely by the KNA and the Tongjihoe. The KNIL nevertheless made it clear that it too would join the unity movement if the KNA and the Tongjihoe successfully united.[38]

Initially, the joint conference for unification proceeded smoothly. At the third meeting it was agreed that the organizational structure after unification would be democratic.[39] At the fourth meeting it was agreed to continue the publication of the *Kungminbo* as it had been, while the *Korean Pacific Weekly (T'aep'yŏng'yang Chubo)* would be published in English.[40] At the seventh meeting it was decided the name of the united organization would be Taehaninhoe, or the Korean Association.[41]

As the series of meetings approached their conclusion, however, several problems arose, including the criteria for membership and how best to deal with each group's property and debts. The issue of membership in particular was closely related to the election of the future president and vice president. Which group would hold the higher position became a problem. Both sides began to discuss the election of a president and vice president at the ninth meeting, which was held on November 30, 1938. At the tenth meeting Cho Pyŏng-yo of the KNA and Kim Ŭi-jae of the Tongjihoe were advanced as candidates for president in the upcoming election.

Unfortunately, the two groups could not reach a final agreement concerning the method of election. The KNA insisted on allowing only those regular members who paid membership dues to vote, whereas the Tongjihoe insisted on allowing all Koreans in Hawai'i to vote without regard to their organizational affiliations. The reason behind this difference was that the KNA believed that it had an upper hand in the number of members, with 463 dues-paying members while the Tongjihoe maintained only about 80.[42] Although we cannot accept these KNA figures to be accurate, it appears that the KNA did have a larger membership than the Tongjihoe, as the Tongjihoe's membership records were inaccurate.

Tongjihoe's opposition to the KNA on the method of selecting the president of the new organization does not appear to have come merely from its disadvantage in membership. The Tongjihoe had maintained the position all along that the unification movement was to embrace all Korean organizations in Hawai'i.[43] Thus, its position was consistent with the principle the Tongjihoe had adopted for the unification movement. The KNA on the other hand insisted that voting rights should be given only to those who were dues-paying members. The KNA's position made it difficult to accept the demand of the Tongjihoe. Thus, KNA representative and acting chairman of the joint conference An Wŏn-gyu stated: "it will be impossible for the conference (for unity) to be successful unless the

Tongjihoe, which has smaller memberships, withdraws its position and makes a big concession (on the election method)."[44]

Both the KNA and the Tongjihoe held firm on the issue of how to select the officers of the new organization, each with a justifiable reason. But in the end they failed to reach a final agreement even though they had come so close to their objective of unification. In the final analysis, the issue was who would control the new organization once it was created. By not backing down on its own position, both sides sought to gain control of the new organization, and for this selfish interest both sides violated the principle of grand unity that they had vowed to adhere to. Thus, during the thirteenth and last meeting held on December 7, 1938, the joint conference for bringing unity in the Korean community ended without success. Despite this, the final meeting terminated peacefully and left hope for yet another attempt at unification in the future. The *Kungminbo* commented that it was not a complete split but only a temporary slowdown, and that further efforts would come in the future. It also reemphasized the need for all Koreans to unite in order to achieve national independence.[45]

This expressed hope became reality in the 1940s. In October 1940 five groups in Hawai'i gathered to found a federal organization called the United Korean Association. In addition, Korean groups in Hawai'i and North America held the "Overseas Korean Conference" and organized the United Korean Committee in America in 1941. It proved to be the final effort toward unification dating back to the 1930s. (For the United Korean Committee, see Chapter 9 of this book.)

CONCLUSION

I conclude this chapter by summarizing the nature and significance of the unification movement that took place in Hawai'i in the 1930s.

First, the unification movement led by Syngman Rhee failed and caused further division in the Hawai'i Korean community because Rhee had failed to follow a democratic process and allow people's participation. The experiences provided valuable lessons for the Korean community and for future unification efforts by the KNA and Tongjihoe in the 1930s, however.

Second, Rhee, who sowed division in the Hawai'i Korean community in the early 1930s, did not involve himself in the unification movement of the late 1930s. He left for diplomatic activity in Europe in November 1931 and did not return to Hawai'i until January 1935. Until he departed Hawai'i again in March 1939 to work for the Korean Commission in Washington, he remained inactive. He did not involve himself in any of the unification activities of the KNA and Tongjihoe in the late 1930s. Knowing that he himself had been largely responsible for the division in the Hawai'i Korean community in the early 1930s, he remained silent. He was also aware of the anti-Rhee mood of the Korean community. His silence did not necessarily mean that he was not interested in the unification movement; rather, he may have believed that he could best achieve the objective of unification by remaining silent.

Third, the Hawai'i Korean community's unification efforts were conducted toward the firm goal of achieving national independence. Therefore, the nature of the unification movement of the period must be understood not simply from the perspective of local unity but from the goal of achieving national independence.

Fourth, the Hawai'i Korean unification movement of the 1930s, though ultimately unsuccessful in the external sense, contributed greatly to the establishment of mutual understanding and a more mature structure and better communication among Koreans in Hawai'i. Upon this foundation the Hawai'i Korean community was able to finally achieve unification in the 1940s.

NOTES

This chapter was written in Korean and translated into English by Yŏng-ho Ch'oe.

1. For sources on the unification movement among Koreans in North America in the 1930s, consult the following: Hong Sŏn-p'yo (Hong Sun-Pyo), "1930-nyŏn-dae chaemi Han'in ŭi t'ong'il undong" (The Unification Movement among Koreans in America in the 1930s), Han'guk tongnip undongsa yŏn'gu (A Study of the History of the Korean Independence Movement) 10 (1996); "Yi Sŭng-man ŭi t'ong'il undong: 1930-nyŏn Hawai tongji Mip'o taep'yohoe rŭl chŏnhuro" (The Unification Movement of Syngman Rhee: Before and after the Hawai'i Tongjihoe Representative Conference of 1930), Han'guk tongnip undongsa yŏn'gu 11 (1997); "1930-nyŏndae huban Hawai haninŭi t'ong'il undong" (The Korean Unification Movement in Hawai'i of the Late 1930s), Han'guk tongnip undongsa yŏn'gu 12 (1998). For sources on the unification movement among Koreans in China, the reader may consult the following: Kang Man-gil, Chosŏn Minjok Hyŏngmyŏngdang kwa t'ong'il chŏnsŏn (The Korean National Revolutionary Party and the United Front) (Seoul: Hwap'yŏngsa, 1991); "Shingminji shidae ŭi minjok t'ongil chŏnsŏn undong" (The Movement for a National Unified Front during the Japanese Colonial Period), in Chaengchŏm Hanguk kŭnhyŏndaesa, vol. 4 (Seoul: Korean Modern and Contemporary History Research Center, 1994); Kim Hŏi-gon et al., Taehan Min'guk Imshi Chŏngbu ŭi chwa'u hapchak undong (The Korean Provisional Government's Unification Movement of the Right and Left) (Seoul: Han'ul, 1995).

2. Shinhan Minbo, August 6, 1925.

3. Hanminjok t'ong'ilŭl wihayŏ" (For Korean National Unity), Shinhan Minbo, March 15, 1928.

4. "Hanminjok t'ong'il ch'oksŏnghoe sŏn'ŏnsŏrŭl" (After Reading the Declara-

tion of the Korean National Unification Promotion Association), *Shinhan Minbo,* March 24, 1928.

5. Yi Pok-ki, Yi Wŏn-sun, Kim Yun-bae, and Yi Sang-ho (*Shinhan Minbo,* May 3, 1928).

6. Ch'oe Ch'ang-dŏk, Min Ch'an-ho, An Wŏn-gyu, Kim Yŏng-gi, Kim Yu-sil, and Chŏng In-su (ibid.).

7. Cho Yong-ha, O Un, An Ch'ang-ho, Mun Tto-ra, Hwang Hae-su, Chŏng Wŏn-myŏng, Pak Sang-ha, Hong Han-sik, An Hyŏn-gyŏng, and Chŏng Un-sŏ (ibid.).

8. "Editorial," *T'aep'yŏng'yang Chubo (Korean Pacific Weekly),* May 9, 1931.

9. "Hawai Hanin hyŏphoe chojik" (The Organization of the Hawaii Hanin Hyŏphoe), *Shinhan Minbo,* March 13, 1930.

10. Chŏng Tu-ok, "Chaemi Han'in tongnip undong shilgi," in *Han'gukhak yŏn'gu,* 3 "pŏlchip" (Inha Taehakkyo, 1991), 77–78.

11. "Tongjihoe 3 taejŏnggang" (The Three Great Principles of the Tongjihoe), *T'aep'yŏngyang chapchi (The Korean Pacific Magazine)* (September 1930).

12. "Tongjihoe Chorye" (The Tongjihoe Articles"), *T'aep'yŏngyang chapchi* (July 1930).

13. Syngman Rhee, "Hawai Han'in haptong" (For the Unity of Koreans in Hawai'i), *T'aep'yŏngyang chapchi* (May 1930). There was rumor that Pak Yong-man may have betrayed the Korean nationalists by being bought off by the Japanese, and Rhee in this article strongly defended Pak as a man of great patriotism and integrity.

14. *T'aep'yŏngyang chapchi* (May 1930): 48.

15. "Tongjihoe kanch'inhoe humun" (News of Tongjihoe Social Meeting), *T'aep'yŏngyang chapchi* (July 1930).

16. "Kongp'osŏ" (A Declaration), *T'aep'yŏngyang chapchi* (September 1930).

17. "Tongjihoe naejŏng" (Tongjihoe News), *Tongji pyŏlbo,* October 22, 1930.

18. "Kongmun" (Public Notice), *T'aep'yŏngyang chapchi* (September 1930).

19. "The Case of Korean National Association," 5.

20. Kim Wŏn-yong, *Chaemi Hanin osimnyŏnsa (A History of Fifty Years of Koreans in America)* (Reedly, Calif., 1959), 216; "Kawai huwŏnhoe" (The Kauai Supporters' Association), *Shinhan Minbo,* June 2, 1932.

21. "Ch'ŏng'nyŏn undong chinbo ch'agcha'k" (The Steady Advance of the Youth Movement), *Shinhan Minbo,* November 5, 1931.

22. "Imsijŏngbu Wahiawa huwŏnhoe" (Wahiawa Association to Support the KPG), *Shinhan Minbo,* June 2, 1932.

23. "Sasŏl" (editorial) and "Chung'ang isahoerok" (The minutes), *T'aep'yŏng'yang chubo (The Pacific Weekly),* December 19, 1931.

24. On Syngman Rhee's diplomatic activities in Geneva, see Pang Sŏn-ju, "1930-nyŏn chaemi han'in ŭi tongnip undong" (The Independence Movement

among Koreans in America in the 1930s), *Hanminjok Tongnip undongsa* (A History of the Korean People's Independence Movement) 8 (1990): 437–48; Yu Yŏng-ik (Young-ick Lew), *Yi Sŭng-manŭi samgwa kkum* (The Life and Dreams of Syngman Rhee) (Seoul: Chung'ang Ilbosa, 1996), 174–88.

25. *Shinhan Minbo*, June 29, 1933.

26. *Shinhan Minbo*, August 10, 1933.

27. Chŏng Tu-ok, "Chaemi Han'in tongnip undong shilgi," 81.

28. Kuksa P'yŏnch'anuiwŏnhoe, ed., *Han'guk tongnip undongsa charyojip* (A Collection of Documents relating to the History of the Korean Independence Movement) (Seoul, 1975), 7:1011–30.

29. For the movement to revitalize the KNA, see Chŏng Tu-ok's articles in *Kungminbo*, May 6 and 13, 1931.

30. Still, the KNIL's organization was not dissolved. *Shinhan Minbo*, November 8, 1934.

31. *Kungminbo* (The Korean National Herald), August 11 and 18, 1937.

32. *T'aep'yŏng'yang Chubo (Korean Pacific Weekly)*, January 15, 1938.

33. *Kungminbo*, September 29, 1937.

34. *Kungminbo*, October 10, 1937.

35. "Hapdongjusŏnŭi chinhaeng" (Progress in Efforts toward Unification), *Kungminbo*, August 17, 1938.

36. "Che 5ch'a hoeŭi" (The fifth meeting), *Kungminbo*, September 14, 1938.

37. *Kungminbo*, September 14 and November 23, 1938.

38. "Che 6ch'a sokhoe" (The sixth meeting), *Kungminbo*, November 30, 1938.

39. "Che 3ch'a sokhoe" (The third meeting), *Kungminbo*, November 23, 1938.

40. "Che 4ch'a sokhoe" (The fourth meeting), *Kungminbo*, November 23, 1938.

41. "Irŭmgwa silsang" (Name and Reality), *Kungminbo*, November 30, 1938.

42. "Editorial," *Kungminbo*, December 10, 1938. But Tongjihoe membership had once reached about three hundred.

43. This point is clearly outlined in one of the Tongjihoe's resolutions; see *T'aep'yŏngyang chubo*, November 26, 1938.

44. *T'aep'yŏngyang chubo*, December 17, 1938.

45. "Editorial," *Kungminbo*, December 14, 1938.

8

How Koreans Repealed Their "Enemy Alien" Status
Korean Americans' Identity, Culture, and National Pride
in Wartime Hawai'i

WORLD WAR II was a race war. For Americans, it was a race war against the Japanese. Outraged by the surprise Japanese aggression at Pearl Harbor on December 7, 1941, the American people, along with Congress, fully supported President Franklin Roosevelt in declaring war against Japan. Americans, public officials and ordinary citizens alike, knew very little about the Japanese and their culture, and this unfamiliarity and ignorance helped foster fear and racism. Americans readily ascribed notorious and inhumane—even beast-like— qualities to the Japanese as their natural and inherent characteristics. As historian John Dower convincingly documents in his book, *War Without Mercy: Race and Power in the Pacific War,* this racist attitude toward the Japanese played itself out on the battlefront, resulting in an especially cruel and violent war in the Pacific.[1] On the home front, the most public display of racism against the Japanese was the unprecedented internment of 120,000 Japanese aliens and Americans of Japanese ancestry living in the United States.[2] This was one of the most racist actions taken by the American government against its own citizens, violating the constitutional rights of Japanese Americans. Something about the Japanese led the American people beyond reasonable hatred of the enemy. The source of this unreasonable hatred partially arose from the fact that the Japanese were Orientals (as Asians were then called)—a foreign race from the East whose culture and traits were vastly different from those of such European enemies as the Germans and Italians.[3]

Within this framework, race became a crucial factor in the experience not only of Japanese and Japanese Americans, but of all Asians and Asian Americans living in the United States during World War II. American racism was directed specifically at the Japanese, but this racism affected all Asians and Asian Americans who looked similar to the Japanese. In the public eye, Japanese Americans were easily identifiable because of their physical appearance, and although other Asian Americans of non-Japanese ancestry lived in the United States at the time, Americans often could not tell the difference or make distinctions.

Thanks to many historians of the Japanese internment and former internees who subsequently wrote about their experience, the hardship and degradation Japanese Americans endured in the United States during World War II is well documented. Some historians have addressed the legal issues of the evacuation of the Japanese while others have concentrated on the social injustices of the internment. All, however, focus exclusively on the experiences of Japanese Americans and mention virtually nothing of other Asian Americans living in the United States.[4]

Scholars of Asian immigration who discuss World War II and its impact on immigrants from Asian countries do not give this topic the full attention it deserves. Their treatment of the issue is brief, as it is usually only a segment of their larger study, and their discussion most often highlights the positive changes World War II brought Asian immigrants and their children. Thus, historians have conventionally dubbed American entrance to World War II as "the watershed" year of opportunities for Asian Americans.[5] There is no denying that in the name of wartime mobilization, Asian Americans served in the armed forces for the first time and acquired jobs hitherto closed to them. But Asian Americans were not the only group of people who enjoyed marginal economic gain during World War II. Due to increased wartime production, other Americans on the bottom rung of the socioeconomic ladder also found better-paying jobs. By emphasizing economic mobility, historians of Asian immigration have failed to take into consideration that Asian Americans, by virtue of their looks and racial affiliation with Japanese Americans, became the central target of American racism as the United States entered the war. Therefore, we need to frame World War II and Japanese internment as a decisive instance of racism affecting all Asians and Asian Americans living in the United States.

In viewing Japanese internment from this angle, I do not mean to disparage the injustice and inhumanity that Japanese and Japanese Americans endured. Nor do I wish to imply that Asians and Asian Americans somehow stood on a common racial ground or shared a strong racial identity in the United States during World War II. Rather, by insisting that we broaden the examination of American racism directed at the Japanese to other Asians and Asian Americans, I am arguing that since Asians and Asian Americans were often lumped together and mistaken for Japanese, they were forced to confront a racial identity imposed upon them by the dominant culture. Thus, how non-Japanese Asians and Asian Americans coped with this time of newly exacerbated hatred toward people who looked just like them and how they protested this racism to which they were subjected by virtue of their physical appearance are important questions not yet fully addressed.

My chapter seeks to answer these questions through an investigation of one such group's experience: Koreans living in Hawai'i and the continental United

States during World War II.[6] Koreans make an interesting case study, for they found themselves in a peculiar position on the brink of America's official entry into the war. Because Korea was under Japanese rule at the time of the American declaration of war against Japan and had been since 1910, Koreans were officially considered subjects of Japan. Thus, despite their long history of hatred toward the Japanese for subjecting Korea to over thirty years of harsh colonial rule, Koreans now faced de facto and de jure association with the Japanese: legally, they were classified as Japanese and enemy aliens, and their physical appearance often led to a mistaken identification as Japanese. In this predicament, Koreans in Hawai'i sought freedom from their forced identification with the Japanese as well as the independence of their homeland, Korea. The goal of this chapter is three-fold. I first untangle the complex history of the Korean enemy alien status and its impact on the lives of Koreans in Hawai'i. I then examine the rationale U.S. officials used to justify Korean enemy alien status. Finally, I analyze the strategies the Korean community employed in their struggle to escape unscathed from racism against the Japanese on the home front during World War II.

KOREANS AS ENEMY ALIENS

In the February 2, 1942, issue of *Time* magazine, the editors declared, "Koreans have the unique distinction of getting on Japanese nerves."[7] This statement, despite its unsubstantiated generalization, was much needed and welcomed by the Korean communities in Hawai'i and the continental United States. After American entry into World War II following the attack on Pearl Harbor on December 7, 1941, Koreans faced what they considered a humiliating fate. Even though they were allowed to register as Koreans under the Alien Registration Act of 1940, they were classified as subjects of Japan and, therefore, enemy aliens. Unlikely Japanese sympathizers, Koreans found themselves in the strange category of loyal Japanese subjects. If anything, Koreans hoped for Japanese defeat, for they believed this would lead to Korean independence.

The development of Korean enemy alien status has a complicated, if confusing, history. It is important to note that from the onset of the war Attorney General Francis Biddle and the Department of Justice made a distinction between the *citizens* and *subjects* of Germany, Italy, and Japan. On January 26, 1942, the Department of Justice announced that Austrians, Austro-Hungarians, and Koreans—all enemy aliens by virtue of their mother country's colonized state—were exempt from having to apply for a Certificate of Identification if they had registered as their native citizenship under the Alien Registration Act of 1940 and "provided that such persons have not at any time voluntarily become German, Italian, or Japanese citizens or subjects."[8] Short of granting them friendly alien status, Attorney General Biddle made an indirect acknowledgment that he and the Department of Justice were aware that Austrians, Austro-Hungarians, and Koreans were Germans and Japanese only by circumstances.

This acknowledgment translated into something more concrete when Attorney General Biddle lifted the restrictions imposed upon enemy aliens by the Department of Justice for subjects of the Axis Powers on February 9, 1942: "Exempt from restrictions imposed upon alien enemies are: Austrians, Austro-Hungarians and Koreans who registered as such under the Alien Registration Act of 1940 and who have not since that time voluntarily become citizens or subjects of Germany, Italy, or Japan."[9] Biddle quickly added that these newly exempt nationals were still "subject to arrest and detention as enemy aliens if at any time their apprehension is regarded as necessary to maintain national security."[10]

While this was great news for Koreans, any celebration was premature. This new ruling only applied to Koreans on the U.S. mainland, Puerto Rico, and the Virgin Islands, excluding the large majority of Koreans living in Hawai'i.[11] Because Hawai'i was under martial law immediately after Pearl Harbor, the final word on Hawaiian affairs belonged to the military governor of Hawai'i. Thus, although Koreans on the U.S. mainland were exempt from the restrictions on enemy aliens after February 9, 1942, Koreans in Hawai'i, who made up the majority of the Korean population, still faced the same restrictions as the Japanese. Furthermore, all Koreans, in both Hawai'i and the continental United States, were still considered subjects of Japan and remained enemy aliens, albeit only in name for U.S. mainland Koreans.

The irony of the situation was almost intolerable for Koreans in Hawai'i. Sharing physical characteristics with the Japanese could not be helped, but legal classification as "Japanese," Koreans believed, could surely be changed if U.S. officials understood the history of Korean enmity toward their Japanese conquerors. Furthermore, to recognize Koreans as enemies of Japan, not the United States, would only be fair and right. An editorial in the February 25, 1942, issue of the *Korean National Herald-Pacific Weekly* filed a polite, poignant complaint in English about the Korean predicament:[12]

> If the Korean is an enemy of Japan, that which he is, he should be welcomed as a friend of the allied nations. The fact that every Korean born is an enemy born for Japan is evidenced by the continuous stationing of Japan's best armed forces within the Korean peninsula at strategic points of large Korean population. And Japan has never trusted the Koreans inasmuch as they hate the Japanese.
>
> Since December 7, the Korean here is between the devil and the deep sea for the reason that the United States considers him a subject of

Japan, which the Korean resents as an injustice to his true status; and he had never renounced his national heritage in line of a Japanese subject.

In China and Russia the Korean is not considered as a Japanese and he has proved himself worthy of their sympathy and encouragement for his national aspirations. A free Korean army composed of exiled Koreans in conquered territories is fighting side by side with the Chinese and allied forces in the Far East. Their number is yet small but their fighting valor and tactics against the enemy Japan have been recognized in admiration.

What is the status of a Korean in the United States? Is he an enemy alien? Has any Korean ever been in Japanese espionage or in subversive activities against the land where he makes his home and rears his children as true Americans?

Since 1903 the Koreans came here and have been classified as Koreans. In the National census they were enumerated as distinct nationals. In the time of national crisis, the Koreans as a minority do not desire to burden the Washington and local authorities with their complaint for an honorable and just clarification. But they do hope with almost an avidity that the ambiguity of their present status be speedily clarified so as to keep up their morale.[13]

Using words carefully chosen not to offend the American officials, Koreans made their plea for clarification of their status and reiterated their commitment to aiding the United States in defeating Japan. The editors specifically addressed the issue of enemy alien status not being lifted for Koreans in Hawai'i, as residents of a territory of the United States under martial law, but the crux of the complaint lay in having to share the same identity with the Japanese for Koreans in both Hawai'i and the continental United States.

This forced identification with the Japanese, and the consequent humiliation for Koreans, went beyond the legal classification. Indeed, more than any inconveniences and stigma attached to being labeled an enemy alien, what Koreans protested the most was being put in the same category with the Japanese. Even the slightest implication that Koreans were Japanese, or that they shared common goals, was a serious insult to their national pride and a mockery of their sorrow at losing Korea to Japan. The daily mistaken identity as Japanese was even harder to endure than the legal classification because of its pervasiveness. The abuses Koreans suffered for being mistaken as Japanese were usually verbal, but sometimes physical violence occurred. Carl Chung Lim of California, for example, had a brick thrown through the window of his gift shop. When he filed a complaint with the Justice Department, he received "a letter of sympathy" explaining that "inasmuch as people cannot tell the difference between a Korean and a Jap such things are bound to happen."[14]

As enemy aliens in Hawai'i, Koreans were denied many rights, some significant and others minor. Lt. Gen. Walter C. Short, commander of the Army's
Hawaiian Department, issued General Orders No. 5 prohibiting the following
activities for enemy aliens:

> unseemly behavior in public; possession or use of firearms, weapons or
> implements of war or component parts thereof, ammunition, bombs,
> explosives or material used in the manufacture of explosives, short-wave
> radio receiving sets, transmitting sets, signal devices, codes or ciphers,
> cameras, papers, documents or books in which there may be invisible
> writing; photograph, sketch, picture, drawing, map or graphical repre-
> sentation of any military or naval installation or equipment or of any
> arms, ammunition, implements of war, advice or thing used or intended
> to be used in the combat equipment of the land or naval forces of the
> United States of any military or naval post, camp, or station; flight in the
> air in any aircraft, balloon, or flying machine of any sort, whether owned
> governmentally or commercially, except upon written authority of the
> Provost Marshal; change of abode or occupation or travel without per-
> mission; any anti-government proclamation or activity.[15]

Unofficially, Koreans were exempt from some minor restrictions, for local
authorities did distinguish between the Japanese and Koreans in Hawai'i. In a
letter to a Korean leader, Secretary of War Henry Stimson noted, "The Com-
manding General of the Hawaiian Department has advised me that the relations
between the military authorities and the members of the Korean community in
Hawaii have been very satisfactory." "As a consequence of the spirit of cooperation of the Korean nationals in Hawaii," he added, "many privileges have been
granted to them not generally granted to alien Japanese."[16] No arrests were
made, for example, if Koreans possessed cameras or shortwave radios, and
Koreans could work on the waterfront, which was prohibited for the Japanese.[17]

Koreans still suffered, however, from some of the more inconvenient restrictions affecting their day-to-day activities. One of the memos from Military Governor Robert C. Richardson Jr. noted that "it has been the consistent policy of
the Military Governor to classify alien Koreans as enemy aliens for the purpose
of the curfew law, the possession of explosives, arms, and ammunition and radio
transmitting sets, etc., all of which have been considered by both Navy and
Army Intelligence essential restrictions in the interest of internal security."[18] In
complying with the curfew laws, Koreans had to be off the streets during blackout hours, which began earlier than the curfew for the general population. The
blackout and curfew hours for both the general public and enemy aliens were
from 6:00 p.m. to 6:00 a.m. initially. Then the beginning of the curfew hours
for the general public was changed to 9:00 p.m. in February 1942, and again to

10:00 p.m. in May 1942. Blackout hours varied from month to month in accordance with the sunset. As the blackout hours were earlier than the curfew for the general public, Koreans, as enemy aliens, had to carry a special permit after the blackout hours. So, in effect, the blackout and curfew hours were the same for enemy aliens like Koreans and Japanese.[19] As one article in the *Korean National Herald-Pacific Weekly* indicated, observing early curfew and blackout hours significantly shortened and altered their antecedent daily schedule. The author of the article sarcastically complained: "And it's pretty hard to grope blindly with the walls of single room as the confines of nightly wandering—and then you've got to fight to sleep. Who wouldn't, going to bed by seven or eight? And, honestly, we believe the sheep we've counted these last few weeks must be more than the stars we've aimlessly watched when slumber was far beyond and out of reach."[20] Koreans also lacked the right to purchase some common items like liquor, drugs, and medical supplies. They had to obtain a special permit before they could buy them.[21] Most Koreans complied, however grudgingly, with the restrictions put upon them as enemy aliens, but a curfew violation by a Korean leader would open up the question of why Koreans in Hawai'i should continue to be subjected to the same restrictions placed upon Japanese when the U.S. Department of Justice had deemed it safe and logical to lift them from Koreans in the continental United States.

CURFEW VIOLATION AND IMPENDING JUSTIFICATION OF KOREAN ENEMY ALIEN STATUS IN HAWAI'I

During the trying time of being classified as enemy aliens and enduring the inconveniences and shame that followed, the editors of the *Korean National Herald-Pacific Weekly* encouraged their fellow Koreans to abide by all the rules: "Let us be careful now more than ever not to violate any of the laws and avoid any incidents that may bring shame to our people."[22] Korean leaders in Hawai'i believed it was in their best interest not to give the U.S. officials any reason to suspect they were engaged in subversive activities or that they were not fully supportive of the U.S. war efforts. For the most part, Koreans won the sympathy of the local and U.S. officials as law-abiding residents of Hawai'i. An arrest of one Korean created a legal as well as political focal point around which Koreans and other supporters rallied, however.

On March 10, 1943, Korean alien Syung Woon Sohn (Son Sŏng-un) was arrested for being on the street without a pass after the curfew hours after his car broke down on Liliha Street. It was only 8:15 p.m., and had he been a regular Hawai'i resident he would not have been violating any law. As an enemy alien, however, Sohn was arrested since it was after the blackout time of 7:45 p.m. Sohn had not planned on being out after the curfew hours and, thus, did not have a special permit with him. Two police officers arrested him, and the case of Syung Woon Sohn was heard in the provost court of Hawai'i on March 29, 1943.[23] Lt. Col. Moe D. Baroff, provost judge, ruled Sohn guilty of curfew violation as an enemy alien and fined him $10 and suspended payment on April 30, 1943.[24] Col. Baroff stated that since the military governor's office had not issued any statement changing the status of Koreans from enemy to friendly aliens, he was required to find Sohn guilty as charged.[25] The $10 penalty was not by any stretch of the imagination severe, but the ruling in this case and upholding of the sentence by the military governor triggered a ripple of protests from the leaders and friends of the Hawai'i Korean community and raised the question of why Koreans in Hawai'i should continue to be subjected to the same restrictions placed upon Japanese.

The question at hand, whether or not Attorney General Biddle's exemption of the restrictions on Koreans in the continental United States should apply to Koreans in Hawai'i, was sufficiently weighty to involve the president of the United States. Sympathetic Iowa Democratic Senator Guy Gillette sent a letter dated May 11, 1943, to President Franklin Roosevelt, which began with the statement, "I deem the situation of enough importance to justify this letter to you." He reminded the president of the absurdity of accusing Koreans of loyalty to Japan:

> I know that you are as fully cognizant as any of us who have been particularly interested in the Koreans that these people have been not only fully loyal to the United States but in this war situation have rendered timely and worthwhile aid to the United States and her interests. They are bitterly opposed to Japan and her government. They are avidly hungry for the restoration of their Nation to an independent status. Thousands of them are fighting with the Chinese armies and tens of thousands are aiding in every possible way outside of the armed services of the allies. They are not Japanese citizens excepting on claim of Japan. They do not consider themselves so, nor do they render homage or assistance to Japan as citizens of that country excepting under compulsion that becomes irresistible.
>
> To list these Koreans who are resident among us as enemy aliens simply because their Nation had been destroyed as an independent entity by Japan is to attach to them a stigma which they do not deserve and might possibly impede assistance which they have been giving and desire to continue giving to the United States.[26]

Thus, the senator first tried to appeal to the president on the merits of justice alone in granting Koreans in Hawai'i friendly alien status. Then he proceeded to remind him that to do so was also in the best interest of the United States, lest Koreans withdraw their support for the United States out of their frustration and feelings of having been victims of injustice.

Korean leaders rushed to file complaints regarding the Sohn case and tried to use this incident as propaganda for repealing enemy alien status for all Koreans. Syngman Rhee's letter to Secretary of War Henry Stimson on May 17, 1943, called for U.S. officials to devote "urgent attention to the legal status of the Korean people in the United States, including Hawai'i." On April 30, 1942, Stimson had sent a letter to Rhee promising to lift the enemy alien restrictions only for those Koreans in Hawai'i who were in the military service. The letter read in part:

> The War Department has issued instructions to all field commanders to inform all concerned that Koreans who registered as such under the Alien Registration Act of 1940 and who have not, since that time, voluntarily become citizens or subjects of enemy nations, shall be exempt from restrictions imposed upon enemy aliens. Field commanders have been directed to examine into the handling of the matters brought out in your communication and to take immediate action to correct any injustices done to your countrymen and their descendants.[27]

Manipulating the content and purpose of this letter, Rhee urged Stimson to overturn the ruling in the Sohn case.

Rhee also raised the issue of the military governor of Hawai'i overriding the decision of the Department of Justice, calling it "a clear case of conflicting orders, not only between the civil and military authorities, but between the military authorities also, creating a grave situation in a time of world crisis." His strategy also included pointing out the illogicality of classifying Koreans as enemy aliens given the historical animosity Koreans had harbored against the Japanese:

> The Japanese promise the Koreans and all other conquered peoples of the Orient every benefit of the so-called "co-prosperity" in their attempts to win them over. Why the military authorities in Hawaii should insult and alienate the national sentiment of the Korean people is beyond understanding. The fact that the Koreans are the worst enemies that Japan has in all the world is proverbial. They are the only people who defeated Japan not once but many times in the past. They are the first victims of Japanese military aggression, and as such they have suffered more than any other conquered people of Europe and Asia. They have been fighting the Japanese singlehandedly ever since 1905.

Finally, Rhee reemphasized that "every Korean will grab the first chance, if it is ever given, to fight for the United States," because "by fighting for the United States he can fight for the freedom of his own nation."[28]

Another, less publicized, curfew violation committed by a Korean woman named Mrs. Do Kyung Lee drew even more protest. Rev. Peong Koo Yoon (Yun Pyŏng-gu), the general director of the Society of Soldiers' and Sailors' Relatives and Friends in Los Angeles, wrote to Secretary of War Henry Stimson and made an emotional appeal to the secretary: "To us Koreans, there is nothing so unjust as this ruling of the Honolulu Provost Judge because of the fact we consider Koreans in this country are no more alien enemies than the Poles, the Hollanders, and the French in this country whose fellow-countrymen in their native countries are conquered and ruled by Germany." Here, he did not explicitly say it, but Rev. Yoon implicitly called attention to American racism behind insisting that Koreans in Hawai'i were subjected to the same enemy alien restrictions as the Japanese, while European subjects of the Axis Powers escaped unscathed.

Rev. Yoon also claimed Koreans' unique position to despise and fight the Japanese due to the history of colonization of their motherland:

> As you know, Korea is the first victim of Japan's ruthless conquest. That Japan's cold-blooded method of subjugation in Korea in the past thirty three years has made Koreans submissive outwardly but it has never conquered the hearts nor the spirit of the Koreans. On the contrary, Japan's guns and swords, which have destroyed countless Koreans, have made Koreans hate Japan as an eternal enemy.

Therefore, Rev. Yoon argued, as many others had, it was only logical and just that Koreans be granted the friendly alien status they deserved:

> To such bleeding and tortured but heroic Koreans in Asia, and her sons and daughters in America, sympathy rather than the stigma of an enemy alien should be shown by the lovers of justice, like you and the President of the United States. Therefore, we bring the aforesaid case to your attention with hope and prayer that after careful review of the Koreans' status of Hawai'i in the light of justice and mercy, your Department may proclaim Koreans no more as enemy aliens there.[29]

Koreans in Hawai'i, thus, counted on and drew support from Koreans in the continental United States, who, even though they were not personally affected, cared about the legal status of their fellow Koreans in Hawai'i and the conditions under which they lived during the time of national crisis. But all the protests from residents of both Hawai'i and the continental United States produced no positive results. When Sohn's lawyer, Willson Moore, appealed the verdict, Delos C. Emmons, then military governor of the Territory of Hawai'i, stated pointblank that "the findings and judgment of the Provost Court are sustained" without offering further justification.[30]

Clearly, the officials of the U.S. Justice Department and the Office of Military Governor of Hawai'i were not unaware of Koreans' hatred toward the Japanese. Why, then, did they still insist on keeping the enemy alien status for Koreans and enforce certain restrictions on Koreans in Hawai'i? In the same way that American officials justified Japanese internment as "military necessity," military officers in charge of Hawai'i used the same rhetoric of national security to sustain the enemy alien status of Koreans in Hawai'i. To otherwise categorize these people who had apparent ties with the Japanese, the argument went, would be a threat to national security.

In the name of national security American Army and Navy Intelligence, along with the Federal Bureau of Investigation (FBI), spent a great deal of time and effort in monitoring the activities of Koreans in both Hawai'i and the continental United States.[31] After the Sohn case, U.S. officials sought advice from the Military Governor's Office. In a memo to Assistant Secretary of War John McCloy, dated May 19, 1943, a Hawaiian official stated that "Koreans as a class are generally recognized to possess an intelligent and crafty character and are regarded as shrewd and unscrupulous opportunists who have been used as spies by the Japanese in the past and it would seem natural and logical for the Japanese to employ Koreans as espionage agents."[32]

Another rationale arguing why Koreans should remain enemy aliens was offered by Robert Richardson Jr., who had succeeded Delos Emmons as the military governor of Hawai'i. In a memo to the assistant chief of staff of the War Department, Richardson stood by his office's decision not to adopt Attorney General Biddle's exemption of enemy alien restrictions for Koreans in Hawai'i. He stated that imposing enemy alien status on Koreans was "deemed essential to the interests of internal security," which was decided "only after careful consideration by the Hawaiian Department Military Intelligence, Naval Intelligence, 14th Naval District, and the Federal Bureau of Investigation." He added that "the Navy Intelligence office was particularly insistent that alien Koreans in Hawai'i should retain their present status as enemy aliens and should not be regarded as friendly aliens."[33]

All of the reasons Richardson cited—some of which could be better described as paranoia—demonstrated intense fear of the Japanese as well as unwillingness, almost a refusal, to trust Koreans despite their demonstrated hatred for the Japanese. First, Richardson contended that Koreans' apparent ties to Japan, willing or not, made Koreans dangerous because they had "families or relatives in Korea or Japan itself," and, moreover, many of them had even "made trips to Korea and Japan."

Second, Richardson was fearful that Kilsoo Haan (Han Kil-su), one of the prominent, if controversial, Korean independence movement leaders, might "sell [his] services to the highest bidder," that is, to Japan.[34] Haan was a source of mystery for U.S. government officials, and the FBI kept close tabs on him. He had made many predictions regarding possible moves Japan would make, including sudden sabotage in the United States, not unlike the Pearl Harbor attack.[35] Given that Haan was employed by the Japanese consulate in Honolulu from 1935 to 1937, U.S. officials suspected that Haan might be an espionage agent working for the Japanese government. Haan's explanation for working for the Japanese consulate was that he could thereby spy on the activities of the Japanese government. Notwithstanding the lingering suspicion of Haan, FBI reports did acknowledge that "Haan was known to be bitterly anti-Japanese, both prior to and subsequent to this employment with the Japanese Consulate."[36] But because U.S. officials regarded Koreans as "shrewd and unscrupulous opportunists," they did not wish to take a chance with Haan and other Koreans.

Sadly, Koreans themselves sometimes fueled this kind of suspicion on the part of U.S. officials. In one of the FBI reports conducted in Detroit, Michigan, Mrs. Line, a Korean woman married to an American, said that "the Japanese now send Japs into Korea to assume Korean names, to learn the Korean language and customs, and to falsely represent themselves to be Koreans purely for the purpose of spying on their Korean subjects," and, therefore, "you cannot trust anyone there or in the United States who represents himself to be a Korean unless you are familiar with his ancestral background." She added, furthermore, "in the United States today, there are many Japanese citizens who are masquerading as Koreans, when, as a matter of fact, they are truly Japs by birth and sympathy." Such statements made any nonsuspecting U.S. officials sit up and take notice of how easily many Japanese might try to pass as Koreans and spy on the United States, whether it was true or not.[37]

Third, Richardson was well aware that Korean leadership in both Hawai'i and the mainland United States, despite efforts to present a united front, was deeply divided, and he held it against them: "The leaders of the Korean nationalist movements appear to be opportunists who are more interested in personal aggrandizement than they are in organizing a movement representing a sincere expression of a people who desire to maintain their own national integrity." In fact, when the Korean leaders were zealous in protesting the verdict and ruling in the Sohn case, U.S. officials saw their objections as stemming from a desire to further their own personal ambition and status in the Korean community rather than from genuine concern for Sohn or the Korean people.

Fourth, Richardson argued that the recognition of near impossibility of telling Koreans apart from Japanese and the fear of Korean-speaking Japanese made Koreans a threat to national security: "Language considerations would make counter intelligence and police coverage more difficult if alien Koreans were classified as friendly aliens. It is almost impossible to distinguish between Koreans and Japanese by sight alone, and Japanese who speak Korean might try to represent themselves as Koreans." And this was precisely the reason why Koreans in Hawai'i were exempt from certain enemy alien restrictions such as being able to have a liquor license, but not exempt from the curfew laws, which required police officers and other officials to be able to tell Koreans apart from Japanese on the spot. If Koreans were regarded as enemy aliens and had to abide by the same curfew laws as the Japanese aliens, then there would be less chance of Japanese who spoke Korean passing as Koreans.

Fifth, Richardson considered the effect granting Koreans friendly alien status would have on other disenchanted ethnic groups, like Formosans (Taiwanese) and Okinawans: "Recognition of the Koreans as friendly aliens might provide an opening wedge for the Formosans, Okinawans, and other colonists not of pure Japanese blood." He worried that because Formosans and Okinawans were also groups considered Japanese due to their unwilling association with Japan, they too might petition to become friendly aliens if Koreans led the way with their campaign.

Sixth, and last, Richardson claimed that the United States need not bother with how Koreans were affected or inconvenienced by their enemy alien status; not only was the number of Koreans considered enemy aliens small, Richardson argued, but to begin the process of granting Koreans friendly alien status would create unproductive demands on the U.S. intelligence services:

> Under the present policy the restrictions for purposes of internal security are not severe and it only affects approximately 2,500 alien Koreans in the community. On the other hand, to exempt these Koreans from these restrictions would put an unnecessary strain on the intelligence agencies. The limited restrictions presently imposed on alien Koreans have provided sufficient control without this necessity for processing through Alien Hearing Boards. To subject these Koreans, both citizens and alien, to hearing board processing as has been done with numerous Japanese would, we believe, invite further unrest and give their leaders a stronger platform for protest.[38]

This kind of contradictory thinking clearly revealed Richardson's hypocrisy as well as expediency: the number of Koreans suffering the enemy alien status was too small to bother caring about, but if those Koreans were granted friendly alien status, the extra work created for the U.S. intelligence services would be too great. Thus, the Military Governor's Office and the U.S. officials combined illogicality, dismissal of facts, paranoia against the Japanese, and racism to preserve the enemy alien status for Koreans.

RECLAIMING THEIR IDENTITY, CULTURE, AND NATIONAL PRIDE

In a time of a national crisis such as World War II, Americans came together in wartime mobilization. Likewise, Koreans in Hawai'i, in the face of their predicament as enemy aliens, tried to set aside their differences and combine their energy into waging a rigorous campaign to repeal their enemy alien status and reclaim their personal and political identity as Koreans. To be sure, there were differences and divisions within the Korean community in Hawai'i during World War II, but the purpose of the following discussion will be to examine the various tactics Koreans as a community employed in their attempt to escape unscathed from American racism. Koreans were aware of the injustice and racism on the part of the U.S. government to keep insisting on lumping Koreans together with the Japanese. Koreans in Hawai'i were not in a position to condemn or offend the Military Governor's Office. Instead, their strategies focused on complying with the martial law and the restriction imposed upon them as enemy aliens. They wanted to prove themselves valuable allies to the United States and win the sympathy of the local and U.S. officials, which they hoped would eventually lead to the repeal of their enemy alien status, recognition of the provisional Korean government in China, and ultimately liberation of Korea.

Because Koreans were treated as Japanese in the public eye as well as in the court of the law, it became imperative for Koreans to identify themselves physically as not of Japanese ancestry to protect themselves from both the American public and government officials. On January 28, 1942, the Korean section of the *Korean Herald-Pacific Weekly* announced: "The United Korean Committee will be issuing identification cards for all Koreans which will read 'I am Korean.' Please bring two small photos with you to our office."[39] This announcement generated an overwhelming response from Korean readers. They were unable to wear these identification cards on the outside of their clothing as they hoped to. The Public Morale Section in the Territorial Office of Civilian Defense, established in Hawai'i to monitor the attitudes and behaviors of different ethnic groups, prohibited such blatant advertisement in order to minimize ethnic tensions.[40] Nevertheless, carrying the identification cards proved to be a handy and effective tool for Koreans when they needed to prove their ethnic background to evade hostility.

Koreans in the continental United States followed the same tactic, and so did some Japanese. It was precisely this sort of incident—in which the Japanese passed for Koreans—that American authorities feared and wanted to avoid. The February 25, 1942, issue of the *Korean National Herald-Pacific Weekly* reported that "the Japanese of Los Angeles have been wearing counterfeit Korean identification buttons," and "the Federal Bureau of Investigation and the city police . . . are now on the watch." The article gave detailed descriptions of the three different kinds of counterfeit buttons the authorities had identified up to that point and added that "the wearing of the Korean identification badges by enemies may endanger public safety and devaluate the importance of identifying Koreans from enemies at this time as it has so well served those who have worn them so far."[41]

Aside from physical identification, the first and foremost strategy of Koreans to evade heightened racism was to distance themselves from the Japanese in every possible way. Intellectually, Koreans tried to convey their profound differences in character and tradition from the Japanese. "The conflicting ideology of Japan's brutal Jingoism with that of our noble heritage and humanitarian culture—imbued in us generation after generation—can never mix," one writer for *Free Korea* boldly declared.[42] In fact, Koreans believed, they were just the opposite of the Japanese: the Japanese were barbaric, blood-thirsty imperialists, and Koreans were innocent, peace-loving victims, "with calm nerve and hidden courage."[43] Such a self-image of Koreans was supported by Pearl Buck, a Nobel prize–winning writer and longtime advocate of the U.S. sympathy for China. Buck praised the Koreans as "likable people, humane, and approachable."[44]

Koreans even employed the rhetoric of white supremacy to prove their superiority over the Japanese. The *Korean National Herald-Pacific Weekly* proudly quoted Dr. Ales Hrdlicka of the Smithsonian Institution, "one of the foremost anthropologists of the world," who recently announced that Koreans are "nearer white men than any other peoples of Eastern Asia." Koreans also "have many white physical characteristics," according to Dr. Hrdlicka, and "seem to 'think like white men' more than either Chinese or Japanese."[45] It is not clear whether Koreans truly believed in white supremacy as this article would imply or if this was simply one of their more desperate measures to differentiate themselves from the Japanese as a race.

Informing the American public of their cruel and inhumane treatment under the Japanese government was the best weapon Koreans had not only to differentiate themselves from the Japanese but also to demonstrate their understandable enmity. Appearing on the Pittsburgh broadcasting station, KDKA, Samuel S. Lee, a longtime resident of the city and a native Korean, spoke of his personal experience of Japanese atrocities:

> My knowledge of the Japanese came quite early when I was a boy in school. They came in gradually there, eating up the country little by little; and no one outside paid very much attention to them. But my father knew. He and the other patriots of our village, they refused to acknowledge the Japanese; so they were seized by the invaders. My father was put into prison and tortured. . . . But you do not know the methods of the Japanese. I have seen my friends and the friends of my father emerge

from their hands . . . some crippled in body . . . some whose minds were completely gone. . . . But there were those who were never again seen alive. I bear their marks on my body myself. They will always be on me until the day I die. But the marks I bear on my soul are the marks I will never forget. . . . They go with me to tell me what to do.[46]

Similarly, the March 1, 1944, issue of *Korean Independence* carried a photo with the following description: "Our photograph shows Koreans a minute after their execution by Japanese soldiers for having shouted 'Long Live Korea,' in connection with the March 1 Movement. The victims were placed in a kneeling position, their arms extended straight out and attached to the arms of rudely constructed crosses. With their eyes bandaged and their heads and bodies securely tied to the upright of the cross they awaited the firing squad."[47]

By emphasizing their willful survival under the Japanese occupation, Koreans also effectively positioned themselves as something of Japanese experts. One editorial in *Free Korea* openly admitted: "We are trying to convince our readers that the Koreans are the only race in the world who can most closely detect the Japanese psychology; since for over thirty years we have been tortured and enslaved under the monkeyish Japanese domination. So, we can tell most correctly what the Japanese would feel, and we can predict almost exactly what the Japanese psychology would choose in a problem or dilemma."[48] Making a similar claim, one editorial in the *Korean National Herald-Pacific Weekly* asserted, "To know the Japs became a second instinct to the Koreans through their bitter experience."[49] On occasion, Koreans took the liberty of warning Americans as to what to expect in their war with Japan. With their "barbaric instinct and force," one article cautioned, "the Japanese will always hit below [the] belt."[50]

Such a statement fit Americans' image of the Japanese, but Koreans believed Americans still underestimated the Japanese. Americans did not understand, Koreans thought, just how cruel and determined the Japanese could be, as they knew from their own experience. An article entitled "Jap Psychology vs. German Psychology" asserted that while the approach of Hitler and his German soldiers to the war was "Win or Lose," the Japanese who were "born in Shintoism, educated in Mikadoism, and trained in Harakirism" fought the war with a "Win or Die" mentality. Again, the implication here was that the Japanese with their peculiar psychology would bring their barbaric determination to the battlefront, making them an especially dangerous enemy—even more so than the Germans.[51] Thus, Koreans' persistent efforts to portray negative images of the Japanese coincided with and even contributed to the racist fears of the American people.

Another important strategy for Koreans to differentiate themselves from the Japanese was to convey their mutual interest in defeating Japan and their active participation in the war effort, both civil and military. "To help win this war with America is our task," declared Won Soon Lee (Yi Wŏn-sun), the chairman of the United Korean Committee.[52] To make this goal more pronounced Koreans created victory buttons, which read "Koreans for Victory with America!" against the background of American and Korean flags.[53] These buttons served a dual purpose of identifying them as Koreans and showing their support for American victory. Almost every issue of the *Korean National Herald-Pacific Weekly* included encouragement for Koreans to give willingly and generously to the war effort. "It is the duty of every Korean residing beneath the Stars and Stripes," one editorial reminded its readers, "to so conduct ourselves and so cooperate with the American war efforts."[54] Koreans demonstrated their full support for what they saw as the aim of the war—"human liberation."[55]

One of the most concrete ways to participate in the war effort on the home front for both Koreans and Americans was to purchase war bonds. Each of the three Korean newspapers carried advertisements for war bonds in every issue: the *Free Korea* used the slogans, "Buy War Bonds to Insure Freedom" and "For Victory, Buy United States War Bonds," the *Korean Independence* also urged readers, and the *Korean National Herald-Pacific Weekly* recommended spending 10 percent of one's income for purchasing war bonds—"Be 100% with your 10%: Buy War Bonds." After financial restrictions on them were lifted, Koreans did not hesitate to purchase war bonds. Taking more initiative than simply giving money, Koreans also organized many American Red Cross fundraisers and benefit shows that featured Korean dances and performances, drawing Korean and American spectators alike. In reference to a Red Cross benefit show on May 3, 1942, a writer for the *Korean National Herald-Pacific Weekly* noted that "the performance made us so nostalgic that we felt like we were on the top of a mountain in Seoul, celebrating our independence." The show raised over $1,000.[56]

Korean participation in the war effort was not limited to civil services. Many Korean men and women joined the armed forces to both fight and serve as interpreters of Japanese. The first-generation Koreans who came to the United States in their adult years were fluent in Japanese because they were forced to learn Japanese while growing up under Japanese rule.[57] Bong-Youn Choy, a Korean scholar, in his autobiographical sketch recalls postponing his studies for a year because he was asked to work for the U.S. government as a translator of Japanese after Pearl Harbor. He also served as an instructor of Japanese for the special Army Training Program classes.[58] Thus, Koreans contributed in big and small ways to the war effort and demonstrated their support for American victory. They wholeheartedly rooted for the United States out of a desire to repeal their enemy alien status and a belief that the American victory was the key to Korean independence.

Despite all their efforts, however, Koreans in Hawai'i remained enemy aliens

KOREANS---HELP RAISE THE RIGHT FLAG!

Every country is entitled to its own flag, its own government, its own religion! Since 1910 Korea has suffered the domination of the Japanese. If you want to help lower the flag of the hated conqueror and raise that of old Korea— help put over the American-Korean Victory Fund Drive. Every cent raised during this drive (ending August 29th) will be sent directly to President Roosevelt to use AS HE SEES FIT! Send your generous contribution to: AMERICAN-KOREAN VICTORY FUND DRIVE, 1306 Miller St., Honolulu —or—HAWAII MUSIC CO., 1184 Fort St., Honolulu.

11 "Koreans—Help Raise the Right Flag," an advertisement for the American-Korean Victory Fund Drive in Hawai'i. (Following this drive, a sum of $26,265 was donated to President Roosevelt in August 1943.)

until late in the war. General Orders No. 45 issued on December 4, 1943, finally exempted Koreans from the curfew restriction, which, according to Michael E. Macmillan, "had come to symbolize enemy-alien status itself." This exemption of curfew restriction for Koreans followed the Cairo Declaration, in which the United States, Great Britain, and China announced their commitment to freeing Korea.[59] But Koreans in Hawai'i did not fully become friendly aliens until May 6, 1944, by General Orders No. 59.[60] Given that their friendly alien status became a reality so late in the war—only after it was certain that the United States would win the war—it would be fair to speculate that Koreans in Hawai'i would have remained enemy aliens as long as the threat of Japan's power loomed large in the war.

To be sure, the irony of Korean enemy alien status was a byproduct of American racism and fear directed at the Japanese. Evading racism does not necessarily require speaking out against it, and Koreans trying to survive heightened racism in Hawai'i during World War II found other, more effective means to minimize discrimination. Their priority lay, not in speaking out against racism, but in protesting that they were not Japanese and did not deserve to suffer discrimination. Even if their protests fell on deaf ears and may not have had much impact ultimately on repealing their enemy alien status, passive acceptance of their ironic, if humiliating, fate was not an option Koreans considered. Forced to share a legal and practical identity with the Japanese, Koreans waged a vigorous and persistent campaign to clear their status in American society and reclaim their identity, culture, and national pride in being Koreans. More than any inconveniences they suffered as enemy aliens, Koreans' bruised national pride and cultural identity provided the fuel for the determination to end their legal ties to the Japanese. For Koreans in Hawai'i, however, gaining their new status as friendly aliens was only half the battle, for they still needed to fulfill their long-lived dream of the liberation of Korea from Japanese rule.

NOTES

I wish to thank Professors Yŏng-ho Ch'oe and Ned Shultz for inviting me to participate in the symposium on "Korean Americans in Hawai'i: Their Life and Experiences," held at the Center for Korean Studies, University of Hawai'i at Manoa (January 13–15, 2000), where I originally delivered an earlier version of this chapter. I have greatly appreciated their support for my scholarship over the years. I am also grateful to Michael Macmillan and Roberta Chang for generously sharing with me their vast knowledge of the history of Korean American communities in Hawai'i.

    1. John W. Dower, *War Without Mercy: Race and Power in the Pacific War* (New York: Pantheon Books, 1986). In his explanation of the unusually cruel war

fought in the Pacific, Dower emphasizes the "subhuman" characteristics Americans and the Allies assigned to the Japanese, using images of apes and vermin. Dower remarks that Americans portrayed the Japanese as "inherently inferior men and women who had to be understood in terms of primitivism, childishness, and collective mental and emotional deficiency." They believed the Japanese were "a uniquely contemptible and formidable foe who deserved no mercy and virtually demanded extermination" (9).

2. Roger Daniels, *Concentration Camps USA: Japanese Americans and World War II* (New York: Holt, Rinehart and Winston, 1971), xiii.

3. In 1988, the attorney general of California officially recommended the public use the term *Asian* rather than *oriental* to refer to people of Asian ancestry. He reasoned that the term *oriental* implicitly mystified and exoticized Asians and Asian Americans. See *Attorney General's Asian and Pacific Islanders Advisory Committee Final Report,* December 1988.

4. Personal testimonies and scholarship on the experience of Japanese Americans during World War II, particularly their internment experience, boasts a vast list. See, for example, Allen R. Bosworth, *America's Concentration Camps* (New York: Norton, 1967); Donald E. Collins, *Native American Aliens: Disloyalty and Renunciation of Citizenship by Japanese Americans during World War II* (Westport: Greenwood Press, 1985); Daniels, *Concentration Camps USA;* Roger Daniels, *Concentration Camps: North America Japanese in the United States and Canada During World War II* (Malabar, Fla.: Robert E. Krieger Publishing Company, Inc., 1981); also by Roger Daniels, *Prisoners Without Trial: Japanese Americans in World War II* (New York: Hill & Wang, 1993); Richard Drinnon, *Keepers of Concentration Camps: Dillon S. Meyer and American Racism* (Berkeley: University of California Press, 1987); Audrie Girdner and Anne Loftis, *The Great Betrayal* (New York: Macmillan, 1969); Bill Hosokawa, *Nisei: The Quiet Americans* (New York: Morrow, 1969); Jeanne Wakatsuki Houston and James D. Houston, *Farewell to Manzanar* (New York: Bantam Books, 1973); Peter H. Irons, *Justice Delayed: The Record of the Japanese American Internment Cases* (Middletown: Wesleyan University Press, 1989); Charles Kikuchi, *The Kikuchi Diary: From an American Concentration Camp,* ed. John Modell (Urbana: University of Illinois Press, 1973); Donna K. Nagata, *Legacy of Injustice: Exploring the Cross-Generational Impact of the Japanese American Internment* (New York: Plenum Press, 1993); Sandra C. Taylor, *Jewel of the Desert: Japanese American Internment at Topaz* (Berkeley: University of California Press, 1993); Yoshiko Uchida, *Desert Exile: The Uprooting of a Japanese American Family* (Seattle: University of Washington Press, 1982); Michi Weglyn, *Years of Infamy: The Untold Story of America's Concentration Camps* (Seattle: University of Washington Press, [1976], 1995).

5. The most prominent historian to mark American entrance to World War II

as the watershed year for Asian Americans is Ronald Takaki. As his chapter title, "The Watershed of World War II," suggests, Takaki sees World War II as a unique, unprecedented opportunity in which Asian immigrants and their children who had been hitherto viewed as "strangers from a different shore" were given a chance to participate in the war effort as Americans, particularly in the armed forces. Ronald Takaki, *Strangers from a Different Shore: A History of Asian Americans* (Boston: Little, Brown and Company, 1989), Chapter 10. Takaki is not alone in this assessment. See also Sucheng Chan, *Asian Americans: An Interpretive History* (Boston: Twayne Publishers, 1991), Chapter 7, and Yen Le Espiritu, *Asian American Women and Men: Labor, Laws, and Love* (Thousand Oaks: Sage Publications, 1997), Chapter 3. Both of these scholars emphasize the economic mobility and improved lives of Chinese, Koreans, Filipinos, and Asian Indians in the United States due to the fact that "their ancestral nations were allies of the United States" (Espiritu, *Asian American Women and Men,* 49). To include Koreans in this category of allies is misleading as they were in fact considered "enemy aliens" along with the Japanese in the United States.

6. A word about the spelling of Hawai'i. With the current presence of strong sovereignty movements in Hawai'i, there has been a conscious effort to reintroduce the two diacritical marks the Hawaiian language uses, the macron, or *kahako,* and the *'okina,* or glottal stop. Out of respect for this new initiative to revive Hawaiian language in Hawai'i, I observe the practice of inserting glottal stops in the word *Hawai'i.* Hawai'i was an independent kingdom from 1810 to 1893. It became a republic in 1894 and remained so until the United States annexed it in 1898. (The laws of the United States did not begin to apply to Hawai'i until passage of the Organic Act in June 1900.) Hawai'i remained a territory of the United States until 1959, when it became the fiftieth state of the United States. Similarly, I refrain from using "mainland" to refer to the continental United States, which, I believe, unfairly privileges and implies greater power of the continental United States over Hawai'i.

7. "Japanese Obsession," *Time,* February 2, 1942, 21.

8. "For Release" by Department of Justice, January 26, 1942, Record Group 319, Army-Intelligence Decimal File, 1941–1948, Box 394, Folder 291.2 Koreans, National Archives II, College Park, Md.

9. As quoted in Syngman Rhee's letter to Secretary of War Henry L. Stimson, January 14, 1943, Record Group 319, Army-Intelligence Decimal File, 1941-1948, Box 394, Folder 291.2 Koreans, National Archives II, College Park, Md.

10. "Biddle Exempts 2 Alien Classes," *New York Times,* February 10, 1942, 21.

11. According to 1940 census figures, there were only 1,711 Koreans in the continental United States, 962 of whom were American-born citizens and 749 aliens.

12. The *Korean National Herald-Pacific Weekly* was a Korean newspaper published weekly in Honolulu, Hawai'i, before the war. The *Korean National Herald*

and *Pacific Weekly* were two separate publications run respectively by the Korean National Association and Tongjihoe (sometimes spelled Donjihoe or Dong Ji Hoi), two Korean political organizations in Hawai'i. But General Orders No. 14, issued three days after Pearl Harbor, banned publication of all foreign-language newspapers in Hawai'i. The two papers merged to obtain permission to resume publication for the duration of the war. The new English section was added, according to the editors, J. Kyung Dunn (Chŏn Kyŏng-mu), Young K. Kim (Kim Yŏng-gi), and Henry C. Kim (Kim Hyŏn-gu), "in respect to the second generation and the American public in expression of both Korean and American thoughts in the ameliorative process of Hawai'i's cosmopolitan life." "Local Korean Papers are Merged into One," *Korean National Herald-Pacific Weekly*, January 21, 1942, 1. It is not clear, however, whether the Korean editors truly wanted to add the English section or added it only to negotiate the resumption of publishing the paper. It could also have been required by the military governor as a condition of lifting the publication ban. As J. Garner Anthony notes, the military governor easily controlled the press through a military censorship in wartime Hawai'i. J. Garner Anthony, *Hawaii Under Army Rule: The Real Story of Three Years of Martial Law in a Loyal American Territory* (Honolulu: University of Hawai'i Press, [1955], 1975), 39–40. The contents of the English section (usually one page) were not simply a translation of the Korean section (three pages). January 21, 1942 was the first issue under the merger.

13. "The Editorials," *Korean National Herald-Pacific Weekly*, February 25, 1942, 1.

14. "Is He a Jap?" *Free Korea*, June 2, 1942, 5.

15. General Orders No. 5, Office of Military Governor, December 8, 1941, Honolulu, University of Hawai'i.

16. Secretary of War Henry Stimson, to Rev. Peong Koo Yoon, undated, Record Group 319, Army-Intelligence Decimal File, 1941–1948, Box 394, Folder 291.2 Koreans, National Archives II, College Park, Md.

17. Lauriel E. Eubank, "The Effects of the First Six Months of World War II on the Attitudes of Koreans and Filipinos Toward the Japanese in Hawai'i" (unpublished M.A. thesis, University of Hawai'i, 1943), 74.

18. Robert C. Richardson Jr., Military Governor of the Territory of Hawaii, to Assistant Chief of Staff, G-2, War Department, Record Group 319, Army-Intelligence Decimal File, 1941–1948, Box 394, Folder 291.2 Koreans, National Archives II, College Park, Md.

19. Michael E. Macmillan, "Unwanted Allies: Koreans as Enemy Aliens in World War II," *The Hawaiian Journal of History* 19 (1985): 183. Gwenfread Allen, *Hawai'i's War Years, 1941–1945* (Honolulu: University of Hawai'i Press, 1950), 112–14.

20. "We are In War Business," *Korean National Herald-Pacific Weekly,* January 28, 1942, 1.

21. Macmillan, "Unwanted Allies," 184. Macmillan points out that the Japanese were not allowed to obtain such a permit.

22. "War Time Living," *Korean National Herald-Pacific Weekly* (Korean Section), March 4, 1942, 4.

23. Copy, "Excerpt From Court Proceedings," included in Record Group 319, Army-Intelligence Decimal File, 1941–1948, Box 394, Folder 291.2 Koreans, National Archives II, College Park, Md.

24. *Honolulu Star-Bulletin,* April 30, 1943.

25. *Honolulu Star-Bulletin,* May 5, 1943.

26. Guy M. Gillette, to President Franklin Roosevelt, May 11, 1943, Record Group 319, Army-Intelligence Decimal File, 1941–1948, Box 394, Folder 291.2, National Archives II, College Park, Md.

27. As quoted in a letter, Syngman Rhee, to Secretary of War Henry Stimson, May 17, 1943, Record Group 319, Army-Intelligence Decimal File, 1941–1948, Box 394, Folder 291.2 Koreans, National Archives II, College Park, Md.

28. Syngman Rhee, to Secretary of War Henry Stimson, May 17, 1943, Record Group 319, Army-Intelligence Decimal File, 1941–1948, Box 394, Folder 291.2 Koreans, National Archives II, College Park, Md.

29. Peong Koo Yoon, to Secretary of War Henry Stimson, August 31, 1943, Record Group 319, Army-Intelligence Decimal File, 1941–1948, Box 394, Folder 291.2 Koreans, National Archives II, College Park, Md.

30. Delos C. Emmons, Military Governor of the Territory of Hawaii, to Willson C. Moore, Attorney for Syung Woon Sohn, May 31, 1943, Record Group 319, Army-Intelligence Decimal File, 1941–1948, Box 394, Folder 291.2 Koreans, National Archives II, College Park, Md.

31. For example, declassified FBI reports on Koreans in the continental United States during World War II reveal extensive efforts of the U.S. intelligence services to track every move of Koreans. Even when there were no known Koreans living in certain locations, FBI agents conducted thorough interviews with respected local authorities and residents to seek out information about any Koreans living in their area, unidentified by the Alien Registration Act of 1940. Cities the FBI investigated included Washington, D.C.; Seattle, Washington; Jackson, Mississippi; Philadelphia, Pennsylvania; San Francisco, California; Detroit, Michigan; Baltimore, Maryland; Los Angeles, California; Phoenix, Arizona; and Honolulu, T.H. Koreans were very few in number especially in some of these cities. This strikes me as an extraordinary amount of resources and energy devoted to finding out exactly what Koreans were doing.

32. An unsigned memo to Assistant Secretary of War John J. McCloy dated

May 19, 1943. Records of the Assistant Secretary of War—Race File: Koreans [5988]. Papers of the U.S. Commission on Wartime Relocation and Internment of Civilians. Reel 5, Box 6 (Microfilm).

33. Robert C. Richardson Jr., Military Governor of the Territory of Hawai'i, to Assistant Chief of Staff, War Department, Washington, D.C., Record Group 319, Army-Intelligence Decimal File, 1941–1948, Box 394, Folder 291.2, National Archives II, College Park, Md.

34. It should be noted that Kilsoo Haan was not even living in Hawai'i at the time. He was residing in California.

35. Haan apparently took credit for more than he had actually accomplished in Japanese espionage work. He claimed to have stolen a book entitled *Three Power Alliance* by a Japanese named Matsuo from two retired Japanese army officers who belonged to the Japanese Black Dragon Society in California, when in fact, the book had been available in bookstores in Los Angeles. Regarding Haan's alleged "confidential agents" from whom he claimed to get information about Japan, a fellow Korean leader, Jacob K. Dunn advised FBI agents that "much of the material appearing in Haan's releases are data concerning current newspaper dispatches, also gossip among Koreans generally, for which Haan would not need any agents to advise him." "Survey of Korean Activities in Washington Field Division," Federal Bureau of Investigation, April 29, 1943, Record Group 319, Army-Intelligence Decimal File, 1941–1948, Box 394, Folder 291.2 Koreans, National Archives II, College Park, Md.

36. "Survey of Korean Activities in Washington Field Division," Federal Bureau of Investigation, April 29, 1943, Record Group 319, Army-Intelligence Decimal File, 1941–1948, Box 394, Folder 291.2, National Archives II, College Park, Md.

37. "Survey of Korean Activities in the Detroit Field Division," The Federal Bureau of Investigation, November 3, 1943, Record Group 319, Army-Intelligence Decimal File, 1941–1948, Box 394, Folder 291.2, National Archives II, College Park, Md.

38. Robert C. Richardson Jr., Military Governor of the Territory of Hawaii, to Assistant Chief of Staff, War Department, Washington, D.C., Record Group 319, Army-Intelligence Decimal File, 1941–1948, Box 394, Folder 291.2 Koreans, National Archives II, College Park, Md.

39. *Korean National Herald-Pacific Weekly* (Korean Section), January 28, 1942, 4.

40. Eubank, "The Effects of the First Six Months of World War II," 85.

41. "Japanese Counterfeit Korean Identification Buttons in California," *Korean National Herald-Pacific Weekly*, February 25, 1942, 1.

42. James Charr, "An Appeal to U.S.A.," *Free Korea*, June 1942, 7.

43. "The Editorials," *Korean National Herald-Pacific Weekly*, September 30, 1942, 1.

44. As quoted in "Our 25,000,000 Forgotten Allies of Korea," *Free Korea,* February 1944, 1.

45. "Dr. Hrdlicka Asks for Korean Restoration," *Korean National Herald-Pacific Weekly,* February 25, 1942, 1.

46. "Korean Tells of Japan's Brutal Rule in Korea," *Korean Independence,* October 27, 1943, 1.

47. "Symbol of Japan's Benevolence to Koreans," *Korean Independence,* March 1, 1944, 1.

48. "Sinful 'Optimism,'" *Free Korea,* June 1942, 2.

49. "The Editorials," *Korean National Herald-Pacific Weekly,* November 25, 1942, 1.

50. "Beware Japanese Feint," *Korean National Herald-Pacific Weekly,* March 25, 1942, 1.

51. "Jap Psychology vs. German Psychology," *Free Korea,* June 1942, 2.

52. Won Soon Lee, "An Open Letter," *Korean National Herald-Pacific Weekly,* January 20, 1942, 1.

53. "Victory Button Arrived," *Korean National Herald-Pacific Weekly* (Korean Section), May 20, 1942, 3.

54. "The Editorials," *Korean National Herald,* November 8, 1944, 1. Starting with the January 19, 1944, issue, the name of the newspaper became just *Korean National Herald* as Tongjihoe withdrew from the United Korean Committee and subsequently used the publication of the paper to show its continued support of Syngman Rhee, who had a serious falling-out with the Committee for misuse of funds.

55. "War of Liberation," *Korean National Herald-Pacific Weekly,* April 15, 1942, 1. (See Chapter 9 of this book.)

56. "The Red Cross Benefit Show," *Korean National Herald-Pacific Weekly* (Korean Section), May 6, 1942, 4.

57. My father, who spent the first thirteen years of his life in Korea under Japanese rule, can (or claims to) still read and speak Japanese.

58. Bong-Youn Choy, *Koreans in America* (Chicago: Nelson-Hall Publishers, 1979), 326.

59. Macmillan, "Unwanted Allies," 194.

60. General Orders No. 59, Office of Military Governor, May 6, 1944, Hawaii War Records Depository, University of Hawai'i, Honolulu, Hawai'i.

9

"Unity for What? Unity for Whom?":
The United Korean Committee of North America, 1941–1945

A s overseas nationalist organizations throughout the Korean diaspora worked to liberate their homeland from the yoke of Japanese colonial rule, by the 1930s, Korean nationalist organizations based in Hawai'i and the continental United States emerged at the forefront of the independence movement. This was the result of a number of factors, including the degree of political freedom available for Korean immigrants in the United States to pursue independence activities, the sympathy of many influential American political and religious leaders concerning the plight of Korea, the emergence of a leadership cohort attuned to the American political system, and the ability of U.S. Korean communities to have the financial means to support such pursuits. This milieu provided ample opportunity for the proliferation of numerous Korean nationalist organizations. While the liberation of Korea may have ostensibly served as the common denominator for such groups, however, the means for liberation, the rebuilding of Korea, and the aspirations of individual leaders of these organizations covered the entire political spectrum.

SETTING ASIDE OLD DIFFERENCES: THE LAUNCHING OF THE
UNITED KOREAN COMMITTEE

Recognizing that the American entry into World War II signaled the best hope for Korean liberation, Korean nationalists of all political stripes were eager to seize this moment. Acutely aware of the necessity of presenting a united front to the American public and, more important, to the U.S. government, nationalist leaders worked to bridge the many political and personal differences that existed within Korean communities. As a result, during the last week of April 1941, a mass meeting of Korean nationalist organizations was convened in Honolulu, Hawai'i. For over a week, nationalist leaders young and old debated strategy and worked to make political unity a reality.

The result of the convention was the formation of the Chaemi Hanjok Yŏnhap Wiwŏnhoe, the United Korean Committee of North America (UKC). This umbrella organization included the Korean National Association (KNA) of Hawai'i, the KNA of Los Angeles, the Tongjihoe (also spelled Dongji Hoi: Comrades Society) of Hawai'i, the Tongjihoe Society of Los Angeles, the Tongniptang (Independence Party) of Hawai'i, the Korean Patriotic Party, the Sino-Korean People's League, the Korean Student Federation of North America (KSF), the Korean National Revolutionary Party (KNRP), the Korean Women's Relief Society of the Tongjihoe of Honolulu, and the Korean Women's Relief Society of the KNA of Honolulu.[1] The coalition of these organizations effectively represented nearly all the Koreans in Hawai'i and North America, especially since many Koreans had overlapping memberships in these organizations.

The explicit mission of the UKC was to support the Korean Provisional Government (KPG) in Chungking, China, and Syngman Rhee, who directed the Korean Commission, the representative arm of the Provisional Government in Washington, D.C. Well aware that when the United States entered the war, the political status of Koreans would be uncertain since they were classified as Japanese nationals, the UKC clearly outlined that it was an organization that was "voluntarily motivated by patriotism and furthermore of war efforts against Japan" while simultaneously aiding the United Nations for the recovery of Korean independence.[2]

By the spring of 1941, given the inevitability of U.S. military involvement,

해외한족대회
대표초대연
대한인부인구제회

인국십삼년오월일일   호노루루항

12   Delegates of the United Korean Committee were honored by the Korean Women's Relief Society in May 1941.

UKC leaders clearly understood that if Koreans in the United States were to have a stake in postwar Korea, they needed to present a united front to the international community. Fashioning a united front, however, was no easy task given the long history of political differences within the Korean independence movement. This chapter, in tracing the activities of the UKC between 1941 and 1945, works against conventional historical interpretations that have largely dismissed the efforts of the UKC as ineffectual or as "too little, too late." Instead, this chapter focuses on the ways in which the UKC emerged as an important site to consider how generational struggle, personal ambitions, transnational politics, and the political lessons that a new generation of nationalist leaders learned in the late 1920s and 1930s in the United States transformed the Korean independence movement in the 1940s.

After a surge of political action in the aftermath of the March First Movement, nationalist activity in the United States and Hawai'i waned in the late 1920s and 1930s, as rank-and-file Koreans grew increasingly disenchanted with the inability of nationalist organizations to advance the cause of Korean independence in any significant way. Simultaneously, in the face of the Great Depression, Korean communities, composed primarily of working-class families, found it difficult to support such organizations financially. While larger nationalist institutions such as the Korean National Association (KNA), the Tongjihoe, and the Korean Student Federation (KSF) in Hawai'i and on the mainland continued to function, albeit in a lesser capacity, smaller organizations such as the Bureau of Information, the Korean Commission, the Independence League, the Sino-Korean People's League, and the Korean Women's Patriotic Society either went defunct or entered into a period of hiatus.[3] While individual nationalist leaders and their supporters continued their pursuits of independence activities, these activities hardly matched the grand ambitions of the movement in the early 1920s.

The decline of political activity on the part of Koreans in the United States should not be interpreted as an abandonment of independence activities, however. Instead, these years should be considered an essential incubating period for the events of the 1940s, as organizations and individuals increasingly familiarized themselves with the American political system, defined their political agendas, honed their political skills, and grappled with issues of generation and national belonging.

TWO HEADS, ONE BODY

Due to the geographic expanse between Honolulu and Los Angeles and the concern over the potential abuse of political power, the UKC established two bureaus, UKCLA (Los Angeles) and HONUKC (Honolulu), each with its own governing body and specific function. While each individual bureau was responsible for the collection of funds in its respective locale, the UKCLA was charged with overseeing the general dispersal of monies while the HONUKC dealt with the actual programs of the UKC. From its inauguration, the UKC appeared destined for strife given its organizational structure. The appointment of UKC officers required careful negotiation to guarantee that each organization received adequate representation in proportion to its membership.[4] While this arrangement appeared democratic, assigning executive officers in proportion to the membership roles of their respective organizations ensured that both the Hawai'i and Los Angeles bureaus would be dominated by leaders from the two largest organizations, the Tongjihoe and the KNA. Along with this arrangement came the attendant conflicts between the two organizations, especially the KNA's longstanding distrust of the Tongjihoe's unquestioning support of Syngman Rhee. Further exacerbating this situation was the fact that while individual organizations were at least in theory willing to work together under the banner of the UKC, each organization continued to function autonomously as it pursued its particular interests, which oftentimes undermined the efforts of the UKC.

In light of its complicated organizational structure it is not surprising the UKC found it difficult to function as a coherent body. As individual nationalist groups worked to put aside political and personal differences for the greater good, it was clear that years of factionalist politics had left their mark. In addition to the blatant power struggles between organizational leaders and their organizations, the UKC faced enormous obstacles even in the day-to-day operations of coordinating its activities between the Honolulu and Los Angeles offices. While these rifts were an acknowledged and accepted fact within Korean circles, these divisions were significant enough to merit attention from the U.S. War Department. Commenting on the "lack of unity" and the desire of "leaders to dominate the local program for Korean independence, to the exclusion of their rivals," the Military Intelligence Division of the War Department found the UKC to be united in name only.[5]

THE "OLD MAN" AND THE UKC

The central figure in the UKC dramas was Syngman Rhee with his political aspirations.[6] Accustomed to operating in many ways as a "lone wolf," Rhee chafed openly at working within the organizational structure of the UKC. It was clear that Rhee had envisioned the UKC as an organization created not only to support the Korean Provisional Government but to also support his own political agenda. After years of understanding and representing himself as the spokesman for Korea, Rhee found it enormously difficult to support a vision of the nation that did not place him at the center of power. Rhee was politically savvy enough, however, to recognize that as the United States mobilized for war, an organization such as the UKC could serve his interests, particularly his need for financial support for his diplomatic efforts.

If in 1941 Rhee believed that the UKC could advance his political agenda, likewise, the UKC needed Rhee. While many within the leadership ranks of the UKC were not fans of Rhee and his supporters, they recognized the political capital of Rhee and advocated unity at any cost, especially given the possibility that even with the end of Japanese colonial rule, Korea could be placed under trusteeship of a Western nation if Koreans appeared incapable of self-rule. UKC leaders were acutely aware that the U.S. input on the fate of Korea would be based on firsthand experiences with Koreans in the United States who, despite their common goal of Korean liberation, had attracted attention primarily for their bitter factionalist struggles. As a result, many members of the UKC tempered their dislike for Rhee and worked to maintain a cohesive body even as Rhee became increasingly difficult to work with.

To be sure, Rhee was a significant hindrance to the UKC as it attempted to move forward. Even as his popular support waned in the late 1920s due to his alleged involvement in a series of community scandals in Hawai'i, Rhee as a former president of the KPG continued his diplomatic efforts to gain official U.S. recognition for the Korean Provisional Government. While it is unclear whether Rhee was shunned at large by the majority of Koreans in Hawai'i or on his own volition kept his distance, his isolation in this period aside from his Tongjihoe supporters allowed him to pursue his interests with impunity. Although limited financial resources due to the Depression certainly curtailed Rhee's program for independence, in many ways a decade of relatively unchecked politicking hardened Rhee's resolve that he alone represented the leadership of the independence movement in the United States.

Consequently, Rhee expected the UKC to indulge his financial and personal demands. Whereas many older first-generation Koreans would have indeed acquiesced to Rhee's requests in the 1910s and 1920s, given his educational accomplishments in the United States (a doctorate from Princeton) and his nationalist activities in Korea including a seven-year prison sentence, which made him a hero in many eyes, by the end of the 1930s it was clear that Rhee no longer commanded such a following, as a new generation of nationalist leaders stepped forward. Often called the "in-between," or the *haksaeng* (student), generation, the majority of these individuals were college educated, articulate, bilingual, and intimately familiar with the American political system. While they shared the common goal of Korean independence with their senior compatriots, they differed not only in their strategies to achieve liberation but also in their explicit desire to improve Korean immigrant communities in the United States.

One important leader from this younger generation was Jacob Kyuang-moo Dunn (Chŏn Kyŏng-mu, also known as J. K. Dunn).[7] Immigrating to the United States at the age of four, Dunn overcame grinding poverty and by 1925 received his master's degree in English literature from the University of Michigan. Throughout his career as a student in the 1920s and the 1930s, Dunn immersed himself in *nara-il* (nation-work). By the 1940s, it was clear that Dunn's time as a student leader in the 1920s and 1930s had been a crucial training ground for his work in the independence movement. The traits that had made him such an effective student leader—his public speaking skills, his ability to work in a group setting, and his commitment to Korean liberation—made Dunn an exemplary candidate for a leadership position within the United Korean Committee. As the impending involvement in World War II reignited nationalist fervor in the United States, many older leaders in the movement turned to this younger generation, who were eager to participate.

Dunn jumped at the chance to work for the UKC for a number of reasons. While much has been made of the hostility and bitter infighting among Koreans in the independence movement, it is important to remember that in a world that deemed Asian immigrants second-class citizens, nationalist organizations offered Korean men and women a safe haven from the daily indignities of living in a racially discriminatory society. For many Koreans, first- and second-generation, especially those individuals with advanced degrees, organizations such as the UKC allowed them their first opportunity to work as professionals. For example, in the case of J. K. Dunn, even upon receiving a master's degree in English literature from the University of Michigan in the late 1920s, he worked on and off throughout the 1930s as a butler and a chauffeur.[8] Dunn's situation was hardly atypical in this period.[9]

Initially, Dunn was recruited from the mainland to serve as the director of public relations for the UKC Honolulu Bureau. He was very much an outsider to nationalist politics in Hawai'i, but this was precisely the reason Dunn was selected. He was perceived as an individual who could transcend the deep fissures within local Korean nationalist politics. Moreover, since Dunn had spent the majority of his adult life in the Midwest he was also a stranger to the factional disagreements between the mainland (primarily the West Coast) and Hawai'i.

As this gradual power shift occurred within the movement, it was apparent that the U.S. government also caught wind of this change and found it acceptable. A 1941 intelligence report stated,

> Jacob Dunn, who had spent most of his life on the mainland, has recently come here, and largely because of his non-partisan background appears to be a likely prospect as a reconciler. His position as Public Relations

Chairman of the United Korean Committee makes it possible for him to be used as such in an official capacity. Dunn is not familiar with all the ins and outs of Koreanism here, and I am impressed by what appears to me to be his innocence and sincerity to act as go-between.[10]

This innocence was fleeting. As a part of the executive committee of the UKC, Dunn quickly discovered that the unity so often touted during the formation of the UKC in many ways was only lip service on the part of older nationalist leaders.

While nationalist organizations in Hawai'i and the mainland were sincere in their efforts to draw (both first- and second-generation) younger Koreans into the independence movement, it was also evident that the older generation expected to maintain their authority within their respective organizations. Thus, by selecting someone with Dunn's "sincerity and innocence" older leaders expected a somewhat malleable individual. Much to their surprise, Dunn demonstrated his political muster early on. An American intelligence report three months later characterized Dunn as "aggressive" and "ambitious" and as an individual who was not just a follower but did things on his own initiative.[11]

One of the key complaints of many UKC leaders such as Dunn was Rhee's abrasive and autocratic style of politics and his refusal to keep the UKC informed of his actions. For example, in August 1942, as Rhee increasingly pressured the U.S. State Department for the formal recognition of the Korean Provisional Government, it was apparent that in the opinion of the UKC Rhee had been too forceful in his approach and had placed the campaign for recognition in jeopardy. Wonsoon Lee (Yi Wŏn-sun), the chairman of the UKC Hawai'i bureau, cautioned Rhee to "hold the pressure on immediate Korean recognition in abeyance temporarily . . . to continue as you have under the circumstance[s] may hurt the cause."[12] Lee concluded his letter with the admonishment, "we may advisedly inform that all offending tactics should never be taken in our present stage. We are pleading, and any form of criticism may injure us."[13] It was apparent that Lee's warning to Rhee stemmed partially from the fact that the UKC learned of Rhee's behavior not through Rhee but via Kilsoo Haan (Han Kil-su), the chairman of the Sino-Korean People's League, one of the charter organizations of the UKC.

Haan's providing the UKC with this information should not be viewed as a gesture aimed at the greater good. Instead, it should be read within the context of Haan's own political ambitions to be recognized as the spokesperson for Korean interests in the United States.[14] Thus, Haan sought actively to undermine Rhee's activities in Washington, and Rhee was well aware of Haan's personal politicking. In a letter to Wonsoon Lee dated August 14, 1942, Rhee attributed the failure of gaining official recognition of the Korean Provisional Government to Haan. Rhee remarked that "Our friendly negotiations with the U.S. State Dept. came to an end about last March. Certain friends in that department, using Kilsoo Haan's agitations as an excuse for delaying recognition, quietly advised us that until such time when the department may see fit to give the recognition."[15]

KOREA FOR KOREANS

Rhee's behavior throughout 1942 supported the UKC charge that he was unwilling to work in a cooperative fashion. Rather than working within the established operational channels of the UKC, Rhee insisted on establishing a coterie of advisors and organizations that were not accountable to the executive body of the UKC. The Korean-American Council was one such organization.[16] It was clear that the Council was not an independent organization interested in the affairs of Korea; it was a group chartered by Syngman Rhee, a fact that the UKC was well aware of. Knowing this, the UKC was understandably reluctant to provide the $5,000 requested by Rhee for the Council to negotiate formal U.S. recognition of the Korean Provisional Government. In a letter to the UKC Honolulu bureau, Rhee implored, "We must produce this sum of money and you will see the results. Please do everything you can to get this required amount at once and wire it to me. If we have it, we will have everything. Borrow it, if possible, and we will raise it later and pay it back."[17]

Given that the Honolulu bureau was responsible for advisory and operational issues and *not* the disbursement of funds, it was evident that Rhee had hoped to capitalize on his long history in Hawai'i and hoped to persuade the UKC in Honolulu to circumvent the authority of the UKCLA given that the Los Angeles office had already denied Rhee's request. The UKC in Hawai'i referred Rhee's plea to the UKCLA and clearly outlined its position for Rhee: "We are more or less an advisory council offering you any suggestion or recommendation for the good of our cause, and we or the L.A. Committee are not in any way trying to block your undertaking. We are not taking any order from L.A. Committee, but we must act as one body for unity and oneness in our purpose."[18] The UKC in Honolulu also pointed out the dangers of Rhee's strategy and reminded him that

> through the united effort of the United Korean Committee, Kopogo
> [KPG] and the Korean Commission receive undivided support financially
> and morally, and in case if we and L.A. Committee disagree on any issue,
> the united organization will be unfortunately wrecked and the subse-
> quent result would be chaos and arguments back and forth among the

Korean organizations. Please have faith in us as much as we have in you.
There is no distinction between your people or our people.[19]

Another complaint of the UKC leadership was Rhee's continued reliance on
non-Korean advisees. Particularly, the UKC took issue with Rhee's dependence
on the Korean American Council in matters of establishing formal diplomatic
relations between the Korean Provisional Government and the United States.
While the Council touted itself as an organization interested in the independence of Korea, the UKC pointed out that the Council was hardly a substantive
organization, given that the membership was "confined to the counting of one's
fingers."[20] The UKC was quick to point out that Council members, while sincere, were "not the sort that can advise Korean negotiations."[21]

"SLEUTHING AND SPYING": KILSOO HAAN AND THE
SINO-KOREAN PEOPLE'S LEAGUE

As the UKC's troubles with Rhee escalated, the UKC was plagued with further
internal strife as Kilsoo Haan and the Sino-Korean People's League,[22] one of the
UKC charter organizations, refused to abide by the UKC's by-laws that established the UKC's legislative and executive branches as the official clearinghouse
for all matters concerning the Korean independence movement in the United
States. Founded in 1933 in Hawai'i by Haan, the League was one of the few
known leftist organizations within Korean nationalist circles. The mission of the
League was to promote anti-Japanese activity in the United States, Korea, and
China and to coordinate aid for the Chinese struggle against Japanese aggression as a way to assist in the campaign for Korean independence.[23]

While the activities of the League throughout much of the 1930s are unclear,
the League resurfaced in the late 1930s as a front for a purported espionage ring
that had infiltrated Japan as well as Japanese-friendly organizations in the
United States. It appears that the League was credible enough in its activities
that it was invited to join the UKC in 1941.[24] It was clear that by the 1940s,
however, that the League had essentially become a platform for Kilsoo Haan's
political career. Despite his willingness to participate in the UKC, Haan was
unwilling to subordinate his interests to the UKC's agenda and ultimately
resigned from the UKC in January 1942.[25] Haan then continued his political
activities and established an office of the League in Washington in 1942 and
designated himself the Washington representative. While the rank and file of the
League were few and the Chinese connections of the organization were negligible, Haan was a consummate showman and managed to gain the favor of the
U.S. State Department for a brief period.

In the immediate aftermath of Pearl Harbor, Haan's hard-line anti-Japanese rhetoric found a receptive audience and was critical in boosting the profile of Koreans in the United States. Just a few months later, however, Haan's activities caused the UKC to argue that "espionaging, ferreting fifth column activities, gaining personal front-page sensationalism, or publicizing the Korean racial suffering for American sympathy is not enough to acquire a lost nation's sovereign rights."[26]

Throughout the spring of 1942, the UKC attempted to rein in both Haan and Syngman Rhee. In an editorial titled "Where the Two Per Cent,"[27] the UKC urged the minority 2 percent to put aside their own interests and coordinate their efforts with the UKC for the cause of Korean independence. The UKC reserved the majority of their displeasure for Haan, however, particularly his proclivity to speak on behalf of the Korean people. This displeasure was compounded by that fact that Haan and his followers and the UKC had parted ways.

> It is admitted that this leader of the minority in his spy role has done much in giving the Koreans and Korea publicity. It is admitted where his espionaging for the United States was accepted for its value or not, he as a Korean has done his best. But the tin-god of the minority can not rest on earned laurels of his nature and declare fiats of his personal like or dislike indiscriminately to the injury of the majority. And because of his background and the sudden gain of undue publicity and lime-light showered on him as a spy does not qualify nor make him an accepted spokesman, or an oracle of his entire people.[28]

By the summer of 1942, Haan's maverick behavior in establishing a Washington office prompted the UKC to pause. In an editorial in the *Korean National Herald-Pacific Weekly*, the official publishing organ of the UKC, the editor, while expressing support for the League's anti-Japanese espionage activities, cautioned the League against operating as a rogue agent:

> All due credit is given to this very small group in endeavoring to call the attention of the United States to the duplicity of the Japanese government and its war plans. However, now that the United States is at war against Japan, espionaging without proper facilities as undertaken by the Sino-Korean Peoples' League has, by circumstances, lost its former significance. It can still continue its mission, but it can by no means equal the American Government's own intelligence service.[29]

In the same editorial it was clear that the UKC had other more pressing issues with the League than potential rogue activity. By June 1942, Haan's activities in Washington began to seriously undermine the fragile unity of the UKC. The UKC urged the League to continue its program of espionage, albeit in cooperation with the State Department, and guaranteed that should this be its agenda, "no Korean organization would object but rather support it." But if the objective of having an office in Washington was to undermine the activities of the Korean Commission, the editor declared that "this minority group is definitely in question to its alleged motive and purpose to work for Korea's independence."[30] Pointedly, the editor went on to specifically address Haan's activities in Washington:

> It has been the recent record of this group's Washington representative to oppose any favoritism shown the Korean Provisional Government. What reason or reasons he enhances for his dilatory and negating stand is of public interest. It is realized he is personally very ambitious. But would he cut off his nose to spite his face? And finally the problem of Korean unity in question cannot be greatly affected by the boisterousness of a few. Truth will [win] out. And facts are the solid basis of constructive development for Korean recognition and independence.[31]

Although the UKC was initially willing to tolerate Haan because of the popular appeal for his anti-Japanese activity, it drew the line at any action that compromised the campaign for the recognition of the KPG, including antagonizing Rhee and the Korean Commission. Calling him a "chameleon poseur" and casting doubts about his loyalty by referring to him as "former Japanese Consulate employee who turned yesterday in metamorphosis a self-styled spy for America's defense, ambitious and groveling now to become a Himmler," the UKC attempted to thoroughly discredit Haan.[32]

Haan was undeterred by the UKC's censure of his activities in Washington. He continued his rounds of the State Department and his frequent press releases and interviews. By July 1942, the UKC declared Haan a "public nuisance" and a "maniac," hinted at the possibility of Haan's involvement in communist activity, and urged the State Department to look into the matter.[33]

> This same "hombre" [Haan] once vehemently denied that he had any connection with the communists or anarchists. Since, however, Russia became one of the United Nations, he boasts of his representation of the ultra-radical group and threatens his fellow countrymen with the power he feels sure to get from the Soviet Republic. All loyal Koreans are nationalists. Yet they tolerate all sorts of "isms" so long as they do not interfere with their national aspirations. They, however, distrust those who are insincere and disloyal. . . . If the State Department would look into this mis-informer, the value of his individuality and his "information" will be readily discernable.[34]

By the end of 1942, the UKC had officially declared Haan *persona non grata*.[35] By February 1943, the relationship between Haan and the UKC had warmed considerably as J. K. Dunn brokered a truce on behalf of the UKC with Haan and the Sino-Korean Peoples' League. Dismissing the rift between the two organizations as a "fight of misunderstood issues," Dunn declared that for the sake of "practical unity, there must never be any wranglings among ourselves or that we should not tolerate any form of factional strife to the dress of deterring our own progress."[36] Amazingly, in a matter of roughly two months, Haan had been transformed from a "chameleon poseur" and a "public nuisance" into an individual that the UKC sought out in their quest to fight the "enemy and become free men and women."[37] This 180 degree turn of events was nothing short of miraculous, given the bitter renunciations cast by the UKC.

This very public reversal on the part of the UKC can only be explained in the context of the UKC's ongoing and escalating difficulties with Rhee, the Korean Commission, and the Korean-American Council in Washington. Unable to wage a battle on two fronts, the UKC decided to extend an olive branch to Haan and the League. At the same time, the UKC was eager to use Haan's location and connections in Washington and capitalize on his anti-Rhee sentiments to keep abreast of the activities of Rhee and his associates and to consolidate the political power and agenda of the UKC.

THE COLLAPSE OF COMITY

With the Haan situation resolved, the UKC turned its full attention to Rhee. The difficulties of working with Rhee had been an ongoing issue throughout 1942 and in February 1943, the UKC sought to remedy the situation by restructuring the relationship between the UKC and Rhee. Clearly, the activities of the UKC threatened to displace Rhee from the cynosure of the independence movement. Unwilling to play a supporting role, Rhee continued to operate with impunity. As a result, in the fall of 1942 the UKC sent J. K. Dunn and Warren Kim (Kim Wŏn-yong), another executive member of HONUKC, to Washington to investigate matters.

Two weeks after Dunn and Kim arrived in Washington, Dunn sent a confidential note to the HONUKC outlining Rhee's position on the UKC, Rhee's estimation of Dunn, and Dunn's strategy in dealing with Rhee. In October 1942, despite the difficulties between Rhee and the UKC, reconciliation seemed possible. As Dunn chronicled Rhee's discontent at being financially dependent on the UKC, he also pointed out that Rhee wanted his confidence but Dunn needed to prove his loyalty to him.[38] Dunn's principal strategy in dealing with Rhee was to work through a series of intermediaries, including Henry DeYoung (Henry Chung, also Chŏng Han-gyŏng) and members of the Korean-American Council. Dunn was especially interested in ingratiating himself with the Korean-American Council, given Rhee's confidence in the Council.

Ultimately, Rhee's continued intransigence in Washington, D.C., prompted a memorandum from the UKC. The memo stipulated that the Korean Commission should establish better channels of communication with the HONUKC and the UKCLA; organize and appoint a chairman, a spokesman, a treasurer, and a secretary; maintain a clear and separate identity from the Korean-American Council, both politically and financially; and work in conjunction with the UKC to immediately coordinate efforts with the KPG and the U.S. State Department to send a formal UKC delegation to Chungking.[39] An addendum to the memo also required Rhee to accept Henry DeYoung as a member of the Korean Commission, for Rhee to sever any official ties to the Korean-American Council, and that Rhee and the Commission publish any "circular letters or their like" in already recognized media outlets, namely, *The New Korea (Shinhan Minbo)* and the *Korean National Herald-Pacific Weekly (Kungminbo)*.[40]

In response to the increasing pressure levied by the UKC on the Korean Commission to be made accountable to the UKC for its activities, Rhee attempted to justify his unwillingness to work in tandem with the UKC by arguing that since the "Chairman of the Korean Commission [Rhee] was appointed Envoy Extraordinary and Minister Plenipotentiary, the Commission actually possesses the status of Legation and/or Embassy," and as an official agency of the Korean Provisional Government, "no private agency nor individual can encroach upon its authority."[41]

In making this distinction, Rhee co-opted the UKC's missive that argued for a clear separation of powers and responsibilities between the two UKC bureaus, the KPG and the Korean Commission. While the UKC had laid out these guidelines for the purpose of limiting and managing Rhee's role in the UKC and to coordinate the efforts of the UKC and the Korean Commission, Rhee interpreted these provisions as a license to continue his autonomous rule of the Commission. Thus, he called for a "line to be drawn between the Korean Commission and the two United Korean Committee[s]."[42] In exchange for this understanding Rhee declared that it would be unnecessary to "continue the weekly Korean Bulletin which the Commission had been issuing recently."[43] To further deflect UKC criticism of the Commission, Rhee countered by turning the conversation to the controversial subject of finances: "It is my suggestion that you and each of you should publish a financial report at least every three months, if not every month, for the information of the Korean people whose contributions make possible the good works of the Committees."[44]

Rhee's steadfast refusal to comply with the directives of the UKC prompted Young-ki Kim (Kim Yŏng-gi), whose relationship with Rhee dated to the 1920s, to rebuke Rhee.[45] Drawing on their long history, Kim urged Rhee to be more amenable to the UKC by reminding Rhee of the urgency of Korean liberation:

"For myself, I did not agree with you on many occasions in which you were so stubborn but since December 7, I, putting aside all my personal pettiness and feeling, pledged myself to support you without reservation, not for your personal glory or gain but for the cause which is so dear to our nation of Korea at this moment."[46] Kim went on to urge Rhee to forego personal politics for the sake of the greater good and work with the UKC leadership. He asked Rhee pointedly, if he was unwilling to work with the UKC, "how do you expect to carry on the work yourself?"[47]

Kim did not mince words as he informed Rhee that the UKC could not "stand any longer as often as your so-called friends here create dissension and disunity by circulating your confidential news from you" or to tolerate the "faithful friends of yours [who] hinder our work left and right."[48] Finally, Kim was willing to voice the unspoken advantage of the UKC that other leaders danced around—money. Kim spelled it out explicitly:

> One thing I want to bring out at this time is the attitude you take toward the Korean people and organizations. As long as the financial support comes from the Korean citizens for the maintenance of KOPOGO [KPG] and the Korean Commission cannot assume an arrogant attitude to the Koreans, expecting them to obey blindly without question.[49]

Furthermore, while many of his UKC cohorts skirted the issue of Rhee's legitimacy given his high public profile, Kim addressed it directly: "Assuming that you are officially appointed by KOPOGO to represent Korea at Washington, such utterance as 'you must obey the order from me' only creates false impression and dictatorial implications. You know very well you cannot force the people to obey in the name of KOPOGO."[50] In closing Kim extended Rhee an olive branch by informing him, "As long as you are reasonable in dealing with your co-workers, we will not tolerate anybody or organizations to interfere with your work."[51]

RHEE LEAVES THE UKC

As the relationship between the UKC and Rhee continued to deteriorate through December 1942, Rhee's followers rallied around their beleaguered leader by organizing the Korean People's Convention of Central California (KPC) in Dinuba, California, on January 16, 1943, which was held jointly with the Korean People's Convention of Los Angeles. In a proclamation, the KPC predictably pledged their loyalty to the cause of Korean liberation and denounced the UKC. In their vilification of the UKC, Rhee's followers were careful to reserve their censure for UKC leaders and not the rank and file of the UKC. As a result, the KPC declared:

Alas, however, a few unscrupulous and selfish persons in the Los Angeles Office of the United Korean Committee in America, usurping the good name of that organization and misusing the privileges of their official positions therein, have now launched themselves into acts of individual self-aggrandizement at an incalculable expense to public good, and thus at this most critical moment have deliberately caused a decision among our people in America, brought disgrace to the good name of the Korean race, willfully attempted to retard and sabotage our leaders' Independence efforts, and threatened the head of the Korean Commission, the official plenipotentiary representative of the Korean Provisional Government.[52]

In closing, in a vote of no confidence with the UKCLA, the KPC declared its jurisdiction over the collection of the Tongnipkŏm (Independence fund).

By November 1943, the politely worded criticisms of Rhee disappeared in the *Korean National Herald-Pacific Weekly* and the *New Korea.* Instead, the UKC mounted a serious offensive against Rhee and his followers. Disgusted by Rhee's continued attempts to discredit the UKC through his non-UKC sanctioned newsletter, the *Bulletin,* his unflagging support for the Korean-American Council, and his general contempt for the UKC, the UKC began to document and offer evidence of Rhee's incorrigible behavior toward Koreans in the United States as well as to the American public.

On November 17, 1943, the UKC had reached its breaking point. In this particular incident, Rhee published in his private circular, the *Bulletin,* a letter addressed to him from Won Kiu Ahn (An Wŏn-gyu), the chairman of the HONUKC. In the letter, in addition to addressing fiduciary issues of the Korean Commission, the UKC advised Rhee that he was "swiftly losing the support of the Korean public" and, more important, that his incessant factionalization was a threat to any future political aspirations on his part. Ahn wrote:

> On the contrary you have spent more time in building your own factions among the Koreans on the mainland and Hawaii which has led us today to face a near-collapse. By your bulletins you have and continue to create confusion. Through them you blame and accuse your fellow-countrymen and with play of words you have been endangering our cause and unity which in consequence has been losing for you popular support that you need to become a leader.[53]

Continuing in its hard-line vein the UKC issued Rhee an ultimatum:

> Now it is very necessary for you to make a definite decision whether to cooperate with us or to lose our support. You can, of course, separate yourself with a handful of your blind supporters. But we know what that

will result for you. And you can, of course, display all your authority and any show of arbitrary authority will fall far short of forcing anything on the public against its will.[54]

Regarded strictly as private correspondence between the UKC and Rhee, the letter was not intended for public distribution. Yet, Rhee violated that confidentiality by publishing the letter in its entirety in the *Bulletin*. Furthermore, Rhee printed the letter out of context by neglecting to include *his* letter that prompted the UKC response. The UKC was acutely aware that such a chastisement of Rhee combined with their apparent unwillingness to release funds collected from the rank and file would make them appear just as autocratic as Rhee. Consequently, the UKC decided to go public with the matter and published both letters in the *Korean National Herald-Pacific Weekly*. Rhee's letter to the UKC provided an entirely different context for the UKC's harsh response. In his letter, Rhee decried the UKC for failing to support the Korean-American Council by publishing an article "criticizing the American friends and warning them to keep their hands off."[55]

By the fall of 1943, Rhee and the Korean Commission were in a beleaguered state as the UKC called for accountability. Put on the defensive, Rhee took on a bunker mentality and refused to address the UKC's demands. Instead, utilizing a network of his personal supporters, Rhee continued to work to undermine the efforts of the United Korean Committee. Specifically, Rhee attempted to subvert the UKC's existing policy of the dispersal of funds with the "establishment of local commissions to act as collection agents to forward funds directly to him."[56] This type of activity coupled with Rhee's refusal to keep the UKC informed of his dealings in Washington further exacerbated an already tense situation.

The fall of 1943 did indeed mark a "turning point," as the UKC decided that it would no longer allow Rhee to operate with impunity. More important, the UKC began to move away from the decades-old campaign for official recognition of the Korean Provisional Government. To be sure, these decisions were intimately connected, given Syngman Rhee's long history and obsession with the project of KPG recognition. By making the question of recognition a nonissue, the UKC effectively made Rhee's politicking a moot point. Consequently, instead of KPG recognition, the UKC began to direct its resources and efforts to causes closer to home. Predictably, Rhee had no plans to abandon his political ambitions as he continued on in his campaign to discredit the UKC. This was evident as he formally withdrew his membership as well as that of the Tongjihoe from the UKC.

With the departure of Rhee and the Tongjihoe, and despite the harsh feelings and recriminations that lingered, the UKC struggled mightily to maintain a façade of unity. In public, the UKC was careful not to place blame on Rhee and his followers. Instead, the UKC urged Koreans to see the Tongjihoe's withdrawal as a patriotic act: "That Dongjihoi had withdrawn for freedom to give its unquestioned loyalty and support to Syngman Rhee is not to be criticized. It is its prerogative and now its principal objective. In its views, this must be judged, its patriotic stand and in its regard the best means of regaining independence. We wish it well."[57] At the same time, the UKC elected not to spend any more time rehashing the terms of the dispute and declared that Koreans would not "make progress in impassion[ed] talks of unity centered on any one man—for no one Korean is above another. . . . Working [for] Korean unity is [as] hard as before through the United Korean Committee. There is no further need of expensive and time-consuming pow-wows. Therefore, 'Damn the torpedoes; full speed ahead!'"[58] Pledging its continued support to the Provisional Government, the UKC rededicated itself to the struggle for Korean independence.

IN DUE COURSE

In November 1943, the heads of the three Allied powers—Roosevelt, Churchill, and Chiang Kai-shek—issued the Cairo Declaration, in which they declared that Korea would be free and independent "in due course" following the defeat of Japan. Korean nationalist organizations in the United States initially rejoiced in the Cairo Declaration, which finally recognized their greatest desire—Korean liberation. But, Korean nationalist leaders expressed their misgivings about the phrase "in due course" and demanded "unconditional freedom and independence" upon the end of the war.[59] In particular, Koreans feared that without unconditional and immediate freedom, Korea would be placed under the political control of an Allied power after the war. Ironically, what should have been a moment of unity among Korean nationalists of all political stripes quickly dissolved into dissent that plagued the independence movement well into the spring of 1944.

The heated nature of these debates prompted J. K. Dunn of the UKC to urge his fellow compatriots to focus on the task at hand, the defeat of Japan, and demonstrate their unity to the world:

> Save the fireworks. Let's get together on what we want in the way of giving hell to the Japs. We have not advocated any mandatory [sic] or supervision of Korea by any power. We are accepting the political decree as given; for right now there is nothing we can do without appreciable fighting strength of our own arms and recognized diplomatic agents; and spouting of words in dissent and denunciation will not bring true Korean independence or change history. Our own unified and balanced organization with increasing strength for United Nations' participation and giving

proof of our stability and ability as a people is the course now to be followed.[60]

Dunn was also quick to point out that "in due course" was not a move to delay Korean sovereignty but a pragmatic measure given the weakened state of Korea in the wake of thirty years of colonial rule. Dunn reminded his fellow Koreans that

> if the Koreans had been deprived of their government in 1937, as recently as the time of the renewed Japanese offensive against the Chinese, or if the Koreans are capable in their own way of driving the Japanese out of Korea now or in the progress of the war, or even in the closing stage of this war, and can immediately establish a government of their own in Korea, civil or military, to assume strong administrative functions, "in due course" may have been written "at once."

Dunn, especially in light of his visit to Korea a decade earlier, recognized the reality of the Korean situation more cogently than many of his co-ethnics. He pointed out:

> But as circumstances exist with Korea, a part of the Japanese empire since 1910 and Korean independence contingent on the allied forces driving the Japanese from Korea, it may be safe to assume that some form of allied administration will be the natural course to take place until such a time as Korean strength and organizational permanency is seen. Certainly when the Japanese are driven out of Korea, the Japanese will arrange beforehand to take out all wealth in despoliation, if they have not already stripped the country for causes of war, and the sudden Japanese organizational collapse will leave Korea in chaos unless and until there is a government with a police force sufficient to control matters. In our interpretation it is to avoid just such a chaotic situation that the phrase "in due course" was written in.[61]

Even as the UKC attempted to take a pragmatic approach on the Cairo Declaration, the issue of "in due course" caused further strife for the UKC as both the Korean National Revolutionary Party (KNRP) and the Korean Student Federation of North America (KSF) broke ranks with the UKC and began to critique UKC policies openly. In a statement that asserted that "Koreans Want Independence, Not Protectorate," the KNRP challenged the UKC's position on the matter of "in due course." The KNRP called J. K. Dunn "irresponsible" and said that his support of some form of Allied intervention in Korea was "detrimental to the very cause of our Korean independence movement" and that such utterances ran "counter to the fundamental spirit of Korean independence as well as to the wishes of the Korean people."[62]

By 1944, both the Sino-Korean People's League and the KNRP soundly rejected diplomatic means for the liberation of Korea. Revisiting a nationalist approach advocated by nationalist leader Youngman Park (Pak Yong-man) in the 1920s while simultaneously censuring the UKC, Inez Kong Pai, reflecting the position of the League and the KNRP, declared:

> The stage of publicity, propaganda and appeals for recognition is past. The emphasis has shifted from the public and political maneuvers to the military. Instead of spending thousands upon thousands of dollars sending delegates hither and thither, calling expensive conferences on the slightest pretext and wasting time trying to compose the petty factional differences—the Koreans in the United States and Hawaii should pool their resources and buy materials and supplies for our men in China and work toward getting them there. If we can accomplish this, other things will follow—political solidarity among ourselves, respect, attention and aid from the United Nations.[63]

Importantly, the debates over "in due course" represented more than the issue of Korean sovereignty; it was also a critique of U.S. imperialism. Consequently, members of the KNRP asked "how far is 'in due course'?" and were quick to point out the Cairo Declaration was in many ways wartime propaganda.

> And yet, the Cairo proclamation as bold as it may be is actually only a psychological attack upon the enemy and a psychological build-up of the morale of the people of Asia. The physical materialization of this great promise will depend upon the interpretation and action of the meaning of "In Due Course"—the conditional clause attached to the Cairo roar.[64]

Additionally, the KNRP described the "in due course" clause in the Cairo Declaration as the price tag attached to "the beautiful bouquet of National Independence."[65]

> In the minds of Koreans it arouses the inevitable suspicion that perhaps, after all, the independence of Korea will conform only to the pattern of the postwar arrangement of big powers. This suspicion and apprehension goes even deeper. The Cairo condition to national liberation places a great question mark upon the Allies' basic concept of the freedom and equality of men and nations.[66]

The heated debates over the UKC's support of "in due course" were significant enough for the UKC to issue a statement at the end of March 1944, which declared:

It is difficult to believe that the three great powers envisioned a mandated
Korea. The Korean people's determination concurs with a statement
issued by Kim Koo [Kim Ku], head of the Korean Provisional Government in Chungking, that Koreans will fight for "unconditional freedom
and independence right after World II." The Korean people who have
fought for their freedom for the past forty years cannot accept any form
of mandate status.[67]

This attempt on the part of the UKC to distance itself from its earliest stance on
the matter of "in due course" came too late, however.

Even as the UKC reassessed its position on the Cairo Declaration and committed financial support for Korean military action in China against the Japanese, it was clear that many Koreans found these measures to be a superficial
gesture at best especially since one of the resolutions passed by the UKC in
the wake of the Cairo Declaration earmarked $30,000 for opening an official
UKC Washington bureau. The opposition to the proposed Washington bureau
prompted the KNRP and the Korean Student Federation to withdraw formally
from the UKC. Insisting that a Washington office would challenge the authority of the Korean Commission already established there and destroy "national
unity," the KNRP reasserted its commitment to a program of military action:

> the most effective diplomacy for us to resort to is to carry out positive
> military action with all of our own strength. Notwithstanding this, should
> the wealth of Koreans in this country be squandered by collecting money
> both individually and publicly under the pretext of diplomacy which has
> no substantial value whatsoever, it would be nothing but an act of put-
> ting the cart before the horse from the standpoint of the entire Korean
> independence movement; on the other hand, it would expose to the eyes
> of Americans our ignorance of diplomacy, thereby giving rise to misun-
> derstanding among them regarding our sincerity toward our liberation.[68]

Simultaneously, the KNRP in its criticism of the UKC also rejected the longstanding Korean nationalist strategy of diplomacy.

Importantly, the marginalized position of the KNRP allowed it to comment
freely on the activities of other Korean nationalist organizations. The KNRP
was acutely aware that its marginalized position in the independence movement
was the direct result of its advocacy of revolutionary means that was comprised
of an active support of military action and the steadfast rejection of Korean liberation premised on "in due course." Even in the face of the marginalization the
KNRP faced, they fervently believed that they could speak for the nation, noting that the more mainstream nationalist organizations despite their rhetoric
of unity ignored the "importance of unity between their countrymen" and

"laugh[ed] at any revolutionary ideas entertained by their fellowmen and disrespect[ed] the leaders of their fellowmen."[69] The fact that the KNRP could operate as a dissenting voice at the height of U.S. wartime nationalism and in the face of more popularly supported nationalist organizations speaks volumes to the ways in which Korean immigrants could and did articulate more radical visions of the Korean nation.

By the summer of 1944, the tensions between Syngman Rhee and the UKC had reached their zenith as a series of furious letters by Sidai Hahn (Han Si-dae), the executive chairman of the UKCLA, were dispatched to Kim Koo (Kim Ku), the chairman of the Korean Provisional Government in Chungking, China. While disgusted with the departure of Rhee and his followers from the UKC, Hahn reserved the full brunt of his outrage for Rhee's duplicitous politicking in Washington, as Rhee opened a Washington office under the title of the United Korean Committee, which caused enormous confusion to Koreans and non-Koreans alike given that the UKC had at an earlier date established an official Washington bureau. Hahn regarded Rhee's move as a "most despicable and fraudulent attempt to confuse the work of the United Korean Committee in America."[70]

Hahn's letter also carried a more ominous message as he related Rhee's political activities in the United States as a "subtle plan of establishing himself as the titular head of [the] Korean government."[71] Hahn's concerns were not without merit especially in 1944 as Rhee worked assiduously to cultivate a public persona as the de facto leader of Korea. Indeed, Hahn found Rhee's activities in the United States so counterproductive to the interests of Korea that he objected to Rhee's continued role as the officially accredited agent of the Korean Provisional Government. Remarking that Rhee could not "add luster or achievement for our Korean cause," Hahn declared that an "immediate solution must be had. And if the present status is unchanged only disastrous consequences can face us all."[72]

Rhee's attempt to short circuit the endeavors of other nationalist organizations and consolidate his power as the chairman of the Korean Commission in 1944 and the response by other Korean nationalists to these attempts represents a clear moment of struggle over the way in which Koreans "imagined the nation." While the Korea Rhee strived to speak for was one that emphasized elite control by educated men like himself, other nationalist visions demanded a "true democracy," which included democratic representation that had to begin at the fundamental level as part of a means to independence. Unwilling to let Rhee and his cohorts justify their behavior as a means to an end, the UKC denounced their actions:

> How strange and audacious it all sounds to us, when the people who
> destroy unity call for unity! That the people who dictate should call for

cooperation! And even as they require unity and cooperation should shout "GET THE HELL OUT OF WASHINGTON." And dare suggest "if we cannot unite and coordinate our efforts in the United States, let us stop all political activities." We know that there are less than 10,000 Koreans in the United States, including Hawaii, Mexico and Cuba. Their numbers are not legions, but those that there are have done much for Korea's cause, and when totaled they have achieved much in their own way.[73]

REORGANIZATION

As the tensions between the UKC and Rhee escalated, the KPG, who had been kept abreast of the situation through a flurry of telegrams by nearly every nationalist organization in the United States, in August 1944 instructed nationalist organizations in the United States to convene a Korean Commission Reorganization Conference to "unify and strengthen the Korean diplomatic front in this country."[74] In hopes of easing the tensions among nationalist groups in the United States and to foster unity, the KPG ordered the reorganization of the Korean Commission and the UKC into a new representative body under the name Korean Diplomatic Mission. Moreover, during this period of reorganization, the KPG declared a cessation of all diplomatic activity by any nationalist organization until the restructuring was complete.

This move to reorganize the Korean Commission and the UKC was part of the growing realization by the KPG in the waning months of the war that Korean independence was imminent upon the defeat of Japan by the Allied powers. Consequently, instead of focusing on the actual means of independence, the Provisional Government turned its attention to making sure that it would have a place in postwar Korea. Despite the fierce debates over the "in due course" clause, nationalists of all political persuasions were acutely aware that the United States would play an integral role in postwar Korea and, to have any input on U.S. policy decisions in Korea, the Korean representatives of the KPG in the United States would have to present a united front.

In response to the KPG's proposal, representatives of thirteen nationalist organizations held a Reorganization Conference in Los Angeles in October 1944.[75] Initially, Koreans in the United States agreed to the KPG's request to include representatives from every Korean nationalist organization in the United States in the Reorganization Conference. In light of the much-circulated proposition that Syngman Rhee be retained as "advisor without executive power," however, Rhee and the Tongjihoe withdrew from the convention to reorganize the Korean Commission. The *Korean Independence* questioned this move:

Does the Dongjihoe take the present action because it knows that its president Dr. Syngman Rhee, present chairman of the Korean Commission who has been to date a source of bickerings, controversy and friction among the Koreans abroad, instead of inspiration of patriotism or national unity, will be denied a chance to retain his present position and prestige? Whatever the reasons for the Dongjihoe's action may be, the Dongjihoe's noncooperative spirit is far from commendable.[76]

The exit of Rhee and his followers dissolved any pretense of unity as the Conference split along conservative and radical lines, with the UKC advocating diplomacy with a UKC-led Commission and the KNRP rejecting diplomatic efforts in the United States in favor of directing all resources to the expansion of Korean military forces. With much negotiation, the Conference managed to bridge this ideological divide, and the representatives for the Korean Diplomatic Mission were democratically elected. Importantly, the Conference outlined eight key proposals:

1   Unification of the Korean activities in the United States by strengthening the United Korean Committee.
2   Reorganization of the Korean Commission.
3   Promotion of the Korean military campaign in the Far East as a contribution to the speedy defeat of Japan.
4   Measures to raise fund[s] and use it for the cause of the Korean movement.
5   Separation of the diplomatic organ from civilian organizations.
6   Publication of an organ by the United Korean Committee.
7   Training of those who will serve Korea by sending Koreans of ability to American universities with scholarships.
8   The drafting of necessary documents to be submitted by the Korean people to the Peace Conference.

While these proposals provided an uneasy alliance, disapproval of this new political order prompted continued criticism. One longtime nationalist leader called the Reorganization Conference a "waste" and declared:

it has neither direction nor sense of value of time. Can we mention it as the Korean Independence Movement? Suppose here is a Korean who regardless of the inside of the Korean society leads an easy life in the nation's capital, attempting to cover the eyes of the foreigners and deafen their ears and who is busy making a round of calls upon lower officials of the State Department with their titled name cards or entertaining his American friends to the chop suey dinners once in a while. Does he think that by practicing this sort of thing the Korean provisional government will be recognized or that Korea will become free and independent?[77]

In many ways, the Reorganization Conference was a "waste" since the KPG refused to honor the nominations proposed by the conference because the nominations did not include Rhee or the Tongjihoe since they had declined to attend the meeting. Instead, the KPG issued a "final order" that recognized the nominations of Commission members at large, but kept Rhee as the chairman of the Korean Commission.[78] In deference to the Provisional Government, however, the UKC and the other organizations accepted this decree despite serious misgivings. Sidai Hahn, the executive chairman of the UKCLA, remarked that the KPG's continued sympathy for Rhee would create a situation where the Provisional Government would not "be respected here any more."[79]

In the aftermath of the Reorganization Conference, the UKC worked assiduously to chart a new course. In addition to Korean independence, it wholeheartedly committed itself to "take up actively the problems for Korean welfare in the United States and elsewhere."[80] The concern over the welfare of Koreans in the United States was hardly a new phenomenon. From the very onset of Korean emigration, Korean immigrants established numerous organizations, religious and secular, to ameliorate the harsh conditions of immigrant life in the United States. What was new in 1944 was the explicit recognition of a long-term future in the United States for Korean immigrant communities. Acutely aware that many immigrants, particularly the earliest immigrants who were in their sixties, seventies, and eighties would be ill equipped to pick up their lives in a Korea they had not set eyes on in nearly fifty years, and that many first-generation immigrants with American-born children and grandchildren were not willing to abandon the lives that they had painstakingly built with years of arduous labor in the United States, the UKC sought to improve the lives of Korean immigrants in America.

For the UKC improving the lives of Korean immigrants in the United States and the campaign for Korean independence were two sides of the same coin. Recognizing that the war had brought enormous financial and political opportunities for Koreans in the United States, the UKC believed that a strong postwar Korea would only continue to improve this situation.

> Economically, for most they [Koreans] are out of the red for the first time and they build substantially for their children to be Americans on American standards. And the Korean-Americans have an equal footing in the unique opportunity of developing and interpreting best the economic and cultural ties of postwar Korea and America. They stand best to gain most in the future Korean-American relations.[81]

The establishment of an official Washington bureau of the UKC inaugurated this new strategy for the UKC. Relaunching the previously thwarted Chungking trip emerged as the most urgent matter. For the UKC, this face-to-face meeting with the leadership of the Provisional Government represented not only a way to coordinate UKC and KPG activities, but in the context of Rhee's personal political aspirations, it was also a way to further legitimacy of the UKC as the sole agency that represented Korea in the United States.

Aside from the Chungking plan, the UKC continued its offensive against Rhee by generating a series of directives that assessed Rhee's inability to yield any real political gains for Korea. In a letter to the KPG, J. K. Dunn, the UKC public affairs director, provided an explicit account of Rhee's shortcomings. In addition to demonstrating Rhee's responsibility in destroying the comity of Korean independence activities in the United States, Dunn pointed out Rhee's failure to bring about the formal recognition of KPG, a failed lend-lease plan for the Korean military, Rhee's inability to secure representation at various UN conferences in the United States, and Rhee's shortcomings in generating positive press for Korea.[82]

It was evident that even after Rhee's official withdrawal from the UKC, the acrimonious relationship between the UKC and Rhee continued to simmer. As a result, in February 1945, J. K. Dunn felt compelled to author a report explicitly outlining the agenda of the UKC. While the report revealed the valiant struggle of the Committee to maintain a high profile through a number of public events including a lecture series, radio interviews, and the issuance of a Korean commemorative stamp, it was clear that Rhee's continued hostilities toward other nationalist interests aside from his own had resulted in the UKC operations under the "greatest handicap and the severest strain."[83] The strain was further compounded by the fact that given staff shortages, Dunn, as the executive director of the Washington bureau in addition to serving as the secretary of public relations, worked full-time in dealing with "office administration, daily correspondence, local and distant contract for keeping and giving mutual advice for organizational cooperation."[84]

In an effort to thwart Rhee's endeavors to co-opt the UKC name, the UKC worked resolutely to legitimate and distinguish itself as the bona fide UKC. One such tactic was an extensive campaign of publicity spearheaded by J. K. Dunn out of the Washington bureau. In his quest to maintain the integrity of the UKC name, Dunn worked to establish relationships with any government and private agency that dealt with foreign policy, East Asia, or public affairs. For example, in a request to be placed on the mailing list of the Foreign New Bureau of the Office of War Information, Dunn declared: "Our organization is the representation of the Korean people in the United States and Hawaii with offices in Los Angeles and Honolulu. Our Washington office is here for the purpose of undertaking research, publicity and public relations on behalf of the Korean people's for war participation and for their national liberation."[85] Other organizations included the U.S. Government Printing Office, the Foreign Policy Association, the Institute of Pacific Relations, the Yale Institute of International Studies, the Public Affairs Press, the American Council on Public Affairs, and the *Far Eastern Survey.*

This publicity campaign was particularly important when it came to the UKC's relationship with the U.S. State Department. In order to make a favorable impression, especially in the light of Rhee's name recognition factor, the UKC routinely offered the services of its members to the U.S. government. By 1944, while many Koreans, especially Korean-born college students fluent in Japanese, had already been absorbed into the U.S. war machine, the UKC was envisioning a more expansive role that would not be limited to contributions to the war effort. The UKC found such an opportunity with the Division of Cultural Cooperation (DCC), a government office housed in the U.S. State Department.[86]

In the 1940s, the agenda of the DCC included offering financial assistance to foreign students and the "building of cultural relations between the American Government and the peoples of occupied countries of the Far East to be liberated."[87] In presenting the UKC as the Korean authority in the development of such a relationship, on behalf of the UKC Dunn offered the DCC a list of Korean students in the United States suited for such a program. Dunn outlined the DCC requirements:

> It is to the applicant's advantage to have received a degree. He must be an alien Korean as the planning takes into consideration aiding the education of those Koreans who will return to Korea where they purpose to serve. The applicant may designate any college or institution, and pursue any line of study that meets his desire with intent of returning to Korea.[88]

At a time when the United States was grappling with the status of foreign students and of Asian immigrants in general, a program that clearly detailed the return of Korean aliens to Korea must have seemed attractive. For the students interested in the program, the financial support offered by the DCC filled an immediate need, especially since the war had left many Korean students who depended on funds from Korea in a tenuous position.

Compared to the early days of the independence movement in the United States, by the 1940s it was clear that many Korean nationalist leaders in the UKC had learned a few lessons in American politics along the way. While the invoking of American patriotic ideals especially in the context of the war remained very much the same, the level of political acumen on the part of independence leaders was a significant departure from the scattershot efforts of political mobilizations of the past. Rather than relying on a charismatic personality as the primary method by which to advance their political demands, by the 1940s Koreans in the United States had established a sophisticated ethnic political machine.

A glimpse of this new political style can be seen in a missive Dunn sent out to various leaders of the UKC as well as the leaders of individual organizations. Dunn provided an organizational blueprint for political mobilization for S. 730, a Senate bill that called for the naturalization of Korean immigrants and the establishment of an immigration quota. He recommended the formation of an advisory committee composed of "known Americans whose support and advice are almost a pre-requisite to any and all efforts as may be made by Koreans for successful legislative consideration of the bill."[89] It was also obvious that the larger percentage of second-generation Koreans in this period influenced the political strategy of independence leaders. In the formation of sectional committees, Dunn suggested that "organizations interested in the bill should make contacts with American civic, religious and educational bodies to inform and to obtain support for the proposed legislation—and at the proper time to advise their Congressmen to vote."[90] He also advocated that Koreans directly contact not only their congressional representatives, but also Immigration and Naturalization officials. Finally, Dunn urged Koreans to take advantage of American media outlets as well as the lecture circuit.

Even despite criticism from members of the Korean community, the newly organized Korean Diplomatic Mission and particularly the efforts of the UKC were applauded by the KNRP, who praised this new political order: "The Overseas Korean Conference [sponsored by the UKC] is commendable for its remarkable liberal and democratic attitude, for it demonstrated its sincere desire to seek the common and collective opinions of the majority of people and act on the basis of the collective wishes of the people. . . . This is a sign that the Koreans in this country are moving one step ahead, spiritually, morally, and ideologically."[91]

THE UN CONFERENCE

Despite the reorganization of Korean organizations in the United States under the banner of the Korean Diplomatic Mission, both the UKC and Rhee pursued their own agendas through the winter of 1944–45. But, as the end of the war appeared imminent, Korean nationalist organizations began in the spring of 1945 to consider the postwar future of Korea actively. Central to these plans was gaining an official delegation status at the upcoming United Nations Conference on International Organization to be held at the end of April in San Francisco. Well aware that campaigning for recognition to attend the UN Conference would require a united effort, the KNRP asked: "shall we Koreans still wander and hesitate before our ultimate goal—the liberation and independence of our homeland?"[92] The KNRP also pointed out the urgency of the situation:

> Our compatriots, let us not look back upon our past which is dead but to endeavor to make the best of our reality. If we are united now, we as a nation shall survive and if we wander, hesitate, shrink, and scatter ourselves, the future of our nation is anything but bright. . . . The failure by us to demonstrate our capacity of making united action at this time will forever remain as an ineraseable [sic] on the pages of our history.[93]

That this sentiment was expressed by an organization that had long rejected the diplomatic efforts of the UKC and the Korean Commission indicates the importance the UN Conference and the fervent desires of these organizations to have a stake in the reconstitution of the Korean nation. Consequently, a meeting was called by the UKC in Los Angeles in April 1945 to organize a strategy for representation in San Francisco.

By the end of the UKC conference it was clear that sending any type of official delegation to San Francisco would be next to impossible given that the U.S. State Department refused Koreans in the United States to represent the KPG at the UN Conference, contending that the Korean Provisional Government lacked formal recognition by any nation. At the same time, Koreans were also denied permission to attend as civilian delegates, which forced the UKC to devise other plans. In light of this situation the UKC declared:

> There are now three alternatives for the Koreans to take; the first is to seek the permission for the Koreans to attend the San Francisco Conference as observers or spectators; the second, to attempt to submit to the conference a memorandum regarding the case of Korea, in the case that the first alternative fails; and third to attempt to appeal to the delegates of the United Nations through private contact with them, in case the aforesaid two alternatives prove futile.[94]

Notably absent from the UKC's Overseas Conference was Rhee and the Korean Commission. As the UKC, the KNRP, and the Sino-Korean People's League struggled to present a united front, Rhee and his supporters were making their own plans in regards to the UN Conference and had separately petitioned the State Department for recognition. In petitioning the State Department independently Rhee, under the auspices of the Korean Commission, thwarted the much-desired unity proposed by the UKC and others. Angry and frustrated the UKC declared: "The cancer of the Korean community in the United States, which has existed for the past decades, still remains to be removed, for it is much to be deplored that we cannot have a unity among us at this moment when it is vitally needed."[95] The UKC went on to remark on the absurdity of the situation: "In asking for permission to send the delegation representing a nation—two opposite groups of the same nation submitted petitions independently of each other and it is not difficult to conjecture that either the U.S. State Department or the United Nations refuse to take into [consideration] this kind of petition."[96] The UKC demanded democratic representation and asserted: "This is the time when the bureaucracy and aristocracy of the Eighteenth and Nineteenth Century must be abrogated. Modern government is for the people; therefore, without the support of the majority of people no government can stand."[97] Most important, the UKC made clear that any discussion of a postwar Korea at a fundamental level needed to be grounded in principles of democracy:

> We live under the protection of a democratic country, but a dozen of leaders of Korean organizations disregarding public opinion, wield legislative and executive powers of their own accord. Where did they get that power anyhow? If these leaders really want to serve the cause of people and independence, they should first of all formulate the best plans and then put them to vote among their followers before attempting to put them into execution. That is the fundamental principle of democracy.[98]

Ultimately, the efforts of all nationalist organizations failed to get a Korean delegation seated at the UN deliberations. Instead, the only way that the UKC and other nationalist organizations managed to attend the UN Conference was under the guise of "press correspondents." Under the auspices of the *New Korea*, the *Korean National Herald*, and the *Korean Independence*, key nationalist leaders including J. K. Dunn and Kilsoo Haan were in San Francisco, where they and others focused on making private appeals to other national delegations on the matter of Korean independence. Simultaneously, Syngman Rhee, representing himself as the "head of the Korean Provisional Government delegation," focused on providing interviews about the postwar future of Korea to national press outlets including the *Washington Post*, the *New York Times*, and the *San Francisco Chronicle*.[99]

CONCLUSION

The end of World War II was in many ways anticlimatic. While Koreans in exile throughout the world openly rejoiced at the liberation of Korea, it was immediately clear that this freedom would be sharply circumscribed by the Allied occupation of postwar Korea. Viewed as a temporary measure, Koreans in Korea and abroad never anticipated the division of Korea into two occupied zones and the subsequent civil war that took the lives of so many. Nor did they expect the political ascendancy of Syngman Rhee as the president of South Korea. While these developments outraged many in Korean communities in the United States, it was also clear that for many Koreans in the United States this was not a Korea that they knew or recognized, given that by the 1940s the majority of first-generation Koreans had resided in the United States for nearly a half century. With lives established in the United States, especially with children and grandchildren, and the liberalization of U.S. naturalization laws in the 1950s, the prospects of returning to a postwar Korea ravaged by decades of colonial rule and civil conflict seemed remote at best. Ironically, many Koreans who had so ardently participated in the Korean independence movement for the majority of their lives in the United States chose to stay rather than repatriate to Korea. It was clear their immigrant experiences allowed them to craft an ethnic American identity that envisioned a viable future in the United States. This, however, did not occur in the "watershed of World War II" as many historians have suggested. The negotiation of this identity was a continual process from the arrival of the first Korean immigrants in the first decade of the twentieth century.

The liberation of Korea also signaled the beginning of the end of the UKC. While the UKC did send a delegation to Korea immediately after World War II, in light of the chaos and political confusion on the Korean Peninsula combined with the escalation of Cold War tensions, the UKC delegation quickly discovered that the American military government had opted to support Syngman Rhee. The American support of Rhee guaranteed that the UKC would have very little influence in Korea, which precipitated the decline of the UKC.[100]

In the end, perhaps the saddest and most tragic outcome of the postwar Korean situation was for those Koreans in the United States who had challenged Rhee throughout the 1930s and 1940s and had hoped to return and contribute to the rebuilding of Korea. As if the pain of the division of Korea was not enough, once Rhee assumed the presidency of South Korea it was nearly impossible for any of these leaders to enter the country, since Rhee refused to provide entry visas.[101] Consequently, some of the most critical nationalist views were excluded from the rebuilding of the Korean nation. Simultaneously, the international politics of the Cold War guaranteed that Koreans in the United States would not have a role in the development of North Korea. It is not clear to what degree such input would have dramatically altered the course of Korean politics in the postwar period, especially in light of Cold War geopolitics. The efforts of organizations like the UKC and others suggest that the postwar Korean situation was not a foregone conclusion, however.

NOTES

Ilhan New, "Is There Something Wrong With Korean Organizations?" *The New Korea*, August 12, 1943.

　　1. FA-2 Registration Statement in compliance with the 1938 Foreign Agents

Registration Act, 1941. Heisop Chin Collection, United Korean Committee Papers, Box 4, UCLA. In the FA-2 statement, the Tongjihoe of Los Angeles was not listed but it was evident that the Tongjihoe of Los Angeles operated as a distinct organization.

2. Ibid.

3. The most prominent activity of organizations such as the KNA, Tongjihoe, and the KSF was the publishing of organization-supported newspapers and newsletters. The KNA in Hawai'i published the *Kungminbo (Korean National Herald)*; the KNA, first in San Francisco and then in Los Angeles, published the *Shinhan Minbo (The New Korea)*; the Tongjihoe in Hawai'i published the *T'ae-p'yŏngyang Chubo (Pacific Weekly)*; and the KSF published the Korean Student Bulletin.

4. Notably, neither branch of the Women's Patriotic League received a titled position. Instead, a member of each branch was assigned to be a member at large.

5. Annex No. 2 of the G-2 Periodic Report, RG 165, Military Intelligence Division, Islands Hawaii, 1922–44. National Archives and Records Administration (NARA) II, College Park, Md.

6. Letter to Warren Y. Kim from J. K. Dunn, October 16, 1942, Folder 9, Box 4, Heisop Chin Collection, UCLA.

7. For a more detailed account of Dunn's experiences in the 1920s and 1930s, see Chapter 3 in Anne S. Choi, "Border Crossings: The Politics of Korean Nationalism, 1919–1945" (Ph.D. diss., University of Southern California, 2003).

8. Interview with Ellen Thun (J. K. Dunn's cousin and adopted sister) by author, July 4, 2002.

9. Even Syngman Rhee, the future president of South Korea, had worked as a "houseboy" during his college years.

10. Gordon T. Bowles quoted in Wayne Patterson, *The Ilse: First-Generation Korean Immigrants in Hawai'i* (Honolulu: University of Hawai'i Press, 2000), 190.

11. Ibid.

12. Letter to Syngman Rhee from Wonsoon Lee, August 12, 1942, Heisop Chin Collection, United Korean Committee Papers, Folder 9, Box 4, UCLA.

13. Ibid.

14. Unlike Syngman Rhee, despite his political ambitions Haan maintained his affiliation with the UKC for a number of reasons, including the fact that Haan's supporters via the Sino-Korean People's League remained small in comparison to Rhee's supporters in the Tongjihoe. Additionally, Haan lacked the nationalist pedigree that Rhee possessed, which most likely encouraged him to remain friendly with the UKC.

15. Letter to Wonsoon Lee from Syngman Rhee, August 14, 1942. Folder 9, Box 4, Heisop Chin Collection, United Korean Committee Papers, Box 4, UCLA. Given that these letters were mailed from Honolulu it is unlikely that Rhee had

received Wonsoon Lee's letter dated August 12, 1942, that related Haan's proclivity for sharing information about Rhee to UKC officials.

16. Hereafter, referred to as the Council.

17. Letter to Won Soon Lee from Syngman Rhee, August 14, 1942, United Korean Committee Papers, Folder 9, Box 4, Heisop Chin Collection, UCLA.

18. Excerpt from a letter to Syngman Rhee from the UKC, Honolulu, September 16, 1942, United Korean Committee Papers, Box 4, Heisop Chin Collection, UCLA. This letter in excerpt form was part of a larger case file that was evidence of Rhee's unwillingness to work within the UKC and to explain his withdrawal from the organization. Hereafter, cited as UKC Case File.

19. Ibid.

20. Sidai Hahn to Kim Koo, June 16, 1944, UKC Case File, Box 4, Heisop Chin Collection, UCLA.

21. Ibid.

22. Hereafter, referred to as the League.

23. The slogan of the League was "To Help China, Let's Help Korea Too!" This slogan was part of the official letterhead for the League.

24. An editorial in the *Korean National Herald-Pacific Weekly*, June 10, 1942, states that the League was largely defunct through the 1930s.

25. "Kilsoo Haan Resigns," *Korean National Herald-Pacific Weekly*, February 25, 1942.

26. "What of the Koreans?" *Korean National Herald-Pacific Weekly*, March 18, 1942.

27. It is assumed that Kilsoo Haan and Syngman Rhee each represented one percent.

28. "Where Are the Two Per Cent?" *Korean National Herald-Pacific Weekly*, April 29, 1942.

29. "A Korean Case," *Korean National Herald-Pacific Weekly*, June 10, 1942.

30. Ibid.

31. Ibid.

32. "Let's Be Frank," *Korean National Herald-Pacific Weekly*, July 15, 1942.

33. "Public Nuisance," *Korean National Herald-Pacific Weekly*, September 23, 1942.

34. Ibid.

35. "UKC Stands," *Korean National Herald-Pacific Weekly*, January 27, 1943.

36. "Dunn Meets with Sino-Korean Peoples' League, Feb. 14," *Korean National Herald-Pacific Weekly*, February 10, 1943.

37. Ibid.

38. Letter to United Korean Committee, Honolulu, October 24, 1942, United Korean Committee Papers, Folder 9, Box 4, Heisop Chin Collection, UCLA.

39. "Memorandum," October 22, 1942, UKC Case File, 19-20, United Korean

Committee Papers, Box 4, Heisop Chin Collection, UCLA. In addition to the personal rivalries between Rhee and various UKC members, political infighting within the Provisional Government in Chungking, China, translated into further strife for the UKC. While political upheaval had dominated the KPG for much of its existence, by 1942 the situation became intolerable as factions within KPG argued whether the provisional government would support the Chinese nationalists or the Chinese Communists. These disputes escalated to the point that the UKC felt the need to intervene, as it appeared that the KPG would implode. The decision was made to send a UKC delegation composed of Kim Ho, the executive chairman, and J. K. Dunn, the public relations secretary, to Chungking to investigate and to mediate between the disputing factions. At the same time, for the UKC the Chungking mission emerged as a key opportunity to define their organizational platform apart from the factionalism that marked nationalist politics before World War II. In sending a delegation to China, the UKC sought to build direct political ties with the provisional government without Syngman Rhee and the Korean Commission as the intermediary. Importantly, as the UKC leadership attempted to secure the proper documentation and negotiate the passage for the trip to Chungking, they made it explicitly clear that their mission represented more than political strategizing; the Chungking mission was characterized as the critical link between the KPG and Koreans in America. The initial planning of the mission was quite successful as the UKC secured the approval of the American State and War Departments. Unfortunately for the UKC, the plans for the Chungking mission were in the end short-circuited by Rhee.

40. "A Memorandum," no date, UKC Case File, 25-26, United Korean Committee Papers, Box 4, Heisop Chin Collection, UCLA. An annotation to this document notes that this addendum was negotiated at a conference between Jacob Dunn, Henry DeYoung, Ilhan New, and members of the Korean-American Council. Rhee "absented himself at the conference" and the redrafted memo was never accepted by Rhee.

41. Letter to Charles Ho Kim and J. K. Dunn from Syngman Rhee, November 28, 1942, UKC Case File, 27, United Korean Committee Papers, Box 4, Heisop Chin Collection, UCLA.

42. Ibid.

43. Ibid.

44. Ibid.

45. Kim was appointed the director of public relations for the HONUKC after J. K. Dunn's departure for Washington.

46. Ibid.

47. Ibid.

48. Ibid.

49. Ibid.

50. Ibid.

51. Ibid.

52. "A Proclamation," The Korean People's Convention of Central California, January 16, 1943, United Korean Committee Papers, United Korean Committee Papers, Box 4, Heisop Chin Collection, UCLA. Notably, the KPC did not include the HONUKC in their proclamation. Rhee and his followers despite their ongoing disputes with the Honolulu Bureau, particularly J. K. Dunn, directed their animus toward UKCLA over the issue of financial support since the Los Angeles Bureau made the fiscal decisions for the UKC. The "Joint Resolutions" of the KPC declared: "We support the patriotic attitude and proper carriage of the Legislative Branch of the United Korean Committee in the Hawaiian Islands; at the same time we most indignantly censure the illegal and unpatriotic actions and behavior of the Executive Branch of the United Korean Committee in Los Angeles." See "Joint Resolutions," The Korean People's Convention of Central California and the Korean People's Convention of Los Angeles, United Korean Committee Papers, Box 4, Heisop Chin Collection, UCLA.

53. Letter to Syngman Rhee from Won Kiu Ahn, September 25, 1943, published in the Korean National Herald-Pacific Weekly, November 17, 1943.

54. Ibid.

55. Letter to Won Kiu Ahn from Syngman Rhee, September 11, 1943, published in the Korean National Herald-Pacific Weekly, November 17, 1943.

56. "The Turning Point," Korean National Herald-Pacific Weekly, September 29, 1943.

57. "Dongji Hoi's Withdrawal," Korean National Herald-Pacific Weekly, January 22, 1944.

58. Ibid.

59. "Provisional President Speaks Out on 'In Due Course' Phrase," The New Korea, December 9, 1943.

60. "An Answer to the Hecklers," The New Korea, March 1, 1944.

61. J. K. Dunn, "In Due Course," The New Korea, March 1, 1944.

62. "Koreans Want Independence, Not Protectorate," Korean Independence, February 16, 1944.

63. Inez Kong Pai, "To a New Approach," Korean Independence, March 1, 1944.

64. "How Far Is 'In Due Course'?" Korean Independence, March 1, 1944.

65. Ibid.

66. Ibid.

67. "Communique by UKC," Korean Independence, March 29, 1944.

68. "KNRP and Korean Student Federation Withdraw from UKC," Korean Independence, February 16, 1944.

69. "Road to Liberation of Korean People," *Korean Independence,* November 15, 1944.

70. Sidai Hahn to Kim Koo, June 19, 1944, Folder 9, Box 4, Heisop Chin Collection, UCLA.

71. Ibid.

72. Ibid.

73. Ibid.

74. "Road to Liberation of Korean People," *Korean Independence,* November 15, 1944.

75. Kim Wŏn-yong, *Chae-Mi Han'in 50-nyŏn sa,* 439.

76. "As to Korean Commission Reorganization Conference," *Korean Independence,* October 25, 1944.

77. Il Kyu Paik [Paek Il-gyu], "Korean Patriot's Outspoken Self-Criticism of Korean Independence Movement," *Korean Independence,* December 20, 1944.

78. Telegram to UKCLA from KPG, Chungking, China, November 21, 1944, Papers of the United Korean Committee, Korean American Digital Archives, Korean Heritage Library, University of Southern California.

79. Telegram to KPG from Sidai Hahn, UKCLA, November 15, 1944, Papers of the United Korean Committee, Korean American Digital Archives, Korean Heritage Library, University of Southern California.

80. Ibid.

81. "Thought for Korean American Future," *Korean National Herald-Pacific Weekly,* February 2, 1944.

82. J. K. Dunn to Kim Koo, July 24, 1944, Folder 9, Box 4, Heisop Chin Collection, UCLA.

83. J. K. Dunn, "Report United Korean Committee in America," Washington Office, Folder 9, Box 4, Heisop Chin Collection.

84. Ibid.

85. Letter to the Foreign New Bureau of the Office of War Information from J. K. Dunn, July 17, 1944, Korean American Digital Archive, University of Southern California.

86. It is unclear when this office was organized or when it was terminated. It was in operation for the duration of World War II.

87. Letter to John Starr Kim from J. K. Dunn, February 21, 1945, Korean American Digital Archive, University of Southern California.

88. Ibid.

89. Letter to United Korean Committee in America, Honolulu, United Korean Committee, Los Angeles, Korean Civic Club, Honolulu, and the Korean University Club, Honolulu from J. K. Dunn, March 17, 1945, Korean American Digital Archive, University of Southern California.

90. Ibid.

91. "Overseas Korean Conference and Its Significance," *Korean Independence,* April 5, 1945.

92. "Koreans in U.S. to Discuss Representing at S.F. Conference," *Korean Independence,* March 28, 1945.

93. Ibid.

94. "Overseas Korean Conference and Its Significance," *Korean Independence,* April 5, 1945.

95. "In Order to Avoid Greater Frustrations," *Korean Independence,* April 12, 1945.

96. Ibid.

97. Ibid.

98. "San Francisco Conference and Koreans' Urgent Work," *Korean Independence,* April 19, 1945.

99. "Justice is the Foundation of Peace," *San Francisco Chronicle,* April 25, 1945.

100. The UKC was largely defunct by 1950.

101. One exception to this policy was the employment of Koreans from the United States by the American military government.

Judy Van Zile

10

Korean Dance in Hawaiʻi
A Century in the Public Eye

AMONG IMMIGRANT COMMUNITIES in Hawaiʻi dance has played a significant role in establishing or reinforcing an identity related to that of the
homeland, as well as in presenting this identity to the larger community.[1] Dance
can be found in public contexts, ranging from formal, evening-length concert
presentations to large-scale multicultural community events, as well as in private
contexts, which include such things as birthday parties, fundraising activities,
and church events intended for a select audience. Korean dance, brought to the
Islands by immigrants in the early 1900s, has functioned in both of these arenas
for almost a century. During this time countless people have been involved in
performing, presenting, and observing Korean dance. Three women played critical roles in the prominence of Korean dance in public settings: Ha Soo Whang
(Hwang Hae-su), Halla Pai Huhm (Pae Hal-la Huhm), and Mary Jo Freshley.[2]

My purpose here is to outline the history of the public face of Korean dance
in Hawaiʻi through the contributions of these women, delineating the nature of
the roles they played, the types of dance they fostered, and the connections they
had to Korea both before and during their involvement in Hawaiʻi. Because they
resided and worked on the island of Oʻahu, and it was there that the greatest
amount of activity was focused, the emphasis in this chapter is on this island.

SETTING THE STAGE

The stage for Korean dance in Hawaiʻi was set as early as the arrival of the first
immigrants. While the literal stage was likely the soil of the island plantations,
the figurative stage was the nostalgia for familiar practices of the homeland.
According to Bernice Kim, the earliest Korean dance in the Islands was performed by men on informal occasions; at the time respectable women would not
have danced because in Korea this was an activity reserved for female entertainers *(kisaeng)* and shamans who were "beyond the pale of respectability."[3] Kim
states these dances were done under the influence of alcohol on social occasions

intended for relaxation, and involved untrained attempts at movements considered stereotypically Korean today. These were likely the lifting and lowering of the shoulders *(ŏkkae ch'um)* accompanied by a side-to-side swaying, arms extended sideward at shoulder height, and the occasional manipulation of a small scarf or handkerchief held in one hand, movements easily recognizable as those seen in similar contexts in Korea today, where they may be performed by both men and women.

The early absence of women dancers is also likely for religious reasons. Many of the first immigrants were converts to Christianity. In the early twentieth century the church maintained a puritanical attitude toward the body. Religious leaders in Hawai'i spoke out against all forms of dance, specifically criticizing folk dance activities for women and children sponsored by the Young Women's Christian Association (YWCA).[4] This is ironic because the YWCA would later foster dance among many immigrant groups, particularly women and children.

Improvised dancing in social settings continued throughout the twentieth century, and can still be seen at the beginning of the twenty-first century. More formal presentations in the early days took the form of skits, pageants, and enactments of traditional celebrations such as weddings, generally sponsored by the Korean National Association of Hawai'i (Kungminhoe) and the YWCA.[5] It is not until the 1920s, however, that we find references to presentational kinds of dance specifically put before the public eye. The earliest performers and teachers appear to have been members of the Nam-Pung-Sa (Namp'ung-sa?), an organization founded in 1922 by the Korean National Association. Warren Kim notes that the organization's goal was

> to teach the unique Korean arts. The majority of its promoters were old immigrants who had training in the classical music and court dances of Korea. The organization brought musical instruments and other paraphernalia from Korea, taught young people the heritage of Korean arts, and made efforts to introduce them to the American public during its five-year existence.[6]

Apart from names of several probable members of this short-lived organization, little is known about the backgrounds of the older performers and teachers other than the simple statement in Kim's description.[7]

HA SOO WHANG

The first person to assume a pivotal role in fostering Korean dance in the Islands was Ha Soo Whang. Born in 1892 in what is now North Korea, Whang was educated at missionary schools and taught at a Christian girls' school before traveling to the United States.[8] She first went to the mainland United States, where she earned a degree from Athens College in Alabama, and then settled in San Francisco for a brief time. She came to Honolulu in 1919 to take charge of the Korean section of the International Institute at the YWCA.[9] The Institute followed a nationwide YWCA initiative to establish centers throughout the country to aid immigrant women, and Whang was Hawai'i's first Korean social worker.[10] The institutes were designed to help foster relationships between immigrant women and the local community, and to help immigrant women learn English and the practical details of setting up and running a household in their new homeland. An additional goal was identified as "The Conservation of Old World Arts and Activities."[11] In a national YWCA report on standards for the institutes, one of the activities advocated was "old world festivals," which freshened "homesick hearts" and reawakened "old memories," memories that were "of quite as much importance as . . . the event itself."[12] Because of this philosophy, costume pageants, plays, dance performances, and enactments of such traditional activities as wedding ceremonies came to be regular features of events sponsored by the YWCA that highlighted the heritages of the ethnic groups constituting the Institute membership.

In 1927 the YWCA celebrated the opening of its new Richards Street building in downtown Honolulu with performances of Chinese, Japanese, Philippine, and Korean dance. A newspaper article described "a Korean butterfly dance, in which eight little Korean children flitted through a weaving pattern of gorgeous costume-coloring to the strange motions and music of a Korean chant."[13] Although no specific role in this event is attributed to Whang, in the same year she founded the Hyung Jay (Hyŏngje), or Sisters' Club, at the YWCA, and served for many years as its advisor.[14] Among the club's undertakings was "instruction in the Korean traditional arts by lectures and class discussions, and . . . preserv[ing] the knowledge of the traditional arts."[15] Club members, under the guidance of Whang, became frequent performers of Korean dance in public settings.

In the same year the Hyung Jay Club was founded, the Honolulu Academy of Arts opened its doors, and a year later, in 1928, members of the Club danced in a program at the Academy. This was the beginning of a long relationship between the Club, Whang, and the Academy: events performed by Club members had become annual programs at the Academy by 1940.[16] From 1928 to 1940 we find many references to performances of plays Whang wrote and directed, pageants she supervised, and countless music and dance programs she directed.[17]

Only scant performance details on dances during this period can be gleaned from extant records and memories of some older Koreans alive today. Among the most significant of these sources is a film that documents actual movements of one dance. Made in 1931, this film shows three high school girls in an excerpt from a dance titled "Scarf Dance," which vaguely suggests the dance now known as Salp'uri.[18]

Ha Soo Whang's role during this period was that of producer and facilitator. It was her initiation of events and identification of people to be involved in them that made them happen. Older members of the Korean community in Hawai'i today say that she herself never taught or performed dance. Instead, she was adept at identifying individuals who could teach dances based on having studied them before coming to Hawai'i, or who could create dances in a manner they believed to be Korean.

Two individuals worked with Whang on many occasions and were directly involved in the teaching of dance. The choreography for a 1934 Hyung Jay Club performance is attributed to "Mrs. Henry D. Lee, . . . reputed to be the finest Korean musician in the territory,"[19] and dancers in a 1940 YWCA performance were taught by Chai Yong Ha (Ch'oe Yong-ha), described in a newspaper article as a Buddhist monk before arriving in the Islands, who had "a profound knowledge of temple dances of his native homeland."[20]

Susan Chun Lee came to Hawai'i in 1910 and subsequently married Rev. Henry D. Lee.[21] They lived ten to fifteen years in Waialua, on O'ahu's north shore, before moving to Honolulu. Lee had graduated from Ewha Woman's University in Korea, and for many years was editor for the *Korea Times* in Hawai'i. According to her daughters, Lee's brother had studied Western medicine in Japan. He became the first doctor to practice Western medicine in Korea and worked in the royal court. Because of this, Lee saw many upper-class things and may have observed some court dance rehearsals or performances. In addition, her elder sister had studied the *kayagŭm*, giving Lee many opportunities to hear traditional Korean music.

Lee's daughters describe their mother as a talented musician with an innate ability in many art forms. Although she never studied dance, she taught dances in Hawai'i that bear similarities to court dances, the monk's drum dance, and a sword dance, all of which one daughter says came from Lee's "fertile imagination." If she had, indeed, seen court dances in her homeland, when called upon Lee combined her memories with her artistic gifts, which also included the design and construction of costumes, to teach children who performed in many events.

Yong Ha Chai's background is more difficult to determine. Newspaper articles say he came to the Islands in 1905,[22] but logs of ship passengers do not show anyone with this name from 1903 to 1905.[23] The State of Hawai'i census of 1910 indicates that he arrived in 1904, that he was thirty-two years old at the time the census was taken, and that he was working on the Hakalau plantation in the Hilo District on the island of Hawai'i. In 1940 his dance and music abilities became known to Ha Soo Whang, who brought him to the island of

INTERNATIONAL FETE

SPONSORED BY THE Y. W. C. A.

UNIVERSITY OF HAWAII AMPHITHEATRE

July 20, 4:30 p. m.

GENERAL ADMISSION FIFTY CENTS

With photographic privileges, 3-4 p. m., 75 cents

Children's Admission, 25 cents

13   Choi Yongha playing *changgo*, from a flyer announcing a 1940 event sponsored by the YWCA, Honolulu, Hawai'i.

O'ahu to teach dance. A YWCA report of that year states that he taught "royal school dancing," a description probably intended to refer to court dancing.[24] Newspaper descriptions of performances crediting the dance teaching to Chai include references to a sword dance and to "Chin Yang Moo,"[25] the latter likely referring to the court dance Ch'unaengmu. This suggests that Chai was familiar not only with the Buddhist dances mentioned in the 1945 newspaper article, but with court dance and possibly folk dance as well. Unfortunately his dance background is known only through the brief newspaper comments on his religious affiliation prior to arriving in the Islands, an affiliation that cannot be substantiated.

Older Koreans who studied with Chai when they were quite young describe him as a small, wiry old man who could not speak English but who "could beat a mean drum."[26] He refused to perform, and since his young students did not speak Korean he taught by having them imitate his movements. One woman remembers him being extremely graceful, saying that "his whole body, even his toes," came alive when he danced.[27]

While Ha Soo Whang was not responsible for teaching or choreographing dances during this early period, she was responsible for identifying individuals who could undertake these tasks, particularly for establishing Yong Ha Chai as an instructor, and for initiating and organizing a significant number of events in which dance was publicly performed. For her contributions to supporting early Korean immigrant women and to furthering Korean music and dance in Hawai'i she was posthumously recognized as one of twenty-seven eminent Koreans in Hawai'i during centennial celebrations in 2003.

Whang left the Islands in 1943 after establishing a strong Korean dance presence. Yong Ha Chai continued to be credited with the teaching of dances in programs through 1945, at which time various other individuals are identified as teachers and directors for performances.[28] Particularly important for literally showing us what one dance of the mid-twentieth century looked like is a 1948 film about Koreans in Hawai'i.[29] Included here is a dance excerpt in which performers wear very elegant court dance costumes and perform movements that are characteristic of court dances seen today. Many of the dances of this period appear to have been continuations of those taught by Chai and Susan Chun Lee.

In addition to the numerous programs presented by the YWCA and the Academy of Arts, the first half of the twentieth century saw Korean dance presented at local fairs, school programs, and public events celebrating Korea's March First Movement. These were sponsored by such organizations as the Korean Red Cross, the Korean Women's Relief Society, and clubs at schools and the University of Hawai'i.

HALLA HUHM

The arrival of Halla Huhm in 1950 marks the beginning of a second period in Korean dance in the Islands.[30] Born in Pusan, Korea, in 1922, Huhm at the age of five and four siblings went to Japan, where she was raised by a family relative, Pae Ku-ja, a woman she referred to variously as her cousin and her sister, and who became her first dance teacher. Huhm graduated from high school in Tokyo and also earned a university degree in home economics there. At the start of World War II she returned to Korea, and in 1950 immigrated to Hawai'i with her Hawai'i-born Korean American husband.

Huhm differed from Ha Soo Whang in that she had specifically been trained as a dancer. This training began in Japan and Korea with ballet and the changing traditional dance styles growing in popularity in both countries in the first half of the twentieth century. Over time she studied with dancers she helped bring to the Islands from Korea, and returned to Korea on many occasions to learn more traditional dances. Huhm studied traditional dance with Han Sŏng-jun, a man acknowledged throughout Korea for both his retention of traditional movements and innovative choreography; Buddhist ritual music and dance from Pak Song-am, a priest formally recognized by the Korean government for expertise in this area; shaman rituals and dance from Yi Chi-san, a shaman from the Seoul area; salp'uri, a solo dance form considered by many to be the epitome of Korean dance, from Kim Mok-hwa; and court dance from Kim Ch'ŏn-hŭng, a dancer recognized by the Korean government for his traditional dance knowledge and ability.

Huhm's contributions to the public face of Korean dance in Hawai'i lie in her roles as both dancer and teacher. She had performed extensively in Japan, Korea, and China before coming to Hawai'i, and following her island debut as a performer in 1952,[31] quickly became described as "an artist of the first rank."[32] She continued to perform throughout her life. Initially teaching at various locations, including the YWCA and several churches, she eventually opened what has become the longest-lived Korean dance studio in the Islands.[33] In 1959 she also began teaching at the University of Hawai'i, and twenty-four years later, in 1983, she returned to Korea for five years to teach dance at the Ch'ŏngju University of Education.

Halla Huhm taught both the traditional repertoire of her teachers and her own adaptations of dances she learned in various settings. She also created some of her own dances in a Korean style, such as a dance she performed to a piano rendition of the Lord's Prayer at a Christian church service in 1957, and a dance she was invited to choreograph in 1962 to Wind Song, music newly composed by Alan Hovahness.

Before her death in January 1994, Halla Huhm received numerous awards and citations for her contributions to furthering traditional Korean culture. These came from the Government of the Republic of Korea (including citations from the Ministry of Education, the Ministry of Public Information, and the Consulate General of the Republic of Korea), the legislature of the State of Hawai'i (both the Senate and House of Representatives), the American Smithsonian Institution, Soroptomists, Jaycees, and such individuals as U.S. Senator Daniel Inouye. Like Ha Soo Whang, Huhm was recognized posthumously as one of twenty-seven eminent Koreans in Hawai'i during the centennial celebrations in 2003. Halla Huhm's name had become synonymous with Korean dance in the Islands.

Halla Huhm and her students performed frequently in a multitude of settings that put them before the public eye: state fairs, concerts of the Honolulu Symphony, festivals at the University of Hawai'i, tourist programs in Waikiki hotels, events (often fundraisers) sponsored by Korean and non-Korean organizations, and recitals of her own studio as well as those presented collaboratively by studios representing the dances of other ethnic groups in the Islands. For a time Huhm worked with Barbara B. Smith, then professor of music at the University

14   Halla Huhm teaches a class of teachers at the University of Hawai'i, ca. 1958.

of Hawai'i, to present "lecture-recitals" in Honolulu as well as on the other islands of Hawai'i. Through these events Korean dance was presented not just as a form of entertainment, but as an integral component of Korean culture. Performance commentary described the background of the dances presented, frequently noting aspects of traditional Korean court life, religions, and cultural etiquette.

Life was not always easy for Huhm. She was more concerned with perpetuating the art she loved than with charging high fees for lessons at her studio or for performances. While she worked for many years at a travel agency, teaching and performing on weekends and in the evening, her efforts to put Korean dance and culture before the public were relentless. Although she periodically threatened to close her studio because of the challenges involved in sustaining it, each time people would come forward to remind her of the role she played in providing a thread for the continuity of Korean culture in the Islands. Her perseverance and commitment provided a role model for generations of immigrants and their children; at the same time it functioned as a source of pride and a link

15   Halla Huhm performs *To Salp'uri* in 1987.

to the cultural heritage of these people, and a source of exposure to this heritage for those from other cultures.

So many children of Korean ancestry studied at the Halla Huhm Studio that a middle-aged, third-generation Korean-American businessman believes many Korean Americans in the Islands consider studying dance at the studio to be part of their education as young Koreans. Just as many Americans ask, "Weren't you a girl scout?" Koreans in Hawai'i, he says, ask, "Didn't you go to the Halla Huhm Studio?" And these same students continue to place Korean dance before the public eye as they perform in school May Day programs, for beauty pageants, and in activities of numerous organizations.

MARY JO FRESHLEY

Over the years a number of individuals served as assistants to Halla Huhm. The ethnic and national heritage of these people was quite diverse, and included individuals she helped come to Hawai'i from Korea, several young women who had studied in university dance programs in Korea, and local residents of Okinawan, Japanese, and European ancestry. Most maintained their studio affiliation for several years and then moved on to other things. One, Mary Jo Freshley, became deeply committed to Korean dance, assisting Halla Huhm with both business and teaching responsibilities at the studio and traveling, like Huhm, to Korea on numerous occasions to study with recognized dance authorities. Freshley studied with some of the same teachers who had instructed Halla Huhm, particularly Kim Ch'ŏn-hŭng, as well as others, most notably Kim Pyŏng-sŏp, a recognized performer and teacher of *nongak* (Korean farmers' band music and dance), and members of the well-known contemporary Samul Nori group.

Freshley, who was born in 1934 in Ohio of European ancestry, assumed full responsibilities for the Halla Huhm Dance Studio upon the death of Huhm. Although she had studied several kinds of dance in college, Freshley did not become interested in Korean dance until after she moved to Hawai'i in 1961 to teach physical education to elementary-level students. Piqued by her exposure to Korean dance in a University of Hawai'i class taught by Halla Huhm, she continued her studies at Huhm's Studio.[34] Important to note regarding Freshley's involvement with Korean dance is that, unlike Ha Soo Whang and Halla Huhm, she is not Korean. But her dance knowledge and abilities were formally acknowledged by Huhm, who awarded certificates of achievement to students in a manner that is based on a system she learned in Japan and on her own receipt of the name Pai from her teacher. The highest certificate awarded by Huhm to her students gave them the name of her primary mentor, and designated them as instructors in the Pai tradition. Freshley is one of only about a dozen indi-

16   Mary Jo Freshley performs *Hak Ch'um* (Crane Dance), choreographed for her by Halla Huhm, in 2000.

viduals who have earned this certificate; she was given the name Pai Myung-sa in 1975. Her performing abilities have also been validated through awards won in contests for foreigners in Korea. Like her predecessors, Freshley has been publicly recognized for her contributions to Korean dance in Hawai'i with awards from the Hawai'i Heritage Center, the City and County of Honolulu, the Hawai'i Consulate General, and local Korean chambers of commerce and Rotary clubs.

In many ways Freshley continues the roles and contributions of Halla Huhm. Like Huhm she is both a performer and teacher as well as a student, seeks ways to expose the community to a broad spectrum of the kinds of Korean dance (including perpetuating the repertoire of Huhm), maintains strong ties to Korea by inviting guest teachers to Hawai'i and by visiting Korea to expand her own training, and creates some of her own dances. In 1995, for example, she collaborated with several advanced students to create Aloha Changgonori, a piece that wove together elements of the then-popular Korean Samul Nori and instruments used in hula, which Freshley had also studied. After its performance in Honolulu, Freshley and her students were invited by Kim Duk-su (Kim Tŏk-su), director of the original Samul Nori group, to perform Aloha Changgonori at a festival in Korea, where they were awarded second place in the foreigners' division.

Under her leadership she and students of the Halla Huhm Studio have continued to perform in diverse public settings, and through the Halla Huhm Foundation, a nonprofit organization she helped establish, Freshley has collaborated with other groups to bring individual teachers and dance companies to Hawai'i.

Freshley's most significant contribution to Korean dance in Hawai'i may come about simply by virtue of who she is—or rather, is not. Because of her extraordinary knowledge and dedication, and her continual acceptance of requests for students to perform in public venues, the fact that she is not Korean has stimulated the interest of many Koreans in their own culture.

CONTEXTUALIZING AND INTERPRETING THE STORIES OF THREE WOMEN

How does Korean dance in Hawai'i and the story of its three women advocates relate to events happening in Korea and Hawai'i? Ha Soo Whang's arrival in the Islands occurred less than a year after Korea's nationwide March First Movement. With the establishment of Hawai'i as an external base for nationalist activities under the leadership of Syngman Rhee and Pak Yong-man, there was a concern with delineating a Korean identity distinctive from that of Korea's Japanese colonizer. This was evident in the Korean National Association in Hawai'i's 1920s creation of the Nam-Pung-Sa with the explicit goal of teaching

17 Ha-Soo Whang (Hwang Hae-su) on the right, with an unidentified woman (Bishop Museum Archives with permission).

"the unique Korean arts."[35] Coincidentally this concern aligned perfectly with the YWCA international institutes' mandate to advocate traditional cultural activities of members of immigrant communities. Thus, Ha Soo Whang's initiation of countless public performances supported the goals of the YWCA as well as those of Korea's nationalistic efforts. Dances that at the beginning of Korean immigration to Hawai'i were considered inappropriate for performance by women or children because of their association with female entertainers and shamans in Korea quickly came to be an important representation of Koreanness performed largely by women and children.

Halla Huhm's increasingly deeper personal involvement with Korean dance and her concerns with informing the Korean and non-Korean communities alike about traditional culture may have been a legacy of her own upbringing. Her family background is shrouded in a tangled web of Japanese-Korean relationships.[36] Spending her formative years in Japan made her more fluent in the Japanese language than Korean, and many close associates felt that her demeanor —and even some of her early dancing—was more Japanese than Korean. It is possible her commitment to Korean dance was the result of a personal reconciling of her own complex background.[37]

Mary Jo Freshley's involvement with Korean dance emanated from an appreciation of the dance form itself. As she became increasingly immersed in her studies she also became increasingly aware of the multiple facets of Korean culture embedded in the dance, and turned to using dance as a vehicle for helping people—both Korean and non-Korean—to better understand this "other" culture. Freshley describes her goals for students: to gain a sense of what Korean culture is like through its dance and music, to perpetuate Halla Huhm's choreography, to understand the diversity of Korean culture through the diversity of its dances, and to educate both the students and their parents.[38] With new waves of immigrants coming from a greatly modernized and highly Westernized Korean society, and second, third, and fourth generations who are considerably removed from their traditional heritage, Freshley is a repository of knowledge many local Koreans do not have. At the same time she contributes significantly to the public face of Korean dance in the Islands. Her role in the perpetuation of Korean dance has sparked discussions among many as to the appropriateness of a non-Korean continuing this heritage, however.

There are some who would interpret the activities and motivations of these three women in highly political ways. Korean American Peggy Myo-Young Choy, for example, layers issues of colonization and racism onto the period of Ha Soo Whang, criticizing the policies of the institute she worked for and asserting that the role of institute activities during Whang's time was "a microcosm of the larger racist colonial society in the [Hawaiian] islands."[39] If she took into account the concurrent nationalistic movement in Korea and its influence on activities among members of the immigrant community, including the goals of the Nam-Pung-Sa, the Hawai'i arts organization established by members of the nationalistic movement, Choy might focus her colonial concerns on two colonizers, Japan and the United States.

In Halla Huhm's case, speculating on her motivations could shift away from the personal agency I have suggested to an interpretation casting blame on the colonizing powers of Japan that clearly influenced her youth and formative years, leaving wounds she would seek to heal later. As she established her life in Hawai'i this interpretation could further place blame on the need for maintaining uniqueness amid the globalizing push that contributes to an ever homogenizing society, which for many is the result of the power of European-American influence.

Mary Jo Freshley's contributions raise issues of cultural ownership. Those with postmodern inclinations could interpret Freshley's interests and activities as an inappropriate assumption of what rightfully belongs to others—again, the specter of colonization.

Interestingly questions of cultural ownership could be raised in relation to all three women. With her Christian upbringing, activities occurring in Korea during her early years, and the young age at which she left Korea, traditional dance was almost certainly not an integral component of the culture with which Ha Soo Whang was intimately involved.[40] In the case of Halla Huhm, with her immersion in the language and culture of Japan during her formative years, and her early Western-based dance training and involvement with Japanese dance as well as dance forms of other cultures, it could be argued that she, too, ultimately became involved in an aspect of culture that originally belonged to an "other."

It is particularly intriguing that with the exception of Yong Ha Chai the primary forces behind Korean dance in Hawai'i were women. Why women and not men? As a starting point for future considerations in seeking answers to this question a statement by Ananda Coomaraswamy, an Indian art historian and aesthetician, written almost fifty years ago is provocative:

> Even in recent times, in families where the men have received an English education unrelated to Indian life and thought, the inheritance of Indian modes of thought and feelings rests in the main with women; for a definite philosophy of life is bound up with household ritual and traditional etiquette and finds expression equally in folktale and cradle-song and popular poetry. . . . it is often the case that Indian women . . . have remained the guardians of a spiritual culture which is of greater worth than the efficiency and information of the educated.[41]

Since many kinds of Korean dance have traditionally been performed by men, Coomaraswamy's comments suggest an interesting possibility. In the context of a diasporic community, particularly one that was so preoccupied with nationalistic concerns in its home country, was the maintenance of many aspects of the heritage culture left predominantly to women? Esther Kwon Arinaga indicates that this may, indeed, have been the case, but also reveals the dual pulls women experienced: "Despite their small numbers, the Korean women managed to preserve their distinct cultural heritage and resist erosion of their ethnic identity. Still, they cherished the American ideals which had lured them from the country of their birth."[42]

There is no question that Korean dance in Hawai'i has been used at different times for different purposes, sometimes for political, racist, and colonial reasons. As a form of nonverbal communication Korean dance could be easily undertaken by individuals who did not speak the Korean language, and many people assumed that because of its nonverbal nature it could be used to communicate something about Korea or Korean-ness to those of other heritages. Through distinctive ways of using the body and unique musical accompaniment and costumes, dance quickly became a symbol in the Islands of things Korean. It served as a recreational or leisure activity, and as a communal activity that pulled together individuals with a shared heritage. As it was performed in public arenas, it reinforced this shared heritage, serving as a cultural icon. For older Koreans, it was a reminder of a past that lay thousands of miles away. For some younger Koreans, it taught them, through a literally embodied experience, of a past they never knew in its original setting. For non-Koreans, it was a lesson in the culture of a potentially exotic other. For many, it was an identity marker—a symbol of uniqueness.

Among some of the Korean children born in Hawai'i, participating in dance satisfied a familial obligation. Concerns at school revolved around learning Western ways and melding seamlessly into the culture of the land in which the youngsters were born. It was only parental urgings that led them to dance classes and to don clothing from another time and place, urgings that sought continuation, in some way, of a Korean identity. For many, young and old, there was a more fundamental reason for engaging with Korean dance in Hawai'i, one that allows for strong agency on the part of those directly involved, a purpose that places even dance in political contexts in a different light. The arts play a powerful role in simply enjoying activities of the body. Korean dance in Hawai'i has played, and continues to play, many roles, one of which is precisely the pleasure of involvement with aesthetic experiences, either as a performer or a viewer. Since the beginning of immigration in the early twentieth century, Korean dance in the Islands has maintained clear links to Korea, whether in the form of remembered dances, return visits to Korea by local dancers, or visits to Hawai'i of dancers from Korea. At the same time, however, it has been performed in new contexts, has merged with movement stylings of other dance forms, and been performed and taught by individuals not of Korean ancestry. For more than a hundred years Korean dance in Hawai'i has embraced the other—whether that other is defined as individuals born in the Islands, individuals whose ancestry is traced to cultures and countries beyond Korea, or the country and culture of Korea itself.

EPILOGUE

In tracing the history of Korean dance in Hawai'i through the stories of three women who contributed in important ways to it, I do not claim to speak for those who lived the experience. The study of the past, even the recent past, can be little more than an attempt to ascertain what might be factual, and to seek to understand it and its contribution to the present. The voices of the past can seldom speak directly to us. For those alive today, the past may be better or worse than it actually was. It may be remembered in whole or in part. By attempting to listen to the voices of the past in whatever way they present themselves— through photographs, newspaper stories, letters, and personal remembrances— we ultimately seek to understand them.

As I sought the voices of the past I looked for answers from them: What dance training could Ha Soo Whang, a devout Christian when she came to the United States at an early age, have possibly had? Why did Halla Huhm turn so persistently to some of the most traditional dance forms of her ancestral heritage? Why did Mary Jo Freshley, a European American, become so dedicated to instilling a knowledge of Korean culture in young Korean Americans? Were the young girls who participated in Korean dance in the early years really asserting a stance against colonial and racist attitudes that some contemporary interpreters would have us believe? Were they being dutiful children who followed the requests of their parents? Or were they simply enjoying a particular way of moving?

My own connection with Korean dance began for quite simple reasons: I liked doing the movement. I was not trying to "become Korean," to usurp a manifestation of a culture that was not my own, or to atone for the colonialist or racist "sins" of my European and American ancestors. I liked the way I physically, and ultimately psychologically, felt when I moved my body in the way that is characteristic of many Korean dances.

Strongly established as a contributor to cultural life in the Islands by three pioneering women, Korean dance has been used in Hawai'i to inspire nationalism and to promote identity. But it is likely it was, and still is, an embodied activity enjoyed for kinesthetic and aesthetic reasons by those who participate in it, in whatever way they choose.

NOTES

1. This chapter integrates and expands on several of my earlier works: "Halla Pai Huhm: Portrait of a Korean-American," *Korean Culture* 14, no. 3 (Fall 1993): 34–40; "Korean Dance in Hawaii: Immigrant Issues and Cultural Ownership," in *Haeoe Hanminjok kwa Ch'a Sedae, Che 2-chip* (Koreans Abroad and the Next Generation, Volume 2), ed. Kyemyŏng Taehakkyo Akademia Koreana (Taegu: Kyemyŏng Taehakkyo Yŏn'guch'ŏ, 1998), 335–45; and Chapter IX of *Perspectives on Korean Dance* (Middletown, Conn.: Wesleyan University Press, 2001). Several portions of this text are taken from these sources. For a broad discussion of dance among immigrant communities in Hawai'i, see Judy Van Zile, "Non-Polynesian Dance in Hawaii: Issues of Identity in a Multicultural Community," *Dance Research Journal* 28, no. 1 (Spring 1996): 28–50. For contributions to the research resulting in these and the current study I am grateful to Yŏng-ho Ch'oe for sharing information from his newspaper indexing project supported by a grant from the University of Hawai'i at Manoa's Center for Korean Studies; to the Honolulu YWCA, and in particular Gay Conklin, for allowing me access to the YWCA's rich archives while they were still in the process of being organized and catalogued; to Christine Wilson and Shuzo Uemoto of the Honolulu Academy of Arts for allowing me access to their archives and photo collection; to the staff of the Bishop Museum Archives, particularly DeSoto Brown, for assistance in locating film footage from the Ray Jerome Baker Collection; and to the many older Koreans in Hawai'i who generously shared their memories and scrapbooks with me.

2. Korean names of individuals in Hawai'i are written here with the given name followed by the family name, and are spelled with the commonly used local romanization, since that is how they appear in local sources. Upon first mention, the known, or probable, McCune-Reischauer spelling follows in parentheses.

By focusing on these three women I do not intend to overlook the contributions of scores of other individuals. This focus evolved during research as materials increasingly pointed to the nature and extent of the contributions of the three women, over long periods of time, in placing Korean dance before the Hawai'i public.

3. Bernice Kim, "The Koreans in Hawaii" (M.A. thesis, University of Hawai'i, 1937), 116.

4. See, for example, "Bishop Condemns All Dances, Even Child Folk Steps," *Pacific Commercial Advertiser,* July 29, 1916, section 2, 7, 9; "Bishop Restarick Draws Criticism," *Pacific Commercial Advertiser,* July 30, 1916.

5. References to such events may be found, for example, in "Koreans Will Hold Big Celebration," *Pacific Commercial Advertiser,* January 31, 1914, 1;

"Korean Y.M.C.A. Gives Interesting Program," *Pacific Commercial Advertiser,* May 11, 1914, 2; "Local Koreans Make Merry at Nuuanu 'Y'," *Honolulu Star-Bulletin,* January 13, 1919; "International Institute Entertains for Chinese," *Honolulu Star-Bulletin,* January 3, 1919.

6. Warren Y. Kim, *Koreans in Hawaii* (Seoul: Po Chin Chai, 1971), 45.

7. Although not specifically mentioning the Nam-Pung-Sa, a 1925 newspaper article refers to a performance by "four of the older Koreans in Honolulu [who] will give an old dance which the younger generation in Hawai'i has not learned," and identifies the performers as Chong Soon Chun, Yick Long Kim, Yong Woon Shim, and Han Bong Park ("Korean Program to be Given Sunday by Cosmopolitan Forum," *Honolulu Star-Bulletin,* March 14, 1925, 2). It is likely these were some of the "old immigrants" referred to by Warren Kim.

8. Peggy Choy and Andy Sutton, "Ha Soo Whang: Woman Pioneer of Hawaii (1892–1984)," *Korea Times,* October 16, 1991, Los Angeles edition, 4; Trina Nahm-Mijo, "A Sister's Story Told by Tutu," in "Herstory I" (unpublished anthology of oral histories, 1989), ed. Trina Nahm-Mijo, based on a taped interview c. 1979. Nahm-Mijo states that Whang's older sister helped her run away to a Christian girls' school when she was about eight years old. Additional biographical information on Whang is contained in Nahm-Mijo's essay and Choy and Sutton's newspaper article.

9. "Korean Secretary for Women's Work Arrives on Sachen," *Pacific Commercial Advertiser,* December 9, 1919, 1. Choy and Sutton, "Ha Soo Whang," state that Whang began work at the YWCA in 1922, and cite interviews with Whang and several other older Koreans as sources for their information. The 1919 newspaper article, together with records at the YWCA, indicate that Whang began her work there very shortly after her 1919 arrival, and Whang is generally identified as founding the YWCA's Korean Mothers Club, which began in 1920. Based on these latter sources, I believe the 1919 date is accurate.

10. *Silver Anniversary, 1900–1925,* YWCA brochure (September 1925–April 1933 scrapbook, YWCA Archives).

11. "Philosophy of the International Institutes" (unpublished typescript excerpted from San Francisco Study on Program Planning, 1932), YWCA Archives, Folder—International Institute: Reports, Standards 1930–1935.

12. Ibid.

13. Elizabeth Green, "New Home of the Y.W.C.A. In Honolulu Opens Its Doors," *San Francisco Chronicle,* July 17, 1927.

14. Kim, *Koreans in America,* 45.

15. Ibid., 4–5. This article appeared in a San Francisco newspaper. Strong ties between local branches of the YWCA and the international institutes across the country undoubtedly contributed to this Hawai'i news appearing in a California

newspaper, as did the fact that Ha Soo Whang worked in San Francisco prior to taking on responsibilities at the Honolulu YWCA.

16. Edgar Schenck, director, letter to Miss Ha Soo Whang, May 25, 1940, Archives of the Honolulu Academy of Arts.

17. These references are contained in printed programs in Academy archives and the personal collections of local people, as well as in newspaper articles.

18. In 1931, Ray Jerome Baker made a film showing the multicultural nature of the McKinley High School student population. (This film is contained in the archives of Hawai'i's Bishop Museum.) Following a segment of the school's football team in action and head-shots of team members bearing captions of their ethnicity are segments of dancers and musicians of Chinese, Japanese, and Filipino heritage, and a segment of a Korean scarf dance.

19. "Korean Girls to Dance Here," *Honolulu Star-Bulletin,* May 19, 1934, 4.

20. Captioned photograph, *Honolulu Advertiser,* March 18, 1945, section 2, 20. Susan Chun Lee and Yong Ha Chai are the most frequently mentioned teachers or individuals responsible for staging/directing dance portions of programs. Others only occasionally identified in newspaper articles and printed programs include a Mrs. W. Chung, Ms. Nodie Kimhaikim, Sarah K. Lee, Rose Shon, Mrs. D. W. Lim, Ms. Fannie Nahm, Sin Bok Kim, Mrs. Sarah Yang, and Lily Shin. Because of the vague language used in describing the roles of these individuals (e.g., "directed by," "arranged by"), it is not possible to determine their precise input to individual performances. Ms. Lily Lim Ahn was often involved in directorial responsibilities, particularly at the Honolulu Academy of Art, and may have been involved in originally locating Yong Ha Chai.

21. Henry Lee, whom she married after divorcing her first husband, had been a student at Mid-Pacific Institute in Honolulu. Information about Susan Chun Lee is based on January 2001 interviews with two of her daughters, Stella Lee and Dorothy Lee.

22. See, for example, "Korean Play To Be Given," *Honolulu Advertiser,* May 19, 1940, 10.

23. Duk Hee Murabayashi, compiler, *Korean Passengers Arriving at Honolulu 1903–1905* (Honolulu: Center for Korean Studies, University of Hawai'i, 2001). Available online at www.koreancentennial.org/resource/passlist.pdf. Consulted April 20, 2001.

24. "Evaluation of Group Work 1940" (unpublished typescript), YWCA Archives, Folder—International Institute.

25. "Korean Program Next Wednesday At the YWCA," *Honolulu Star-Bulletin,* March 14, 1940, 12.

26. Elizabeth Ahn Toupin, interview with author, June 13, 2002.

27. Clara Ahn, interview with author, February 18, 2001.

28. A June 1945 program indicates "dances by Mrs. Sarah Yang" and "dance directors" as Mrs. Ethel Kim and Hyung Kwon Chun ("Love of Spring Bud, Korean Play, To Be Given Friday Night," *Honolulu Star-Bulletin,* June 27, 1945, 9), and a July 1947 program states that the evening, which included Korean dance, was "directed by Mrs. Moses Ome" (*Dances of the Orient,* 1947 [printed program for July 1 performance at the Honolulu Academy of Art], personal collection of Stella Lee).

29. Moo-goong-hwa-Dong-san (Mukunghwa Tongsan—Hibiscus Garden) was produced by Chul-young Ahn (An Ch'ul-yong). A copy of this film is available at the Center for Korean Studies, University of Hawai'i.

30. The name of the woman known in Hawai'i at various times as Halla Huhm, Halla Pai Huhm, and Pai Halla is not entirely clear. She herself gave different explanations to different people at different times. The most consistent explanation is that she was born Pae Yong-ja, Pae being her family name and Yong-ja her personal name. At some time she took Halla as her personal name, from Mount Halla in Korea. According to Joann Keali'inohomoku (interview with author, February 2000), the name Halla, from Mount Halla on Korea's Cheju Island, was given to Huhm by her father. Huhm was the family name of John Huhm, the Korean American she eventually married but then divorced. From the time she lived in Hawai'i, she consistently romanized Pae as Pai. Because her mentor, Pae Ku-ja, recognized her as an official carrier of the Pae Ku-ja dance style, possibly actually bestowing the name Pae Ku-ja II on her (Mary Jo Freshley, interview with author, February 14, 1999), Halla Huhm may have decided to sustain this recognition by keeping Pae, romanized Pai, as part of her name. Pai, the romanization Huhm used, is retained here.

31. "War Bride Exponent of Korean Classical Dance," *Honolulu Advertiser,* April 6, 1952, section 3, 13.

32. In Emery Nemethy, "Dancing Diplomat Halla Huhm," *Paradise of the Pacific* 68, no. 2 (1956): 27.

33. For a history of the Halla Huhm Dance Studio, see Ann Kikuyo Nishiguchi, "Korean Dance in Hawaii: A Study of the Halla Pai Huhm Korean Dance Studio" (M.A. thesis, University of California, Los Angeles, 1982).

34. In the early days, Freshley's classes were mostly private lessons, since she was older than most of the other students. Interestingly, at the time a number of students were of Japanese ancestry. (Halla Huhm had lived many of her formative years in Japan and spoke Japanese fluently. When she first came to Hawai'i she associated a great deal with the Japanese community, and the travel agency she eventually worked for was owned by a Japanese man. Some people believe she was much more comfortable with Japanese people during her early days in Hawai'i, and that is why some of her early students were Japanese.)

35. Kim, *Koreans in Hawaii,* 45.

36. For some suggestion of this background, see Walter Wolf, "Nobu Yamamoto's Fantastic Tale," *The Santa Barbara Independent* (Santa Barbara, California), March 1–8, 2001, 39–41, which recounts the life of Nobu Yamamoto, the Japanese name under which Pae Ku-ja (probably Halla Huhm's sister or cousin, and also her mentor) lived during her residence in the United States until her 2003 death. For some related comments, as well as descriptions of the relationship between Pae Ku-ja and Halla Huhm, see Halla Huhm, "Onni, Pae Ku-ja" (My Sister, Pae Ku-ja), *Chum,* Part 1, 17, no. 7 (July 1977): 70–78; Part 2, 17, no. 8 (August 1977): 24–30.

37. The popularity of her studio in the 1970s may have been partially the result of increased concerns with ethnic identity across the United States.

38. Mary Jo Freshley, interview with author, February 17, 1997.

39. Peggy Myo-Young Choy, "Anatomy of a Dancer: Place, Lineage and Liberation," *Amerasia Journal* 26, no. 2 (2000): 234–52.

40. Several older-generation Korean women say that Whang was not at all well-informed of cultural aspects of Korea, and that her involvement with Korean dance was supported and informed by the advice of others in the community.

41. Ananda Coomaraswamy, *The Dance of Shiva* (New Delhi: Sagar Publications), 1968 (revised from 1957 version), 100–101.

42. Esther Kwon Arinaga, "Contributions of Korean Immigrant Women," in *Montage: An Ethnic History of Women in Hawaii,* ed. Nancy Foon Young and Judy R. Parrish (Honolulu: General Assistance Center for the Pacific, College of Education, Educational Foundations, University of Hawai'i, 1977), 79.

Contributors

Yŏng-ho Ch'oe (Ph.D., University of Chicago) is professor emeritus in the Department of History at the University of Hawai'i at Manoa.

Anne Soon Choi (Ph.D., University of Southern California) is assistant professor of American Studies at University of Kansas, Lawrence, Kansas.

Sun-Pyo Hong (Lit.D., Hanyang University) is research fellow at the Institute of Korean Independence Movement Studies and adjunct professor at Soonchunhyang University, Ch'ŏnan, Korea.

Do-Hyung Kim (Lit.D., Kookmin University) is research fellow at the Institute for Korean Independence Movement Studies, Ch'ŏnan, Korea.

Lili M. Kim (Ph.D., Syracuse University) is Luce Assistance Professor of History and Global Migrations at Hampshire College, Amherst, Massachusetts.

Richard S. Kim (Ph.D., University of Michigan) is assistant professor of Asian American Studies at University of California, Davis.

Brandon Palmer (University of Hawai'i) is assistant professor of history at Ohio University, Athens, Ohio.

Mahn-Yol Yi (Lit.D., Seoul National University), professor emeritus of History at Sookmyung Women's University, Seoul, is chairman of the National Institute of Korean History, Republic of Korea.

Judy A. Van Zile is professor of dance in the Department of Theatre and Dance at University of Hawai'i at Manoa.

Index

Production Notes for
Ch'oe / From the Land of Hibiscus:
Koreans in Hawai'i, 1903–1950

Cover and interior design by Leslie Fitch
with text in Sabon and display in Requiem

Composition by Josie Herr

Printing and binding by Edwards Brothers

Printed on 60 lb. Finch Opaque, 500 ppi